Governance and Public Management

IIAS Series: Governance and Public Management
International Institute of Administrative Sciences (IIAS) – *Improving Administrative Sciences Worldwide*

Website: http://www.iias-iisa.org

Governance and Public Management Series
The *Governance and Public Management* series, published in conjunction with the International Institute of Administrative Sciences (IIAS), brings the best research in public administration and management to a global audience. Encouraging a diversity of approach and perspective, the series reflects the Institute's conviction for a neutral and objective voice, grounded in the exigency of fact. How is governance conducted *now*? How could it be done better? What defines the law of administration and the management of public affairs, and can their implementation be enhanced? Such questions lie behind the Institute's core value of *accountability*: those who exercise authority must account for its use – to those on whose behalf they act.

More information about this series at
http://www.palgrave.com/gp/series/15021

Andreas Ladner • Nils Soguel
Yves Emery • Sophie Weerts
Stéphane Nahrath
Editors

Swiss Public Administration

Making the State Work Successfully

palgrave
macmillan

Editors
Andreas Ladner
IDHEAP
University of Lausanne
Lausanne, Switzerland

Nils Soguel
IDHEAP
University of Lausanne
Lausanne, Switzerland

Yves Emery
IDHEAP
University of Lausanne
Lausanne, Switzerland

Sophie Weerts
IDHEAP
University of Lausanne
Lausanne, Switzerland

Stéphane Nahrath
IDHEAP
University of Lausanne
Lausanne, Switzerland

Governance and Public Management
ISBN 978-3-319-92380-2   ISBN 978-3-319-92381-9 (eBook)
https://doi.org/10.1007/978-3-319-92381-9

Library of Congress Control Number: 2018948702

This Palgrave Macmillan imprint is published by the registered company Springer Nature Switzerland AG
The registered company address is: Gewerbestrasse 11, 6330 Cham, Switzerland

Preface

In 2013, the Institut de hautes études en administration publique (IDHEAP) at the University of Lausanne published the first handbook on Swiss public administrations both in German and in French. This handbook became quite a success within the civil service and proved to be very useful for teaching. This completely rewritten and much shorter volume concentrates on the main characteristics of public administrations in Switzerland and makes the content of the handbook accessible to a broader English-speaking public. It responds to an increasing interest in Swiss political and administrative institutions and policy solutions.

The book was written to be presented at the 2018 Conference of the European Group of Public Administration (EGPA) organized at the IDHEAP in Lausanne. One of the goals was to give our colleagues some ideas about the organization and the functioning of Swiss public administration. We hope it gives answers to questions which usually come up while considering another country and provides insights into an administrative system which is quite different and complex but rather successful.

To write such a volume in a relatively short lapse of time was quite a challenge, and we would like to say thank you to all those who contributed to it, especially all the authors for their significant contributions. Our thanks also go to the University of Lausanne, the Faculty of Law, Criminal Justice and Public Administration, and the Graduate School of Public Administration (IDHEAP) for their financial support.

A very special thank-you goes to John Bendix, who not only translated the French and German texts into English, and corrected our attempts to use the language of Shakespeare, but also shared with us his huge knowledge of the topic and prevented us from being unclear or incorrect. A special thank-you also goes to Merita Buzuku, who brought all the numerous documents in the form requested by the editor.

Lausanne, Switzerland
April 2018

Andreas Ladner
Nils Soguel
Yves Emery
Sophie Weerts
Stéphane Nahrath

Contents

Notes on Contributors

Laure Athias is Associate Professor of Public Economics at the Swiss Graduate School of Public Administration (IDHEAP) at the University of Lausanne, Switzerland. Her areas of research contribute to the understanding of the problem of effective public service delivery and draw on political economy as well as on contract theory and incentive theory in economics.

Marion Baud-Lavigne is a research assistant at the Swiss Graduate School of Public Administration (IDHEAP) at the University of Lausanne. She specializes in the evaluation of public policies, political steering, and the institutionalization of evaluation.

Giuliano Bonoli is Professor of Social Policy at the Swiss Graduate School of Public Administration (IDHEAP) at the University of Lausanne. His research has focused on pension reform, active labor market policies, and family policies, both in Switzerland and comparatively.

Jean-Loup Chappelet is Professor of Public Management at the Swiss Graduate School of Public Administration (IDHEAP) at the University of Lausanne. He was Director of the Graduate School from 2003 to 2012. He specializes in the public policy of sports and the governance of sport organizations.

Yves Emery is Professor of Public Management and Human Resource at the Swiss Graduate School of Public Administration (IDHEAP) at the

University of Lausanne. His areas of research include HRM strategies, work identities, and the motivation and competencies of civil servants and public managers.

Manuel Fischer is a senior researcher at the Swiss Federal Institute for Aquatic Research and Technology (Eawag) and at the University of Bern.

Alexandre Flückiger is Professor of Public Law and Vice-Dean of the Faculty of Law of the University of Geneva. His areas of research include constitutional and administrative law, environmental and planning law, data protection law and transparency, as well as better lawmaking.

Christine Guy-Ecabert is an honorary professor at the Law Faculty of the University of Neuchâtel. Her areas of research focus on urban planning and territorial development, alternative dispute resolution, and lawmaking.

Katia Horber-Papazian is a professor at the Swiss Graduate School of Public Administration (IDHEAP) at the University of Lausanne. Her areas of teaching, research, and expertise, in Switzerland and internationally, focus on the steering and evaluation of public policies, the institutionalization of evaluation, multi-level governance, and institutional and territorial reforms.

Karin Ingold is a professor at the Institute of Political Science and the Oeschger Centre for Climate Change Research at the University of Bern, and Head of the Policy Analysis and Environmental Governance cluster at the Swiss Federal Institute for Aquatic Research and Technology (Eawag).

Andreas Ladner is Professor for Political Institutions and Public Administration at the Swiss Graduate School of Public Administration (IDHEAP) at the University of Lausanne. His areas of research include the quality of democracy, political institutions and public administration, local government, political parties, and voting advice applications.

Moudo Macina is a researcher at the Swiss Graduate School of Public Administration (IDHEAP) at the University of Lausanne. His research interests include public service delivery, public health policy, and culture and development economics.

Pascal Mahon is Professor of Swiss and Comparative Constitutional Law at the Faculty of Law of the University of Neuchâtel. He is also President of the Swiss Judicial Academy and Member of the Board of Directors (in the thematic cluster migration) of the Swiss Center of Expertise for Human Rights. His research interests focus on constitutional law and institutions, judiciary systems, and procedural and human rights.

Tobias Mettler is Associate Professor of Information Management at the Swiss Graduate School of Public Administration (IDHEAP) at the University of Lausanne. His research areas include the study of digital government transformation and innovation as well as the design of methods for technological forecasting and evaluation of digital government initiatives.

Stéphane Nahrath is Professor of Public Policy at the Swiss Graduate School of Public Administration (IDHEAP) at the University of Lausanne. His areas of research include comparative public policy, sustainable resource management, and circular economy.

Martial Pasquier is Professor of Public Management and Marketing at the Swiss Graduate School of Public Administration (IDHEAP) at the University of Lausanne, where he is also Vice-Rector. His research focuses on transparency, public communication, and public agency management.

Amalia Sofia is a researcher at the Swiss Graduate School of Public Administration (IDHEAP) at the University of Lausanne. Her interests focus on the privatization of migration policy.

Nils Soguel is Professor of Public Finance at the Swiss Graduate School of Public Administration (IDHEAP) at the University of Lausanne. His research interests include public sector financial management, fiscal policy, and fiscal federalism.

Philipp Trein is a senior researcher at the Institute of Political, Historical and International Studies at the University of Lausanne. His research interests include comparative public policy and administration, comparative and European politics, and economic voting.

Frédéric Varone is Professor of Public Policy and Head of the Department of Political Science and International Relations at the University of Geneva.

Sophie Weerts is Associate Professor of Public Law at the Swiss Graduate School of Public Administration (IDHEAP) at the University of Lausanne.

Her research interests include constitutional and administrative law, the sources of public law, human rights, language policies, and gender policy.

Pascal Wicht is a research fellow at the Swiss Graduate School of Public Administration (IDHEAP) at the University of Lausanne. His research focuses on the modes of provision of public services, in particular, public–private partnerships.

List of Figures

List of Tables

Introduction: Swiss Public Administration—Key Characteristics and Challenges

Swiss citizens approve of their government and the way democracy is practiced in the country. They trust their authorities and are satisfied with the range of services Swiss governments provide. This seems to be quite a contrast to many other countries which find it increasingly difficult to form stable governments and witness growing disenchantment with politics among their citizens. This goes hand in hand with complaints about a too rigid and not very effective and efficient bureaucracy, and the political and administrative difficulties in finding solutions for the pending challenges to old-age pension schemes, education, energy supply, health, unemployment, and other public policy issues.

We do not claim throughout this book that Switzerland has solved these problems or that political institutions, politics, and public administration make all the difference. Government certainly matters, but there are other things which also make a country successful. We nevertheless believe that Switzerland is an interesting case to look at from a theoretical as well as from a more practice-oriented perspective. Though confronted with the same problems that exist in other countries, Switzerland occasionally offers different solutions; some of them seem to work particularly well.

We begin with the history and formation of Swiss political institutions and describe the horizontal and vertical organization of the state, the role of the different levels of government, the territorial units, and other actors who provide public services. We also provide information about the number of employees working in the public sector and compare Swiss public administration to public administration in other countries. The second part is devoted to the legal system, mainly focused on the federal level. It introduces classic legal concepts, as understood in the country, and presents some of the legal mechanisms and institutions. The Swiss legal system, like many others, is confronted with structural transformations and has its debates about the loss of legitimacy and the lack of efficiency of legal instruments in addressing issues of governing. Part 3 looks at managerial aspects of the Swiss administrative system and examines the principles on which it is based as well as its most recent reforms. We also look at aspects related to human resource management and at public employees who are no longer career civil servants. Following this, part 4 takes up the question of public financing. It stresses the distinctive features of the financial process and how taxing power, tax competition, and financial equalization are organized, as well as how they affect the financial situation of the different levels of Swiss government. The final part looks at select public policies such as social security, health, climate, and telecommunication, and highlights interesting findings of how politico-administrative arrangements are designed in these policy domains. It also explains how and why policy evaluation has been institutionalized in Switzerland. The sections which follow summarize key aspects discussed in each of these five parts.

Part 1: "Bottom-Up State Organization, Diversity, and New forms of Policy Coordination"

It is helpful to briefly look at the foundation of the modern Swiss state to better understand its political institutions and the genesis of Swiss public administration. That the entire Swiss territory was never part of a strong monarchy but was instead a loose confederation of more or less independent territorial subunits (cantons) led almost inevitably to creating a federalist structure. This seemed the only practicable solution for uniting a religiously and linguistically heterogeneous territory. With residual power in the hands of the cantons, the price for the transfer of competencies to the national government was to introduce direct democratic mechanisms and to integrate the various political forces by having them share in the responsibility for governing. Each transfer of tasks to the national government needs the consent of the majority of the citizens and the majority of the cantons. This bottom-up type of state-building is also why the federal (national) government was long limited in its powers and saw an expansion of these powers relatively late, comparatively speaking. The execution of many tasks still remains in the hands of cantons and municipalities, and widespread cooperation with private and semi-private actors has also contributed to the country having an only modest state sector.

Swiss federalism is based on cooperation between the different levels of government, and competition between them is considered positive. Unity explicitly allows for diversity, and the cantons still fiercely defend their autonomy; the principle of subsidiarity is also upheld. Most civil servants work for cantonal governments, and cantonal expenditures, taken as a whole, are much higher than those at local and national levels. This is not only due to the relatively high number of cantons (26) for such a small country but also of the increasing importance of policymaking in the domains of education and health, both of which are largely cantonal responsibilities. Despite attempts to more strictly follow the principle of fiscal equivalence and to concentrate the regulation, funding, and execution of specific tasks at only one level of government, various forms of cooperation between different levels of government are still the rule. In some areas, they have even increased, and there is extensive cooperation between cantons whose aim is to better coordinate autonomous policymaking—and to increase their collective influence on the higher, national level of government.

The complexity of political arrangements has also increased through a partial outsourcing of activities formerly organized by public authorities. This is very much in line with the international debates about administrative reform in the context of new public management, and is in line with the existing Swiss tendency of intense cooperation between social and economic actors. Switzerland thus has all the characteristics of what is often called multi-level governance. Even with this, there are many attempts to introduce new forms of policy coordination which are less hierarchical, to reach across the different levels of government, and to involve the private sector in fulfilling public tasks.

Part 2: "Strengthening the Legitimacy and Efficiency of Swiss Law"

As in neighboring France or Germany, the Swiss legal system is part of the civil law family that originated in the Roman Empire. There is a written (and frequently amended) constitution, which contains fundamental rights, separates the legislative, executive, and judicial organs of the federal state, and fixes the distribution of powers between cantons and federal authorities. Its judiciary is federally and hierarchically organized, with a Supreme Court at the top. In terms of the relationship between international and national law, Switzerland follows the 'monist' tradition, meaning that international law is part of the Swiss legal order. The Swiss legal system is also unique owing to its many instruments of direct democracy at both federal and cantonal levels.

Yet structural changes have strongly influenced both legal systems and public administrations. Laws are more and more frequently produced in international forums. Executive branches today play an increasingly important role in developing legal norms. New forms of normativity have emerged which employ informal mechanisms and involve private actors, thereby circumventing legal rigor and increasing the flexibility of public action. Within the classic conception of the separation of powers, the judiciary plays an increasing role in expanding constitutional review. All these developments generate questions about the continued legitimacy and efficiency of the law, including in Switzerland.

One issue is that the growing diversity in legal norms seems to be leading to a loss of legitimacy of the existing legal system. The proliferation comes in part through the development of international law, but arises as well from the technicality of enacted laws and the sheer complexity of the legal system. The instruments of direct democracy have the potential both of supporting and of undermining lawmaking processes, so various rules and practices have been developed to help build political consensus. This is done in part by identifying different forms of law and specifying the competent actors but also through a legislative process that is cautiously organized. That process includes a very elaborate consultation procedure that brings together public administrations with political and private actors and covers both domestic and international law. The organization of the judiciary and a (formally) limited degree of constitutional review of federal laws on the part of the Federal Supreme Court support the separation of powers notion.

Another issue, one which also affects legitimacy, is the desire for greater efficiency in politics and administration. The criticisms are well known: the lawmaking process is too slow, legal language is too abstract and technical, there are too many regulations, legislative instruments are inadequate for managing contemporary social issues, and so forth. This section addresses the efforts by lawmakers to address such problems, while also discussing the openness of the Swiss public law to other forms of normativity. Even if the acts of 'soft law' are not part of the sources of law, they are used by the public authorities and circumvent existing formal constraints.

Part 3: "An Outcome-Oriented and Open Civil Service"

From the perspective of management and human resources, Swiss public administration is a particularly interesting case of what the literature calls 'post-bureaucracy'. This is a hybrid universe which combines the values and methods employed in traditional management with those of private management. Politicians and public managers in Switzerland have always been open to the private sector, which helps explain the success in introducing 'new public management' methods in Switzerland. But rather than privatizing the public sector, these new methods complement more conventional public administration principles which include legality and the equality of treatment. These remain very present and have been joined to more entrepreneurial principles, including cost control, efficiency, attention to the quality of services provided to the population, and evaluating the effectiveness of administrative acts. Similarly, human resource management in public administration today combines private sector practices such as performance-based pay and the facilitated termination of employment with traditional safeguards that include guarantees under public law for such work relationships. This is in the context of often quite favorable working conditions: the levels of remuneration in public sector employment are often higher than those found in the private sector, as the statistics regularly show. Such a marriage of public and private elements is not self-evident and may represent a unique 'Swiss way' of management.

Part 4: "A Sound Fiscal Policy Thanks to Strong Fiscal Institutions"

Swiss fiscal institutions have distinctive features. Parliaments, whether at federal or cantonal levels, are not under the thumb of their executive councils. For many years now, the federal constitution and the constitutions of the cantons have set hard budget constraints on spendthrift governments. Switzerland's instruments for direct democracy—popular referenda and initiatives—also apply to legislation involving tax and expenditures. These elements build systems of checks and balances that have led, particularly in the last two decades, to sound public budgets with relatively low debt levels.

The strongly decentralized and federalist structure of the country has also contributed to this outcome. It enables effective competition between local governments. Tax competition is part of the picture, with direct taxes the main source of financing for the cantons and the municipalities. Local governments have also implemented high-quality financial and management accounting systems; these governments are the main providers of public services which are financed according to a 'user-pays' principle. Thanks to these rather technical characteristics, the financial statements prepared by Swiss federal, cantonal, and local governments have high levels of accountability and transparency.

Perhaps surprisingly, the governments' favorable financial situation is not due to high taxes. Even though Switzerland makes extensive use of direct taxation, the tax burden in Switzerland is lighter than elsewhere for both households and companies. A repeated criticism is that indirect taxation, notably value-added tax (VAT), should be used more. True, VAT engenders fewer fiscal distortions compared to other taxes. However, the fact that income tax dominates compared to VAT makes it one of the drivers of fiscal federalism and tax competition. To reduce its predominance would weaken both of these advantages of Swiss institutions.

The existence of tax competition in a highly decentralized context in which local and cantonal governments are fiscally extremely autonomous raises the specter of a 'race to the bottom' which would exacerbate the inequalities between financially strong and weak governments. However, the financial equalization schemes that have been implemented at both national and cantonal levels mitigate this risk. Indirectly, they guarantee that tax competition can continue to exist, just within acceptable and accepted boundaries.

Part 5: "Public Administration as Policy Broker"

Particular aspects of the Swiss political system—notably (cooperative) federalism, (neo-) liberalism, and subsidiarity—affect the organization and operation of politico-administrative arrangements in the course of policy formulation and implementation. These arrangements are characterized both by great heterogeneity (involvement and responsibility of private actors) and high fragmentation (extent and complexity of policy networks), which allows for competition between cantons, between municipalities, and, in some cases, between private and public organizations. Both heterogeneity and fragmentation are magnified by the substantial cantonal and local autonomy in designing politico-administrative arrangements.

Private actors in Switzerland also may be rule-makers and rule-takers. Thus, one often finds professional organizations strongly influencing policy decisions or even issuing guidelines, norms, and standards which can become part of the policy design. In terms of implementation, significant elements of federal laws or cantonal tasks may be delegated, through various contractual instruments, to private actors. Thus, a non-trivial part of public service delivery is provided in Switzerland by professional, nonprofit (NGOs, foundations, associations, cooperatives), or even for-profit (companies) organizations.

Policy brokering and coordination also play a crucial role in limiting certain negative outcomes of cooperative federalism. Cantonal autonomy is an efficient way of adapting policy designs to regional specificities, but it can lead to negative side effects such as the unequal treatment of citizens or an uncoordinated implementation. Inter-cantonal associations play an important role in countering this by coordination efforts during the implementation stage (e.g., in health and social security policies), or in limiting (but not entirely removing) the unequal treatments of citizens.

Yet social network analysis also shows that policy brokering on the part of public administration units can help find solutions to conflicts which arise in the policy formulation or implementation phases. Their high 'reputational power' allows them to substantially influence policy formulation (and the choice of policy instruments) in acting as a policy broker or as a member of an advocacy coalition. Still, nowadays public administrations need to share their power with private actors—paradoxically, it appears, by renouncing their previous role as the dominant actor.

Problems and Challenges

Political systems and public administration in Switzerland are, of course, far from perfect. Some of the more fundamental questions turn on the territorial organization of the state. Although decentralization and a high degree of autonomy of the lower units are seen as rather positive features, there seem to be by far too many municipalities and cantons for such a small country. Through mergers, the number of municipalities has shrunk by about one-fourth since the 1990s, but many are still very small and the entire population of certain cantons does not even reach the size of a single larger city. It is even more problematic that the political units no longer coincide with the actual territory people live and work in, which challenges not only a territorially based taxation system but also the way democratic decisions are reached.

A country with both fast-growing and less-dynamic areas raises questions about how competencies and resources can be symmetrically distributed. Metropolitan areas are the drivers of economic growth but have different needs than more remote rural areas, so how far should equalization schemes go and with what aim? The Swiss system allows for diversity, but there are very large differences in individual tax burdens (based on local and cantonal residence) which are difficult to justify.

Cooperation between the different municipalities and between cantons as well as across the different levels of government makes politics much more complicated and—despite the many elements of direct democracy—tends to move political influence away from citizens and even parliaments. Top-level civil servants and executive bodies have gained importance, and technocratic solutions increasingly replace political decisions. One of the challenges is to find efficient and democratically legitimate forms of cooperation in public decision-making.

While the mechanisms of direct democracy help reinforce the legitimacy of legal rules domestically, they create difficulties in the application of international law to Swiss political decisions, and lead to tensions between domestic and international law. This puts Switzerland, in turn, under strong internal and external pressure, as it can make it appear a too mercurial political and economic partner.

The ever-present threat of a popular referendum pushes political actors to cooperate and negotiate already in the pre-parliamentary phase of legislation, but that also has the effect of slowing the process of lawmaking. Moreover, despite very well-organized lawmaking procedures, non-obligatory acts (soft law) have also developed. If some view this as a good sign, it also shows that classic legal acts and processes cannot cover all state activities, and there is a need to imagine alternative procedures and new mechanisms to guarantee classic obligations will also be fulfilled.

With respect to the courts, and especially the Federal Supreme Court, the re-election of justices and the limited constitutional review the Supreme Court can exercise over federal laws underline the importance of the Federal Assembly. At the same time, such rules mean the judiciary cannot play the role of a countervailing power at the federal level.

The hybrid nature of the Swiss administration, as well as the institutional characteristics described above, makes managing public administration difficult. There is resistance of various kinds, not least because of claims that a kind of 'reform mania' is at work—leading to discrediting the reforms initiated as well as wearing out the civil servants. The methods introduced have not always taken the specificities of public administration sufficiently into account and lead to a clash of values between those who support a classical vision of administration, one far removed from the managerial requirements of efficiency and effectiveness, and those who promote a more pragmatic view of an administration that is seen as a provider of (quality) services to the population. There is the suggestion that the enacted reforms have led to an excessive 'managerialization' of public administration and thus to having economic objectives overtake political objectives. Some political authorities even had the impression they were losing control of their own administrations, while others skillfully used the new management tools to increase their power. All this was against a backdrop of a Swiss administration perceived, even before the advent of new public management, as having too much power (or expertise) relative to the political institutions.

In terms of public finance, the schemes which guaranteed success in the past may not necessarily be conducive to future successes. Economic crises, international competition over business taxation, migration, and the aging of the population are all factors which cast shadows over public budgets, in Switzerland as elsewhere. Switzerland's strong institutions will no doubt be able to meet these socio-economic challenges but will probably also need to be adapted. And while the tools of direct democracy have their advantages, they can also be a brake on the rapid reform of institutions and laws. This is particularly the case when changes mean that the current generation of citizens and voters must give something up. This often leads voters to refuse projects which they perceive as having a negative outcome for them personally.

The large difference in tax burdens, while tolerated until now, may not be accepted in the future. The differences themselves can be explained by citizen preferences to receive better or costlier public services. But these differences can also, or even mostly, be explained by a non-uniform distribution of economic activities (and thus of the tax base) over the entire country. Geography and topography are partly responsible, but so is the tax competition between cantons and municipalities.

One solution here would involve strengthening financial equalization. At the same time, the tyranny of the majority (by jurisdictions benefitting from transfers compared to jurisdictions financing the transfers) has already reached its limit. Another solution would be to unify tax deductions and tax rates, though in the past, Switzerland's federalist instinct pushed voters to refuse this kind of solution. A more extreme solution could be to withdraw all or part of the taxing power cantons and municipalities have thus far enjoyed, but this would undermine a key element of Switzerland's success.

As in other countries, we can also find the typical 'principal-agent dilemma' in Switzerland. It is difficult for the federal government and its administration to control cantonal and local authorities, and there are contradictions between the interests of (private) implementing actors and of those who benefit from various policies. There are also tensions, or even contradictions, between the principles of cantonal autonomy and the equal treatment of citizens. And there is a continuing, and perhaps increasing, need for strengthening inter-policy coordination in a context of an increasing trans-territoriality in public problems.

Switzerland: A Model Case?

In a contextualist understanding, every country is different and has to be treated as a particular case. Quite often, this is used to justify that something which works in one country could never work in other countries. Such a position is often defended when it comes to the Swiss political and administrative system. Direct democracy, or a multiparty federal (or cantonal) government on a voluntary basis whose majorities shift from case to case, a high degree of decentralization and diversity, and a far-reaching fiscal autonomy are possible in Switzerland—but could this work anywhere else?

There are less controversial lessons that can be drawn from the Swiss case. To find good and lasting policy and managerial solutions takes time, especially if the solutions are to be supported by employees, citizens, and a majority of the parties alike. More inclusive policymaking, by the same token, increases the legitimacy of the decisions and helps guarantee compliance. To be close to citizens, owing to strong and effective decentralization, allows for a more direct orientation to the needs, wants, and thoughts of citizens. Smaller governmental units are also easier to manage, at least in principle, and it brings the public sector closer to the people. In the current political climate, this is also what many people around the globe say they want.

IDHEAP
University of Lausanne
Lausanne, Switzerland

Andreas Ladner
Nils Soguel
Yves Emery
Sophie Weerts
Stéphane Nahrath

PART I

General Aspects

CHAPTER 1

Society, Government, and the Political System

Andreas Ladner

1.1 Introduction

Switzerland, at least by the commonly used measures (GDP, competition, and innovation rankings), is a very successful and prosperous country. Its residents esteem Swiss political institutions and trust the authorities, and they are content with the range of services Swiss governments provide. In Europe, along with the Scandinavians, the Swiss are among the most satisfied with their national government and with the functioning of their democracy.[1] An important contribution to this esteem comes from an effective and well-functioning public administration.

The organization, functioning, and performance of public administrative bodies are directly linked to government configurations, political institutions, and the key values which undergird them. These frameworks set the conditions under which public administration works, along with

[1] See the European Social Survey (ESS5–2010, ed.2.0; own calculations), and Denters et al. (2016).

A. Ladner (✉)
IDHEAP, University of Lausanne, Lausanne, Switzerland
e-mail: andreas.ladner@unil.ch

A. Ladner et al. (eds.), *Swiss Public Administration*, Governance and Public Management,
https://doi.org/10.1007/978-3-319-92381-9_1

the goals or directions, pursued. Knowledge of the basic principles of a political system, the institutional configuration, and the values underlying the system and the institutions are key to understanding, and analysing, a public administration.

Without meaning to invoke historical determinism, the genesis of the governmental structures in the country gives insights into the reasons for its current organization and reveals the principles and ideas guiding it. This helps to understand the limits or prospects for making administrative adjustments or carrying out reforms. Of particular interest is the question of how malleable governmental institutions are. To what extent is the organization of a government determined by the past (path dependency)? To what extent do structural and cultural factors (such as small size or the differences between language regions or religious faiths) play a role? To what extent might changes and adjustments be the result of conscious agenda-setting and political decisions taken (for more on this, see Ladner 2011)?[2]

We begin by briefly looking at the foundation of governmental structures in Switzerland and their subsequent expansion. We then turn to its most important structural and cultural characteristic and the basic elements of the political system. In doing so, we refer to the effects this institutional, political, and historical framework has, and has had, on how Swiss public administration functions.

1.2 From Confederation to Federal State: Bottom-Up Nation-Building

The key to understanding the Swiss state and its institutions is the fact that it developed from the bottom up. Unlike in countries with a monarchical past, a strong, centralized government never existed on Swiss soil, or at least not prior to the founding of the modern Swiss state in 1848. The history of the country as an independent political entity instead began with a loose alliance between a few rural cantons gradually joined by other cantons. This alliance acquired, controlled, and exploited various territories which now form modern Switzerland.

It was only with Napoleon's occupation and the subsequent creation of the Helvetic Republic (1798–1802) that cantons were put on an equal footing and a national, centralized administration was introduced.

[2] These are precisely the questions raised by various 'neo-institutionalist' approaches.

However, the re-organization of the country on the French model was only a brief historical interlude, and the country soon reverted to earlier habits, though with the difference that the sovereignty of the individual cantons was now no longer questioned. The Congress of Vienna in 1815 set the territorial boundaries of the country. This Congress also ensured Switzerland would be neutral, a status desired not just by the Swiss. The Great Powers wanted to prevent one another from trying to exert influence on what was a geopolitically significant area at the heart of Europe. In the course of the nineteenth century, the forces arguing for democratization and a modernization of government gradually gained influence.

One consequence—and one can certainly draw parallels here to the later development of the EU—was the introduction of conditions creating a unified economic area. Tolls and tariffs between cantons were repealed,[3] and a common national currency was introduced. Efforts to create a modern, centrally organized national government led to a very brief civil war in 1847 (*Sonderbundskrieg*) which pitted liberal, business-friendly circles interested in modernizing government and society against Catholic-dominated cantons and conservative forces antagonistic to centralization.

The liberal forces triumphed, and after a successful constitutional plebiscite, the modern Swiss federal state was founded in 1848. However, though the proposed constitution made concessions to the Catholic losers—who had argued for more independence for the cantons—they were not persuaded. The 1848 Constitution was turned down by clear margins in the Catholic cantons of Uri, Schwyz, Obwalden and Nidwalden, Zug, Wallis, Ticino, and Appenzell Innerrhoden. Approval of the proposed constitution was also helped along by more questionable means. To achieve the needed majority of cantons, the positive decision by Fribourg's then liberal government was counted, though it was a Catholic canton, and in the case of Lucerne, also Catholic, it was decided to count non-voters as having voted in favour. The new constitution was therefore accepted.

Because individual cantons were reluctant to see their former competencies centralized, many powers remained reserved to the cantons, including much of the administration of justice, tax law, police, and transportation, along with control over education and the churches (Maissen

[3] According to the federal customs inspectorate, as of 1844 there were still about 370 customs stations at cantonal borders, of which 147 stood at the country's external borders and more than 180 were found inside the cantons (see Polli-Schönborn 2006).

2010: 200 et seq.). Moreover, it was important to guarantee the cantons appropriate political influence at the national level. Institutionally, this was ensured by creating a territory-based upper house (*Ständerat*), to which each canton sent two representatives; its powers were equal to those exercised by the population-based lower house (*Nationalrat*). The cantons with small populations, many of which had been on the losing side of the 1847 *Sonderbund* civil war, were over-represented in this upper house. Still, when the 1848 Constitution came into force, the prior loose confederation of cantons was transformed into a federal state, and some of the competencies cantons previously had were transferred to the national level.

The new national government pursued goals which included creating an entity capable, over the longer term, of acting in a uniform manner vis-à-vis other nation-states, articulating and pursuing Swiss interests abroad, taking responsibility for external security, and asserting both independence and neutrality. To this were added guarantees given to promote public order and ensure domestic security, as well as a broadly formulated goal to 'promote the common welfare'; there was also a general mandate to erect 'public works' (see Maissen 2010: 202). The creation of a benefits-disbursing welfare state at the national level, and the creation of a national consciousness, came later. But in comparative terms, Switzerland developed into a democratically organized country relatively early.

The price of unity, however, was a pronounced federalism and a weak national government. Residual competencies, meaning everything not explicitly defined as within the power of the national government, remain even today in the hands of the cantons. Every additional competence the national government is to acquire, or every new task it is to carry out, requires the approval of both voters and cantons. The Catholic and conservative opponents of a federal state thereby received a high degree of protection; with respect to the future development of the national government, it was necessary to take their concerns into account.

1.3 Structural and Cultural Heterogeneity

Which tasks can and should a state assume? Despite many commonalities, there are differences with respect to the tasks and challenges a state faces which depend on its size, its social and cultural composition, and its geographic circumstances. Of course, what needs to be coordinated among eight million residents is decidedly less than what it takes to coordinate a nation of a billion people, but it is also true that a country heterogeneous in language and religion requires greater efforts to integrate than does a more homogeneous society. And there is also the question to what degree a government wants to regulate and redistribute. Every additional regulation means more involvement and greater responsibility. This not just calls for a willingness to implement but also requires mobilizing the needed resources for the task. Political attitudes differ about social justice, along with the degree of redistribution and its consequences.

In terms of territory and population, Switzerland belongs to the smaller countries. About 8.3 million people inhabit a territory which is about 42,000 km^2 in area, though the largest part is uninhabitable due to the Alps. Most of the population is concentrated in the lower-lying areas called the *Mittelland*. About 25 per cent of the population is foreign, even though more than half of those without a Swiss passport were either born in Switzerland or have lived in the country for at least a decade. The foreign population largely comes either from European Union (EU) or from European Free Trade Association (EFTA) countries (e.g., Italy, Germany, Portugal).

The density of political units in the territory is striking, and includes 26 largely sovereign cantons and 2255 (as of 1 January 2017) relatively autonomous communities (for more on this, see Chap. 2). The large number of territorial sub-units means most of them are quite small, and that there is considerable variation in their population size. The smallest Swiss communities have less than 100 inhabitants; the largest cities hold several hundred thousand. The largest canton (Zurich) has more than a million inhabitants, while the smallest cantons (Appenzell Innerrhoden, Uri, Obwalden, and Glarus) are in the low ten thousands. In spite of these large differences, no asymmetries exist under public law, and all communities are formally equal to one another, as are all cantons. Pronounced decentralization and the large independence accorded to decentralized political units is a distinctive characteristic of Swiss political culture.

Also characteristic is Swiss cultural heterogeneity, particularly in terms of religion and language. About 70 per cent of the inhabitants belong to a Christian faith. Catholics form a majority of the permanent resident population in 11 cantons, while in seven others, they are less than 30 per cent. The proportions in the remaining eight cantons are less clear.[4] Switzerland is also a multilingual country with four national languages: 63 per cent

[4] See Bundesamt für Statistik: Strukturerhebung der eidgenössischen Volkszählung 2015: Sprachen und Religionen.

speak (Swiss-) German, 23 per cent speak French, 8 per cent speak Italian, and 0.5 per cent speak Romansh. English, Portuguese, and Albanian, each spoken by 3–5 per cent, are also relatively common.

Cultural differences call for considerable efforts at integration on the part of both society and government. In cultural terms, this requires accepting a degree of diversity and by respecting and considering the concerns of minorities. As can be seen in the next section, the political institutions make an important contribution here. Switzerland also profits—especially if one adds economic capacity—from the fact that its cleavages do not line up but are instead cross-cutting. Thus, rather than having rich, Protestant, German-speaking cantons opposing poor, Catholic, French-speaking cantons, one instead has Protestant and Catholic, and economically stronger as well as economically weaker, cantons in both German-speaking and French-speaking parts of the country.

1.4 The Model of the State and the Extent of State Activity

Switzerland does not belong to the category of 'Scandinavian-style welfare states', and unlike Germany or Austria, it also does not clearly endorse the 'social market economy' model. If one looks at the ratio of government expenditures (33.6 per cent) or tax revenues (27.7 per cent) to GDP,[5] then these are markedly lower than in most European countries and are more comparable with the values found for Australia and the US.[6] Nevertheless, it would be a mistake to regard the Swiss model of the state as being that of 'minimal state'. The Swiss state in the nineteenth century, dominated by the Liberals (*Freisinn*, now *FDP.Die Radikalen*), was not a 'night-watchman state' (Gruner 1964) concerned only to guarantee enough scope for economic interests, providing the infrastructure for modern trade and making workers available. Within the 'extended family' of the *Freisinnige* at the time, one could find not only adherents of the Manchester School but Democrats and Radicals as well. The latter made efforts, first at the level of individual cantons, to pursue socially balanced fiscal and social policies based on social justice and the provision of bene-

[5] See Bundesamt für Statistik: Kennzahlen der öffentlichen Finanzen im internationalen Vergleich 2015.

[6] See OECD Economic Outlook 90, Annex Table 25: General government total outlays in per cent of nominal GDP.

fits, including free public education and the founding of cantonal banks to provide cheap 'popular credit'[7]. Towards the end of the nineteenth century, not least as a consequence of the economic crises during the 1880s, the national government increasingly influenced the economic framework (Code of Obligations 1881; Copyright Act 1883; Trademark Protection Act 1890; Patent and Invention Law 1883) and took measures to protect vulnerable groups (the Factory Law; the promotion of vocational training; support provided for agriculture in 1884).

Swiss politics at the national level was always dominated by centre-right, employer-friendly forces. It was only at the end of the 1950s that left-wing parties, along with the Catholic People's Party that had become more centrist, and then later, particularly with the help of the Greens, that it was possible to form majorities around certain topics. Earlier, certain cantons, and especially certain cities, achieved left-wing majorities, and in recent years, nearly all large Swiss cities have been dominated by coalitions of Social Democrats, Green and left-wing parties.

Economic peak associations played an important role early on in Switzerland. They were successful at convincing the national government to subsidize their association offices (e.g., general-secretariats) already by the late nineteenth century (Mach 2006: 273). Their political involvement was strengthened in particular by governmental interventions during the economic crises of the interwar period. Their middle-class-oriented economic policies were also expanded and strengthened through corporatist arrangements (*Sozialpartnerschaft*). A series of protectionist decisions—limiting imports, barriers to market access, measures to limit competition, binding collective agreements by private economic associations—and economic arrangements—price fixing, participation in production costs, or eased access to capital—worked to the benefit of a whole series of sectors (Linder 1983: 278 et seq.). The peak associations made use of the government not just to protect their interests, but themselves became implementers of governmental policies to protect the market (Ackermann and Steinemann 1981: 86 et seq.).

The Second World War intensified the nexus between government and economy, one which was eventually ratified through revisions made, in 1947, to various articles of the Swiss constitution that addressed the economy. The clause concerning the freedom of trade now included a

[7] See Linder (1983: 260 et seq.) on this, with the corresponding references to Gruner (1964).

caveat giving the national government the power to pass measures against cartels (especially if they had socially or economically damaging effects), the power to 'preserve a healthy farming estate', and to protect those parts of the country which were economically threatened. In addition, associations were to be explicitly included in preparing as well as implementing laws, and the binding force of collective bargaining agreements was confirmed. Finally, more formally, what had been constitutional articles designed to combat crises were now changed into constitutional articles to promote the economy.[8]

The proximity of government to economy can be seen in the significance para-state organizations are awarded.[9] Through its branch associations, the private sector is involved in helping formulate and implement government policies. Traditionally, such organizations had particular influence in agriculture but also in other economic sectors (see Farago and Kriesi 1986); para-state organizations take on important roles in implementing policy, in market regulation, or in organizing vocational education. Such strong interlinkage between government and economy in carrying out tasks is called 'neocorporatism' in the political science literature (Schmitter 1974).

In calculating the ratio of government expenditures to GDP, part of the expenditures for social insurance is not included. Similarly, when calculating tax revenues relative to GDP, certain compulsory costs which residents in Switzerland must pay—for example, for the occupational pension scheme (the 'second pillar') or for medical insurance—are not counted. In other countries, these costs, to a lesser or greater degree, are included in the taxes residents pay.

Therefore, the low values found for the ratio of government expenditure or tax revenue to GDP do not reflect a limited set of benefits or a particularly efficient provision of services but are to some degree the result of a differing structure for meeting government obligations. If one includes mandatory payments into the pension funds and mandatory medical insurance payments, for example, then the ratio of tax revenues to GDP would rise (by about ten percentage points) to a little over 40 per

[8] In the current Swiss constitution, economic associations are wholly integrated and noted in Art. 94–104 (Economy) as well as in Art. 110 (Labor).

[9] A parliamentary investigation carried out in 1983 found 232 para-state organizations, employing nearly 12,000 people, at the national level; the received one billion CHF in subsidies. These figures do not include health insurance funds or organizations devoted to the handicapped. See Germann (2002).

cent.[10] Similarly, social insurance costs not included in government expenditures account for an additional 10 per cent of GDP.

The history of the Swiss state, like that of other comparable states, is one of growth, increased differentiation, and shifting emphases. At the beginning, the primary goal was to secure independence externally (e.g., establish sovereignty) and to ensure domestic peace and security. Subsequently, rights to participate or co-determine were added, and civil liberties had to be guaranteed. It also became important to create the necessary preconditions for the economy to develop. These preconditions included lowering barriers to trade and increasing government commitments to expand infrastructure (transportation, energy) and education. Over time, the national government took on more tasks related to health care and social security as well. Crises and structural changes also meant that business cycle and economic policies increased in importance. Maintaining the natural environment and sustainable development have become governmental tasks only in the more recent past.

Increased governmental activity can be illustrated by public outlay figures. When the modern Swiss federal state began in 1850, total expenditures at federal, cantonal, and local levels were about 50 million Francs. The federal share of this was only about 10 per cent, or 4.5 million Francs (Weber 1969: 17), and the remainder was about equally divided between the other two levels (Guex 1998: 102).[11] By 2014, this had risen to 207.6 billion Francs (Federal Finance Administration 2016: 5). Of this, federal or national outlays constituted 64.7 billion (25.5 per cent), cantonal 85.2 billion (32.6 per cent), and community outlays 46.4 billion (18.3 per cent) Francs. To this, one can add expenditures for social security of about 59.8 billion (23.6 per cent).[12]

However, increases in government expenditures relative to GDP did not do so linearly. Until the late 1950s, they increased more or less parallel

[10] See the answer of the Federal Council to the interpellation of Jean-Pierre Graber on 29 September 2011 (Curia Vista 11.3970).

[11] Cantonal and community expenditures in this era are very difficult to establish because the data is very spotty or available only for certain places (e.g., Zurich or Bern).

[12] If one adds these four sums together, one arrives at a value of more than 256 billion; these are gross expenditure figures. However, the national government transfers money to the social security system and to the cantons (transfer payments between the levels) which in turn record the money they pay out as expenditures (e.g., a 'duplicated' outlay). The totals do not include such duplications, but they are included in the calculation of the percentages.

to economic activity, meaning the ratio of government expenditure to GDP remained both low and relatively stable.[13] The 1960s saw a significant expansion of government activity, and the average real growth rate, at all governmental levels, exceeded the growth rate of real GDP (Kirchgässner 2004: 2). At the beginning of the 1960s, government outlays at all three levels were still considerably under 20 per cent of GDP.

Outlays may be contrasted with income. Interestingly, and typically for Switzerland in international comparison, all three governmental levels control their own tax income, as well as raise their own income taxes. As they have taxing autonomy, cantons and communities set their own tax rates. The highest tax rates the national government can charge, however, as well as the level of the value-added tax, are set out in the Swiss constitution.[14] The authority given to the national government to raise taxes is also laid out in the constitution, and has a (renewable) time limit.[15] This constitutional anchor means, for example, that to raise the national tax rate requires amending the constitution, and hence also calls for the approval of both the people and the cantons. Only the national government levies a value-added tax, and in European comparison, it is at a relatively low level. The cantons participate, partly, in the tax revenues gathered by the national government.

National revenue in 2014 stood at about 65 billion Francs, and of that, tax revenue constituted 58 billion Francs (Federal Finance Administration 2016). Of that 20 billion Francs (32.9 per cent) were generated from the value-added tax and 18 billion (28.5 per cent) from direct federal tax. Direct income taxes play a rather larger role at the cantonal and community levels. Total cantonal income stands at about 83 billion Francs. Of that 43 billion (52 per cent) comes from tax revenue, with 31 billion of that coming in turn from the direct taxation of natural persons and 25 billion (30 per cent) from transfer payments. Total income at the community level is about 45 billion Francs, 27 billion (60 per cent) from tax income and 5 billion (11 per cent) from transfer payments.

[13] Following Tanzi and Schuknecht (2000: 6), the ratio of government expenditure to GDP in 1870 was about 16.5 per cent; in 1960, it stood at 17.2 per cent.

[14] Article 128 of the Swiss Constitution sets the maximum tax rate at 11.5 per cent. Article 130 sets the normal value-added tax rate at 6.5 per cent, though has been raised to 8 per cent until the end of 2017.

[15] See the transitional stipulations for Articles 128 and 130. Currently, the constitution stipulates that permission to raise direct federal taxes, as well as to charge a value-added tax, will run out in 2035.

Switzerland is not just strongly decentralized. It also has a public sector, at least in the classic sense, which is relatively small. Certain tasks which elsewhere are the responsibility of the public sector have traditionally been provided in cooperation with private actors. This goes along with the idea that government, economy, and society need not be antagonistic. Switzerland is often characterized as a liberal variant of the neo-corporatist model (Katzenstein 1985).

1.5 Political Institutions

The political institutions help integrate different segments of the population as well as the regions, but also contribute to holding the country together and maintain the country's (considerable) political stability. These institutions enjoy broad support among Swiss, ensuring the legitimacy of political decisions and political actions taken.

Political observers agree[16] that the three cornerstones of the political system are provided by federalism, 'concordance'—meaning all important political actors and interests are involved in the decision-making process—and direct democracy. These factors are often cited as reasons for Swiss 'distinctiveness' if not its idiosyncrasy.[17] What they have in common is that they all either serve to limit the exercise of power or they encourage the sharing of power. Federalism divides power between the federal and cantonal levels, as well as between the cantons, while the 'concordance' system divides power between the parties and interests, and direct democracy divides power between the authorities and the people.

1.5.1 Federalism

It has already been noted that a federalist solution was the only possible path to pursue when the Swiss nation-state was founded in 1848. The 26 cantons (called *Stände* in Swiss usage) each have their own parliaments, their own executives, their own courts and their own constitutions, though cantonal constitutions cannot be in contradiction to the Swiss national

[16] See Linder (2005), Kriesi and Trechsel (2008), and Vatter (2016).

[17] Some authors also refer to the 'militia' idea of volunteering one's time to perform political and social tasks communities need, an idea which is still widespread. Neutrality is also often cited, though both it and the 'militia' character of politics, while they exert influence over politics and administration, have a less pronounced institutional character than federalism, 'concordance', and direct democracy.

constitution. Cantons implement national laws and directives but otherwise organize their own activities according to their own needs. They have considerable leeway, for example, in how they organize education and hospitals, in the area of culture, as well as with respect to the police. Each canton levies its own income and wealth taxes to finance its cantonal tasks.

Cantons also participate in political decision-making at the national level. The primary locus for this is the upper house of Parliament (*Ständerat*), in which each full canton has two seats. Additionally, cantons have a special status in the context of Swiss direct democracy (see below), but what is decisive is the principle that every proposed extension of powers at the national level must be approved by a majority of the cantons. Cantons also exercise influence when new laws are being drafted, at which time their representatives, as experts, are consulted. Finally, they play an important role in implementing policies decided at the national level, and in doing so, have some degree of freedom.

The hundreds of inter-cantonal agreements (*Konkordate*), many of which involve infrastructure arrangements, play a special role as do cantonal inter-ministerial meetings (e.g., of the finance ministers of all the cantons). There is also a Conference of Cantonal Governments whose goal is to coordinate political policies among the cantons. One goal of this Conference is to keep political tasks from drifting up to the national level and thereby diminishing the influence of the cantons.

Swiss federalism is noteworthy particularly for its readiness to accept, and respect, different kinds of solutions; it also has an explicitly competitive orientation. Unlike German federalism, there is no constitutionally based mandate to ensure that the same living conditions prevail throughout the country. The logic of Swiss federalism operates much more with an eye to ensuring minimal standards that are to be ensured with the help of a nationwide financial equalization scheme which in essence takes from the rich(er cantons) and gives to the poor(er cantons). Tax competition between cantons (and communities) leads to considerable variation in the tax burden on individuals.

A comprehensive reform designed to bring about greater financial equalization between economically strong and economically weak cantons came into effect at the beginning of 2008. As part of the new rules, certain tasks were unbundled, cantonal cooperation was reorganized, and cooperation between cantonal and national levels was reconfigured. Still, increasing centralization remains an issue, as more and more tasks call for uniform regulation, and some of the pressures to do so derive from international rules formulated outside of Switzerland. Education, health, and social expenditures, which have grown significantly in recent years, pose additional challenges for the cantons. Large differences and the small size of some cantons make inter-cantonal cooperation increasingly important, with the result that decisions are increasingly taken by executives and administrators rather than by voters.

1.5.2 Direct Democracy

Another key element of the political system is provided by the extensive direct democratic tools at hand. All changes to the constitution, as well as accession of the country to collective security or international organizations, call for a mandatory referendum. Here, it is not enough to obtain a majority of the votes; a majority of the cantons must also be in favour. Citizens can also launch popular initiatives to alter the constitution, for which they must collect 100,000 signatures within 18 months of launching the proposal. For a popular initiative to be successful, a majority of the votes as well as a majority of the cantons are also needed. Finally, citizens can also launch a referendum, if they so wish, against a new law that has been passed, as well as against certain international treaties. To do so, 50,000 signatures need to be collected within 100 days. If no (simple) majority is reached, the existing law stands. Individual cantons can also launch initiatives, and eight cantons together can launch a so-called cantonal referendum, though both happen quite rarely.

Direct democracy in Switzerland goes back to the 1830s, when St Gallen and Basel-Land first introduced a veto right for voters (Kriesi and Trechsel 2008: 4). Proposed amendments to the constitution requiring the approval of voters and cantons triggered a mandatory referendum already as of 1848, and a limited and relatively complicated version of the right to launch an initiative was introduced then as well, with whose help one could demand a total revision of the constitution. The 1874 revised national constitution introduced an optional referendum for laws that had been passed; in 1891, the initiative for a partial revision of the constitution was also introduced. More recent important changes have included extending these direct democratic tools to cover foreign policy issues, understandable in light of the increasing importance of supranational associations and international treaties.

There is no doubt that the existence of the referendum mechanism slowed the expansion of tasks the government could undertake. A series of modernization and centralization proposals failed during the early years of the federal state, largely due to the opposition from Catholic and conservative cantons (Kölz 2004: 633). Otherwise too, the expansion of the state—and not least of the social welfare state—was relatively slow and remained at a low level (Linder 2005: 263 et seq.).

The threat of a popular referendum leads to the integration of the most significant political forces into the government, thereby contributing significantly to the third major element, 'concordance'. A referendum gives interest group associations, political parties, and other organized groups the chance to defeat unloved changes made to constitution or law. To prevent this, strong political parties are represented in the government and participate in formulating proposals. Hence, they are, at least morally, obligated to support the resulting formulations. Efforts are also generally undertaken to include legitimate arguments brought by the opponents of a proposal in order to make them 'referendum-immune' (Neidhart 1970). Witness the extensive consultations (*Vernehmlassungsverfahren*) with all the interested groups, cantons, and parties that form part of the legislative process. Those groups less well represented in the political system, however, can articulate their concerns through the popular initiative process, and thereby can also exert influence on politics and policy-making.

Direct democracy not only means that politicians must be more strongly attuned to the 'popular will' but it also means the citizens' will carries greater weight in the work of the public administration. In the end, proposed laws or changes must convince a majority of the citizens, making ballot box decisions particularly relevant to administrative activities. It may go too far to ascribe a 'citizen-orientation' to administrators that results from the use of such direct democratic tools, but it is true that the verdict reached by the voters has a different valence than instructions received from the government.

1.5.3 The 'Concordance' System

The term 'concordance'[18] refers to the more or less willing inclusion of the most important parties in the executive, as well as the willingness to govern in common with changeing majorities. As a rule, all the largest parties are represented in the executive, whether this is at community, cantonal, or

[18] See Arend Lijphart's conceptualization of consensus democracy and division of power (Lijphart 1999).

national levels. The Federal Council (*Bundesrat*), Switzerland's national executive, is composed of seven members who have equal status, and who not only come from the various regions of the country but also are members of the four largest political parties. The Federal Council makes decisions collegially, its members oriented to reaching a consensus which will allow policy to be carried out. Outwardly, individual members of this Council represent the collegial consensus which has been reached—even when it goes against their personal convictions or against the position of the political party they belong to. Unlike in other countries, there is no clear distinction between government and opposition in Switzerland. There is no single party, or a coalition of parties, which determines policy for the duration of a legislative period. Instead, the individual representatives of various parties craft temporary majorities; these may shift, depending upon the issue. The executives at the lower levels of the Swiss system function similarly; parliaments and commissions have shifting majorities, depending on the issue, and their major task is to find sufficient support, from whichever political direction it may come, to create a majority for a given proposal or policy or law.

The 'concordance' system does have certain indirect effects on administrative activity. Though individual departments are headed by the representatives of various political parties, the political orientation of a department overall is more heterogeneous than in a system where the post as head of an administrative unit is filled by a person representing the current party in power. Thus, top civil servants do not necessarily belong to the same party as the (nominal) head of their department. That does not mean that civil servants do not quickly learn which proposals are likely to find greater favour with their administrative superiors, but it does mean that there is room for differing positions and arguments. In the end, proposed projects need to not only find favour in the ranks of one's own political party but also convince other members of the executive as well as other parties; otherwise, they will not achieve majority support either in Parliament or among the voters.

Aside from these 'soft' effects of 'concordance' and direct democracy on administrative activity, one also finds quick direct implications. Political processes take their time until all the political hurdles have been taken, and the great challenge is to suggest proposals which will find majority support. These, inevitably, are the creatures of compromise, and may call for—sometimes quite costly—concessions to be made to the various stakeholders.

The effects of federalism and community autonomy paired with the commitment to subsidiarity are even more dramatic and incisive. They lead to a pronounced segmentation, both horizontally and vertically. This makes it easier to take account of social and cultural differences, and to create much more homogeneous sub-units. However, the consequence, along with the considerable diversity it permits, is a small-scale partitioning of what is already a very small nation-state. Corporative networks between the various levels are needed if the many necessary tasks are to be fulfilled by government and administration, and it is not surprising that in many areas, and in many places, it has not been possible to establish professional administrative structures. As we will see in Chap. 2, governmental tasks have therefore had to be carried out with the aid of private sector organizations and the help of many ordinary citizens who, in what Swiss call a 'militia system', volunteer their time to help govern communities.

References

Ackermann, C., & Steinmann, W. (1981). Historische Aspekte der Trennung und Verflechtung von Staat und Gesellschaft in der Schweiz – die Genese der Verschränkung. *Forschungsprojekt Parastaatliche Verwaltung, Projektbericht Nr. 14.* ETH Zürich: ORL-Institut.

Denters, B., Ladner, A., Mouritzen, P. E., & Rose, L. E. (2016). Reforming local governments in times of crisis: Values and expectations of good local governance in comparative perspective. In S. Kuhlmann & G. Bouckaert (Eds.), *Local public sector reforms in times of crisis: National trajectories and international comparisons* (pp. 333–345). London, UK: Palgrave Macmillan.

Farago, P., & Kriesi, H. (Eds.). (1986). *Wirtschaftsverbände in der Schweiz.* Grütsch: Verlag Rüegger.

Federal Finance Administration. (2016). *Finanzstatistik der Schweiz 2014. Zwischenbericht.* Bern: Schweizerische Eidgenossenschaft.

Germann, R. E. (2002, December 18). Öffentlicher Haushalt. *Historisches Lexikon der Schweiz.* http://www.hls-dhs-dss.ch/textes/d/D10342.php. Accessed 7 May 2012.

Gruner, E. (1964). 100 Jahre Wirtschaftspolitik. Etappen des Interventionismus in der Schweiz. *Schweizerische Zeitschrift für Volkswirtschaft und Statistik, 100*(I/II), 34–70.

Guex, S. (1998). *L'argent de l'Etat – Parcours des finances publiques au XXème siècle.* Lausanne: réalités sociales.

Katzenstein, P. J. (1985). *Small states in world markets: Industrial policy in Europe.* Ithaca: Cornell University Press.

Kirchgässner, G. (2004). Die langfristige Entwicklung der Bundesfinanzen 1960–2002. Hintergrundpapier zu, 3. Teil des Jahresberichts 2004 der Kommission für Konjunkturfragen. Universität St. Gallen.

Kölz, A. (2004). *Neuere schweizerische Verfassungsgeschichte. Ihre Grundlinien in Bund und Kantonen seit 1848*. Bern: Stämpfli.

Kriesi, H., & Trechsel, A. H. (2008). *The politics of Switzerland. Continuity and change in a consensus democracy*. Cambridge: Cambridge University Press.

Ladner, A. (2011). Die wichtigsten institutionellen Reformen zwischen 1970 und 2010 in Bund, Kantonen und Gemeinden: Welche Rolle spielt die konjunkturelle Lage? In N. Soguel (Ed.), *Des politiques au chevet de la conjoncture* (pp. 149–174). Lausanne: Presses polytechniques universitaires romandes.

Lijphart, A. (1999). *Patterns of democracy. Government forms and performance in thirty-six countries*. New Haven: Yale University Press.

Linder, W. (1983). Entwicklung, Strukturen und Funktionen des Wirtschafts- und Sozialstaats in der Schweiz. In A. Riklin (Ed.), *Handbuch des politischen Systems der Schweiz, Band 1. Grundlagen* (pp. 255–381). Bern: Haupt.

Linder, W. (2005). *Schweizerische Demokratie. Institutionen, Prozesse, Perspektiven*. Bern: Haupt.

Mach, A. (2006). Associations d'intérêts. In U. Klöti, P. Knoepfel, H. Kriesi, W. Linder, Y. Papadopoulos, & P. Sciarini (Eds.), *Handbuch der Schweizer Politik, 4th completely* (revised ed., pp. 369–392). Zürich: Neue Zürcher Zeitung libro.

Maissen, T. (2010). *Die Geschichte der Schweiz*. Baden: Hier + jetzt.

Neidhart, L. (1970). *Plebiszit und pluralitäre Demokratie. Eine Analyse der Funktion des schweizerischen Gesetzesreferendums*. Bern: Francke.

Polli-Schönborn, M. (2006, November 6). Zölle. *Historisches Lexikon der Schweiz*. http://hls-dhs-dss.ch/textes/d/D13765.php. Accessed 30 May 2012.

Schmitter, P. (1974). Still the century of corporatism? *Review of Politics, 36*(1), 85–131.

Tanzi, V., & Schuknecht, L. (2000). *Public spending in the 20th century: A global perspective*. Cambridge: Cambridge University Press.

Vatter, A. (2016). *Das politische System der Schweiz*. Baden-Baden: Nomos UTB.

Weber, M. (1969). *Geschichte der schweizerischen Bundesfinanzen*. Bern: Haupt.

CHAPTER 2

The Organization and Provision of Public Services

Andreas Ladner

2.1 Introduction

The residents of many countries which are comparable to Switzerland all have access to more or less the same types of public services. However, how services are provided varies widely. Health care in the UK, for example, is provided by the National Health Service, but to a large degree in Switzerland, health care is provided by the cantons and communities. Swiss cantons play a central role in education; in France, it is far more centrally organized.

The key to understanding how public services are provided lies in how a country is territorially organized. As a rule in federalist countries, the middle level plays a larger role, potentially at the expense of the communities or of the central state. In unitary countries, by contrast, more tasks are performed directly by the central state, but there are also countries like Denmark or Sweden, where the communities play a very important role.

One also needs to take the relationship between different levels into account. In dual systems, one of the two levels is wholly responsible for a given task and how it is regulated, financed, and implemented, while

A. Ladner (✉)
IDHEAP, University of Lausanne, Lausanne, Switzerland
e-mail: andreas.ladner@unil.ch

A. Ladner et al. (eds.), *Swiss Public Administration*, Governance and Public Management,
https://doi.org/10.1007/978-3-319-92381-9_2

in cooperative systems, more than one level is involved in providing a given service. It is also possible, though for various reasons not always desirable, that different levels address the same task largely independently. In cooperative systems, the relations between different levels can be hierarchical or can be a partnership. Tasks can be performed by decentralized (or deconcentrated) administrative units, implementation can be carried out at lower levels (*Vollzugsföderalismus*), or task fulfillment can be achieved using negotiated contracts for specific programs or outcomes (*Programmvereinbarungen*).

Terms used today, such as the 'guarantor state' (*Gewährleistungsstaat*), the 'activating state', or 'governance', point to the fact that not all tasks have to be fulfilled by public administration bodies, but that a government must ensure that all the necessary services are available in the desired form. This blurs the distinction between public and private sectors; rather than clear, hierarchical structures, services are provided through political networks.

This chapter briefly sketches the development of state functions and describes the various areas of responsibility of different administrative levels. Expenditures at different levels for specific tasks are addressed separately. Relations between the different levels of government are an additional aspect, as is the relationship to private sector providers and the current forms cooperative efforts take.

2.2 The Development of State Functions in Historical Perspective

Prior to 1848, expenditures at the national level were limited to paying for diplomatic representation abroad, and covering the costs of the head of state (*Landammann*), the Chancellery, and a small part of the army—at the time, the cantons had jurisdiction over the latter. Beyond military expenditures, the cantons paid for roads, education, the judiciary, and the police (Stalder 2010). Social welfare was a community responsibility but only to a limited degree: when family networks proved inadequate, either the community or private institutions stepped in.[1]

At the national level, immediately after the Swiss nation-state came into being in 1848, the largest single category of outlays (55–65%) was for the military. The amount expended for administration (3%) was minimal by

[1] This section is based on Ladner (2013) and on the detailed analysis of the development of state activities found in Linder (1983).

comparison. Still, the national government did provide subsidies for cantonal roads, bridges, correcting river courses or lakes, and for reforestation in the higher mountains. With the founding of the Federal Polytechnical School in 1855 (renamed the Swiss Federal Institute of Technology or ETH (Eidgenössische Technische Hochschule) in 1911), the national government began to pay for a tertiary education institution (Halbeisen 2010). Expenditures at the cantonal level, particularly for primary education (*Volksschule*) and scientific research, had begun to play a greater role, along with cantonal spending for administration, the judiciary, the police, health care, and the military.

The military began to centralize in the period from 1874 to 1913. National-level outlays in other areas only began increasing in the 1890s, and included repurchasing railway concessions previously granted to the cantons (1898) as well as the subsequent expansion and creation of a nationwide public railroad system. Subsidies were also given for agriculture, for vocational education purposes, and for primary school teaching (after 1902). In 1884, such subsidies for civilian purposes amounted to only 7.5% of all outlays, but by 1913, this had increased to 40% (Halbeisen 2010). Such increases occurred at the same time as the founding of the Swiss National Bank (1905), the medical insurance system (1914), and the Swiss National Accident Insurance Fund (1918).

Even before the First World War, communities and cantons had begun to build an electricity industry, creating intercantonal enterprises under private law that were funded with public capital. Communities at the turn of the century were primarily engaged in expanding their water supply as well as building residences, with larger cities also expanding their public transportation networks (Linder 1983: 268). Education expenditures also grew in significance at community and cantonal levels: by 1910 in the canton of Zürich, they comprised 30% of public outlays. Spending on health care was over 20% of the canton of Bern's outlays at this time as well. Depending on the canton, there were also significant spendings for poor relief and the churches, or for agriculture and forestry.

In the war and crisis-ridden years, the national government not only faced large expenditures for military defense but it also had to ensure the country was supplied with adequate food and raw materials, alleviate inflation effects, and combat unemployment (Weber 1969: 17 et seq.). Overall, foreign affairs, agriculture, transportation, social insurance, education, and research increased in importance. Though there were fluctuations, there was a steady increase in outlays at the national level.

This began to change after the Second World War. From 1890 to 1950, the Swiss economy grew 2%, on average, but now the increase was over 5%. With a little delay, state expenditures 'explosively' increased in the 1960s, first in the outlays for infrastructure. Considerable investment, not least by the communities and cantons, was made in roads, schools, and hospitals, as well as in supply and disposal (Linder 1983: 238). Swiss higher educational institutions expanded and the national road system was enlarged.

New tasks and functions were also transferred to the state. The overall regulation, or steering, of the economy increasingly became a public responsibility, with measures to combat crises added to those meant to ensure the economy did not overheat. Economic imbalances created through urbanization and rural flight, for example, were addressed through regional planning stipulations added to the constitution (1969) and by a regional planning law passed a few years later (1976). Some of the consequences of economic growth were also countered with new water pollution and environmental protection laws (both 1971). Characteristic for these times were efforts to coordinate policy proactively, and over a longer term, by using tools such as regional and financial planning, government directives, and formulating nationwide strategies for defense, transportation, or energy (Linder 1983: 291 et seq.). This was the heyday of the interventionist and performance-oriented state.

During the worldwide recession from 1974 to 1976, the national-level measures to address crises again come to the fore. In addition to the existing instruments, anti-cyclical measures to support specific economic sectors came into play, including investment programs, housing subsidies, and export risk guarantees along with the expansion of unemployment insurance (Linder 1983: 296). Unlike during economic booms, however, the incurred costs could be covered less and less by revenue, and a discussion over the limits to the interventionist, performance-oriented state—as well as about state regulation—began. A pragmatic phase followed, one no longer oriented to bringing about larger reforms or nationwide strategies but instead to 'perpetuating' or 'freezing what already exists' (Linder 1983: 298). The center-right, in particular, criticized the increasing imbalance between revenues and outlays, and this resulted in freezing new hires in the federal administration and to a greater scrutiny of costs. In the 1990s, efforts to increase efficiency merged into larger reforms known as New Public Management (NPM; see the next chapter as well as Hablützel 2013). Parallel to this, liberal demands for deregulation focused on making labor law (and shop opening hours) more flexible, as well as preventing the creation of cartels (1996), limiting the expansion of the social welfare state, and reducing taxes (Maissen 2010: 316).

Such reforms affect the organization of services governments provide. Outsourcing efforts have increased, as have efforts to eliminate government-controlled monopolies such as in postal, telephone, and telegraph services which were state-run until the late 1990s. Reforms were carried out with two goals in mind: one was to increase, in an environment more oriented to market forces, the 'entrepreneurial' scope in providing public services; the other was to rein in the growth of the state—or to have an answer for those who criticized such perceived growth. Outsourced enterprises and 'agencies' (Pasquier and Fivat 2013) now no longer appear (wholly) in the state expenditure column, though what they do—in the case of the Swiss Federal Railroads, the post office, Swisscom, cantonal banks, hospitals, and road traffic offices—can continue to be counted as part of what the state, in a broader sense, provides.

Despite the demands for more deregulation and greater liberalization, economic downturns in the early 1990s, as well as the economic and financial crisis at the end of the 2000s, again necessitated greater government intervention. The role the national government played in 2001 (the grounding of Swissair) and in 2008 (bailing out the UBS bank), and in more recent interventions in response to a weak Euro, has made state interventions in the economy appear necessary. Still, increased globalization sets limits. The bilateral agreements with the EU, reached in the wake of the 1992 Swiss referendum turning down EEA (European Economic Area) membership, along with the fundamental need to find transnational political solutions nowadays, means that in this international context, Swiss public administrators face increasing demands which are difficult to meet if they are based only on domestic political mechanisms.

In sum, the state has continually increased in importance, and steadily taken on new tasks. This is mirrored in the figures. Per capita expenditures in 1848 stood at 24 Francs; in 2010, they were 22,680 Francs. Even when taking inflation into account, per capita expenditures today are more than 60 times greater than they were 160 years ago (Ladner 2013: 31). The growth of the state, however, goes hand in hand with a more complex fulfillment of different tasks.

2.3 Tasks Undertaken Today by the Three Levels of Government

As noted in the first chapter, one of Switzerland's characteristic features is its three-tiered, federalist, and pronouncedly fine-meshed, territorial division into about 2200 communities and 26 cantons. As also noted, the tasks delegated to the national level only gradually increased over time, not least because this alteration or expansion of mandates calls for a change to the national constitution, and these must be approved by the voters and the cantons.

Several basic principles, set out in the constitution, guide the division of tasks and responsibilities, particularly between the national level and the cantons. One of these is that in allocating and performing state tasks, 'the principle of subsidiarity must be observed' (Art. 5a). The national level only undertakes tasks cantons are unable to perform or that require uniform national regulations (Art. 43a (1)). By doing so, the principle of fiscal equivalence has to be respected; it states that whichever 'collective body' benefits from a public service also bears its costs (Art. 43a (2)) or putting it another way, the collective body paying for a public service can also decide about the nature of that service (Art. 43a (3)). The same principles guide the division of tasks and responsibilities between cantons and communities, though depending on canton, these principles may be interpreted or implemented differently.

It is contested whether such principles are applicable to every case, but at least they do offer some guidance. In the case of subsidiarity, one can argue about what calls for uniformity in regulation, or when exactly the power of the cantons is exceeded. The answers depend in part on political preferences and values. There is also a danger, under the subsidiarity principle, that the weakest cantons become the touchstone when it comes to allocating tasks. The smallest cantons reach their limits faster than do the bigger cantons in trying to perform certain tasks, which partly explains why certain responsibilities are shifted and performed by higher levels. In the case of fiscal equivalence, which links together regulation, provisioning, financing, and utilization, it is unclear how directly this utilization must incur. Not everything can be financed by those who directly utilize or can be provided by those who regulate, or regulated by those who provide. (((Drop the next sentences, the system did not accept it))) Not everything can be financed by those who directly utilize or by the providers who regulate or by regulators themselves. One should also not forget, finally, that there can be deviations from basic principles arising through constitution and law, and that certain international obligations may take no account of domestic regulatory principles.

Following the logic of how the Swiss state was structured, the national-level tasks are explicitly limited and stipulated in the constitution. Article 1 (1) of the Swiss constitution states that: 'The Confederation (*Bund*) shall carry out the duties assigned to it by the Federal Constitution'. There are 81 articles (Title 3, Ch. 2 and 3, Arts. 54–135) in the Swiss constitution listing specific tasks and competencies allocated to the national level, including the following:

- Foreign relations
- Security, national defense, and civil defense
- Education, research, and culture
- Environment and spatial planning
- Public works and transportation
- Energy and communications
- The economy
- Housing, employment, social security, and health
- Temporary and permanent residence of foreigners
- Civil law, criminal law, and weights and measures
- The financial system

The competencies, the form regulations take, the degree of national involvement and participation in provisioning, and the financing share vary by task area.[2] There are various tasks the national government shares with the cantons. The classic form of cooperation between the national government and cantons is described in Art. 46 (1): the cantons are to implement national law in accordance with the national constitution and national legislation. This organizational form is commonly referred to as implementation federalism (*Vollzugsföderalismus*). This arrangement is often criticized, since cantons receive no guarantee they will be able to participate in decision-making and may simply be required to carry out superordinate tasks—which they may even have to partly finance.

More recently, and as part of the reform of the financial equalization scheme, it has become common to talk of joint tasks (*Verbundsaufgaben*). These include those which, as part of deconcentration or 'unbundling' efforts, cannot be assigned to one or another level. The idea is that the

[2] For a detailed typology, see the 2006 corporate governance report from the Federal Council (Bericht des Bundesrates zur Auslagerung und Steuerung von Bundesaufgaben), and Waldmann and Spiess (2015).

responsibility for carrying out and financing (the fulfillment of) a given task should be shared by the national and cantonal levels, on the basis of a new type of partnership. Examples of such joint tasks include the official cadastral survey, the penal and correctional system, scholarships, nature and cultural heritage preservation, major roads, flood control, transportation in metropolitan areas, noise control, water pollution control, supplementary benefits entitlements, reduction of health insurance premiums, and improvements to structural development in agriculture, forestry, hunting, and fishing.

Within their area of competence—Art. 3 of the constitution states that they exercise all rights not vested in the national government—cantons themselves decide which tasks, and to what extent, they wish to fulfill. In that sense, cantons possess what is called a 'Residualkompetenz' (residual competencies). This also means that the portfolio of tasks will vary from canton to canton.

In recent years, cantonal constitutions have increasingly included lists of cantonal tasks and goals, in an effort to make citizens better aware of them. These give a useful survey of what the 'collective body' at this level is responsible for (Buser 2011). Detailing all the differences between the cantons would go too far, but the following list of responsibilities noted in Bern's cantonal constitution gives some idea of the scope:

- Environmental protection
- Protection of nature and cultural heritage
- Regional/land-use planning and building codes
- Transportation and roads
- Water and energy supply
- Sewage treatment and waste disposal
- Maintaining public order and security
- Social welfare
- Labor
- Habitations
- Health care
- Schools
- Universities and polytechnics
- Media
- Culture
- Leisure, sports and recreation
- Agriculture and forestry
- Cantonal usage rights (to salt, water, mountains, hunting, and fishing)
- Cantonal bank

Communities, in turn, carry out tasks determined by local, cantonal, and national policies, and in so doing, distinguish between those in their own sphere of influence and those delegated to them by canton or the national government. In delegated tasks, the community is charged with implementing decrees from canton or national government. Federal law is carried out by the communities, for example, when implementing water pollution or food inspection laws, or by civil defense regulations; cantonal laws are carried out, for example, in the school system.

Statutory regulation is also in a community's jurisdiction. Unlike tasks delegated from above which must be carried out, having this power means communities have the right to set their own laws and administrative procedures, and can on occasion even administer justice, as when they set penalties for violating community regulations (Steiner and Kaiser 2013: 150). Within a community, one can distinguish between obligatory and self-chosen tasks. In the case of obligatory tasks such as land-use planning or setting building codes, these must be carried out in accordance with national or cantonal law. Self-chosen tasks, inasmuch as they do not lie within the sole jurisdiction of the national government, the canton, or other organizations, and inasmuch as they serve the general good, may include such things as building a multipurpose community hall or a community tennis court.

In practice, it is not always easy to establish which tasks belong to which level; it often calls for an interpretation of the relevant regulations. Wastewater disposal in the canton of Zurich, for example, is a community-level task, but because cantonal law and regulations have an influence on the financing, there is little scope for communities to act as they might wish.

The tasks carried out, or services provided, by communities and their administrators vary from canton to canton. The following is a list of what is often provided (Steiner 2002):

- Kindergarten, primary school, and middle school (lasting three years)
- Welfare, outpatient care, elder care, and certain social insurance tasks
- Wasser, wastewater, refuse, and electricity
- Public transportation within the community
- Community zoning and land-use planning, building inspection, nature and cultural heritage preservation, roads and paths, sports infrastructure, and cultural institutions
- Appointment or election of officials, organization of the administration, and personnel management

- Budgeting and accounting, administering the community's property and wealth, and setting the community's tax rate
- Fire prevention authorities, traffic police, and workplace inspectors
- Granting community citizenship to foreign residents

The guiding principle behind dividing tasks between canton and community is again that of subsidiarity. Communities, inasmuch as this is objectively feasible and leads to results that are both qualitatively and quantitatively acceptable, should take on as many tasks as possible. The hope is that this will lead to better legitimation and greater responsiveness in governmental action, as well as to both more effective and more efficient service provision (Steiner and Kaiser 2013). The division of tasks between cantons and communities, however, is also a result of historical developments and political power relations. In the last ten years, numerous Swiss cantons have newly regulated the division of tasks between them, in keeping with the restructuring of tasks brought about by changes to the financial equalization scheme and the redefinition of national and cantonal tasks. Noteworthy here is the shifting of tasks upward from the communal to the cantonal level, a move often justified with reference to the greater professionalism and stronger financial position of the cantons. Smaller communities are no longer in a position to fulfill their tasks. New regulations promulgated at the federal level are often the trigger, as they call for changes to cantonal law, as in the reordering of the civil registration system in the 1990s or in changes made to child and adult protection laws in the 2010s.

2.4 Fulfilling State Tasks in Light of Revenues and Expenditures

Increasing governmental responsibilities and the importance of the various actors in fulfilling tasks is mirrored in the finances. This is all the more significant because each level in Switzerland has its own sources of income and its own budgets, and must pay for its own expenditures. This is particularly true for the communities, as there is relatively little vertical transfer of funds. Of much greater significance are the transfers between the national level and the cantons, a large part of which is made up of contributions from the national level to joint tasks and implementation costs.

In terms of expenditures, when the Swiss federal state began in 1850, the national level was the least significant: communities accounted for 47% of the expenditures, and cantons 45% (Guex 1998: 102). By 1913, the national level accounted for 22%, the cantons for 40%, followed by communities at 38%. The national level continued to increase in importance, so by the 1950s, it was the most significant source of expenditures, with communities now comprising less than 30% of the total. This trend reversed after 1960, with cantonal expenditures reflecting the expansion of the state and the economic boom. The trend has persisted: in 2014, cantons accounted for 43.4%, the national level for 33%, and communities for 23.6% of expenditures.

The low proportion of outlays at the community level is striking, particularly in international comparison. If one includes social insurance in calculating total expenditures, as is done in comparative Organisation for Economic Co-operation and Development (OECD) studies, then Switzerland belongs, at less than 20% as of 2009, to the countries with low community expenditures (OECD 2011). The share of community expenditures is still lower in German, Austrian, Spanish, and Greek communities but higher in Italy, Norway, and the Netherlands (30–35%). They were exceptionally high in Sweden (about 50%) and Denmark (over 60%). This is in contrast to the repeated assertion of how significant communities are in Switzerland. Yet this is not really so surprising, given the small average size of Swiss communities and their consequent limited ability to provide services. The part of the national level is also comparatively small. By contrast, the share of social insurance costs is large (in other countries, these form part of the expenditures of a central state, or these costs are integrated into the communities), as is the share of the cantons, an administrative and political level that is only significant in federalist countries.

If one looks at the national-level expenditures for specific tasks, then at 33.4%, social welfare—a responsibility accepted haltingly and relatively late (early nineteenth century) in Switzerland—takes the lion's share (see Table 2.1). The second largest category, considerably smaller, is transportation (11.8%), followed by education (9.5%) and the military (8.5%). Especially noticeable, historically speaking, is the relative decline in importance of the army, and the relative increase in importance of education, transportation, and the environment. That health expenditures by the national level are so low is due to the fact that the provision of health services is organized by the cantons and communities. Furthermore, the costs of treatment are borne to a very large extent by privately run health-care insurance funds, so their expenditures do not form part of state expenditure tallies.

Table 2.1 National, cantonal, and community expenditures, plus social insurance (2014)

2014	*National govt.*		*Cantonal govts.*		*Local govts.*		*Social insurance*		*Total*		
	↓	→	↓	→	↓	→	↓	→	*Total*	↓	→
	In %	*In %*	*In %*	*In %*	*In %*	*In %*	*In %*	*In %*	*In mil. CHF*	*In %*	*In %*
General administration	9.3	34.3	7.7	37.4	10.7	28.3	0.0	0.0	17,476,676	6.8	100
Public order and security, defense	8.5	***34.0***	9.0	***47.6***	6.4	18.4	0.0	0.0	16,185,942	6.3	100
Education	9.5	14.5	**28.1**	***56.6***	**26.3**	28.9	0.0	0.0	42,259,405	**16.5**	100
Culture, sports, leisure, Churches	0.7	8.8	2.0	31.2	7.0	***60.0***	0.0	0.0	5,397,629	2.1	100
Health	0.4	2.0	**14.1**	***84.9***	4.0	13.1	0.0	0.0	14,153,441	5.5	100
Social security	**33.4**	20.2	**20.2**	16.2	**18.5**	8.0	**99.3**	***55.6***	106,797,417	**41.7**	100
Transportation and communication	**13.8**	***45.5***	7.3	31.6	9.6	22.9	0.0	0.0	19,592,226	7.6	100
Environmental protection, planning	1.4	14.1	1.7	21.9	9.2	***64.0***	0.0	0.0	6,655,877	2.6	100
Economy	8.1	***45.8***	5.2	39.0	3.7	15.1	0.0	0.0	11,458,646	4.5	100
Finances and taxes	14.9	59.5	4.7	24.6	4.6	13.2	0.7	2.6	16,174,834	6.3	100
Total	100	33.0	100	43.4	100	23.6	100		256,152,093	100	
	64,726,027		85,220,441		46,403,528		59,802,097				

Source: Federal Finance Administration, financial statistics

Education (28.1%) is the large single expenditure category at the cantonal level, followed by social security (20.2%) and health (14.1%). Education is also the largest category of outlays for communities (26.3%), followed by social security (18.5%).

If one combines expenditures at all three levels, and adds social insurance outlays to it (independent of territorial entity), then the distribution of expenditures proves to be quite lopsided: more than 40% flows into social security, followed by a little more than 15% into education. All other expenditure categories are under 10%. Adding the full costs of health care (including health insurance) means more than 70% of all public spending goes to social security, health, and education.

However, listing the expenditures for specific task areas at the three political levels provides only limited information about how much leeway there is or how large an influence a particular level has in a given case. If one level is responsible only for covering the costs and another has decision-making power or room to act, then, despite contributing more funds, the significance of the former will be markedly smaller. In the cooperative federalism typical for Switzerland in which the national level lacks its own implementing administrators—unlike, say, in the US—an expansion of tasks at the national level can therefore lead to more implementation activity at the cantonal level. This increased importance of the cantonal level is thus sometimes the result of the increased scope of federal-level tasks (Vatter 2006: 223).

Cantons, and at times communities as well, have complained since the 1970s that tasks and costs increasingly are being shifted to them without a corresponding increase in decision-making power. The political interlacing (*Politikverflechtung*) of the system makes it generally more cumbersome, and it can be accompanied by a lack of clear responsibilities. Changes to the financial equalization scheme, and the reassignment of tasks,[3] particularly to be in accordance with the principle of fiscal equivalence anchored in the constitution, along with a reorganization of 'vertical cooperation', were attempts to counter such tendencies.

The largest share of revenues, which are gathered at all three levels, is provided by income taxes (see Fig. 2.1). The maximum tax rate which the national level can levy is laid out in the constitution, but cantons and communities—within certain limits—are free to set their own level of taxation

[3] The corresponding Federal Council decision of 3 October was clearly accepted by a plebiscite of the people and the cantons (64.4% and 18 5/2 cantons in favor; the electoral participation rate was 36.9%) on 28 November 2004, and came into force at the beginning of 2008.

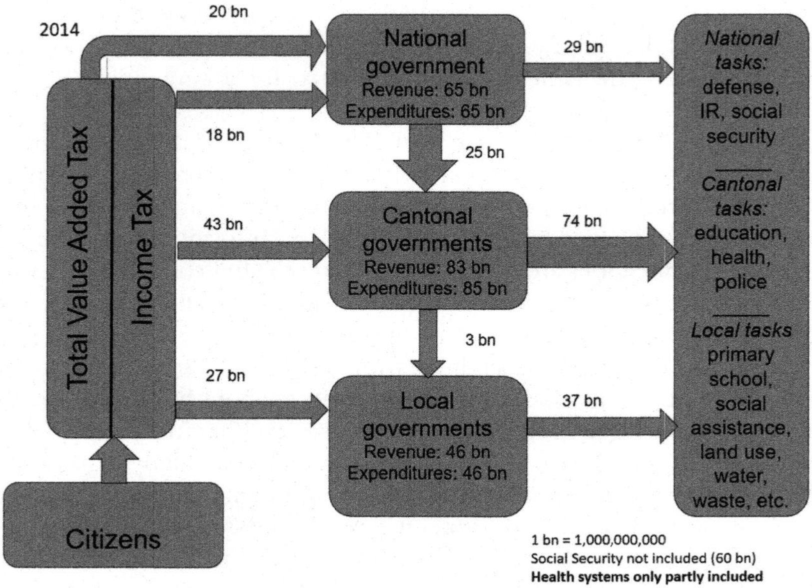

Fig. 2.1 Expenditures and revenues of the three political levels

according to their needs. As a result, the tax burden varies quite widely depending on where one lives. Most political communities also have balanced budget requirements, forcing them to keep expenditures and revenues in balance. In European comparison, the value-added tax is low and currently stands at 8%; this tax is paid directly to the national government and is its most important source of revenue.

A clear division of tasks, or of revenue sources, between political levels was not strictly observed even when the Swiss federal state began in 1848. Over time, however, the interlacing has increasingly meant lower levels carry out or implement decisions they did not participate in, with the financial flows becoming ever more complex and opaque. As noted several times, reform of the financial equalization scheme in 2008 was undertaken precisely in order to counter this tendency and to 'revitalize' Swiss federalism. But despite a new division of tasks, the financial autonomy of the individual political levels, and a declared commitment to fiscal equivalence, considerable interlacing, especially between the national level and the cantons, remains. Of the 63 billion Francs revenue received at the national level in 2010, nearly 19 billion (nearly 30%) of that was transferred to the cantons, and about 14 billion was transferred to social insurance, especially for pensions and disability insurance. Most of the transfers to the cantons, which amount to more than 11 billion Francs, are linked to tasks performed by the cantons and come in the form of contributions, compensation, or investment. The cantonal share of federal revenues run to about 4.5 billion (direct federal tax, withholding tax, gasoline tax, heavy vehicle tax, etc.), and about 3 billion are accounted for by the federal share of the financial equalization scheme between the cantons.

That the higher level spends less money directly than it receives, and that a part of its revenues flows to the lower level, is a phenomenon one finds in all (federalist) states (Anderson 2010: 50). Herein also lies the justification for a central state to steer activities at the lower level, as well as to equalize the differences between the various territorial bodies. Characteristic of Switzerland, however, is how low the national share of total expenditures is, and how much of that flows, as transfers, into other public budgets. The national government, and this can be read out of how it developed historically, was in many areas never given the sole competence to provide state services. It was also not given independent power to increase its resources by raising value added or direct federal tax rates. The power to do so is set out in the constitution, and such increases cannot even be decided by parliament but must be approved by a majority of the voters and of the cantons.

2.5 Intergovernmental Relations and Cooperation with the Private Sector

If one examines the expenditures, one can see that the political levels are seldom solely responsible for a given policy area or for fulfilling a specific task. Instead, vertical cooperation between political levels as well as horizontal cooperation between cantons, or between communities, matter considerably more.[4] To this one should add the cooperation with private sector actors, at all three levels.

2.5.1 Vertical Cooperation

In the case of vertical cooperation, the first question is how hierarchical, or conversely how egalitarian, the relationship between the three levels is—and more to the point, how independent lower levels are. The relationship

[4] On intergovernmental relations in Switzerland, see Ladner (2010).

between the national level and the cantons is often discussed in terms of sovereignty, and that between canton and community is often couched in terms of autonomy.

The determinative question is who is responsible for which aspects of task performance and to what degree. Without going into too much detail, one can distinguish between regulation, financing, and implementation. Following the principle of fiscal equivalence (see the constitutional articles noted above), these three should coincide—though this is not always possible to achieve in jointly implemented tasks.

As a rule, authority to set regulations lies at higher levels, with lower levels given less or more decision-making scope in this process. But part of the financing and implementation are in the competency of the cantons. Depending on the particular area, the national government may help finance but as a rule is not involved in actual implementation: Article 46 (1) explicitly states that the cantons are the implementers of federal law.

Reform of the financial equalization scheme in 2008 tried to modernize, and clarify, vertical cooperation in the country. As part of the 'program agreements' (*Programmvereinbarungen*), cantons and the national government (at times, with the communities and in consultation with private sector service providers) may sign four-year agreements which clearly define the tasks to be undertaken. They also contain a fixed funding formula. The idea is to complete stated tasks based on a partnership, one in which strategic questions are handled at the national level and the operative implementation is left to the cantons.

Cooperation between communities and cantons is less complex, though communities, of course, do insist on their independence and resist efforts to increase the financial burdens they already bear. Generally speaking, and in international comparison, Swiss communities have a very high degree of autonomy (Ladner et al. 2016). However, they are weaker than Scandinavian communities when it is a matter of political discretion they are granted in fulfilling tasks.

As far as vertical cooperation is concerned, the standard view has been that the national level negotiates with the cantons, and the cantons then negotiate with the communities. In more recent times, this model has proven inadequate, since there are cases of multi-level policy-making (tripartism) of this kind found in descriptions of multi-level governance. Art. 50 provides the constitutional basis, as it not only guarantees the autonomy of the communities, in accordance with cantonal law, but also explicitly states that the national government must take the possible consequences of policies for communities into account. Indeed, the national government is also obligated to take the special position of cities and urban regions, as well as that of the mountain regions, into account. Regional planning in urbanized areas or integration/inclusion policies are examples of policy areas coordinated through tripartite practices.

2.5.2 Horizontal Cooperation

Horizontal cooperation plays an important role in carrying out tasks at lower levels; here it refers to cooperation either between the cantons or between the communities. For a long time, the former played a relatively subordinated role, but this has changed and now is of considerably more importance (Bochsler 2009). Such cooperation includes coordination between cantons over policy areas (without including the national government), exchange of information about cantonal experiences with policies, representing common cantonal interests vis-à-vis the national government, and in more recent years, organizing common implementation of political tasks (Bochsler and Sciarini 2006; Vatter 2016: 468).

The organizational expression of such cooperation includes the Conference of Cantonal Governments (since 1993), four regional (Western, Northwestern, Eastern, and Central) conferences of cantonal governments, policy-specific conferences (Cantonal Finance Directors' Conference, Cantonal Education Directors' Conference, etc.), as well as intercantonal meetings between specialized officials. More than 500 such bodies exist in the various branches of the cantonal public administrations, which create a dense and influential network of relationships (Iff et al. 2010). The organizational center for this activity is the House of the Cantons in Bern—and this degree of activity has led to some grumbling that it competes with the *Ständerat*, the upper house of Parliament which represents the cantons.

There are also more than 800 *Konkordate* ('concordats', meaning contracts or agreements) between the cantons, the vast majority of which are less than 40 years old (Bochsler 2009). Their main purpose is to regulate intercantonal and regional cooperation. About three-quarters of the concordats are bicantonal; only a dozen or so involve all the cantons (Vatter 2016: 470). Most concordats address tax or finance, education, research, or cultural issues.

Intercantonal cooperation efforts are often criticized for their ponderousness and a tendency to be technocratic or over-determined by administrators and executives. Cantonal parliaments do have less influence in preparing and carrying out concordats than they have in the case of cantonal laws, though there have been efforts to address this through greater cantonal inter-parliamentary cooperation.

A special form of intercantonal cooperation is laid out in Art. 48a of the Swiss constitution, which identifies areas (including cantonal higher education institutions, cultural institutions of supraregional importance, urban transportation, and advanced medical science) over which the national government, at the request of interested cantons (as a rule, 18 are needed), can declare intercantonal agreements to be binding or can require cantons to participate in them. This constitutional article was a direct result of changes made to the financial equalization scheme. Interestingly, it is a way cantons can initiate nationwide rules without the national parliament being involved in shaping them. That no such generally binding agreements have yet been crafted shows that this invitation for cantons to coordinate their efforts works.

Cooperation between communities is equally widespread, following a variety of organizational models. The 'community seat' model (*Sitzgemeindemodell*) foresees a (larger) community fulfilling certain defined tasks for other communities or a special purpose association (*Zweckverband*, a juridical entity) can be designated as the entity responsible for fulfilling a certain task. Communities do cooperate in service provisions, including in common fire brigades, providing medical services, school cooperation, wastewater and sewage systems, eldercare, or in waste disposal. Most Swiss communities say they work with at least one other community in providing such services (Steiner and Kaiser 2013: 164). Numerous newer cantonal constitutions also have articles which make it possible to force communities to cooperate should they not themselves be in the position of providing certain services in a satisfactory manner.

The small size of certain communities and cantons is a factor which favors cooperation. Very small communities may not be able to have their own schools for lack of pupils and therefore cooperate with neighboring communities to provide education. In consequence, inter-community cooperation is often seen as an alternative to community mergers—which have increased sharply in recent decades. Similarly, the smaller cantons do not have their own universities, so it has been necessary for them to find cooperative solutions with the cantons which do.

2.5.3 *Cooperation with Private Actors and Outsourcing*

Public tasks are fulfilled not only by the state in a narrower sense, but also in cooperation with the private sector. These can range from dependent institutions given contracts to provide services to private enterprises given public sector contract to fully private enterprises which provide services that are of a public nature.

Enterprises, institutes, or agencies under public law, which belong fully to the national government but which may be separate legal entities, include the Swiss Institute for Intellectual Property, the two Federal Institutes of Technology (ETH), and the Federal Pension Fund (Publica). Furthest away from the core of the administration one finds enterprises under public law or under special provisions in which the national government is the sole or majority owner. This includes former state monopolies, such as the SBB(Schweizerische Bundesbahnen)/the Swiss Railway, Swisscom, and the Swiss Post. Similarly, the maintenance and production facilities of the Swiss army have been turned into Ruag, a joint stock company under private law; it describes itself as engaged in aerospace defense technology. Similarly, the national government's former control of Swiss airspace and air navigation, both civilian and military, is now in the hands of Skyguide, a joint stock company.

According to 'The Cantons as Enterprises' (Meister and Rühli 2009), a 2009 study, cantons cooperated with or participated in about 600 independent (private) enterprises in the following sectors:

- 190 in public transportation
- 146 in financing (banks, insurance companies, credit or surety cooperatives)
- 102 in energy
- 56 in education
- 42 in health (esp. hospitals)
- 447 other (esp. in agriculture)

Our own community surveys (see *Gemeindemonitoring* 2017) found that in areas such as the computerization of administrative services, zoning and regional planning, energy supply, or supplementary childcare, one in five communities made use of private sector providers.

In addition to certain entrepreneurial freedoms granted in Switzerland, the subsidiarity principle is at work here too, though in its horizontal manifestations. In keeping with the tradition of Catholic social thought, this principle argues that as much as possible, all tasks should be carried out through private efforts. The state should only intervene when this is objectively justifiable, thereby reinforcing the reluctance to having a strong state.

A further force encouraging cooperation with the private sector is size. Many communities, and even certain cantons, are too small to be able to afford an extensive, efficient public administration, so it is not surprising that relief is sought from the private sector. Preparations for construction permits or local land-use plans, the maintenance of streets, or the care provided to the elderly are given into the hands of private providers. The call for greater private involvement in public tasks in the 'provider' or 'guarantor' state (*Gewährleistungsstaat*) also comes from advocates of NPM. This effort is meant, among other things, to create competitive structures as well as to profit from greater entrepreneurial and economic liberties.

2.5.4 New Cooperation Forms: Multi-level Governance

Multi-level politics and cooperation with private actors merge into an organizational form called multi-level governance in the literature. Cooperation between the political levels is no longer hierarchical, and both public and private actors participate in shaping politics and implementing policies. With this, all the characteristics of the concept of governance, as suggested by Kersbergen and Van Waarden (2004: 152) and others, are fulfilled. One can see it illustrated in urban development or integration policies, in the various program agreements, or in national policy discourses about welfare, health, energy, or culture. Given their experience(s), private service providers, together with local, cantonal, and national authorities, are involved in helping to formulate policy.

However, studies of this new organizational form, not to speak of experience with it, are still largely lacking, so that one cannot yet speak of a new, promising form of policy coordination and policy steering. But there are certainly efforts being made to address ever more complex demands being made on the various policy areas.

References

Anderson, G. (2010). *Fiscal federalism: A comparative introduction*. Oxford: Oxford University Press.

Bochsler, D. (2009). Neighbours or friends? When Swiss cantonal governments co-operate with each other. *Regional & Federal Studies, 19*(3), 349–370.

Bochsler, D., & Sciarini, P. (2006). Konkordate und Regierungskonferenzen. Standbeine des horizontalen Föderalismus. *LeGes, 17*(1), 23–41.

Buser, D. (2011). *Kantonales Staatsrecht. Eine Einführung für Studium und Praxis*. Basel: Helbing & Lichtenhahn.

Guex, S. (1998). *L'argent de l'Etat – Parcours des finances publiques au XXème siècle*. Lausanne: réalités sociales.

Hablützel, P. (2013). Bürokratie – Management – Governance: Schweizer Verwaltungsführung im Wandel. In A. Ladner, J.-L. Chappelet, Y. Emery, P. Knoepfel, L. Mader, N. Soguel, & F. Varone (Eds.), *Handbuch der öffentlichen Verwaltung in der Schweiz* (pp. 93–108). Zürich: Neue Zürcher Zeitung libro.

Halbeisen, P. (2010). Öffentlicher Haushalt. *Historisches Lexikon der Schweiz*. http://www.hls-dhs-dss.ch/textes/d/D26197.php. Accessed 7 May 2012.

Iff, A., Sager, F., Herrmann, E., & Wirz, R. (2010). *Interkantonale und interkommunale Zusammenarbeit. Defizite bezüglich parlamentarischer und direktdemokratischer Mitwirkung (unter besonderer Berücksichtigung des Kantons Bern)*. Bern: KPM Verlag.

Kersbergen, K., & Waarden, F. (2004). 'Governance' as a bridge between disciplines: Cross-disciplinary inspiration regarding shifts in governance and problems of governability, accountability and legitimacy. *European Journal of Political Research, 43*(2), 143–171.

Ladner, A. (2010). Intergovernmental relations in Switzerland: Towards a new concept for allocating tasks and balancing differences. In M. J. Goldsmith & E. C. Page (Eds.), *Changing government relations in Europe: From localism to intergovernmentalism* (pp. 210–227). London: Routledge/ECPR Studies in European Political Science.

Ladner, A. (2013). Der Schweizer Staat, politisches System und Aufgabenerbringung. In A. Ladner, J.-L. Chappelet, Y. Emery, P. Knoepfel, L. Mader, N. Soguel, & F. Varone (Eds.), *Handbuch der öffentlichen Verwaltung in der Schweiz* (pp. 23–46). Zürich: Neue Zürcher Zeitung libro.

Ladner, A., Keuffer, N., & Baldersheim, H. (2016). Measuring local autonomy in 39 countries (1990–2014). *Regional & Federal Studies, 26*(3), 321–357.

Linder, W. (1983). Entwicklung, Strukturen und Funktionen des Wirtschafts- und Sozialstaats in der Schweiz. In A. Riklin (Ed.), *Handbuch des politischen Systems der Schweiz, Band 1. Grundlagen* (pp. 255–381). Bern: Haupt.

Maissen, T. (2010). *Die Geschichte der Schweiz*. Baden: hier + jetzt.

Meister, U., & Rühli, L. (2009). Kantone als Konzerne. Zürich: Avenir Suisse. https://www.avenir-suisse.ch/publication/kantone-als-konzerne/. Accessed 31 May 2018.

OECD (Organisation for Economic Co-operation and Development). (2011). *Government at a glance 2011*. Paris: OECD Publishing.

Pasquier, M., & Fivat, E. (2013). Die autonomen öffentlichen Organisationen oder Agencies. In A. Ladner, J.-L. Chappelet, Y. Emery, P. Knoepfel, L. Mader, N. Soguel, & F. Varone (Eds.), *Handbuch der öffentlichen Verwaltung in der Schweiz* (pp. 183–198). Zürich: Neue Zürcher Zeitung libro.

Stalder, H. (2010). Öffentlicher Haushalt. *Historisches Lexikon der Schweiz.* http://www.hls-dhs-dss.ch/textes/d/D26197.php. Accessed 7 May 2012.
Steiner, R. (2002). *Interkommunale Zusammenarbeit und Gemeindezusammen schlüsse in der Schweiz.* Bern: Haupt.
Steiner, R., & Kaiser, C. (2013). Die Gemeindeverwaltungen. In A. Ladner, J.-L. Chappelet, Y. Emery, P. Knoepfel, L. Mader, N. Soguel, & F. Varone (Eds.), *Handbuch der öffentlichen Verwaltung in der Schweiz* (pp. 149–166). Zürich: Neue Zürcher Zeitung libro.
Vatter, A. (2006). Die Kantone. In U. Klöti, P. Knoepfel, H. Kriesi, W. Linder, Y. Papadopoulos, & P. Sciarini (Eds.), *Handbuch der Schweizer Politik*, 4th completely revised edition (pp. 203–232). Zürich: Neue Zürcher Zeitung libro.
Vatter, A. (2016). *Das politische System der Schweiz.* Baden-Baden: Nomos UTB.
Waldmann, B., & Spiess, A. (2015). Aufgaben- und Kompetenzverteilung im schweizerischen Bundesstaat. Typologie der Aufgaben und Kompetenzen von Bund und Kantonen. Institut für Föderalismus. Gutachten im Auftrag der Konferenz der Kantonsregierungen (KdK).
Weber, M. (1969). *Geschichte der schweizerischen Bundesfinanzen.* Bern: Haupt.

CHAPTER 3

The Characteristics of Public Administration in Switzerland

Andreas Ladner

3.1 Introduction

As the history of the country, the founding of the modern Swiss state and its political institutions, the organization of public services, and the understanding of state task fulfillment as the basis for public administration have been addressed already, this chapter is devoted to the characteristics of its various administrations. The plural is deliberate. The federalist structure, along with the many cultural differences in the country, means one cannot treat public administration in Switzerland as a unitary entity. The Confederation, the cantons, the cities, and the communities each have their own administrations which differ from one another—beyond their common basic responsibilities.

For Switzerland, as elsewhere, public administration has increased in importance vis-à-vis politics, due to the greater professionalization and specialization which go hand in hand with the heightened complexity of political tasks nowadays. As the locus of important decisions shifts to higher, or even international, levels, the administrators who carry out decisions come to have more and more influence and distance themselves

A. Ladner (✉)
IDHEAP, University of Lausanne, Lausanne, Switzerland
e-mail: andreas.ladner@unil.ch

A. Ladner et al. (eds.), *Swiss Public Administration*, Governance and Public Management,
https://doi.org/10.1007/978-3-319-92381-9_3

from the policy makers. Also the 'militia' manner in which public services are organized and delivered that is still widely used in Switzerland nowadays only works if politicians can rely on strong administrations.

Switzerland does not have a politicized administration that is replaced when a new government comes to power, and party affiliation is not a precondition for employment in the higher civil service. Still, such affiliation can be important when filling top administrative posts: it is not uncommon for successful applicants to belong to the personal political network, and hence to the party, of the elected politician who selects them. At the local level, some of the community secretaries (*Gemeindeschreiber*), the highest civil servant, are still elected, though less often so than in the past.

Despite various criticisms, the degree of bureaucratization in Switzerland remains relatively low, and the various public administrations are generally not perceived as authoritarian, superordinate powers one must submit to. That the aspect of service provision is more prominent may in the end be due to a direct democratic system in which the voters have the last word—and perhaps also that voter's tax monies directly pay the wages of administrators. This becomes particularly visible at the local level. The level of satisfaction with administrative service provision is exceptionally high, particularly at the community level and also compared with such satisfaction levels in other prosperous countries (Denters et al. 2016). Residents are highly satisfied with the accessibility and performance of their administrators, and this makes the Swiss civil service system interesting to outside observers.

This chapter describes the scope of the public sector and administration in a narrower sense, followed by a description of how the various governmental levels are organized. The more important characteristics of the Swiss administrations are then discussed, as well as reforms which have been carried out in recent years. The chapter closes with a brief comparison of the Swiss system of public administrations with those in other West European countries.

3.2 The Delimitation and Scope of Public Administration

It is not that easy to determine the scope of public administration, nor its changes over time, due to the relatively fluid boundary between public and private sectors in Switzerland, and also because the attribution of tasks has changed through the years. There is a gray area where governmental bodies provide services also provided by private actors, or where mixed-economy and private enterprises are charged with providing public services. Demarcation problems arise, on the one hand, in trying to separate core administration in a narrower sense from what other governmental actors do, and, on the other hand, in clearly separating public and private sectors. Employees of the postal service or the national railroads, for example, are not counted as part of public administration in a narrower sense, yet they provide public services and are employed by the government (formally, as *Staatspersonal*). Hospital employees too, depending on who owns their place of employment, may either count as public sector employees (e.g., of a canton) or as part of the private sector.

The nomenclature used by the Swiss Federal Statistical Office bases its determination of what counts as part of the public sector on the legal form a given administrative entity takes.[1] Public administration in a narrow sense thus includes national, cantonal, district, and community administrations, along with public corporations. Commercially oriented entities over which the government holds a controlling majority are counted among the public enterprises,[2] as are the public enterprises of the cantons, the districts, the communities, the public enterprises of a corporate body, as well as entities under public law. The public sector is composed of these public enterprises and entities, along with the public administrations in a narrower sense.

As of 2015, the Swiss public sector comprised about 575,000 full-time positions (see Table 3.1),[3] or about 15 percent of all full-time positions. Just under two-thirds of these positions were in the public administrations, and a little more than a third were in public enterprises. In the case of the former, the largest share, at a little more than half, is accounted for by cantonal public administrations. About one-quarter of these positions are in the communities, and about 10 percent are at the national level. Among public enterprises, the largest share by far consists of positions in the public institutions, followed by the cantons and the communities.

[1] The NOGA (*Nomenclature générale des activités économiques*) makes it possible, based on their economic activity, to classify the statistical units 'enterprises' and 'workplaces'. NOGA 2008 is the current version.

[2] The legal entities which fall under corporate law (such as stock companies, sole proprietorships or unregistered partnerships) can also offer public services. However, they are not counted as part of the public sector and instead belong to the private sector.

[3] See BFS – STATENT.

Table 3.1 Full-time equivalent (FTE) positions, public sector employees, by legal form (2015)

Legal form	*FTE*	*In %*	*In %*
Public sector	572,044.3		100.0
Public administrations	373,969.5	100.0	65.4
National administration	36,071.3	9.6	6.3
Cantonal administration	190,145.6	50.8	33.2
District administration	1072.1	0.3	0.2
Community administration	92,329.9	24.7	16.1
Entities under public law[a]	54,350.6	14.5	9.5
Public enterprises	198,074.8	100.0	34.6
Cantonal public enterprises	40,075.7	20.2	7.0
District public enterprises	824.7	0.4	0.1
Community public enterprises	26,511.9	13.4	4.6
Corporate body public enterprises[b]	14,438.6	7.3	2.5
Entities under public law	116,223.9	58.7	20.3

Source: BFS – STATENT: https://www.pxweb.bfs.admin.ch (consulted on September 2, 2017), published values (provisional)

[a]These are public corporations which cannot be listed as falling under national, cantonal, district, or community administration, such as municipal associations, administrative districts, the public bodies responsible for schools in certain cantons (*Schulgemeinden*), and administrations managed by several corporate bodies. See Datenstandard eCH-0097, Version 3.0

[b]Public enterprises which cannot be listed under national, cantonal, district, or community enterprises, such as the forestry enterprises of residents' communities (*Ortsbürgergemeinden*) in certain cantons. See Datenstandard eCH-0097, Version 3.0

The growth of the public sector has been a repeated subject of political controversy. However, the statistics show that the share of the public sector has actually diminished, at least in recent years. My own calculations based on Federal Statistical Office figures show the numbers shrank by around 2000 full-time equivalents (FTEs) from 2012 to 2015. If one looks at the changes in FTEs relative to population increase, then the reduction is even clearer. In 2012, there were 72.2 FTEs per 1000 residents; in 2015, this stood at 69.4 FTEs. Hence there was a reduction in the public sector share of all positions from 15.4 to 14.9 percent, largely due to changes in public enterprises and entities under public law. Among the public administrations, however, FTEs increased from 44.9 per 1000 residents in 2012 to 45.4 FTEs in 2015, or from 9.6 to 9.8 percent of all employees.

The figures from the 2001, 2005, and 2008 business censuses showed no great shift of positions from the private to the public sector, either.[4]

[4] See Branchenporträt des öffentlichen Sektors (2015), p. 9 and 10.

Unfortunately, such figures do not allow one to follow developments over a longer time period, and the constantly changing definitions and categories do not make a definitive assessment easy. There is still a notion in Switzerland that the public sector generally, and public administration in a narrower sense, continue to increase in importance, at least in terms of positions and wages.[5] The empirical evidence, however, is less unanimous or conclusive.

The proportion of Swiss public sector employees is markedly lower than in most other comparable countries. In Scandinavia, especially Denmark and Norway, it lies near 30 percent; at about 10 percent, Switzerland is right behind Germany and well below the Organisation for Economic Co-operation and Development (OECD) average (OECD 2017a). Particularly noteworthy is the low share, at under 10 percent, of those employed at the national level in Switzerland, largely due to the country's federalist political structure. Yet even among federalist countries, this is very low. It may in part be due to a unique understanding of the state as well as to a particularly pronounced decentralization (OECD 2017b).

The largest single public administration in Switzerland is at the national level. If one looks at the development of civil service positions here, then one sees an increase starting around the year 2000 followed by a marked reduction (Fig. 3.1). In the following decade, the numbers again increased, reaching a plateau of about 35,000.[6] As the country's population also increased substantially in this period, then at least in terms of positions per 1000 residents, the tendency since 2003 has actually been regressive. At least some of the reduction in personnel is probably attributable to efforts at rationalizing jobs and increasing efficiency, in turn related to externalizing some activities, dispensing with certain services, and outsourcing specific task areas. There is relatively high political pressure in the country to not increase the outlays for public administration activities.

Evidence for an implicit ceiling of 35,000 also is reflected by figures from the 1970s, 1980s, and 1990s, when between 32,000 and 35,000 national-level administrative positions were recorded. Since 2000, a

[5] See the NZZ, February 3, 2017.

[6] Though the Federal Council had proposed 254 FTEs for 2016, as well as 177.5 additional FTEs based on internal changes, the total actually reduced (−21 FTE, for a total of 34,914 positions) for the first time in six years. This was due in part to cuts in personnel the Federal Council had decided upon, as well as a certain reluctance to recruit (Bericht zur Bundesrechnung R2016, Vol. 1, p. 79).

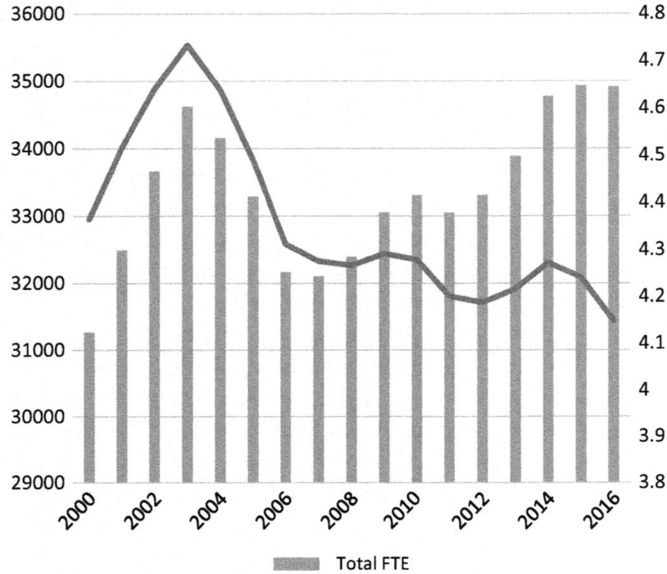

Fig. 3.1 National administrative positions and total positions per 1000 residents

number of entities, including the ETHs (Eidgenössische Technische Hochule) in Zurich and Lausanne, have no longer been listed under the 'general national administration' heading (Varone 2013: 113)—though they accounted for nearly 15,000 positions. Many of these are supported through third-party funding.

The government holds a majority of the shares in a number of large enterprises, such as Swisscom (telecommunications), and controls others (the postal service, the Swiss railroads, the defense company Ruag), and though these are not counted as part of the national administration in a narrower sense, they account together for considerably more than 100,000 FTEs (2015–16). With 44,000 employees in the postal service, 21,000 at Swisscom, and 9000 at Ruag, the current numbers in these enterprises are higher than in previous decades. The national railroads, at 33,000 FTEs, have also increased their employment compared to the turn of the millennium. However, one should not forget that the number of beneficiaries of these services (e.g., railroad passengers) also has increased, as have the services provided.

Most public administration staff, as noted, work at the cantonal level. In 2015, all cantons together employed about 190,000 FTEs, plus an additional 40,000 in cantonal public enterprises. The most populous cantons (Zurich, Bern, Vaud, Geneva) have the largest administrations, though it is noteworthy that Zurich's cantonal administration (19 positions per 1000 residents) is significantly smaller than in these other cantons (26, 28, and 44 positions per 1000 in Bern, Vaud, and Geneva, respectively).

There are various reasons for this. In addition to the respective significance accorded the public sector, how public services are provided, for example, as a division of labor between public and private enterprises, or between canton and community, has an influence on the size of a cantonal administration. The centrality of a canton can play a role as well. Generally, the more urban a canton is (e.g., Geneva, Basel-City), the larger the cantonal administration. French-speaking cantons traditionally also give more weight to the public sector and prefer tasks being carried out at the cantonal rather than at the community level. One can speak of a kind of cantonalization of administration in French-speaking Switzerland but of a municipalization in German-speaking Switzerland.

In 2015, more than 92,000 FTEs worked as municipal administrators, plus an additional 27,000 in municipal public enterprises. Less work at the community than at the cantonal level, and communities have dwindled in relative importance as employers over the last few decades compared with the cantons. This is largely due to the considerable expansion at the cantonal level in education and health sectors.

There is even more variation in the size of administrations at the community level than among the cantons. In the smallest communities (less than 500 inhabitants), of which many still exist, the administration consists of the community secretary (*Gemeindeschreiber*) and at most one or two additional employees who divide less than two FTEs between them. The cities, by contrast, have fully developed and effective public administrations which may employ several thousand people. The relative size of community administrations, defined as the number of employees per 100 residents, takes a U-shaped form. As the number of residents increases, the relative number of community employees at first declines, but then gradually rises—above about 2000 residents—and reaches its highest values in the cities. This confirms findings familiar from research on organizations and administration: with increasing size of an organizational unit, a degree of rationalization can be achieved in fulfilling tasks, but that with increased functional differentiation, coordination efforts, and with it the costs, of administration begin to rise again (Geser et al. 1996).

If one compares the administrative density among the largest Swiss cities, defined as the number of city employees per 1000 residents, Zurich (28.5 positions) has the highest density, followed by Lausanne (27.5). At first glance, the difference between German-speaking Zurich and French-speaking Lausanne does not appear all that large. But in Zurich, one needs to add the 25 positions in the city's public enterprises, while Lausanne has only seven (per 1000 residents). This is corroboration for the point noted above: administration at the community level plays a greater role in German-speaking Switzerland than it does in Western, French-speaking Switzerland. French-speaking Geneva, for example, has only 18.5 positions (per 1000 residents) in city administration, and none at all in city public enterprise, due to a strong cantonal presence in public administration. Likewise, Bern has no positions in the city's public enterprises, and thus has a comparatively low administrative employment of 21 (per 1000 residents). Strong cantonalization is at work here, as is the fact that it plays less of a role as a regional center: the area taken up by the city itself is very small, and it is encircled by larger, high-performing communities.

According to surveys we have repeatedly carried out, the number of community personnel has increased over the last 20 years. In 2016, about 60 percent of the communities (n = 1757) have noted an increase in the number of positions over the last decade, while 30 percent report no change. Increases are largely confined to larger communities and cities.

3.3 Organizational Structure

The Swiss ***national administration***[7] is divided into seven Federal Departments: Foreign Affairs (FDFA), Home Affairs (FDHA), Justice and Police (FDJP), Defense, Civil Protection and Sports (DDPS), Finance (FDF), Economic Affairs, Education and Research (EAER), and Environment, Transportation, Energy, and Communications (DETEC). To this one should add the Federal Chancellery (FCh). The Departments have General Secretariats—four also have State Secretariats—and a variety of Offices and other units below them.

Compared to the Ministries found in other countries, there are few Departments, and this is directly related to the number of Federal Councilors (***Bundesräte***). The national executive, the Federal Council (***Bundesrat***), has consisted of seven members since 1848 (see Chap. 1),

[7] For a detailed overview, see Varone (2013).

and the number of Departments in the national administration reflects this. Some of them are quite large and heterogeneous: the head of the UVEK (Eidgenössisches Departement für Umwelt, Verkehr, Energie und Kommunikation) Department is simultaneously Minister for Transportation, Minister for Energy, Minister for Communications, and Minister for the Environment, and in international negotiations, depending on subject area, must deal with numerous different colleagues.

In terms of national civil service employment, the DDPS (Defense), at 30 percent in 2015, accounts for the largest share, followed by the FDF at about 25 percent, and the FDFA at about 15 percent (see Table 3.2). The other four departments all have less, though the number of employees is not directly related to how much that department spends. Thus, the FDHA, at about one-quarter, has the largest share, closely followed by the FDF; the share of the DDPS (Defense), however, has shrunk, and now stands at less than 8 percent.

The real backbone of the national administration is found at the lower level, in the Offices and other units associated with a given Department (Grisel 1984: 213). The Departments themselves are relatively immobile, so governmental activities occurs at these lower levels; in most departments, the number of such offices and other units have grown in the last century (see Table 3.3). Only in the DDPS (Defense), despite its size, can one see a countertendency owing to recent changes and reorganization efforts. The State Secretariat for Education, Research, and Innovation

Table 3.2 Personnel (positions) and expenditures (million CHF) by departments in 2015

Departments	*Employees (absolute)*	*Employees (in %)*	*Expenditures (in million CHF)*	*Expenditures (in %)*
FCh	216	0.6	46	0.1
FDFA	5537	15.8	3170	4.8
FDFI	2227	6.3	16,870	25.7
FDJP	2410	6.9	2280	3.5
DDPS	11,670	33.2	4850	7.4
FDF	8681	24.7	16,230	24.7
EAER	2150	6.1	12,220	18.6
DETEC	2232	6.4	10,000	15.2
Total	35,123	100	65,666	100.0

Source: Der Bund kurz erklärt 2017: 42 ff

Note: Entities with large degrees of autonomy (the ETHs formally under the FDHA, FINMA under the FDF, or the Competition Commission under the EAER) are not included here

Table 3.3 Number of offices directly under department heads, 1928 to 2017

Year/department	*FDFA*	*FDFI*	*FDJP*	*DDPS*	*FDF*	*EAER*	*DEVEC*	*Total*
1928	1	7	6	15	7	6	3	45
1959	4	12	6	11	8	6	6	53
1980	5	14	8	7	13	7	7	61
1991	6	11	11	7	11	8	7	61
2001	5	11	11	7	10	8	9	58
2006	6	11	9	7	11	8	7	59
2011	6	12	10	6	11	10	8	63
2017	7	11	12	7	12	10	8	67

Sources: Germann (1996: 49) for 1928–91 and Der Bund kurz erklärt 2017 for 2001, 2006, 2011, and 2017

(SERI) and the ETHs, both previously in the FDHA (Interior), were transferred into the newly named Department of Economic Affairs, Education, and Research (previously: Federal Department of Economic Affairs), and together with the Commission for Technology and Innovation (CTI) comprise the new SERI.

The General Secretariats play a significant role in the individual Departments. They coordinate the administrative work of or for the Swiss parliament and the Federal Council, and serve as the interface between the various Offices in a Department and the respective Federal Councilor. In doing so, they undertake planning, coordination, consulting, and controlling or monitoring tasks, exert influence on personnel and finances, and also have the job of communicating messages externally. The individual General Secretariats are also responsible for, and provide, other, partly department-specific services, including for Presence Switzerland [public diplomacy, nation-branding], to aid gender equality, carry out translations, answer consumer inquiries, and so forth.

Certain areas are not directly under the respective Departments and follow a different organizational logic. This includes institutions and enterprises located farther afield as well as the 'militia' administration. In the case of the former, these include the enterprises, institutes, or agencies under public law which belong entirely to the Swiss Confederation, some of which may even be separate legal entities (e.g., the Swiss Institute for Intellectual Property, the two Federal Institutes of Technology [ETH], and the Federal Pension Fund [Publica]). Further from the center, one finds enterprises under public law or under special provisions in which the national government is the sole or majority owner. This includes former state monopolies, such as the SBB/the Swiss Railway, Ruag Holding, Skyguide SA, the Swiss National Accident Insurance Fund SUVA, Swisscom, and the Swiss Post (Pasquier and Fivat 2013: 192). This segment of the Swiss public administration has gradually opened to greater competition.

Extra-parliamentary commissions, brought to life by the Federal Council or by individual Departments to carry out certain public tasks, are counted as part of the 'militia administration'. Their members are mostly not federal civil servants but rather experts, and they are asked to address a large range of political and policy tasks. A commission might take the form of a board of experts or consultants who offer advice to federal administrators, or of interested parties who help with the preliminary work for proposed laws, or they might be those parties interested and involved in implementing specific policies. One study found 223 commissions of this kind in 2010 (Rebmann and Mach 2013: 167, 170).

Examples of such commissions, which gives an idea of just how broad a range of issues this 'militia administration' addresses, include the Anti-Racism Commission, the Commission for Women's Issues, the Tobacco Control Commission, the Consumer Affairs Commission, the Commission for Radiopharmaceuticals, the Regional Planning Council, and the Swiss Delegation for the Regulation of Lake of Geneva. Over time, the work of some of these commissions can result in creating regulatory authorities which themselves may come to play significant roles in the nation's administration. Prominent examples include the Competition Commission (under the EAER), the Communications Commission (under DETEC), FINMA (under the FDF), the Electricity Commission (independent of both the DETEC and the Federal Council), or the Swiss Agency for Therapeutic Products (affiliated with the FDHA) (Gilardi et al. 2013: 203).

Due to the 'implementation federalism' ("Vollzugsföderalismus") which is characteristic of the Swiss political system, the cantonal administrations, in spatial terms, can be counted part of decentralized administration—at least for those public administration tasks which are carried out in common. This category also includes deconcentrated services provided by the national level, for example, the customs directorate.

To some degree, *cantonal administrations* are analogs of the national administration.[8] Public tasks and activities are first divided between

[8] For a detailed overview, see Koller (2013).

Departments (or Directorates) and then distributed among the various Offices (or Services). The cantonal administrations are also supported by the work of various commissions, with at least some cantons (Graubünden, Jura, Luzern, Obwalden, Uri; see Moor 1992: 43) anchoring the existence of such commissions in their constitutions, at least in part.

In the 1990s, the cantons began to simplify their administrative apparatus. Many cantons dissolved departments previously devoted to military or civilian defense, or agriculture, or welfare issues. In some cases, if interior or justice departments were not closed, they might be consolidated. Reorganization of this kind was carried out in nearly all the cantons, though at differing levels of intensity and with different results.

Two models have established themselves since 2006, with either seven or five equally strongly represented departments. Both cantonal departments and the cantonal offices below them have seen increased concentration. The number of cantonal departments has declined, across the country, by 33 percent (from 208 in 1990 to 156 in 2008), while the number of offices only slightly increased (by 4 percent from 1070 to 1110) over the same time period (Koller 2013: 139).

The activities carried out have also seen greater harmonization, reflected not least in the nomenclature used. Every canton at this point has an education department, one also responsible for science and culture, and every canton has a construction, transportation, energy, and environment department. Out of 26 cantons, 23 have police and justice departments, 21 have finance departments, and 19 have health and social welfare departments.

Generally speaking, the number of lower-level offices are proportionate to the size of the department, with education the largest (227 offices in the 26 cantons), followed at considerable distance by the health and social welfare departments (132 offices). As at the national level, six cantons (Aargau, Appenzell Ausserrhoden, Schaffhausen, St. Gallen, Solothurn, Schwyz) had Interior Departments (as of 2001). One more rarely finds offices devoted to newer policy concerns such as the promotion of gender equality (nine cantons); only ten cantons have bureaus devoted to intercantonal cooperation and community reform (Koller 2013: 141).

As for the *community administrations,* there is quite a difference between the larger municipalities and the cities. The structure of city administrations is very similar to that of the cantonal administration, but due to the character of their tasks, they are closer to the citizens and the users of their services. Some of the city administrations are larger than the administrations of smaller cantons, whereas the administrations of the smaller municipalities may only consist of a few people.

The president of a community, despite his or her role as *primus inter pares* in a community's executive or ruling council, also has added competencies, which in quite a few communities means managing the community's employees. Political and administrative responsibility lies with the community's executive body as a whole, with each executive council member responsible for one or more areas—typically construction, finances and taxes, public works, social issues, health, schools, security, and the official registration of the residents.[9] The heads of these departments as a rule are only involved in preliminary consultations, or at best in the implementation of administrative decisions; decision-making power is in the hands of the executive council as a whole, or in a sub-committee it delegates to address certain tasks.

Legislative powers in slightly less than 20 percent of the bigger, or French-, or Italian-speaking municipalities are in the hands of a local council which decides on the budget, public expenditures or projects, and local regulations. In the rest of the municipalities, predominantly German-speaking, or the rather small ones, most decisions are taken in a local assembly. These gatherings of citizens entitled to vote take place about two or three times a year. Prior the vote, typically by a show of hands, the issues at stake are open to debate and amendments and changes can be suggested.

Beyond the executive and legislative, communities also have other organs at their disposal, in particular commissions which are responsible for a very specific sector in the community (e.g., construction, fire prevention, welfare, taxes, schools). On the one hand, they fulfill political purposes, inasmuch as different (political) groups in the community thereby have a chance to participate in decision-making. On the other hand, they fulfill function related to expertise, inasmuch as the occupational or professional skills and knowledge (of individual commission members) can be drawn on. As a rule, a member of the community's executive body presides over these community commissions, and its members are selected or elected by the legislative or the executive if they are not directly elected by the citizens, as it is often the case for school commissions.

In addition to community commissions which are granted independent administrative powers, communities can also create oversight commissions which examine the work of the administrators and of the executive.

[9] For further details, see Steiner and Kaiser (2013).

These include audit commissions, finance commissions, and controlling commissions.

The community secretary plays a particular, and important, role. As the 'chief of staff' of the executive, he or she is at the intersection of politics and administration. His or her responsibilities include organizing the entire administration of the community, preparing meetings (including of the executive council), and advising the political authorities. In communities with part-time executives, he or she may exert a great deal of influence on its political affairs.

Since the 1990s, and influenced by New Public Management (NPM) ideas calling for a sharper division between strategic (political) and operative (administrative) levels, various Swiss communities have increased the duties of the *Gemeindeschreiber* so that he directly manages the entire community administration. As in other European countries, this gives him a position like that of a city manager. In such communities, the executive is then responsible for the political decisions, and this city manager equivalent is responsible for implementation (Steiner and Kaiser 2013: 159).

The basic challenge for every administrative organization is both leadership and coordination. The typical form of organizational division used in Switzerland leads to structuring the second level down by subject or field—education, health, security, planning/construction, culture, and so forth. This runs the danger that departments (or directorates at the cantonal level or municipal level), owing to a certain degree of egoism, make themselves independent, and leave the executive, as a collegial body, having to accept the loss of a degree of control (Thom and Ritz 2008). That the heads of the various departments (at once also members of an executive council) may also have different party allegiances may reinforce this kind of organizational 'silo' culture.

Certain problems are also created for leadership. Though the higher-level civil servants are usually experts in their areas and remain for many years at their posts, the political careers of members of the executive are typically of more limited duration. This is a special issue at the community level, as political candidates often have little experience relevant to administering a community (Geser et al. 2011). It is also here where reforms, including new leadership models developed as part of NPM efforts, underscored by the Swiss Government and Administrative Organization Law of 1997, come into effect. A genuinely collegial leadership of public administration, based on a common perspective shared by all executive council members, has been no more possible to achieve (Germann 1996: 53) neither has a forward-looking, effects-based steering following political guidelines set out by a legislature.

3.4 Characteristics

Characteristic of administrations in Switzerland is their permeability with respect to the private sector, along with the now nearly obsolete status of permanent civil servants (*Beamtenstatus*). There is no particular examination that needs to be passed to become a civil servant, and the often lifelong guarantee of continued employment government officials enjoy in many countries is an exception in Switzerland. Most cantons and communities, as well as the national administration, employ or employed a system of appointment to office for a specified length of time. According to Germann (2011), this reflects a pronounced republicanism, as well as the later direct democratic tradition, one alien to the professionalized civil services which emerged out of monarchical court administration in other countries.

With the new Federal Employment Law, in effect since 2002, the system changed from one in which civil servants were employed for four-year, renewable, periods to one with open-ended employment. With few exceptions (e.g., employees in judicial capacities), all those who work at the national level are employed using individual contracts under public law which can be canceled by either party. During the 1990s, numerous communities and cantons switched to employment relationships under public law.[10]

Nevertheless, in Switzerland, as elsewhere, there is critique of the bureaucratic mentality thought to be found among government employees, and critique of increasing bureaucratization. The perception, at times, is of a state which regulates life more and more with the help of a mighty administration dictating what the country's residents have to do. Overall, though, residents do not have an antagonistic relationship to administrators per se, and also do not perceive them as an authority deserving excessive respect. The strong degree of decentralization in the country and the traditions of direct democracy, coupled with the fiscal sovereignty at each political level, results in a rather different relationship of citizen to state and public administration than seems to be the case in other countries.

[10] In 1997, the Swiss parliament decided to separate postal, telephone, and telegraph enterprises (then: PTT), creating the independent entities of the Post and of the Telecom AG (since 1998: Swisscom). Swisscom employees had earlier already been changed from that of civil servants to being employees under public law. When the new Federal Personnel Act came into force, employees of the postal services and of the federal railroads also lost their status as civil servants.

At the community level, people see exactly what is being done with their taxes, and they have quite direct ways to influence not only policy but also—and in particular—the expenditures of the local authorities. They do so with full knowledge that it is through their taxes that these expenditures will be financed. Correspondingly, they do not just let themselves be 'managed' or 'administered' but expect good quality, efficiently delivered services from 'their' community and 'their' community employees. Local politicians and administrators take this seriously, and make considerable efforts to be both transparent and accessible, and this seems to work extremely well. Residents in Switzerland, especially when compared with other wealthy nation-states like Denmark, Norway, or the Netherlands, are not only happier with the avenues open to them to influence policy locally, but are also happier with the local provision of services (see Denters et al. 2016).

Having part-timers fulfill public mandates contributes to this sense of being in touch with the people. Due to how small many communities are, but also often as a conscious choice, many public tasks are performed not by career administrators but by citizens who also pursue other professions (Geser 1981). Swiss often refer to this as a 'militia' system, and it reaches deep into local administration. In many communities, operational management also is carried out by elected, but part-time, politicians. Other residents, sometimes endowed with the requisite expertise from their 'real' professions, people the local commissions, and while these might only have consultative functions, they can have regulatory or even decision-making powers. Here, too, administrative tasks are carried out in the nebulous area between public responsibility and the private sector.

Since the Swiss political system does not function following a pattern of parties in government and parties in opposition ready to assume power, the politically motivated replacement of top administrators after a successful election, as occurs in the US, is also unknown. The party affiliation of top administrators plays a quite small role in Switzerland, allowing for greater continuity over time as well as more focus on the subject at hand (Krumm 2013: 230). At most, members of the Federal Council might select their personal staff or the directors of certain offices based on their party affiliation, but because the four most important political parties are all permanently represented in the national executive, these parties are also all represented in key offices in the national administration. True, for many years the Liberals (now: FDP. Die Liberalen) dominated the administrative posts, but this party also long dominated Swiss politics. Their predominant position has weakened, so both the left-wing Social Democratic Party (SP) and the Christian Democratic People's Party (CVP) today have numerous officials in important civil service positions. Only the right-wing Swiss People's Party (SVP), whose rise to prominence and power (from 12 percent in 1991 to nearly 30 percent by 2015) has been relatively recent, is underrepresented in top administrative posts.

There is also a general feeling that a multilingual country should try to make sure its major language groups are proportionately represented in the civil service, even though this complicates how both administration and politics function. Some mitigation comes through federalism and community autonomy, since relatively few cities (Biel, Fribourg) or cantons (Valais, Fribourg, Bern, Graubünden—4 of 26) face genuine issues arising from multilingualism in their jurisdictions. Nearly all communities in the country are monolingual, whether in Italian, French, or German; so in terms of politics and administration, it is at the national level where multilingualism is most addressed and most relevant.

Multilingualism does not mean one can interact with the authorities anywhere in the country in one's own language, or even that one has a right to do so. Rather, if a German-speaking family moves to a French-speaking part of the country, then French becomes the relevant language for interacting with local and cantonal authorities. The right that does exist to use one's own language when dealing with the authorities is one that applies, in particular, to dealing with the national-level authorities.

At this national level, more or less successful efforts are undertaken to have the civil service mirror the proportion of those who speak a given language in the Swiss population. As a result, one finds 71.3 percent German-speakers, 21.4 percent French-speakers, 7 percent Italian-speakers, and 0.3 percent Romansch-speakers among civil servants at the national level, numbers which approximate the native speakers of these languages among Swiss (Eidgenössisches Personalamt 2017: 8).

Given this ambition at proportionality, it is perhaps not surprising that controversies arise, whether over the underrepresentation in key positions of those who speak particular minority languages, over the translation of working documents, or about the use of Swiss-German rather than High German in informal conversations. At regular intervals, directives are sent out in an effort to promote multilingualism.[11] As exceedingly few administrators are perfectly trilingual, the operative practice is that everyone uses

[11] See also Kübler (2013).

their mother tongue, under the assumption that everyone understands the other languages quite well. With three languages and complex problems, this can be a challenging standard to meet. The language which ends up functionally dominating is High German, though English is threatening to replace it and become the new lingua franca.

3.5 Reforms and Modernization

The NPM movement reached Switzerland in the 1990s (Lienhard et al. 2005). Here one should distinguish between reforms which concerned the responsibilities for, and the organization of, carrying out public tasks and reforms made to internal administrative processes and service delivery itself. While all of these are reforms to administration, we can call the first external and the second internal (see Kuhlmann and Bouckaert 2016: 4 et seq.),

Switzerland has a tradition of outsourcing public tasks, one established long before NPM emerged. Beginning in the early twentieth century, communities and cantons found numerous ways to fulfill public duties with the help of private and semiprivate providers.[12] This tradition has been strengthened more recently, particularly in areas where the market has been liberalized, with examples of such outsourcing including Swisscom, the defense industries and military workshops now part of Ruag Holding, or the cantonal banks.

At the national level, this trend is manifested in what are called the third and fourth circles.[13] The third includes enterprises and institutions owned by the national government (the ETHs, Swissmedic, etc.) which exist due to dedicated legislation. These enterprises and institutions are chartered or organized under public law, but do not fall under the provisions of the Federal Budget Act. In the fourth circle, one finds public-private enterprises or stock companies chartered under specific laws which fulfill special national tasks (the national railroads, the postal service, Swisscom). This reorganization has led to a reduction in the size of the state sector, as understood narrowly (see Germann and Ladner 2014). At the cantonal level, building insurance and traffic offices have

[12] On this, see Pasquier and Fivat (2013: 190).

[13] This model was introduced as part of NPM reforms. It separated the national administration into four concentric circles, with the innermost containing the core ministerial administration. The second contained the FLAG offices with their performance agreements and global budgets. The third circle included the enterprises and institutions under public law, while the fourth contained the mixed and private enterprises.

been outsourced; communities, by the same token, turn relatively often to private computer technology, spatial planning, or energy providers.

Administrative reforms in a narrower sense, particularly at the national level, also have a certain tradition, and in the past were often part of austerity measures or efforts to increase efficiency. More comprehensive reforms initially primarily affected the second circle of the 'four-circle model' introduced in the 1990s. Offices not primarily involved with political coordination, such as general secretaries or cross-departmental agencies, were gradually transformed into a new steering model given the acronym FLAG (*Führen mit Leistungsauftrag und Globalbudget*—Leading with Performance Mandates and Global Budgets), with the idea of introducing a more outcome-oriented form of administration providing more operative freedom. The differentiation between first and second circles was eliminated as of the beginning of 2017, and in introducing a new, comprehensive leadership model in the national civil service (the German acronym for which is NFB), a format very close to the NPM model is now operating. Administration and leadership are now goal and outcome-oriented, and both transparency and controllability are to be improved at all levels.

During the 1990s, a crisis in public financing, and changes to the economic and ideological environment led to radical administrative reforms in many cantons, including abolishing the tenure of civil servants, introducing NPM reforms, or reorganizing administrative departments (Germann and Ladner 2014). At the beginning of the twenty-first century, more than half the cantons use elements of NPM, most of them across all administrative areas (as in the Aargau, Bern, Luzern, Solothurn, Thurgau, and Zürich).

Efforts to modernize administration were also undertaken in the communities in the 1990s, in part, in response to what NPM called for. However, such changes tended to be carried out in the largest communities, and only rarely were core elements of NPM, such as outcome-oriented steering and the reorganization of the different public activities in the form of products or group of products, which can be quantitatively measured and which have a fixed price, introduced (see Ladner 2016).

The concepts and the goals of these reforms, which replace the interventionist and performance-oriented state model through a 'guaranteeing' state notion, were not fundamentally new to Switzerland, nor was the suggestion contained in these NPM and governance models that public service and tasks could or ought to be provided through greater private sector involvement. In fact, many smaller nation-states have traditions of public-private cooperation and negotiating political solutions across party lines (Lijphart 1999). Noteworthy in Switzerland are the mixed or para-state solutions governments find, making the state appear quite lean despite the density of public services provided.

The Swiss state is certainly liberal in the classical sense, but it has little in common with the minimalist state. It is not that governmental tasks are not carried out. It is instead that they are carried out in other ways and, most particularly, not with the help of a central state apparatus. As history shows, this is not just the product of a consciously chosen strategy, but was in the end, and given the country's cultural differences and the absence of strong, centralized power, the only way a national Swiss state could emerge. This was augmented by appropriate political institutions which shared power both between the cantons and between the cantons and the Confederation (federalism), between the parties ('concordance'), and between the people and the political authorities (direct democracy). All these elements make it difficult to engage in grand and transformative political or administrative acts. The reforms the international literature calls for, however, are not completely unfamiliar to the Swiss administrative system. With its traditionally decentralized form and in light of the services already provided in partnership with the private sector, Swiss public administration is more modern than is often thought.

3.6 Swiss Public Administration in Its International Context

The Swiss system of public administration was long ignored in comparative studies,[14] and in light of the country's small size and minor international importance, this is understandable. But given the country capacities and capabilities, the high degree of acceptance its civil service enjoys in the population, and how accessible its public administration is, it stands as a model that could well be of interest outside its borders.

When the Swiss public administration is included in models, as in Kuhlmann und Wollmann's 2013 study, then it is seen as an example of a continental European federalist nation-state, along with Germany and Austria. This sets it apart from the administrative systems found in France, Italy, or Spain (continental European Napoleonic), in Great Britain (the 'Anglo-Saxon' or English-speaking world), or Denmark and Sweden (Scandinavian).

[14] For more detail, see Giauque (2013).

This can certainly be justified but only up to a point. Like them, Switzerland is federalist as well as a constitutional state under Roman law. Decentralization and a commitment to the principle of subsidiarity are also in common, though the latter is more pronounced in Switzerland.

What is far more alien to the Swiss case are traditions engendered by a hierarchical Prussian state (out of which German state administration grew) or by an imperial dual monarchy (which Austrian public administration has struggled to overcome). There are also differences with respect to public officials. Germany and Austria traditionally regarded their officials as 'servants of the state' who occupied a place above society (Kuhlmann and Wollmann 2013: 26). In Switzerland, civil servants are more often seen as 'employees of the people'. The boundary between public and private professional roles is more porous in Swiss administrations, and 'the state' has been regarded far less as a lordly, superior authority than in Austria or Germany. The acceptance of diversity, coupled with adamant assertions about cantonal sovereignty and community autonomy, together with strong elements of fiscal federalism, also sets Switzerland apart from its neighbors.

There are a number of parallels with the administrative systems one finds in Scandinavia. These include an openness toward public employees with respect to recruitment and career, as well as an openness toward the citizenry with respect to transparency, citizen participation, and a kind of 'user democracy'. The Swiss also would seem to have some affinities with the liberal, utilitarian understanding of government found in the English-speaking world: the government is seen as one which acts, rather than as one whose existence is of 'inherent value' (Kuhlmann and Wollmann 2013: 27). If one puts all these differences (vis-à-vis Switzerland's German-speaking neighbors) and similarities (with Scandinavia or with England) together, then one can with good reason refer to the Swiss system as a hybrid model (Giauque 2013).

References

Bundesamt für Statistik. (2015). *Branchenporträts des öffentlilchen Sektors (konsolidierte Daten 2012)*. Neuchâtel: Bundesamt für Statistik.

Denters, B., Ladner, A., Mouritzen, P. E., & Rose, L. E. (2016). Reforming local governments in times of crisis: Values and expectations of good local governance in comparative perspective. In S. Kuhlmann & G. Bouckaert (Eds.), *Local public sector reforms in times of crisis: National trajectories and interna-*

tional comparisons. Governance and public management (pp. 333–345). London: Palgrave Macmillan.

Eidgenössisches Personalamt. (2017). *Reporting Personalmanagement 2016 Bundesverwaltung*. Bern: Eidgenössisches Personalamt.

Germann, R. (1996). *Administration publique en Suisse: L'appareil étatique et le gouvernement*. Berne: Haupt.

Germann, R. (2011). Beamte. *Historisches Lexikon der Schweiz*. http://www.hls-dhs-dss.ch/textes/d/D10346.php

Germann, R., & Ladner A. (2014). Verwaltung im 19. und 20. Jahrhundert. *Historisches Lexikon der Schweiz*. http://www.hls-dhs-dss.ch/textes/d/D10342.php

Geser, H. (1981). *Bevölkerungsgrösse und Staatsorganisation. Kleine Kantone im Lichte ihrer öffentlichen Budgetstruktur, Verwaltung und Rechtsetzung*. Bern: Peter Lang.

Geser, H., Höpflinger, F., Ladner, A., & Meuli, U. (1996). Die Schweizer Gemeinden im Kräftefeld des gesellschaftlichen und politisch-administrativen Wandels. Abschlussbericht des Nationalfondsprojekts Nr. 12-32586.92. In *Aktuelle Wandlungstendenzen und Leistungsgrenzen der Gemeindeorganisation der Schweiz*.

Geser, H., Ladner, A., Meuli, U., Steiner, R., & Horber-Papazian, K. (2011). *Exekutivmitglieder in Schweizer Gemeinden. Kapitel Gemeindereformen*. Chur/Zürich: Rüegger.

Giauque, D. (2013). Die schweizerische Bundesverwaltung im internationalen Vergleich: auf der Suche nach einer Verwaltungstradition. In A. Ladner, J.-L. Chappelet, Y. Emery, P. Knoepfel, L. Mader, N. Soguel, & F. Varone (Eds.), *Handbuch der öffentlichen Verwaltung in der Schweiz* (pp. 47–60). Zürich: Neue Zürcher Zeitung libro.

Gilardi, F., Magetti, M., & Servalli, F. (2013). Regulierungsbehörden in der Schweiz. In A. Ladner, J.-L. Chappelet, Y. Emery, P. Knoepfel, L. Mader, N. Soguel, & F. Varone (Eds.), *Handbuch der öffentlichen Verwaltung in der Schweiz* (pp. 199–217). Zürich: Neue Zürcher Zeitung libro.

Grisel, A. (1984). *Traité de droit administratif*. Neuchâtel: Ides et calendes.

Koller, C. (2013). Die kantonalen Verwaltungen. In A. Ladner, J.-L. Chappelet, Y. Emery, P. Knoepfel, L. Mader, N. Soguel, & F. Varone (Eds.), *Handbuch der öffentlichen Verwaltung in der Schweiz* (pp. 127–148). Zürich: Neue Zürcher Zeitung libro.

Krumm, T. (2013). *Das politische System der Schweiz. Ein internationaler Vergleich*. München: Oldenbourg Verlag.

Kübler, D. (2013). Verwaltungsorganisation in einem mehrsprachigen Land. In A. Ladner, J.-L. Chappelet, Y. Emery, P. Knoepfel, L. Mader, N. Soguel, & F. Varone (Eds.), *Handbuch der öffentlichen Verwaltung in der Schweiz* (pp. 75–92). Zürich: Neue Zürcher Zeitung libro.

Kuhlmann, S., & Bouckaert, G. (Eds.). (2016). *Local public sector reforms in times of crisis: National trajectories and international comparisons*. London: Palgrave Macmillan.

Kuhlmann, S., & Wollmann, H. (2013). *Verwaltung und Verwaltungsreformen in Europa: Einführung in die vergleichende Verwaltungswissenschaft*. Wiesbaden: Springer VS.

Ladner, A. (2016). Administrative reforms in Swiss municipalities over the last twenty years – The end of new public management? *Lex Localis, 14*(2), 185–207.

Ladner, A., Chappelet, J.-L., Emery, Y., Knoepfel, P., Mader, L., Soguel, N., & Varone, F. (Eds.). (2013). *Handbuch der öffentlichen Verwaltung in der Schweiz*. Zürich: Neue Zürcher Zeitung libro.

Lijphart, A. (1999). *Patterns of democracy. Government forms and performance in thirty-six countries*. New Haven/London: Yale University Press.

Moor, P. (1992). *Droit administratif*. Berne: Staempfli.

OECD (Organisation for Economic Co-operation and Development). (2017a). General government employment across levels of government. *Government at a Glance 2017*. Paris: OECD Publishing.

OECD (Organisation for Economic Co-operation and Development). (2017b). Employment in general government. *Government at a Glance 2017*. Paris: OECD Publishing.

Pasquier, M., & Fivat, E. (2013). Die autonomen öffentlichen Organisationen oder Agencies. In A. Ladner, J.-L. Chappelet, Y. Emery, P. Knoepfel, L. Mader, N. Soguel, & F. Varone (Eds.), *Handbuch der öffentlichen Verwaltung in der Schweiz* (pp. 183–198). Zürich: Neue Zürcher Zeitung libro.

Rebmann, F., & Mach, A. (2013). Die ausserparlamentarischen Kommissionen des Bundes. In A. Ladner, J.-L. Chappelet, Y. Emery, P. Knoepfel, L. Mader, N. Soguel, & F. Varone (Eds.), *Handbuch der öffentlichen Verwaltung in der Schweiz* (pp. 167–182). Zürich: Neue Zürcher Zeitung libro.

Steiner, R., & Kaiser, C. (2013). Die Gemeindeverwaltungen. In A. Ladner, J.-L. Chappelet, Y. Emery, P. Knoepfel, L. Mader, N. Soguel, & F. Varone (Eds.), *Handbuch der öffentlichen Verwaltung in der Schweiz* (pp. 149–166). Zürich: Neue Zürcher Zeitung libro.

Thom, N., & Ritz, A. (2008). *Public Management – Innovative Konzepte zur Führung im öffentlichen Sektor*. Wiesbaden: Gabler Verlag.

Varone, F. (2013). Die Bundesverwaltung. In A. Ladner, J.-L. Chappelet, Y. Emery, P. Knoepfel, L. Mader, N. Soguel, & F. Varone (Eds.), *Handbuch der öffentlichen Verwaltung in der Schweiz* (pp. 111–126). Zürich: Neue Zürcher Zeitung libro.

PART II

The Legal System: Law and Courts

CHAPTER 4

The Law and the Principle of Legality

Sophie Weerts

4.1 Introduction

In the European legal tradition, the law embodies the privileged instrument of public action since the emergence of the modern state. Its legitimacy comes from its author—a democratic organ—its content—its presumed rationality—and its formalism—its procedure of adoption and publication. Nevertheless, since the 1990s, social transformations occurred and blurred the concepts of law and state. The foundations of administrative law are particularly involved (Mockle 2007; Caillosse 2015). The law—taken broadly—sees its field of intervention competing with non-obligatory instruments that bring out the idea of 'soft law'. Such a phenomenon questions what lawyers call the sources of law (Hachez et al. 2010). As for the state, traditionally described by models of liberal state and then social state, fits the model of the 'propulsive state' (Morand 1991) or the 'state - resource manager' (Moor 2005: 63) better. Sovereign powers and social competencies are no longer the main concepts used to analyze the state's actions. A more dynamic concept of public policy has been adopted in which the law takes different forms of normativity. These two trends indicate a general transformation of the law.

S. Weerts (✉)
IDHEAP, University of Lausanne, Lausanne, Switzerland
e-mail: Sophie.Weerts@unil.ch

A. Ladner et al. (eds.), *Swiss Public Administration*, Governance and Public Management,
https://doi.org/10.1007/978-3-319-92381-9_4

More specifically, in the field of statute law, more and more legal norms are generated by the executive branch. The democratic legitimacy of the law is also called into question when international rules are the basis of public action. Private bodies adopt standards which sometimes are later included in the law (Uhlmann 2013). This evolution highlights a shift in the center of gravity of power that is no longer located in the (representative) democratic body. Normative instruments which are less formalized, such as soft law, are emerging as a new category in the typology of (formal) sources of law. Finally, the infallibility of the law has been questioned with the development of constitutional justice. From the point of view of legal science, some identify the beginnings of a global administrative law (Kingsbury et al. 2005). Others consider that the principle of legality must be revisited (Popelier 2012: 48–54).

In Switzerland, all state activities are based on, and limited by, law (Art. 5 (1), Federal Constitution, abbreviated as Const.). Nevertheless, the definition of the word law is not easy to grasp and does not always fit perfectly with the idea of statutory law. Since the 1990s, Swiss legal scholars have worked on the issue of the law, noting the contextual and structural transformations of state activities (see Moor 1990, 2005; Morand 1991; Müller 2006; Flückiger 2007, 2008).

The following four chapters address many of the issues surrounding the figures of the law. Chapter 5 presents a particular stage in the formation of the law: the pre-parliamentary phase. It evokes the hypothesis of the shift of the center of gravity of the parliamentary to executive power and presents the 'compensation mechanisms' that have been instituted in Swiss law. Chapter 6 deals with the development of international law. Here, the federal administration plays an important role in maintaining the coherence of the Swiss legal system and making it congruent with its international commitments, while respecting the exercise of political (or popular) rights. Chapter 7 examines the phenomenon of soft law in Swiss public law and shows how this mode of public action developed with respect to legislation (the main formal sources of law, called 'hard law'). Finally, the last chapter addresses one of the singularities of Swiss public law: its limited ability to review the constitutionality of laws. Each of these chapters addresses the challenges faced by Swiss law and, in turn, challenges for the public administration which must act within the framework and the limits of the law.

In that context, some basic legal notions are worth presenting. A first one is the understanding of the concept of law (in Swiss law) (Sect. 4.1).

Indeed, from the strictly legal point of view, it constitutes the first formal source of law within the meaning of Article 1 of the preliminary title of the Civil Code and is understood as written law (statute law). Its corollary is the principle of legality (Sect. 4.2), which is essential in all the activities of the state as stated in Article 5 (1), Const. Both are indispensable for understanding the main features of the legal framework Swiss public administration acts within.

4.2 The Law

The law takes many forms which vary according to legal traditions. In the continental legal tradition, the law is defined as any general and abstract rule resulting from a collective will and endowed with binding force. It corresponds to the idea of legislation. Strictly speaking, it is defined as the acts adopted by the legislative branch (primary legislation), as opposed to the acts (statutory instruments) adopted within the framework of the executive branch and by the administrative authorities (delegated or secondary legislation). This distinction echoes the notions of formal law and material law, formulated by German constitutional theory (Sect. 4.2.1). Both are found in Swiss law, which also makes another crucial difference between 'legal rule' and 'decision' (Sect. 4.2.2). Finally, even if some elements indicate the emergence of a more flexible law (see the chapter by Flückiger), a series of procedural mechanisms also shows the strengthening of the democratic legitimacy of the legal norms (Sect. 4.2.3).

4.2.1 The Distinction Between Formal Law and Material Law

The distinction between formal and material law has its origin in German constitutional theory (Popelier 2012: 19 et seq). It allowed the Prince's power to be limited by defining the areas in which he needed to have the support of Parliament. In France, a different conception of the law developed after 1789: the law only rests on the institutions that collectively exercise the legislative function. The government then exercises the executive function and adopts acts to put the law in action. In the French case, the idea of material law was thus not conceivable. In both cases, the explanatory criterion, therefore, lies in the democratic legitimacy of formal law. This is produced by a democratic body, Parliament. This legitimacy justifies its pre-eminence over the acts of government or administrative authorities.

Formal law, however, competes with other sources. International treaties, European law, or the use of delegated legislation for the benefit of executive authorities are all expressions of a form of law which is no longer the result of the deliberate will of a parliament. They embody the concept of material law. In the field of fundamental rights, the European Convention on Human Rights allows restrictions if they are made in accordance with or prescribed by the law (Art. 8 (2), 9 (2), 10 (2) and 11 (2) ECHR). In its case law, the European Court of Human Rights has nevertheless not made the formal character of the law a condition for a restriction to be valid. It considers that an act corresponds to a law, within the meaning of the European Convention on Human Rights, on four conditions: it constitutes a legal basis for public action, it is accessible to all, the consequences of the law must be foreseeable and the law must, if the act is accessible to individuals, be formulated in precise terms to allow everyone to predict the consequences of their actions (ECHR, *Sunday Times* vs. *The United Kingdom*, 1979). Two exceptions, however, are well known. The first is Article 6 ECHR, which guarantees the right to a fair trial. In this framework, jurisdiction must be established by legislation to ensure that an individual is not subject to the discretion of the executive. The second is when a national constitution requires that a matter be regulated by legislation (see Popelier: 26–28).

The determination of the form of law is an important element in Swiss public administration, as any public action involves defining an action tool. However, the distinction between formal and substantive law is also present in Swiss law (Auer et al. 2006: 88 et seq). Indeed, several constitutional provisions require the adopting of a law. This varies according to subject, but also according to the degree of restriction of the autonomy of an individual. The general requirement of a law, for example, is laid out in the context of any restriction of fundamental rights. It is listed in Article 36 (1) Const. The statutory requirement is also stated in Article 164 Const. for federal legislation in general. In both cases, the idea of law is a two-way street. Depending on the circumstances, it is either an act adopted by Parliament or an act adopted by an authority empowered to decide. In the fields of taxation—according to the principle of 'no taxation without representation'—(Art.127 (1) Const.), access to justice (Arts. 29a and 30 Const.) and deprivation of liberty (Art. 31 (1) Const.), the requirement of a law is understood within the meaning of formal law. The extent to which individual autonomy, the keystone of the liberal state, is undermined or at risk justifies the public action being taken by a democratically elected body. It should be added that Swiss law does provide for an exception to the legal requirement: the general police clause. This clause allows the government to act without any legal basis, and to limit fundamental rights, in the event of preventing or putting an end to a serious and imminent infringement of public order (Aubert and Mahon 2003: 325).

4.2.2 The Legal Rule as a Criterion for Distinguishing the Legislation

Between German and French conceptions previously described, Swiss law follows the German tradition. The legislative function can be exercised by the parliament, the people and the executive branch (the Federal Council). The word law—formal law—is reserved for acts adopted by Parliament, possibly with the support of the people. However, the parliament can also adopt ordinances just like the Federal Council. In other words, it is not the author of the legal norms that qualifies the legal act but the content of it.

In Swiss law, when referring to legislation, the determining factor is the legal rules. The notion of a legal rule is defined in Art. 22 (4) of the Federal Act of the Federal Assembly. It refers to the norms of a general and abstract scope addressed to a circle of recipients who are not defined in a precise way (Federal Office of Justice 2007: 229). This could concern all citizens or all motorists. The rule applies to general cases, for example, all instances of speeding, or all taxable income. It is called on to be applied in a repetitive way, that is to say, whenever situations appear which correspond to its abstract hypothesis. It is intended to be sustainable and is presumed stable. These characteristics of generality and stability are key elements in ensuring 'legal certainty' for members of society. Indeed, they allow recipients to predict their actions and the consequences thereof.

However, any act adopted within the framework of public administration is not necessarily a legislative act or a legal rule. If the norm is not general and abstract, then it is called a 'decision'. In this case, the act settles an individual and concrete case. This distinction between legal rule and decision constitutes a fundamental element for the understanding of public administration and Swiss public law in general (see the chapter by Mahon). Indeed, this distinction carries many consequences in terms of the authority's competence, the means of appeal, the mode of communication of the act (official publication of the legislation and notification of the decision) or information contained in the act. In addition, the distinction between the two notions is not always easy to identify. Some urban plans are ambivalent acts with a scope that exceeds the individual, without being of general scope. When the public authority is in doubt as to the form of the law it intends to adopt, it must consider whether, to produce its effects, a legal act still needs to be concretized by individual acts; if so, the legal act to be adopted has an indeterminate scope that is characteristic of a legal rule (Federal Office of Justice 2007: 230).

Where the public authorities have to act by legal rules, the form may still vary. At the federal level, it can take the form of a law or ordinance. The Federal Assembly has the power to adopt laws and ordinances (Art. 163 (1) Const.). It also participates in the ratification of international treaties (Art. 141a Const, see the chapter by Weerts and Sofia). Among all these acts, it is the norms that are qualified as 'important' that must take the form of a law. The Constitution states that this concerns the rules relating to the exercise of political rights, the restrictions on constitutional rights, the rights and obligations of persons, the fiscal field, the tasks and services of the Confederation, the obligations of the cantons in the implementation and enforcement of federal law and the organization of the procedure of the federal authorities (Art. 164 (1) Const.). Norms that do not have such a fundamental dimension for individuals or for federal activities can then take the form of an ordinance, which can be passed by the Federal Assembly but also by the Federal Council and the federal administration (departments and offices).

At the federal level, the author of the legislation is either the Parliament or the Federal Council. The most important legislative body is, of course, the Federal Assembly, which is composed of two elected chambers. Laws adopted by the Federal Assembly may still be submitted to a legislative referendum within 100 days of publication in the Federal Gazette (Art. 141 (1) Const.). In this case, the people participate in the adoption of the law. The Federal Assembly also adopts ordinances. For that, it must draw its competence from the Constitution or the law. All acts adopted by the Federal Assembly are not necessarily legal rules. It can adopt decrees as well. These acts have no normative scope. This form of act is used notably for acts which concern the Federal Assembly. The decree is also the legal act adopted by the Federal Assembly in the framework of the ratification process of international law. Depending on the type of treaties ratified, the decree can be submitted to a legislative referendum (see the chapter by Weerts and Sofia). The Federal Council is the second legislative body. It has the power to enact ordinances, which extend the rules contained in the primary law (Art. 182 Const.). It may also be empowered to adopt so-called substitution orders. In this case, it must have been given the power to legislate under the Constitution or the law. Finally, the Federal Council can also delegate to the departments of the federal administration the power to enact rules of law (Art. 48 (1) Government and Administration Organization Act).

Once the form and the author of the law have been determined and the content has been set in accordance with legislative procedures, the act produces legal effects as long as it is known by everyone. This requirement presupposes a condition of publication and directly shapes the democratic and liberal state (Hangartner 2008). Under Swiss law, the legislation—domestic law as well as international treaties—is published in the official compendium of federal law (Recueil officiel). At the same time, it is gathered by subject in a systematic collection (Recueil signalétique), which facilitates access to legislation and allows everyone to see the state of the law in force. The publication requirement allows everyone to anticipate the consequences of their activity and to comply with the law. For this purpose, the entry into force does not coincide in principle with the date of publication, except for the constitutional provisions (Art. 195 Const.). In essence, publication must take place at least five days before the entry into force of the law (Art. 7, Publications Act). The decision to enter into force usually belongs to the Federal Council, but it may also have been included in the legislative act itself. For international treaties, it is the treaty itself that contains its own rules of entry into force (Mader 2013: 258–259).

These different elements show that in Swiss public law, the notion of a legislative act encompasses the concepts of formal and material laws. It does not follow the institutional distinction between parliament and government. Thus, the type of legislative acts is not determined according to its author but according to its object. Finally, in all cases, legislative acts must comply with formal requirements.

4.2.3 *Strengthening the Procedural Dimension of the Law*

While it is generally observed that the formal law is losing ground in favor of a substantive conception of the law, Swiss public law has mechanisms and practices that reinforce the procedural dimension of the legislation. From this point of view, these mechanisms and practices reflect an attachment to the law as the first formal source of law, which can also be seen in the principle of the immunity clause in the framework of constitutional review (see the chapter by Mahon). These mechanisms and practices illustrate a trend toward an increasing 'proceduralization' of legislation. This can be analyzed as a strengthening of the democratic legitimacy of the law. It accentuates the symbolic value of the law, at the risk of being more focused on a purely formal and non-substantive approach to law. Two elements are a part of such a trend. On the one hand, there is the dissemination of a genuine 'culture of lawmaking' through the federal administration and, on the other hand, the tools of direct democracy.

4.2.3.1 The Culture of Lawmaking

Switzerland has several instruments to ensure the quality of its legislation. All these instruments represent a culture of lawmaking, which can be defined as 'an (applied) science of legislation that seeks to determine the best ways of developing, enacting and applying legal norms' (Chevallier 1998: 15). It addresses the fundamental question of what good law is, a classic theme in the philosophy of law. This concern has become an important aspect of legislative activity when the law is analyzed as one of the resources available to implement state activity in terms of enacted public policies (Knoepfel 2017: 142 et seq.). Several elements can be identified in Swiss public law and public administration as illustrating this approach. Some belong to 'formal lawmaking', others are a part of 'material lawmaking' and both improve the formal and the substantive dimensions of law.

The purpose of drafting formal law is to improve editorial quality and legislative technique. Among the instruments available to Swiss public administration in this area are internal instructions or recommendations of the administration. Another aspect that fits into a culture of drafting formal law is the training of lawyers. Although the drafting of the law is traditionally the prerogative of lawyers, only a few law schools offer courses in drafting law. Such training has therefore been set up in the federal administration and is also open to those without previous legal training. Federal civil servants thus have access to training combining theory and practice, which simultaneously allows the development of a network for sharing experiences. A Swiss Society of Legislation has been created and, under its mandate, three universities offer several courses open to lawyers from cantonal and community administrations. A Legislation Forum has also been created. It is now a network active throughout the executive branch that allows for a fruitful sharing of experiences and which publishes a triennial newsletter.

The purpose of material lawmaking is to improve the law's ability to act on social reality. In Switzerland, it is implemented through legislative evaluation, since following Art. 170 Const., the Confederation must assess federal measures with regard to their effectiveness (Flückiger: 2007). This generalized what had already been practiced in implementing asylum policies or in efforts to combat inequalities, be it against women or people with disabilities (Mader 2015: 69).

The consultation procedure (Art. 147 Const., see the chapter by Guy-Ecabert) constitutes a means of acting on the formal as well as the substantive quality of the law. It enables cantons, political parties and interested parties to comment on important legislative acts. It has acquired a certain importance and several qualities are attributed to it (Mader 2013: 255–256). It expands the collection of information about a proposed legislative project, helping to promote greater relevance of the legislative project to social problems, and likely bringing greater legitimacy to it. It is also hoped that the consultation process will foster consensus among political actors, and makes it possible to test the practicability of the proposal with those who will implement it, namely the cantons. In any case, it promotes a process of learning and information to the public when details about the consultation are publicized.

These different elements contribute to strengthening the quality of the law. They are mobilized when the legislative process is initiated by the executive branch, but also—in the case of legislative evaluation—ex post facto. They are grouped into legislative guides (Flückiger and Guy-Ecabert: 2008). These include not only editorial guidelines but also quality standards, methods of codification or consolidation of the law and a periodic review of legislation. However, they remain imperfect. Indeed, they are of little use when the legislative process comes from the parliamentary or popular initiatives. In terms of substantive law, it is not sufficiently integrated by lawyers in administrative or judicial positions. Indeed, the quality of the law is mainly considered with regard to social or economic objectives. It leaves aside social justice dimensions, that is to say its capacity to participate in the realization of constitutional values such as respect for the rule of law, fundamental rights, democracy and federalism, which are part of the law as well and a keystone of liberal democratic states.

4.2.3.2 Instruments of Direct Democracy

The extension of political rights (or 'popular rights') is the second element reinforcing the procedural dimension of the law. They allow citizens to participate in decision-making through voting. In Switzerland, popular rights are provided at federal, cantonal and communal levels. At the federal level, they have been progressively expanded. They were first instituted with the constitutional referendum (since 1848), then the optional legislative referendum (1874), the constitutional initiative (1891) and finally the referendum on international treaties (implemented progressively in 1921, 1977 and 2003; see Chap. 6, Weerts and Sofia). Their use strengthens the democratic legitimacy of legislative acts, which were historically derived, at the federal level, from their adoption by democratically elected institutions.

At the federal level, the participation of the people in the legislative process varies according to the form of the legal act (Art. 138–142, 193, 194 Const.), of which there are three categories: the constitution, the law and the decrees ratifying the texts of international law. The procedure for popular participation varies according to the form of the legislative act. In some cases, the people must participate in the legislative process, in a broad sense, when there is a mandatory referendum. In other cases, people can intervene in the legislative process (optional referendum).

The procedural requirements are laid out in the Federal Constitution and in the Federal Act on Political Rights (Art. 68 to 76, Political Rights Act). The number of signatures required is set by the Federal Constitution. The referendum is obligatory in the case of revisions of the Constitution and accession to international organizations. These call for a dual majority, of both the voters and the cantons. In this case, there is no requirement to collect signatures (Auer et al. 2013: 810–819). At the constitutional level, people can also propose changes by using the 'popular initiative' (Art. 138 and 139 Const.). If they collect the signatures of 100,000 eligible voters, a vote has to be organized within 18 months after the official publication of their initiative. The optional referendum can be triggered with regard to federal laws but also relative to the ratification of international treaties (Art. 141 (1) Const.; Art. 59 to 67 Political Rights Act). A vote will be held if 50,000 eligible voters or eight cantons request it within 100 days of the official publication of a federal law (Art. 141 (1) lit. a Const.).

Since 1848, 617 federal votes (referenda and initiatives) have been held.[1] Since 1970, their frequency has increased. They peaked between

[1] Federal Statistical Office, https://www.bfs.admin.ch/bfs/fr/home/statistiques/politique/votations.html#1384097411 (consulted on April 5, 2018).

1990 and 1999, achieving a number of 100 votes.[2] In such a trend, one instrument has been very successful: the popular initiative. Thirty-nine of these latter have already been addressed between 2010 and 2018[3] (Federal Chancellery: 2018). This trend indicates an increasing participation of citizens in setting the political agenda, even if such a participation is mainly activated by political parties.

4.3 The Principle of Legality

The other figure of the law is embodied in the principle of legality. This principle is enshrined in Article 5 (1) of the Federal Constitution and reads: 'all activities of the state are based on and limited by law'. The other paragraphs of this Article require the Confederation and the cantons to act or respect the principles of public interest and of proportionality (2), the principle of good faith (3) and international law (4). All these elements are described as constituting the rule of law.

Before its 1999 revision, this principle of legality was not explicitly stated in the constitutional text. However, it already guided the action of the state, having the form of an 'unwritten constitutional principle' unanimously recognized by doctrine and jurisprudence (Federal Council 1997: 133), and having a binding value recognized by all. This is not the only unwritten constitutional principle: not all laws, or all legal principles, are contained in written acts.

The function of the principle of legality is to limit and regulate the activities of the state. For individuals, the principle of legality is an important element in terms of legal certainty and equal treatment. The legal doctrine (Aubert and Mahon 2003: 41) considers that all collectivities and public institutions are intended. It is thus aimed at the Confederation, the cantons, the communes, but also all the individuals who assume, by delegation, tasks of the state. In addition, the principle applies to all activities of the state, meaning not only activities that limit the rights of individuals but also those that provide benefits to individuals or activities related to state organization (Tanquerel 2011: 152).

[2] Federal Statistical Office, 'Évolution de la participation aux votations populaires fédérales'. https://www.bfs.admin.ch/bfs/fr/home/statistiques/politique/votations/participation.assetdetail.3602769.html. Bern: Swiss Confederation (consulted on April 5, 2018).

[3] Federal Chancellery, 'Initiatives populaires ayant fait l'objet d'une votation'. https://www.bk.admin.ch/ch/f/pore/vi/vis_2_2_5_7.html#. Bern: Swiss Confederation (consulted on April 5, 2018).

In Swiss law, the principle of legality contains two aspects (Federal Council 1997: 133). The first aspect is called the 'primacy of the law' (Sect. 4.3.1); the second is the 'reserve of the law' (Sect. 4.3.2). These two aspects mean that the principle of legality embodies the formal dimension of the rule of law (Epiney 2015: 93).

4.3.1 The 'Primacy of the Law' and Its Corollary, the Hierarchy of Norms

The 'primacy of the law' aspect means that the public administration must respect the law. This requirement applies to all laws, formal and material and to all activities. Such an affirmation must be understood in the light of the hierarchy of norms.

Simply put, the hierarchy of norms means that lower-level acts are subordinate to superior acts, thus putting the legal system in order. This subordination implies that every act of public administration respects the higher standards. The hierarchy is first of all between the legal orders (international law/domestic law) and then within each legal order. Thus, a 'decision' must respect a 'material law' and this one must in turn respect a 'formal law'. It should be noted, however, that legal norms have become more complex and call into question the idea of a well-ordered hierarchy. Without going into this debate, it can be noted that the ordering of the legal system is built on the basis of a combination of legal rules enshrined in the Federal Constitution and rules of interpretation (Haller 2016: 20–26; Mahon 2014: 65–68).

A series of legal acts can be identified. First, there is the Constitution itself, which is adopted on the basis of a particular procedure (Art. 192 to 195 Const.). Then the Constitution designates several legal acts which have a federal rank such as statutes (Art. 164 Const.), ordinances and orders. Some of the ordinances are adopted by the Federal Assembly (Art. 163 Const.) and others are adopted by the Federal Council (Art. 182 Const.). Laws and ordinances constitute the essence of domestic law. In a federal system, the legal system also has several subsystems. There is cantonal law (Article 49 Const.). Each canton has a constitution, which in turn sets its list of legislative acts. Thus, within each canton, there are laws—formal law—and decrees or ordinances—material law. Municipal law is still a third tier of the Swiss legal system (Art. 50 Const.). All these federal, cantonal and communal rules are adopted unilaterally. However, Swiss law also has legislative acts that are adopted in a contractual sense.

Among these rules, there are 'intercantonal concordats' (see Chaps. 1 and 2 by Ladner). This form of acts does not belong to cantonal law. It is also not included in federal law, although the Confederation can also—within the limits of its powers—participate in these concordats (Art. 48 para. 2 Const.). Swiss law also incorporates rules of international law. Some are negotiated and adopted between states and take the form of bilateral or multilateral conventions and treaties. As for European regulations and directives, they are generally taken up through the practice of autonomous adaptation. Switzerland creates standards equivalent to European law, these European-inspired standards thus taking the legislative forms of classical federal law.

The Swiss Federal Constitution does not provide for a general rule of organization or articulation between all these legal norms. Several elements, however, make it possible to reconstruct the matrix of the Swiss legal system.

First, from the point of view of international law, every state party to a treaty is bound by the principle of *pacta sunt servanda* ('agreements must be kept'). This customary principle is declined in Art. 26, 27 and 46 (1) of the Vienna Convention on the Law of Treaties. It requires the state which is a party to a treaty to respect its international obligations, regardless of its domestic law. In other words, international law imposes the primacy of international law on the signatory state that has ratified rules of international law.

The Constitution provides also several indications of its commitment to the respect of international law. Articles 139 (3), 193 (4), and 194 (2) Const. indicate that popular initiatives must respect the imperative rules of international law (*jus cogens* or 'compelling law'). In addition, Article 5 (4) indicates that the Confederation and the cantons respect international law. Nevertheless, this does not follow the wording of Article 46 (1) Const. according to which federal law takes precedence over cantonal law. This choice of wording is analyzed as the result of a political compromise (Mahon 2014: 48–49). The case law of the Federal Court (the Schubert case), which had not been consistent on the principle of primacy of federal law over domestic law, explains such a nuance. Since then, however, the Federal Tribunal has been consistent in favor of the primacy of international law. The principle of the primacy of federal law flows from the very nature of the international rule, hierarchically superior to any internal rule (Federal Supreme Court: ATF 131 V 66). In 2012, it indicated that international law takes precedence over domestic law (Federal Supreme Court:

ATF 139 I 16), without addressing a rigid clause of precedent rule (Keller and Balazs-Hegedüs 2016: 717).

However, the question of the primacy of international law over domestic law is a subject of intense political discussions. By virtue of their sovereignty, states may decide to denounce their commitments, but they will take the risk of threatening their international credibility with their partners (Keller and Balazs-Hegedüs 2016: 719). If they violate their international obligations, they then engage their international responsibility (Kolb 2016: 572–573).

Within the Swiss legal system, it is necessary to distinguish between the federal level and the cantonal level. Federal law—Constitution, federal laws and ordinances—prevails over cantonal law (Art. 46 para.1 Const.). Within each level, there are also hierarchical rules according to the type of standards. Thus, the constitution prevails over the law. The supremacy of the Constitution stems from the fact that the other rules of domestic law have their source in the Federal Constitution, which is pre-eminent over other sources of law. Laws are formulated on the basis of the Constitution and they are implemented by the ordinance (Art. 182 Const.).

Courts and legal scholars have developed interpretative methods. The first of them, deduced from the above-mentioned constitutional rules, derives from the maxim *lex superior derogat legi inferiori* ('a law higher in the hierarchy displaces a lower law'). The two others apply in the context of conflict between standards of the same level. The first provides that the special rule derogates from the general rule and the second implies that the subsequent rule derogates from the previous rule. The method of interpretation in conformity with the Constitution is also used by the judge to develop an interpretation of the legal norm in line with the values of the constitution.

All of these provisions and rules of interpretation help lawyers to maintain, as far as possible, coherence between the legal norms within the Swiss legal order.

4.3.2 The Requirement of a Legal Basis

The second aspect of the principle of legality is generally named as the 'reserve of the law'. This is the principle of requirement of the legal basis and means that, except in cases of *force majeure*, any state activities must be based on a legal rule (Schindler 2014: 118). This aspect of the principle of legality allows individuals to foresee the consequences of their actions but also guarantees they will be treated equally.

The requirement of a legal basis can take the form of a formal law but also of a material law. However, it is in this dimension that the principle of legality presents its most flexible aspect, thus being able to fit the contours and specificities of public administration.

As noted above, the choice of the legal basis will depend on the type of intervention. In some areas, such as criminal law or questions of taxation, formal law is a condition for the state's action. In other areas, material law is sufficient. In the event of restricting personal freedom, the greater the degree of infringement, the higher the legislative quality of the rule.

If the legal basis is material law, its legal quality will be assessed according to its accuracy. This element makes it possible to assess the degree of predictability of the law for the citizen. However, practice shows that the degree of accuracy is a criterion that can be easily achieved. This flexibility is accepted on the grounds that, on the one hand, the legislator cannot foresee everything, and, on the other hand, it is also up to the judge to give a more precise content to the legal basis. It is the elements of the hypothesis of application that will then make it possible to determine the degree of precision of the legal rule. In general, the more numerous the persons targeted by the norm, the greater the infringements on personal freedom, the more likely the situations concerned, the more important the accuracy of the norm must be (Tanquerel 2011: 158).

4.4 Conclusion

The aim of this chapter was to introduce two basic legal notions of Swiss law, both crucial for public administration: the law and the principle of legality. Starting with the concept of law, it showed that the law does not only consist in written laws adopted by Parliament (formal law), but includes norms adopted by the executive branch and public authorities (material law). The two aspects ('primacy of law' and 'requirement of legal basis') of the principle of legality each refer to the law as well. Their description made it clear that formal and material laws are part of the Swiss law. In the Federal Council's message on the total revision of the Constitution, the term law was defined as referring to the Constitution, the law and ordinances (Federal Council 1997: 134).

Nevertheless, the law implicitly referred to rules of conflict between norms established by legal doctrine and jurisprudence (Federal Council

1997: 134). In other words, law also referred to something which was not explicitly included in legislation. On this point, another example shows that Swiss law is not limited to statutory law. In the framework of revising the Federal Constitution in 1999, described as a 'fundamental reform' and an 'update' of constitutional law (Federal Council 1997: 20 and 9), the idea of a material constitution was evoked. Adopting this new text was justified by the fact that the 1874 Constitution—a formal law—did not encompass all of Swiss constitutional law. The idea of material Constitution was used to designate all the rules and principles, which form constitutional law (Aubert 1993: 101–103). It referred to constitutional systems without a written constitution, such as those found in the United Kingdom or New Zealand. It then included the practice of the Federal Assembly and the Federal Council, the case law of the Federal Court, as well as many norms of international law, which Switzerland has undertaken to respect (Federal Council 1997: 17). The revision of the Constitution did not codify this entire material constitution, for 'the text of the Constitution never fully restores substantive constitutional law' (Federal Council 1997: 19). This conception of the Constitution, therefore, indicates that Switzerland has a 'living constitution' that has evolved over time, but especially with respect to the scope given to its values. Here, the judge plays a major role. Respect for fundamental rights, democracy and the separation of powers and federalism represent these Swiss constitutional values and contribute to shaping the activities and limits of the state, and that includes Swiss public administration.

Yet, as we have noted, the formalistic dimension of the law develops as well. Several elements show such a trend. This was the case with the requirement of a certain legal quality of laws set in guidelines for specific methods of codification or with the federal consultation procedure. It was also the case with the enlargement of the popular participation in ratification procedure of some international treaties, which has added an extra formal condition to the validity of the ratification.

References

Aubert, J.-F. (1993). *Traité de droit constitutionnel suisse*. Neuchâtel: Ides et Calendes.

Aubert, J.-F., & Mahon, P. (2003). *Petit traité de la Constitution fédérale de la Confédération suisse du 18 avril 1999*. Zurich/Basel/Geneva: Schulthess.

Auer, A., Malinverni, G., & Hottelier, M. (2006). *Droit constitutionnel, vol. I.* Berne: Staempfli.
Auer, A., Malinverni, G., & Hottelier, M. (2013). *Droit constitutionnel suisse* (Vol. I, 2nd ed.). Bern: Stämpfli.
Caillosse, J. (2015). *L'État du droit administratif.* Paris: LGDJ Lextenso éditions.
Chevallier, J. (1998). Vers un droit post-moderne ? *Les transformations de la régulation juridique, Revue du droit public, 3*, 659–714.
Epiney, A. (2015). Art. 5. In B. Waldmann, E. M. Belser, & A. Epiney (Eds.), *Bundesverfassung* (pp. 85–133). Basel: Helbing Lichtenhahn.
Federal Council. (1997). Message du Conseil fédéral du 20 novembre 1996 relatif à une nouvelle constitution fédérale. *Feuille fédérale I*, 1–653.
Federal Office of Justice. (2007). *Guide de législation, Guide pour l'élaboration de la législation fédérale.* Bern: Swiss Confederation.
Flückiger, A. (2007). L'évaluation législative ou comment mesurer l'efficacité des lois. *Revue européenne des sciences sociales. European Journal of Social Sciences, XLV-138*, 83–101.
Flückiger, A. (2008). Qu'est-ce que "mieux légiférer"?: enjeux et instrumentalisation de la notion de qualité législative. In A. Flückiger & C. Guy-Ecabert (Eds.), *Guider les parlements et les gouvernements pour mieux légiférer: le rôle des guides de légistique* (pp. 11–32). Geneva: Schulthess.
Flückiger, A., & Guy-Ecabert, C. (2008). *Guider les parlements et les gouvernements pour mieux légiférer: le rôle des guides de légistique.* Geneva: Schulthess.
Hachez, I., Cartuyvels, Y., Dumont, H., Gérard, P., Ost, F., & van de Kerchove, M. (2010). *Les sources du droit revisitées* (Vol. 4). Limal: Anthemis.
Haller, W. (2016). *The Swiss Constitution in a Comparative Context.* Zurich/St Gall: Dike.
Hangartner, Y. (2008). Kommentar zu Art. 5 BV. In B. Erhenzeller, B. Schindler, R. J. Schweizer, & K. A. Vallender (Eds.), *Die Schweizerische Bundesverfassung. St Galler Kommentar* (pp. 99–125). Zürich/St. Gallen: Dike/Schulthess.
Keller, H., & Balazs-Hegedüs, N. (2016). Anspruch und Realität der «Selbstbestimmungsinitiative». *Aktuelle Juristische Praxis, 6*, 712–724.
Kingsbury, B., Krisch, N., & Stewart, R. B. (2005). The emergence of global administrative law. *Law & Contemporary Problems, 68*(3/4), 15–61.
Knoepfel, P. (2017). *Les ressources d'action publique. Vers une nouvelle lecture du pouvoir.* Zurich/Geneva: Seismo.
Kolb, R. (2016). L'initiative de l'UDC sur l'autodétermination (« juges étrangers »). *Swiss Review of International and European Law, 26*, 567–580.
Mader, L. (2013). Législation. In A. Ladner, J.-L. Chappelet, Y. Emery, P. Knoepfel, L. Mader, N. Soguel, & F. Varone (Eds.), *Manuel d'administration publique Suisse* (pp. 245–265). Lausanne: Presses polytechniques et universitaires romandes.

Mader, L. (2015). Les rôles des clauses d'évaluations dans le processus législatif fédéral. In K. Horber-Papazian (Ed.), *Regards croisés sur l'évaluation* (pp. 67–78). Lausanne: Presses polytechniques et universitaires romandes.

Mahon, P. (2014). *Droit Constitutionnel. Institutions, juridiction constitutionnelle et procédure* (Vol. 1). Basel: Helbing Lichtenhahn.

Mockle, D. (2007). *La gouvernance, le droit et l'État.* Bruxelles: Bruylant.

Moor, P. (1990). Introduction à la théorie de la légalité. In C.-A. Morand (Ed.), *Les figures de la légalité* (pp. 11–28). Paris: Publisud.

Moor, P. (2005). *Pour une théorie micropolitique du droit.* Paris: Presses universitaires de France.

Morand, C.-A. (1991). *L'Etat propulsif: contribution à l'étude des instruments d'action de l'Etat.* Paris: Publisud.

Müller, G. (2006). *Elemente einer Rechstsetzungslehre.* Zurich/Basel/Geneva: Schulthess.

Popelier, P. (2012). La loi aujourd'hui (le principe de légalité). In I. Hachez et al. (Eds.), *Les sources du droit revisitées* (Vol. 2, pp. 17–54). Limal: Anthémis.

Schindler, B. (2014). Art.5 abs 1–2. In B. Erhenzeller, B. Schindler, R. J. Schweizer, & K. A. Vallender (Eds.), *Die Schweizerische Bundesverfassung. St Galler Kommentar* (pp. 103–142). Zürich/St. Gallen: Dike/Schulthess.

Tanquerel, T. (2011). *Manuel de droit administrative.* Geneva/Zurich/Basel: Schulthess.

Uhlmann, F. (2013). Die Normen können bei...bezorgen werden – gedanken zur Publikation und Verbindlichkeit privater Normen. *LeGes, 1*, 89–104.

CHAPTER 5

The Pre-parliamentary Phase in Lawmaking: The Power Issues at Stake

Christine Guy-Ecabert

5.1 Introduction

Swiss law contains a certain number of rules concerning the lawmaking process. In this framework, the federal administration has developed an impressive practice in lawmaking which has been progressively established in specific guides and enshrined in law. The aim of this chapter will not be to present all the lawmaking, but will instead focus on the pre-parliamentary phase during which the federal administration has to act.

Before coming into force, a federal law goes through four phases: pre-parliamentary, parliamentary, referendum, and implementation. Swiss are generally quite familiar with the parliamentary phase of the legislative process; debates in the two chambers of the Federal Assembly are well covered by the media during each of its four annual sessions. By contrast, the pre-parliamentary phase remains relatively unknown if not confidential (Sciarini 2011). Yet it is during this phase that the draft legislation submitted to parliament is negotiated, and this partly determines its future fate. The federal administration plays a major role in this phase, which is why it is worth devoting attention to this preparatory phase when addressing

C. Guy-Ecabert (✉)
Faculty of Law, University of Neuchâtel, Neuchâtel, Switzerland
e-mail: christine.guy-ecabert@unine.ch

A. Ladner et al. (eds.), *Swiss Public Administration*, Governance and Public Management,
https://doi.org/10.1007/978-3-319-92381-9_5

public administration and the lawmaking process at the federal level. To make it more explicit, the dossier on the revision of the Federal Data Protection Act (DPA) will be used to illustrate the room for maneuver available to the federal administration, and more specifically to the federal offices.[1]

Chronological logic is used first to describe the preparatory phase, which focuses more on the process than on organizational issues. Next, we present the supporting material (reference documents) that governs this process, and discuss the limits of their accessibility. Then we contrast how the federal authorities portray the objectives of the pre-parliamentary phase with the results of studies by legal scholars and political scientists. Finally, we examine an underlying issue, namely what is at stake in terms of power in the pre-parliamentary process.

5.2 The Stages of the Pre-parliamentary Process

In federal law, there are several categories of legal instruments. The major ones are laws and ordinances; only the first are considered, as they have to be adopted by the legislature. Moreover, in Switzerland, laws (Art. 164 Federal Constitution, abbrev. as Const.) can be subjected to an optional referendum (Art. 141 Const.). In terms of competencies, because it involves preparing a legislative act at the level of law, it is the responsibility of the Federal Council, the national executive (Art. 181 Const.), to direct the pre-parliamentary phase. This is different if the impulse for the law comes from a parliamentary or cantonal initiative, a rare situation—less than 20%—that will not be considered here (Art. 181 and 171 Const.; Art. 7 Government and Administration Organisation Act (GAOA); Federal Office of Justice 2014: 100).

We draw here on the many federal guidelines which govern the pre-parliamentary process (for a particularly critical stance, see Jochum and Ledermann 2009: 92), and follow the chronological development: the design of the legislative project (Sect. 5.2.1), the preliminary draft and its explanatory report (Sect. 5.2.2), and the external consultation on the preliminary draft and finalizing the bill (Sect. 5.2.3).

[1] The author would like to thank Simone Füzesséry, deputy head of the Legislation Projects and Methodology Unit, Public Law Division, Federal Office of Justice and co-responsible for the revision of the Federal Law on Data Protection, for answering numerous questions as well as his careful reading of the present text.

5.2.1 *Designing the Legislative Project*

It is at the beginning of the first, conceptualizing, phase that the necessary information for analyzing the problem is collected and a project organization is set up. The scope of knowledge needed depends on the structure of the project, understood as the organization of the project. The choices here are, on the one hand, a function of the staff resources and expertise of the office in charge, and on the other hand, the likelihood of finding a sufficient consensus. In other words, the more complex and politically sensitive the problem is, the larger the group that prepares the project.

Overall, three variants are possible. The first is an internal working group, which presupposes the federal administration has the necessary knowledge. The second is a joint working group, in particular, committees composed equally of federal and cantonal representatives, formed when the latter are particularly concerned. The third, in exceptional cases when specialist expertise seems needed, is a group of experts from outside the administration. The most common is the joint working group, which brings together interdisciplinary skills. Nevertheless, lawyers are very evident in these different types of working groups.

The conceptual phase allows for the construction of a base of knowledge on which the draft law and the explanatory report—called the 'message fédéral'—later rest. It is based on a material lawmaking approach whose goal is to improve the ability of the law to act on social reality (Flückiger 2008). One can see this as a problem-solving cycle with three stages: defining the problem (by analyzing its causes and its dynamic), determining the objectives (describing the desired future state by prioritizing the objectives to be achieved), and deciding on the instruments to use (presenting the variants in conjunction with the various instruments of action available to the government, and roughly assessing them before selecting which to use) (Jochum and Ledermann 2009). Depending on the circumstances, this iterative approach can be repeated at each state of the pre-parliamentary process.

The problem-solving cycle culminates in drafting an outline of a normative act which summarizes—in the form of theses or guiding principles—the material lawmaking approach, without yet expressing it in the form of a normative text. The following sketch also provides variants to the chosen solution (Art. 141 of the Law on Parliament). It is during the conceptualizing phase that the federal administration can best develop its room for maneuver or be at its most creative.

The DPA case: Almost 20 years after it came into force (on 19 June 1992), it was clear that the Swiss data protection law was outdated, superseded by technological and societal developments and the new requirements under European law. Based on an evaluation carried out by an interdisciplinary research group (Büro Vatter 2011*), the Federal Council instructed the Federal Department of Justice and Police to revise the law (Federal Council* 2011*). The Federal Office of Justice, which was responsible for this dossier, established a working group composed of representatives from the federal administration, the cantons, the universities, as well as from consumer protection and economic interest groups. They drew up a report – incorrectly entitled 'Outline of a Normative Act' – which described the basic axes of the revision, the form of the normative act, the general regulatory structure, its normative density, and a timetable for implementation (Federal Office of Justice* 2014*). In fact, no outline will ever be drafted, despite the directive calling for it by the Federal Office of Justice, probably in order to avoid consulting the head of the department again. Instead, the Swiss Institute of Comparative Law was asked to provide expert reports on how data protection is organized in various countries (Germany, France, Italy, the Netherlands, Poland, Sweden, the UK, Finland, Slovenia, Spain, and in Argentina, Japan, New Zealand, Singapore, South Korea, and the U.S.) and what powers data protection authorities have in these countries. Contracts were also given to the Universities of Applied Sciences in Zurich and Lucerne to analyze the jurisprudence and literature on the cost-benefit ratio in the area of data protection.*

5.2.2 Preparing the Preliminary Draft and the Explanatory Report

The outline of a normative act, which summarizes the main political and legal features of the proposed bill, is now transformed into a text, the draft bill. This is where formal legal rules, in particular those governing structuring, are crucial. The original drafting language is most often German, with a parallel French translation. Depending on the available resources, the text is drafted in parallel in two official languages but often in just one. Italian is the poor relation in the federal administration and is generally only a language of translation rather than of formulation.

The DPA case: The working group was composed largely of French-speakers, so the draft data protection law was formulated originally in French and then immediately translated into German. This is exceptional.

Once the draft is prepared, its potential effects are evaluated. According to the letter of the law, this includes speculation about 'the consequences the project, if carried out, will have on the finances and the status of the personnel of the Confederation, the cantons and the communities, the modalities proposed and their financing, the impact it has had or will have on financial planning, and the cost/utility evaluation of the proposed measures'; 'the economic, social and environmental consequences of the proposed project and its effects on future generations'; and the foreseeable 'consequences the project will have on equality between men and women' (Art. 141 (2)(f, g, and i), Federal Act on the Federal Assembly). However, the Confederation limits this type of study, called a Regulatory Impact Analysis (RIA), to an economic analysis (Federal Department of Economic Affairs 2013). In undertaking these prospective evaluations, the administration seeks to improve the preliminary draft and the explanatory report which comments on it.

The DPA case: After having read the 'outline of a normative act', the Federal Council instructed the Federal Department of Justice and Police to formulate a draft law together with three other Departments, and together with the Federal Data Protection and Information Commissioner.

On behalf of the Federal Office of Justice and of the State Secretariat for Economic Affairs, a private firm conducted an RIA (PWC 2016*). According to its conclusions, it is necessary to legislate, in particular due to the evolution of law at international and European levels. The RIA also showed that from the point of view of firms operating in Switzerland, the preliminary draft would significantly affect those companies with medium or high exposure to data protection law. With respect to international competition, companies would nevertheless benefit from Switzerland maintaining its status as a country with an adequate level of data protection. Those concerned would benefit from a strengthening of their position.*

The first part of the explanatory report of 21 December 2016 on the preliminary draft federal law (on the total revision of the data protection law and on the modification of other federal laws) places it in its national and international contexts, discusses the objectives of the revision (adapting Swiss legislation to technological developments and integrating changes in European regulations), provides a comparative study of relevant laws, and addresses implementation issues. Another section addressed the new standards, commenting on them article by article. Finally, the various financial, economic and social consequences on the IT sector are evaluated. The report also addresses various legal issues, in particular the constitutionality of the preliminary draft in terms of case law, compatibility with international agreements, and the form of the draft act.

5.2.3 *Consulting About the Preliminary Draft and Finalizing the Bill*

The consultation process marks the beginning of opening up the pre-parliamentary process. The addressees are organizations which do not belong to the federal administration. Federal judicial authorities are only consulted on projects which affect their own processes or organization (Art. 11, Federal Ordinance on the Consultation Procedure). The cantons, the political parties, local authorities' associations (cities and communities), and those circles interested in drafting federal laws are also involved in the consultation, one which is supposed to take into consideration all the interests at stake. This is a key instrument of cooperative federalism (Federal Council 2004) which allows NGOs to contribute to the formation of public opinion and help establish whether a project of the Confederation is 'materially correct, executable and likely to be accepted' (Art. 2 (2), Federal Ordinance on the Consultation Procedure).

The drafts of federal laws are generally open to consultation, though the federal administration can waive this (Art. 3a, Federal Act on the Consultation Procedure). This takes place in principle over a period of three months. The federal administration drafts the final report, which presents and weighs the expressed opinions. If the Federal Council approves the bill and the preliminary report, it is sent to the Federal Assembly. This marks the end of the pre-parliamentary phase and the beginning of the parliamentary process.

The DPA case: As part of the consultation process, which lasted a little over three months from the end of December 2016 to the beginning of April 2017, the Federal Department of Justice and Police invited 65 organizations – in particular the federal courts, the cantons, the political parties and various interested organizations – to give their opinions about this proposed bill, while 164 other actors, unasked, also provided input. The Department received 222 statements, 176 from relevant circles (Federal Office of Justice 2017: *5). On 10 August 2017, the Federal Office of Justice published a 79-page summary of the results of the consultation process, laying out the main points (an assessment of the need to legislate and a general assessment of the preliminary draft), along with details on the opinions about specific articles. On September 15, 2017, the Federal Council received the 247-page report about a federal law to revise the federal data protection act (as well as about modifying other federal laws), along with a draft bill which contained 67 articles* (Federal Council 2017: 6565).

5.3 Reference Documents and Their Accessibility

Being familiar with a process internal to the administration implies having access not just to the legal instruments that define it abstractly, but also to the files of the preliminary legislative procedures which are in process or are completed. The few normative texts can be found in the classified compilation of Swiss law. Anyone who wants to obtain information on the pre-parliamentary process can readily find the many texts meant to guide the administration in its work—constitutional norms, laws, ordinances, and directives—on the webpages of the federal administration. On the one hand, the documents concern the phase which has external effects, meaning the consultation process (Art. 147 Const., Federal Act and Federal Ordinance on the Consultation Procedure), and on the other hand, they are related to information provided to the Federal Assembly by the Federal Council which defines the content of the explanatory report, which the second addresses to the first (Art. 141 Federal Act on the Federal Assembly).

The Swiss Confederation did not enact a 'law of laws' forcing a legislator to follow a methodical approach in drafting legislation (Flückiger 2008). However, numerous directives guiding the administration can be found on the respective websites. Thus, the *Guide de législation* (Federal Office of Justice 2007) and the three modules (law, regulations, and parliamentary initiative) which complement it as well as the *Directive sur la présentation d'esquisses d'acte normatif* may be found on the website of the Federal Office of Justice. The *Directives sur la technique législative* and the *Aide-mémoire sur la présentation des messages du Conseil fédéral* are available on that of the Federal Chancellery. These texts provide step-by-step guides for the administrators responsible for carrying out the internal procedures. There is thus a mass of information, the largest part of which comes from the good practices of the federal administration. The practice of consultation, for example, is an old tradition which was codified by a Federal Council directive on May 6, 1970, about the preliminary process for legislation (Federal Council 1970: 1003). This was reinforced by a Federal Council order on June 17, 1991; the Law on the Consultation Procedure was only first passed in 2005.

Documents about each draft bill in the pre-parliamentary phase are as readily accessible for the procedures in progress, though only once the external consultation has begun. Electronic records are more or less well-organized; they are provided as a function of the care various offices give to their own webpages.

The DPA case: The 'strengthening data' file of the Federal Office of Justice is particularly well-documented. One finds in it a summary of the political and legal motivations for revising the law and of the preliminary steps taken, the reports from the experts, the documents made available for consultation, the positions taken and the results of the consultation, along with the preliminary report and the bill.

It would be fascinating to add information to this layer of legal and technical information, about what is at stake, in terms of power, at the heart of government. However, Federal Council deliberations are not public (Art. 21, GAOA), nor are the documents it produces. Indeed, despite a Copernican revolution—which has made it a priority to have transparency outweigh secrecy in the access to federal government documents—the Federal Council does not fall under the scope of this law. In the case of documents relating to co-reporting procedures—the final stage of negotiations between the heads of departments which precedes the Federal Council's decision—they too evade the principle of transparency (Art 8 (1–4) Freedom of Information Act).

The reason for this is that a collegial authority must be able to remain silent about how it reaches its opinions and makes its decisions in order to present a united front to the public. The public is deprived of knowledge about the clash of ideas, the political conflicts, and the alliances formed within the executive—certainly for good political reasons—and does not know what the real power issues are that are at stake. It is thus doubtful that the Federal Council might one day risk opening the door of its 'federal chalet'[2] to allow a [Bruno] Latour interested in the Swiss political system to research and publish a work entitled 'The Making of Swiss Law: An ethnography of the Federal Council'.[3] As for the negotiations which take place in the offices and in the working groups in which preliminary drafts and legal projects are conceived, they remain secret. They thus evade the rules of the democratic game which is played during parliamentary debates.

[2] Owing to its decor and furnishings, the room in which the Federal Council meets is given this amused moniker (https://www.admin.ch/gov/fr/accueil/conseil-federal/ou-travaille-le-gouvernement/salle-seance-conseil-federal.html).

[3] See the remarkable work by Bruno Latour (2002), especially the chapter 'Quel étrange atelier d'écriture': 69 et seq.

5.4 The Objectives of the Pre-parliamentary Process

The political organs of the Confederation are in agreement over the two objectives of the pre-parliamentary process. On the one hand, it is meant to contribute to the quality of the law (Sect. 5.4.1); on the other, it is meant to encourage political acceptability in the parliamentary phase and subsequently in the referendum phase (Sect. 5.4.2). After briefly describing the means the authorities put into practice to achieve these objectives, we contrast them with critical studies written by legal scholars and political scientists (Sect. 5.4.3).

5.4.1 To Contribute to the Quality of the Law

The quality of the law can be judged from a legal, editorial, or political vantage point, and it is a topic which always ignites controversy (Flückiger and Guy-Ecabert 2015: 21–45). It is possible to improve the legal quality of the law before it is adopted or published (as a preventive control) or after its publication or its entry into force (as a subsequent control, see the chapter by Mahon). Switzerland does not have the judicial review of federal laws once they are passed, and even if they are unconstitutional, the Federal Supreme Court and the other authorities are obliged to apply them (Art. 190 Const.).

As early as the preliminary phase, the Federal Office of Justice is primarily responsible for monitoring whether draft federal laws conform with higher law (constitutional provisions), whether they are compatible with international law, and whether they are basically accurate. Its Legislation I and II Units and its European Law and Schengen Coordination Unit provide this legislative support. It is not uncommon for a draft bill to be checked six or eight times by the Federal Office of Justice (Mader 2006: 5), and by virtue of this, this office enjoys considerable de facto autonomy (Mader 2006: 7).

Other offices and administrative units come into play when questions relevant to their area of expertise arise. For example, the Federal Chancellery's legal department systematically examines proposed legislative acts from the perspective of legislative technique and the drafting of laws (Art. 7 (3) Federal Ordinance on the Organization of the Federal Department of Justice and Police and Art. 4 (1) (b) Federal Ordinance on the Organization of the Federal Chancellery). As needed, the Federal

Finance Administration checks compliance with budget law and the law on subsidies, the Directorate of International Law checks compatibility with Switzerland's international obligations, the Directorate for European Affairs of the Federal Department of Foreign Affairs monitors compliance with the agreements concluded between Switzerland and the EU, and the Federal Data Protection and Information Commissioner is concerned with data protection. The opinions provided by the Federal Office of Justice and other administrative bodies are certainly not binding. Nevertheless, given the subject matter, if the competent offices do not take up the conclusions reached by the Federal Office of Justice, they must explain why.

Evaluating the quality of the law comparatively would require research into many legal systems, most likely the reason why such studies have yet to be undertaken. It would also be necessary to decide first on a definition of the 'the quality of the law' and establish some means for correlating this 'quality' with the pre-parliamentary process. Nevertheless, some authors cautiously estimate that federal law is 'rather affordable, concise and understandable in international comparison' (Müller and Uhlmann 2013: 49; Flückiger and Guy-Ecabert 2008: 40; Flückiger 2008: 32).

5.4.2 *To Successively Build a Consensus*

In Switzerland, laws passed by the Federal Assembly are vulnerable as they can be subjected to (an optional) popular referendum. The consequence of this Damoclean sword is that the entire pre-parliamentary process is designed and organized so as to progressively build a consensus—in the hope of escaping the threat of a subsequent referendum. This intent is clearly expressed by the Federal Council: 'the question whether a project will be accepted politically is extremely important for legislators in light of the possibilities the referendum provides within the Swiss democratic system' (Federal Council 2004: 498). The search for consensus commences already in the very first stage, the conceptualizing one, of the pre-parliamentary phase when the experts who will work together in the mixed working groups are selected. Consensus is also sought through the joint interdepartmental report intended for the Federal Council: the intent is to iron out the differences between the departments beforehand (Müller and Uhlmann 2013: 148). This consensus-building is also particularly evident during the process of consulting outside interested parties.

This idea of building consensus is not without its psycho-sociological foundation. It is based on the assumption that involving actors in a decision means that, having accepted that they will participate and contribute to a decision, they will also support it later. However, many political science studies show the opposite to be true (Sciarini 2015: 31; 2011: 196). Both in the parliamentary and referendum phases, media coverage of concertation or consultation efforts compels actors to reveal their positions publicly. Positions stated clearly and openly can exacerbate conflicts. Contrary to what might be expected in a good theory of negotiation, consultation may well not encourage an open exchange of opinions and can hinder symmetrical interactions, leading to an escalation of conflict (Papadopoulos 1997: 48). The ability of the actors to negotiate and find compromise can thus be affected by media coverage of the pre-parliamentary procedure.

5.4.3 Critics

The consultation process has its critics. It has the potential of strengthening conservative views by allowing those who reject change to oppose it, leading to solutions close to the status quo. It can also lead to self-censorship on the part of the authorities (Papadopoulos 1997: 47), and even worse, to a large deficit in Swiss innovation policy (Keller 1997: 14).

The DPA case: The EU imposes very severe criminal sanctions for violations of data protection. To be in compliance, the preliminary draft sanctioned various infractions by imposing a maximum fine of 500,000 CHF. Following the consultation process, the draft law halved this amount, though at the risk that the EU could declare the DPA to be insufficiently deterrent.

One criticism is that consultation considerably lengthens the decision-making process. Legislative proceedings last, on average, for 51 months (more than four years), of which just over two-thirds are taken up by the pre-parliamentary process, or a little under three years (Federal Office of Justice 2007: 23).

Despite these critiques, the stakeholders involved in the consultation process are of the opinion that it allows factual elements to be brought in which both improve the draft law and help right the power imbalances between the actors concerned. It also contributes to greater transparency in the decision-making process (Christe et al. 2016: 212). In the end, it also helps counter the centrifugal forces which exist in a multicultural society, and thus helps preserve social cohesion (Papadopoulos 1997: 46).

5.5 Decrypting the Power Issues

We now focus on the question of who has decision-making power, in a material sense, within the domestic legislative process. It can be considered from two perspectives. First, it concerns the relations between the executive—the Federal Council—and the different levels of the federal administration (head of department, offices and general secretariats). Second, it is about the designation of the leading office of a given project.

The Federal Council functions according to two principles: collegiality (all its members collectively assume responsibility for governing), and the departmental principle (each member heads one or more departments) (Auer et al. 2013: 54). In this configuration, the federal administration, hierarchically subordinated to the Federal Council, is not considered as an organ of the state.

As the chronological presentation of the process highlighted, such an organization has an impact on the power game that is played. The executive, meaning the government relying on a public administration is subdivided into offices and agencies, reigns supreme over the first phase of the legislative process. It is here that the major legal and political decisions about a given project are taken. These decisions will only later be submitted, in the form of a bill, to the Parliament. As we have focused here only on the preliminary phase, we must leave aside the very important question of the horizontal balance of power between government and parliament throughout the legislative process (Sciarini 2015). The question which concerns us here is the vertical distribution of power between Federal Council, the departments, the offices of the federal administration, and the general secretariats of the departments. We will approach this from the top down.

In the context of implementing federalism, where the federal executive is transferring the power to implement federal law to the cantons, the 'pre-legislative' phase is important from the point of view of political power. Nonetheless, this power is largely delegated to the federal administration. Though the Federal Council certainly has the right to make decisions, which it makes use of at each stage of the pre-parliamentary process, it in fact exercises its power in the form of a right of veto over the decisions made by the federal administrative offices rather than making collegial decisions within the Council. Indeed, everything is played out, in a formalized decision-making process, called the interdepartmental co-report procedure, prior to the Federal Council meeting, which is to say in the meeting of the department heads to prepare a joint interdepartmental report (Art. 15 GAOA and Art. 5 Ordonnance on Government and Administration Organization; Müller and Uhlmann 2013: n. 147–150).

The first step is consultation at the level of the federal offices inside the departments. This makes it possible to gather proposals and amendments, and establish whether the relevant office will accede or resist. In a second step, the dossier goes back to the heads of other departments. They can express their disagreement in a report addressed to the head of the responsible department, who can in turn take a position in response to it and to the reports submitted by other departments. A last round of replies from the departments to this response is also possible. These reports, signed by the heads of departments, are in fact prepared by the federal offices (Mader 2001: n. 45), and are the veritable 'backbone' of the federal administration (Grisel 1984: 213); they play a major role in the decision of the Federal Council.[4] Unlike the Federal Councilors, the heads of federal offices, managers of domains, or heads of units (Mader 2006) are not subject to re-election. Because they define the principal orientations, they exercise major and lasting influence over the procedure and the bills.

The general secretariats of the departments are also a locus of power. Serving as general staff, they assist the heads of departments in performing various tasks (Art. 143 et seq. GAOA). However, they benefit from having a different position. They are certainly closer to the head of the department than to the heads of the offices and can intervene at the highest level, at the end of the process. On the other hand, they no longer influence the important points which have not previously been considered in the federal offices internally.

At the very beginning of the preliminary procedure, the new legislative project is assigned to one federal office. Although this decision falls within the material competence of the Federal Council, it is not the result of a political negotiation, on a case-by-case basis, between the Councilors. It is based instead on regulations it has enacted about how the seven federal

[4] As Alain Berset confirmed when he exclaimed: 'Heavens – parliament has dismantled my proposed law!' Cited in Flueckiger and Guy-Ecabert (2008: 141–142). The author, now a Federal Councilor, was vice-president of the Council of States at the time.

departments are (to be) organized, establishing such distribution according to subject (e.g., based on the areas of expertise of the various offices). These offices are supposed to organize themselves in such a way that they can assume their respective legislative responsibility.

In fact, they have very different human resources available to produce quality legal texts. Some, such as the Federal Office of Public Health or the Federal Office for the Environment, have legal services with many employees, or even quality assurance systems. Others, by contrast, do not even have positions for lawyers. In such cases, lawyers from the Federal Office of Justice or the Federal Chancellery provide assistance. In this context, the internal legislative process begins in decentralized 'workshops' which bring together various skills and resources. In a Weberian sense, the administrative system 'delineates spheres of competence and powers' and 'prioritizes functions'.[5]

Federal offices enjoy considerable power in making proposals during the pre-parliamentary phase. They are certainly subordinated hierarchically to the head of the department, as well as potentially subject to a Federal Council veto as it decides about each stage of the process, most especially in starting the consultation process (Art. 5 Consultation Procedure Act). Though responsible for the organization of the project, they nevertheless have an impact on the integration of knowledge and the extent of consultation in the drafting of bills.

Compared with other offices, the Federal Office of Justice enjoys important prerogatives, which has earned it the label of being the 'juridical conscience of the administration' (Mader 2006: 3). It guarantees control over the quality of draft laws, carries out legal assessments, and enacts an important part of the directives and formal legalistic guidelines. It also provides training for federal law clerks. This office has, in effect, designed and implemented a complete training concept—something found rarely even among Swiss university law faculties.

Ultimately, while it is formally a power of the Federal Council, it is the federal offices and even the general secretariats which exercise power over the pre-parliamentary process (Mader 2006: 7). This means a strengthening of public administration relative to the executive, so much so that some describe the federal administration as 'the fourth power' in the state (Häfelin et al. 2016: n. 1698). Of the relevant offices, the Federal Office

[5] Michel Crozier, 'Bureaucratie' in Encyclopædia Universalis. http://www.universalis.fr/encyclopedie/bureaucratie/ (consulted on August 25, 2017).

of Justice enjoys a particularly powerful position, a situation not without its problems. Indeed, the control of the preventive control of compliance with the law by an office raises questions of independence. Author of numerous bills—20%, the office also happens to be the relevant office for the subject matter as well as the locus of preventive control, which could lead to conflicts of interest. It is therefore not surprising that, in response to a postulate, the Federal Council issued a report in which it declared itself satisfied with the status quo, while also advocating some modest optimization measures. It is thus perhaps not surprising that the Federal Council also opposes judicial review: if introduced, it could guarantee oversight by an organ of the state which would be independent of the government and parliament (Federal Council 2010).

References

Auer, A., Malinverni, G., & Hottelier, M. (2013). *Droit constitutionnel* (Vol. I). Berne: Staempfli.

Christe, J., Gava, R., & Varone, F. (2016). Consultations et groupes d'intérêt: un aperçu quantitatif. *LeGes, 2*, 211–224.

Federal Council. (1970). Directives du Conseil fédéral du 6 mai 1970 concernant la procédure préliminaire en matière de législation. *Feuille Fédérale I*, 1002–1010.

Federal Council. (2004). Message du Conseil fédéral du 21 janvier 2004 relatif à la loi fédérale sur la procédure de consultation. *Feuille Fédérale I*, 485–512.

Federal Council. (2010). Rapport du Conseil fédéral du 5 mars 2010 sur le renforcement du contrôle préventif de la conformité au droit. *Feuille Fédérale*, 1989–2066.

Federal Council. (2011). Rapport du Conseil fédéral du 9 décembre 2011 sur l'évaluation de la loi fédérale sur la protection des données. *Feuille Fédérale*, 255–272.

Federal Council. (2017). Message du Conseil fédéral du 15 septembre 2017 concernant la loi fédérale sur la révision totale de la loi fédérale sur la protection des données et sur la modification d'autres lois fédérales. *Feuille Fédérale*, 6565–6802.

Federal Department of Economic Affairs, Education and Research. (2013). *Analyse d'impact de la réglementation*. Bern: Swiss Confederation.

Federal Office of Justice. (2007). *Guide de législation, Guide pour l'élaboration de la législation fédérale*. Bern: Swiss Confederation.

Federal Office of Justice. (2014). *Esquisse d'acte normatif relative à la révision de la loi sur la protection des données. Rapport du 29 octobre 2014 du groupe d'accompagnement Révision LPD*. Bern: Swiss Confederation.

Federal Office of Justice. (2017). *Avant-projet de loi fédérale sur la révision totale de la loi sur la protection des données et sur la modification d'autres lois fédérales. Synthèse des résultats de la procédure de consultation.* Bern: Swiss Confederation.

Flückiger, A. (2008). Qu'est-ce que "mieux légiférer"?: enjeux et instrumentalisation de la notion de qualité législative. In A. Flückiger & C. Guy-Ecabert (Eds.), *Guider les parlements et les gouvernements pour mieux légiférer: le rôle des guides de légistique* (pp. 11–32). Genève: Schulthess.

Flückiger, A., & Guy-Ecabert, C. (2008). *Guider les parlements et les gouvernements pour mieux légiférer. Le rôle des guides de légistique.* Zurich: Schulthess.

Flückiger, A., & Guy-Ecabert, C. (2015). La bonne loi ou le paradis perdu? *LeGes, 1*, 21–45.

Grisel, A. (1984). *Traité de droit administratif, I.* Neuchâtel: Ides et Calendes.

Häfelin, U., et al. (2016). *Schweizerisches Bundesstaatsrecht.* Zurich: Schulthess.

Jochum, M., & Ledermann, S. (2009). La démarche légistique entre théorie et pratique. *LeGes, 1*, 87–103.

Keller, M. (1997). Fragen des Vernehmlassungsverfahrens / Quelques interrogations sur la procédure de consultation. *LeGes, 2*, 11–15.

Latour, B. (2002). *La fabrique du droit. Une ethnographie du Conseil d'État.* Paris: La Découverte.

Mader, L. (2001). Bundesrat und Bundesverwaltung. In D. Thürer, J.-F. Aubert, & J. P. Müller (Eds.), *Verfassungsrecht der Schweiz* (pp. 1047–1069). Zürich: Schulthess.

Mader, L. (2006). Das Bundesamt für Justiz: eine Dienerin vieler Herren? In R. Reusser & B. Schindler (Eds.), *L'atelier du droit. Mélanges en l'honneur de Heinrich Koller à l'occasion de son 65e anniversaire* (pp. 3–10). Basel: Helbing & Lichtenhahn.

Müller, G., & Uhlmann, F. (2013). *Elemente einer Rechtsetzungslehre.* Zurich: Schulthess.

Papadopoulos, I. (1997). La consultation: un outil de gouvernabilité? Fonctions et dysfonctionnements de la phase préparlementaire. *LeGes, 2*, 241–260.

PWC. (2016). *Regulierungsfolgenabschätzung (RFA) zur Revision des eidg. Datenschutzgesetzes (DSG).* Bern: PWC.

Sciarini, P. (2011). Les effets de la consultation sur les processus de décision au niveau fédéral. *LeGes, 2*, 191–204.

Sciarini, P. (2015). Introduction. In P. Sciarini, M. Fischer, & D. Traber (Eds.), *Political decision-making in Switzerland: The consensus model under pressure (challenges to democracy in the 21st century)* (pp. 1–23). Basingstoke/New York: Palgrave Macmillan.

Vatter, B. (2011). Evaluation des Bundesgesetzes über den Datenschutz. Institut für Europarecht (Universität Freiburg), Schlussbericht.

CHAPTER 6

The Federal Administration as an Actor in the Domestic Integration of International Law

Sophie Weerts and Amalia Sofia

6.1 Introduction

The twentieth century witnessed a remarkable expansion of international law, and the Swiss federal constitution of 1999 expresses a strong commitment to international cooperation and respect for international law (Rhinow and Schefer 2009: 696 et seq). Nevertheless, the Swiss legal system is distinctive in its commitment to using direct democratic instruments. Indeed, together with federalism and neutrality, direct democracy has become one of the founding myths of Swiss constitutional identity (Hertig Randall and McGregor 2010: 429).

Yet in recent decades, direct democracy has been increasingly seen as potentially threatening to the coherence of Swiss foreign policy (Federal Council 1997: 445; Haller 2016: 38). Swiss public administration faces a dilemma here. On the one hand, it must comply with the rule of law, applying the principle of legality and respecting international law (Art. 5 (1) and (4), Swiss Federal Constitution, henceforth Const.). On the other

S. Weerts (✉) • A. Sofia
IDHEAP, University of Lausanne, Lausanne, Switzerland
e-mail: Sophie.Weerts@unil.ch; amalia.sofia@unil.ch

A. Ladner et al. (eds.), *Swiss Public Administration*, Governance and Public Management,
https://doi.org/10.1007/978-3-319-92381-9_6

hand, it must simultaneously recognize the people's will expressed at the polls if it is to keep the citizens' trust in the system. This chapter intends to show how the federal administration, guided by Swiss law, plays a role in maintaining a balance between direct democracy and respecting international law. It will not offer a detailed description of the rules and practices regulating the relationship between international and domestic law. Instead, it focuses on the legal and political mechanisms which influence how international and Swiss law are articulated in a manner which ensures respect for the country's 'monistic' tradition. A monistic tradition means that international law is part of the domestic legal order, so new obligations created by treaty do not have to be 'incorporated' into national legislation (Haller 2016: 19).

We begin by briefly defining the constitutive mechanisms involved in the development of international law and direct democracy in contemporary Swiss law. Next, we examine the current ratification procedure for international treaties before turning to the implementation phase of international law. In our conclusion, we identify the strengths and weaknesses of the Swiss system, especially in the face of opposition from international law.

6.2 International Law and Direct Democracy as Constitutive Elements of the Swiss Political System

6.2.1 The Development of International Law

After World War II, the main purpose of international treaties was no longer to define geographic borders or regulate peace negotiations, but rather to institutionalize international organizations. These newly created multilateral bodies quickly became a locus producing, coordinating and interpreting international norms. Such international fora have become a privileged location for discussing and regulating a growing number of important policy issues, while also benefiting from the participation of each state. The development of international law takes different shapes and forms which include international treaties, recommendations, guidelines and other soft law instruments (see Flückiger in this volume). This results in a sharp increase of norms and actors in the field of public international law. These norms can have an effect on the activities of states, their administrations and even on the legal situation of private individuals, if treaties include directly applicable provisions (Mader 2013: 247).

Such developments have been taken into account in Swiss constitutional law, particularly in the 1999 complete revision of the Swiss constitution which included a number of new provisions related to international law (Haller 2016: 37). As noted, the Confederation and the cantons 'respect international law' (Art 5 (4) Const.) (Aubert and Mahon 2003: 48 et seq). The Confederation is 'committed...to a just and peaceful international order' (Art. 2 (4) Const). Mandatory provisions of international law also must not be violated when changing the constitution (Art. 193 (4) and Art. 194 (2) Const.). The federal Supreme Court and other judicial authorities 'apply federal acts and international law' (Art. 190 Const.). All these provisions express Switzerland's strong commitment towards international law.

Moreover, the number of texts in force for international law is higher than for domestic law (Federal Council 2016a). Switzerland signed and ratified 121 Council of Europe conventions (Federal Council 2016a: 6828). Switzerland, however, chose not to become a member of the EU, opting instead for a 'bilateral path' (Maiani and Bieber 2016; Maiani 2013) involving numerous individual agreements with the EU which cover a wide array of issues and policies. In that context as well, European law is pervasive and very evident in Swiss law (Maiani 2013).

6.2.2 The Development of Direct Democracy

Direct democracy is one of the hallmarks of the Swiss legal and political system. It allows Swiss citizens to participate in the lawmaking process as well as in revising the constitution. This can be done either to encourage political action (popular initiative) or to alter political actions already taken (via referendum). (Art. 138 to 142 Const.). Also referred to as 'popular rights', the mechanisms of direct democracy exist at communal, cantonal and federal levels. Historically, they emerged first at the cantonal level and were only gradually established at the federal level to complement the system of representative democracy. Switzerland has gradually increased the use of referenda, thereby compensating for the reduced possibility of popular participation in decision-making processes at the international level (Hertig Randall 2016: 166). Changes introduced in 1999 and 2003 gave parliament a right to participate when international treaties were concluded (Federal Council 1997: 231), and popular rights were modified. Democratic participation in international treaties was thereby brought into line with participation in national legislation (Federal Council 2001: 5795).

To date, while the right to launch an initiative is limited to domestic matters (e.g., it can be used only for the adoption of norms on the constitutional level), referenda can—and in some cases must—be held about international matters such as treaties (optional referendum for specified kinds of treaties) or joining a supranational community (mandatory referendum) (Art. 140 and 141).

6.3 The Role of the Federal Administration in the Accession to International Treaties

The UN's Vienna Convention on the Law of Treaties (23 May 1969) sets out the accession procedure to international law for states. When acceding to a Convention, a state either adheres outright to the treaty, thereby indicating it will commit to it, or signs the treaty, pending internal examination. It will then later ratify it. The Vienna Convention leaves it to each state to determine domestically which organs are given the competency to participate on behalf of the government.

Switzerland has a signature phase and a ratification phase (Art. 184 (2) Const.), but the procedure it adopts, and the internal actors involved, can vary according to whether the treaty is bilateral or multilateral.

6.3.1 Signature

The Federal Council is responsible for foreign relations (Art. 184 (1) Const.) and represents Switzerland abroad (Art. 54 (1) Const.). It has the general competence to sign and ratify international treaties (Art. 184 (2) Const.). In some instances, the treaties must be submitted to the Federal Assembly for approval before ratification. The Federal Council can also delegate the concluding of a treaty to a relevant department or office—of the federal administration (Art. 48a GAOA). If an international negotiation is launched, a negotiating mandate is issued by the Federal Council. The negotiating minister must then consult the parliamentary committees responsible for foreign relations, allowing the negotiator to establish the main outlines and directives of the mandate (Art. 152 (3) Federal Act on the Federal Assembly).

In practice, the procedure combines legal rules and certain processes, providing a guide for public action, though the Federal Council must play a nuanced role. The cantons can themselves play an active role internationally by being associated with a foreign policy decision by the national executive

(Art. 55 (3) Const.), and even conclude international treaties in matters falling within their competences. Nevertheless, cantons must act in such a way to ensure the coherence of the Swiss external policy. Their international commitments cannot be contrary to the interests of the Confederation: therefore, prior to the conclusion of a treaty, the federal authority must be informed (Art. 56 Const.; Art. 61c and 62 GAOA; Art. 27o and 27 t of the Ordinance on Government and Administration Organization). If the Federal Council was to consider this cantonal engagement to be against the nation's interests, the Federal Assembly is notified (Art. 186 (3) Const.). The latter shall then give its approval to the convention (Art. 172 para. 3 Const.; Haller 2016: 250; Ziegler 2015: 88). Furthermore, if a field of cantonal competence is covered by the new international norm, cantons may also take part in the negotiation (Art. 55 Const.; Federal Act on the Consultation Procedure). The impetus to the signature of an international treaty can thus come from the Federal Council itself, from the Federal Assembly, or from a canton (Federal Department of Foreign Affairs 2015: 9).

That being said, the proposal to sign generally comes from the Department of Foreign Affairs and, in some cases, other federal departments when the treaty in question falls within their competence (Federal Department of Foreign Affairs 2015: 9). Furthermore, prior to the signature, a collaborative process takes place during which there are many exchanges between the Federal Council, the Federal Assembly and the cantons (and sometimes social and professional organizations) under the aegis of the federal administration. The Department of Foreign Affairs, in particular, early on played the role of general guardian of the development of international law ('juridical conscience'). This role has been remarkable in the treaties adopted within the Council of Europe, and according to Art. 3 of the Statute of the Council of Europe, Switzerland agreed to 'collaborate sincerely and effectively' in the realization of the organization's goals. Accordingly, the Federal Administration follows the Council of Europe's work closely, and, since 1976, a yearly report on 'Switzerland and the Council of Europe's Conventions' have been published. This document provides the reasons why Switzerland should or should not adhere to Conventions elaborated within the Council of Europe. The report is drafted by the offices in the federal administration and then submitted to the Federal Assembly via a preliminary report provided by the Federal Council.

The Federal Council, supported by the federal administration must base its proposal on measurable elements defined in 1969 (Federal Council 2016a: 6829). Switzerland's international commitment is based on the idea that the state can comply with its engagements, all the more necessary as respecting international law is a principle of Swiss law (Art. 5 (4) Const.). As a consequence, determining whether Switzerland will or will not be able to respect its new international commitment is central, and every ratification project should be analysed in terms of its usefulness and necessity from the point of view of the national interest or of the efficiency of cooperation with other state parties. Moreover, only conventions whose ratification is feasible within a reasonable time are suggested.

Furthermore, Article 147 of the Swiss Constitution requires a consultation procedure, with all actors involved, which is coordinated by the Federal Council. Its aim is to test whether the project is correct, executable, and whether it would likely be accepted (Art. 2 Consultation Procedure Act). The consultation procedure is really a key moment for the federal administration, as it gives public administrators an opportunity to point out any fundamental incompatibility between a convention and the domestic legal order. Once the comments and responses have been received, a procedure to iron out the differences is launched, both at the executive and at lower administrative levels. Nevertheless, the current ratification practice makes it possible to submit conventions which are not in line with domestic law to the Federal Assembly for approval. This is notably the case when existing gaps in Swiss law could be filled by directly applicable provisions contained in the treaty. Otherwise, parliamentary approval might be solicited when accompanying legislative measures can be adopted in sufficient time (Federal Council 2016a, b: 6829).

From a procedural point of view, consultation can occur before signature or during the parliamentary phase afterwards (Federal Department of Foreign Affairs 2015: 47). In practice, it usually takes place during the pre-parliamentary phase (see the chapter by Guy-Ecabert in this volume). The actors usually have a three-month period in which they can draft an answer, and cantons, political parties and civil society actors take part, sometimes quite extensively so.

Thus, the signature of a treaty by the Federal Council is part of a much larger political process, much more extensive than the simple signature of a document by a public authority. The procedure shows the implication of different political actors, allowing the Federal Council to evaluate the political support to a treaty. It can reinforce national commitment to a new adhesion and thereby avoid opposition once the international rules are 'incorporated' in the domestic legal order. Such a procedure 'a priori' can thus attempt to limit the chances of a referendum that may arise later.

6.3.2 *Ratification*

The second phase is ratification. The main actors are the Federal Assembly, the people and the cantons. Their intervention formally confirms (or overturns) the Federal Council's proposition. It takes its final form with the adoption of a federal decree.

This phase begins with the Federal Assembly's intervention, as it must give its approval to ratification (Ziegler 2015: 90) in the case where the Federal Council has not an exclusive competence (Art. 166 (2) Const.; Art. 24 (2) Parliament Act). To allow the parliament to reach a decision, a document describing the reasons why Switzerland should ratify the treaty in question is drafted by the relevant federal department. This 'federal message' is received by the Federal Council and communicated to the Federal Assembly (Art. 141 Parliament Act). In this communication, the federal administration gives a global evaluation of the treaty text, specifying the content and the scope of every provision. After the Federal Assembly approves the treaty, it adopts a federal decree.

The adoption by the Assembly does not necessarily end matters. In some cases, Swiss constitutional law requires that the citizens and cantons must be consulted. Indeed, a mandatory referendum is required if the treaty in question concerns the accession to an organizations for collective security or joining supranational communities (Art. 140 (1) (b) Const.). On this basis, a referendum was organized in 1992 where citizens voted on joining the European Economic Area. Though strongly supported by the Federal Council, this project was rejected at the polls. Optional referenda (Art. 141 (1) (d) Const.) are also possible, for which 50,000 voters must sign a petition, or eight cantons ask for such a vote, within 100 days of official publication of the federal decree. Signed treaties of an unlimited term or when withdrawal from the treaty is not permitted may be subject to popular vote (those cases were introduced in 1921 and in 1977, respectively). This is also the case for treaties containing important provisions establishing binding legal rules or whose implementation requires the adoption of federal laws (introduced in 2003).

Here, too, the federal administration plays an active role, as it establishes whether the treaty in question must be subjected to a mandatory referendum. If an optional referendum is held, the federal administration must verify whether one of three hypothesis take place. Assessing whether a treaty contains important provisions establishing binding legal rules is considered as particularly delicate to assess (Ziegler 2015: 115).

It also has to organize the referendum. Documents must be distributed to all electors in order to allow them to cast their vote validly and in accordance with the respective cantonal procedure (ballot, legitimation card, official voting envelope or validation stamp, etc.). The federal administration provides electors with objective and exhaustive information about the proposed treaty, and by law, this should take into account the main views which have been expressed, including those of the federal Assembly, those of the referendum's initiators and of important minorities (Art 10a and 11 Political Rights Act). Inside the federal administration, the Federal Chancellery is in charge of organizing the referendum, and it takes a self-defined neutral position in doing so.

While the federal authorities may plead for a strong commitment to multilateralism, the referendum process may show a desire on the part of the population to be more isolationist. The mechanism itself works to the advantage of adhering to international law; it completes the democratic debate by directly connecting the parties concerned. Moreover, it requires of the federal administration that it deliver a clear explanation to the voters explaining Swiss interests in deepening and extending its international relations, but equally evaluating the impact of international law on the domestic legal system. It makes it possible to directly address the potential conflicts between international and national provisions.

A clear institutional dynamic is at work, with its special characteristics deriving from the institutions of federalism and direct democracy. Of these two, direct democracy appears to be of particular relevance for explaining the flexibility in the Swiss ratification system. It allows a soft control over the federal government's actions in its international commitments. The federal administration is a key factor here, though it must combine sometimes contradictory tasks involving monitoring, coordinating, synthesizing and narrating the debate on ratification.

6.4 The Role of the Federal Administration in the Application of Public International Law

When applying international norms in the domestic legal system, Swiss law is faced with the traditional issues of international law, namely the direct applicability of the international norm (Sect. 6.4.1). Switzerland, however, is also confronted by a particular challenge: the possibility for citizens to launch a popular initiative, even if that initiative potentially contradicts existing international obligations (Sect. 6.4.2).

6.4.1 The Direct Applicability of International Law and Its Position Within the Domestic Hierarchy of Legal Norms

The development of international law raised a number of legal questions, most notably about the effect and legal force international norms would have on the domestic order, both in terms of national law and constitutional law. Such issues have a direct effect on the work of public administration, and here the Federal Supreme Court provided a response.

As already mentioned, as far as direct applicability is concerned, Switzerland is in the 'monistic' tradition (Haller 2016: 19). This means no particular act is required for an international rule to be considered valid in the domestic legal system (decision of the Federal Supreme Court case of 27 October 1994: ATF 120 Ib 360, 366). More concretely, the Federal Supreme Court stated that an international provision is directly applicable if sufficiently precise and unconditional to produce a direct effect. In other words, international provisions must permit the constitution of a basis for a concrete decision (decision of the Federal Supreme Court of 2 September 1986: ATF 112 Ib 183, 184). From then on, such conditions determined by the Court have been used by the Federal Council to determine the impact of an international engagement on Switzerland's internal bodies (preliminary report of the Federal Council 2003: 80; ibid. 1994: 1481). In practice, these conditions are verified and explained when a federal message on a ratification is drafted. If the international provisions do not fulfil those criteria, they are considered not self-executing. It is then for the legislators (cantonal and/or federal) to implement the programmatic provisions (this was notably the case when the Federal Council elaborated the ratification project to the 2006 United Nations Convention on the Rights of Persons with Disabilities 2012: 601 et seq.). Furthermore, over time the Federal Supreme Court has promulgated several interpretations about the legal force of international provisions on Switzerland's legal system.

During the 1920–1930s, the Federal Supreme Court considered international treaties to be on equal terms with national legislation. In this perspective, in case of conflict, it applied the interpretation rule *lex posterior derogat priori*, meaning a later legal rule prevails over an earlier rule. In 1968, the Court recognized the 'principle of interpretation in conformity' with international law. In other words, when facing a conflict, the national legal norm must be interpreted in a manner compatible with the relevant international rule. A national legal rule adopted after the ratification of an international treaty shall also be interpreted in conformity. Moreover, if a conforming interpretation is impossible, the Federal Supreme Court confirms the non-application of the national rule. By doing so, the Court progressively established the idea of the superiority of international over domestic law. Five years later, in 1973, in the Court's 'Schubert' ruling, it halted this idea of superiority in the event legislators expressly overrode international law. In such cases, the national norm outweighs international law (Decision of the Federal Supreme Court of 2 March 1973: ATF 99 Ib 39).

With the acceleration of the development of international law, the Federal Supreme Court did rule in 1991 that Switzerland cannot avoid its international obligations by applying its domestic law. Domestic law has to be interpreted in conformity with the rules of international law (Decision of the Federal Supreme Court of 26 July 1999: ATF 125 II 417, 424; for an analysis of the case law, see Lammers 2015: 80). If a conforming interpretation is not possible, the Court said that then national rules are not applied. Such a solution has been considered as particularly pertinent when a domestic rule breaches an international rule relating to the protection of human rights (Decisions of the Federal Supreme Court of 26 July 1999: ATF 125 II 417, 424; and 26 July 2002: ATF 128 IV 201, 205). Such an interpretation has been retained in the wording of Article 5 of the Constitution of 1999, which said 'the Confederation and the Cantons shall respect international law' and not 'shall comply' as in art. 49 (1) Const. (Aubert and Mahon 2003: 48 et seq; Thürer 2001: 190).

By 2005, however, the Federal Council was taking a more cautious position, referring to the Schubert ruling, when answering a parliamentary question: 'International law has, in principle, precedence over federal law—at least, if the federal legislation did not knowingly adopt a rule in conflict with international law. The place held by international treaties in the internal hierarchy of norms is controversial in both legal literature and case law. The peremptory norms of public international law (*jus cogens*) take precedence over all public law rules and set limitations to constitutional revisions' (Federal Council, written answer d.d. 23 April 2005, Official bulletin of the National Council 2005: 212).

6.4.2 *Constitutional Amendments and International Law*

In practice, it is generally known that Swiss citizens—and, in particular, those political parties failing to find policy decisions which accord with their ideologies—increasingly use the instrument of the popular initiative. One of them, in particular, even seems ready to propose breaching constitutional amendments to achieve its goals.

To prevent an open conflict between international law and the Swiss Constitution, a system to monitor the compliance of popular initiatives with international law has been instituted (Art. 139 (3) Const.). This control is carried out by the Federal Assembly, which verifies that prior to voting, the proposed constitutional provision will not breach the *jus cogens*. The object of this control is limited to the basic norms and principles of international humanitarian law and the safeguards required by international law not subject to derogation. The parliament has no power to block a popular initiative, but it can formulate a counter-proposal (Auer 2016: 399). To date, only one initiative has been ruled invalid because it was deemed incompatible with a peremptory norm in general international law, namely the *non-refoulement* principle (Rhinow and Schefer 2009: 722; Mahon 2014: 115). Other initiatives, which did not violate any of the above-mentioned norms but remained problematic, have been put to vote and, in some cases, adopted. The initiative banning the constructions of minarets, approved by Swiss voters in 2009 (see Art. 73 (3), Const.), is a good example. Clearly targeting one specific religion, the Federal Council judged that it violated norms concerning the freedom of religion as well as the prohibition of discrimination (established in Art. 9 and 14 European Convention on Human Rights (ECHR), but also in 2 and 18 of the UN Covenant II and, possibly, the protection of minorities guaranteed by art. 27 of the Covenant (preliminary report of the Federal Council 2008: 6924)).

In the end, the federal administration, bound by international law, must implement initiatives, respecting the policy aim of the initiative's promoters and the results of the vote. In this case again, the role of the federal administration is important. Indeed, several scenarios to solve a similar situation have been imagined and sometimes tested.

The first scenario is to imagine implementation laws in conformity with international law. This delicate strategy was used to deal with the initiative for the automatic expulsion of foreign criminal offenders, voted in 2008 (Art. 121 Const.). The application of the new constitutional provision can expose some individuals to a dangerous return to a state where they could potentially be threatened with violence or persecution. To avoid this hypothesis, the federal administration applies the norm by implementing the expulsion decision only if the individual's life is not endangered in the country of origin (Hertig Randall and McGregor: 431).

The second scenario, untested today, is to renegotiate or withdraw from the treaties that are in conflict with a newly adopted constitutional norm. The Federal Council began a political discussion with the Federal Assembly in 2015 (Conseil des Etats 2016), which has initiated a bill on the competence to renounce a treaty (Conseil des Etats 2018). The option of renegotiation was evoked when the popular initiative for 'ending mass immigration' was adopted in 2014, requiring the implementation of immigration quotas and giving Swiss workers priority in employment. This new article 121a is viewed as particularly problematic, given the bilateral agreements—especially on the free movement of persons—between Switzerland and the EU, which gives Switzerland access to the single market (Maiani 2013) and also other treaties as the ECHR, the UN Covenant II and the Convention on the Rights of the Child (Erhenzeller et al. 2014: 2196). Nevertheless, given the potential impact of this norm on the Swiss economy, one dependent on commerce with the EU member states, the application of this provision required considerable negotiation between the Federal Council and the EU. After long and intense diplomatic exchanges, the Federal Administration found a solution. They chose to adopt a regulation compatible with the current agreement, thereby maintaining good relationships with the EU without completely negating the new provision in the Swiss constitution.

A third scenario was foreseen by extending the recognized grounds for invalidating popular initiatives. This proposal was abandoned in 2014, after the federal administration discovered during the consultation process that there were fundamental and unbridgeable differences of opinions among the actors involved (Commission des institutions politiques du Conseil d'Etat 2015: 6493).

Finally, 'popular initiatives which are incompatible with Switzerland's international obligation are not new, the violation of international law has in the past been rather accidental than intentional' (Hertig Randall and McGregor 2010: 429). An initiative calling for 'Swiss law instead of foreign judges (self-determination initiative)' is part of the current trend (Kolb 2016). Its aim is to produce a constitutional amendment which would establish the primacy of national constitutional law over international law, thereby reversing the historical trend integrating international law in Swiss law.

6.5 Conclusion

Swiss law shows a variety of interesting norms visible when dealing with the impact of international law on domestic legislation. The distribution of roles and competencies demonstrates sophisticated institutional engineering in terms of treaty ratification. The risk in activating direct democracy mechanisms can be seen as the reason justifying this complex system. With this in mind, direct democracy can be considered as producing a positive, legitimizing effect on the recognition of the place of international law in the domestic order. This allows one to dismiss the argument often put forward by detractors who frequently assert international law is produced by technocratic decision-makers and lacks democratic legitimacy.

The effect of direct democracy can also be unwholesome, particularly in the case of popular initiatives, and serve to promote minority ideologies, whether progressive or conservative. Currently, in the human rights domain, the use of the popular initiative is aimed at calling into question Switzerland's foreign policy engagements, or to reject the autonomous developments of international law. It has advocated an ideology of retreat into national self-interest, in opposition to the humanist perspective found in contemporary international law, echoing the humanitarian tradition of the country, another founding principle of the Swiss constitutional order.

In this particularly tense situation, the federal administration plays a key role. Like a mediator, avoiding the confrontation between actors and legal norms, it contributes to finding a compromise. The key challenge for the federal administration is to maintain this position of equilibrium between the international openness of Switzerland regarding its humanitarian and neutrality traditions and its adherence to a political system defined by its direct democracy mechanisms. From this point of view, the political context seems to show the popular initiative will still represent a challenge in the future.

References

Aubert, J.-F., & Mahon, P. (2003). *Petit Commentaire de la Constitution fédérale de la Confédération suisse du 18 avril 1999*. Zurich/Basel/Genève: Schulthess.

Auer, A. (2016). The people have spoken: Abide? A critical view of the EU's dramatic referendum (in)experience. *European Constitutional Law Review, 12*(3), 397–408.

Commission des institutions politiques du Conseil des Etats. (2015). Conditions de validité des initiatives populaires. Examen du besoin de légiférer du 20 août 2015. *Feuille fédérale*, 6485–6512.
Commission des institutions politiques du Conseil des Etats. (2016). Initiative parlementaire 16.456. Dénonciation et modification des traités internationaux. Répartition des compétences.
Commission des institutions politiques du Conseil des Etats. (2018). Rapport et procédure de consultation. Dénonciation et modification des traités internationaux. Répartition des compétences. https://www.parlament.ch/fr/organe/commissions/commissions-thematiques/commissions-cip/rapports-consultations-cip/vernehmlassung-spk-16-456. Accessed 30 Mar 2018.
Ehrenzeller, B., Hettich, P., & Schweizer, R. J. (2014). Art. 121a. In B. Erhenzeller, B. Schindler, R. J. Schweizer, & K. A. Vallender (Eds.), *Die Schweizerische Bundesverfassung. St Galler Kommentar* (pp. 2190–2212). Zürich/St.Gallen: Dike/Schulthess.
Federal Council. (1994). Message du 22 juin 1994 concernant les initiatives populaires "pour une politique d'asile raisonnable" et "contre l'immigration clandestine". *Feuille Fédérale, III*, 1471–1513.
Federal Council. (1997). Message du Conseil fédéral du 20 novembre 1996 relatif à une nouvelle constitution fédérale. *Feuille fédérale I*, 1–653.
Federal Council. (2001). Rapport du 2 avril 2001 sur Initiative parlementaire (Commission 96.091 CE) Suppression de carences dans les droits populaires. *Feuille fédérale*, 5783–5800.
Federal Council. (2003). Message du Conseil fédéral à l'Assemblée fédérale, du 19 décembre 2003, relatif à l'approbation de la Charte européenne de l'autonomie locale. *Feuille fédérale*, 71–92.
Federal Council. (2005). Réponse écrite donnée par le Conseil fédéral, le 23 février 2005, à une interpellation déposée le 17 décembre 2004 par M. Mörgeli, député au Conseil national. *Bulletin officiel*, 212–213.
Federal Council. (2008). Message fédéral relatif à l'initiative populaire "contre la construction des minarets". *Feuille fédérale*, 6923–6970.
Federal Council. (2016a). Onzième rapport sur la Suisse et les conventions du Conseil de l'Europe du 24 août. *Feuille fédérale*, 6823–6862.
Federal Council. (2016b). Avis du 31 août 2016 sur l'interpellation 16.3304 (développement de la réglementation). https://www.parlament.ch/fr/ratsbetrieb/suche-curia-vista/geschaeft?AffairId=20163304. Accessed 30 Mar 2018.
Federal Department of Foreign Affairs. (2015). *Guide de la pratique en matière de traités internationaux.* https://www.eda.admin.ch/eda/fr/home/dienstleistungen-publikationen/publikationen.html/publikationen/fr/eda/voelkerrecht/Praxisleitfaden-Voelkerrechtliche-Vertraege.html. Accessed 30 Mar 2018.
Haller, W. (2016). *The Swiss constitution in a comparative context.* Zurich/St Gall: Dike.

Hertig Randall, M. (2016). The Swiss federal bill of rights in the context of international human rights protection: Added value and shortcomings. *Revue interdisciplinaire d'études juridiques, 77*(2), 151–177.
Hertig Randall, M., & McGregor, E. (2010). Reconciling direct democracy and fundamental rights: The case of the Swiss Minaret initiative. *Tijdschrift voor Constitutioneel Recht (TvCR), 4*, 428–436.
Kolb, R. (2016). L'initiative de l'UDC sur l'autodétermination (« juges étrangers »). *Swiss Review of International and European Law, 26*, 567–570.
Lammers, G. (2015). *La démocratie directe et le droit international. Prise en compte des obligations internationales de la Confédération et la participation populaire à la politique extérieure*. Berne: Staempfli.
Mader, L. (2013). Législation. In A. Ladner, J.-L. Chappelet, Y. Emery, P. Knoepfel, L. Mader, N. Soguel, & F. Varone (Eds.), *Manuel d'administration publique Suisse* (pp. 245–265). Lausanne: Presses polytechniques et universitaires romandes.
Mahon, P. (2014). *Droit Constitutionnel*. Bâle: Helbing Lichtenhahn.
Maiani, F. (2013). Internationalisation du droit suisse. In A. Ladner, J.-L. Chappelet, Y. Emery, P. Knoepfel, L. Mader, N. Soguel, & F. Varone (Eds.), *Manuel d'administration publique Suisse* (pp. 283–298). Lausanne: Presses polytechniques et universitaires romandes.
Maiani, F., & Bieber, R. (2016). *Précis de droit européen*. Bern: Stämpfli.
Rhinow, R., & Schefer, M. (2009). *Schweizerisches Verfassungsrecht*. Basel: Helbing Lichtenhahn.
Thürer, D. (2001). Verfassungsrecht und Völkerrecht. In D. Thürer, J.-F. Aubert, & J. P. Müller (Eds.), *Verfassungsrecht der Schweiz, Droit constitutionnel suisse* (pp. 179–206). Zürich: Schulthess.
Ziegler, A. (2015). *Introduction au Droit International Public*. Bern: Stämpfli.

CHAPTER 7

Soft Law Instruments in Public Law

Alexandre Flückiger

7.1 Introduction

In Switzerland, the principle of legality establishes that state activity is based on, and limited by, law (Article 5, Swiss Constitution). Its function is to ensure that the democratic will expressed by legislators is implemented by an administration that does not act in an emotional or capricious manner. The instruments available to the state, and through which it acts, are laws, decisions, and contracts, along with the actions it takes to plan and coordinate individuals working together. It is characteristic of such acts that they are legally binding.

Administrative activity is not exhausted by the aforementioned legal acts, however. In fact, administrative practices manifest modes more suited to governance: preferring incentives over obligations, citizen cooperation rather than unilateral decisions, and coordinating multiple actors to the detriment of maintaining a hierarchical order. Such instruments are frequently grouped under the label 'soft law'—in French, *droit souple* Conseil d'Etat 2013; Hachez et al. 2013.

Soft law has often performed an experimental function, to test a possible future legal rule (for 'green' law, see Abi-Saab 1997: 207 et seq., for

A. Flückiger (✉)
Faculty of Law, University of Geneva, Geneva, Switzerland
e-mail: alexandre.flueckiger@unige.ch

A. Ladner et al. (eds.), *Swiss Public Administration*, Governance and Public Management,
https://doi.org/10.1007/978-3-319-92381-9_7

'pre-law', Peters 2011: 34). The state can thus accustom addressees to a new standard which, once sufficiently matured, may become obligatory. An example is the use of seat belts: they were recommended before they became mandatory. Soft law thus guides the behavior of citizens without imposing a legal obligation. It does not replace traditional administrative activity but instead complements and strengthens it in areas where more traditional modes of governance reach their limits (Mader and Rütsche 2004: 18 et seq.; Morand 1999).

The development of this kind of state action, which is at the fringes of the law, poses difficulties for jurists. Indeed, if the ability of soft law to achieve results—in other words, its effectiveness—is likely to legitimize a remedy for a problem, its democratic foundation totters. In fact, the principle of legality, at least initially, was not designed to legitimize such flexible instruments. In addition, the limited formal requirements for carrying out soft law measures make it possible to circumvent the sluggishness of administrative or parliamentary procedures, dampen the resistance of political actors to new policies, prevent adopting regulations which are too binding or, in certain domains, compensate for an absence of competence to pass obligatory measures. From the point of view of legitimacy, this characteristic of soft law instruments is particularly problematic, since under the rule of law, efficiency criteria cannot be allowed to supersede legality.

In the Swiss case, the legal system has a tendency to tolerate or even establish mechanisms of administrative action under soft law. The Swiss Federal Supreme Court even defends this practice: 'It is not necessary that every governmental intervention take the form of a decision. If so, it would affect the proper functioning of the administration. It is often indispensable that the authorities proceed informally' (Decision of the Federal Supreme Court of 9 April 2002: ATF 128 II 156, 163). This flexibility can be understood as an application of the principle of proportionality, as Article 5 of the Swiss Constitution notes that 'state activities must be … proportionate to the ends sought'. The Swiss legal system thus evinces a gradual normativity that reconciles the need for flexibility on the part of the administration. This is an essential ingredient to ensure a degree of efficiency and legitimacy, one indispensable for ensuring a democratic governance of the rule of law.

One thus needs to examine this type of instrument at the disposal of Swiss public administration. To specify this notion of soft law and identify the legal issues involved, we use a typology that covers differing types of state instruments in Swiss public law (Sect. 7.2). Next, we look at the legal effects (potentially) generated when public authorities use this type of instrument (Sect. 7.3). Then, we turn to how effective they are for the functioning of the state (Sect. 7.4). At the end, we return to the need, within the Swiss constitutional framework, to both guarantee the legitimacy of soft law and maintain its effectiveness (Sect. 7.5).

7.2 A Legal Typology of Non-obligatory State Instruments

One can begin with the observation that non-binding state instruments can change the behavior of individuals either by means of a text (more formally, as 'acts of non-obligatory declaration') or by de facto acts ('material acts in the narrow sense'). However, in the case of the former, they can be enacted unilaterally by the state (Sect. 7.2.1) or in a concerted manner (Sect. 7.2.2).

They thus resemble classic legal acts. Like legal norms, they also contain norms of behavior. In the case of legal acts, the norms are mandatory and must be followed. In the case of 'acts of non-obligatory declaration', however, the norms are only recognized inasmuch as they are acknowledged by their addressees. Standards, in their non-legal sense, are not necessarily imperative in such cases. Finally, while such 'acts of non-obligatory declaration' contain rules which may or may not be followed, 'de facto acts' consist of specific actions and contain no norms (Moor and Poltier 2011: 28 et seq.) (Sect. 7.2.3).

7.2.1 Unilateral Non-obligatory Acts

The principal unilateral non-obligatory act at the disposal of the state is to make recommendations; a number of other special cases also illustrate this.

7.2.1.1 Recommendations

Recommendations are declarations which suggest a certain behavior should be followed. They take many different forms. Behind this diversity lie different degrees of emphasis; a warning has a stronger character than a wish or simply a piece of advice.

Giving a recommendation is a classic instrument in international public law and EU law. The resolutions and declarations adopted by the United Nations General Assembly, the most famous of which is the 1948 Universal Declaration of Human Rights, are recommendations, as are the various recommendations made by the Council of Europe. Similarly, declarations made at international conferences, such as at the Rio Summit on Environment and Development in 1992, or the Bologna Declaration about higher education in 1999, are also recommendations (Daillier et al. 2009: 416 et seq.; Guzman and Meyer 2010; Shelton 2008). In European law, recommendations and opinions have been institutionalized, though here too, these acts are not binding (Article 288 of the Treaty on the Functioning of the EU). Thus, the Charter of Fundamental Rights of the European Union was not legally binding before the Lisbon Treaty came into force (Nowak 2011: 134 et seq.). At the international level, some rules which take the form of a recommendation are also produced outside of government. These may come from private, semi-public, or hybrid actors and their influence on internal law may be decisive (Pauwelyn et al. 2012). To some authors, they even appear to be a kind of global administrative law (Cassese 2005).

As will be shown later, recommendations have become a classic instrument in Swiss law. In terms of formulating behavioral rules, recommendations may be either explicit or implicit in nature. Thus, when they directly state what the recommended behavior is, they will be described as explicit. Some examples are provided in Table 7.1 (Moor et al. 2012: 404 et seq.).

However, when state instruments point toward following a behavior without expressing it explicitly, the behavior to be followed stems implicitly from the instrument; its purpose, more or less obviously, amounts to a recommendation. Thus, through the publicity a public authority gives to its exemplary behavior, it can exhort individuals to adapt their conduct (Morand 1999: 178). Furthermore, a public administration thus demonstrates the feasibility of adopting the conduct, and thus increases its credibility.

For example, in public procurement, the incentive effect is reinforced when the state uses its power to issue contracts. They serve their own recommendations and are contained, in turn, in their public policy objectives. Although the potential contractors remain free not to conform to the state's new requirements, they then take the risk of being excluded from the public market (Manfrini 1991). In keeping with the principles of transparency, equal treatment, the prohibition of discrimination, and free competition, the state may lay out certain criteria, particularly ecological or social, before awarding a public contract (Rodondi 2001).

Table 7.1 Typology of recommendations

Recommendations strictly speaking	The grape varieties recommended for cultivation in Switzerland (Art. 3, Ordinance on Grape Varieties)
Alerts	Public warning (Art. 54, Foodstuffs Act)
Advice	The waters protection agencies shall provide advice to the authorities and to private individuals (Art. 50 II, Waters Protection Law)
Notice	The Competition Commission shall provide other authorities with expert reports on competition law issues of general importance (Art. 47, Cartel Law)
Notification	The office notifies the insured about any final decision it intends to take on a claim for benefits (Art. 57a, Disability Insurance Act)
Conclusions of certain reports	The report of the study must include the following information: Conclusions and recommendations (Art. 8 II, HIV Studies Ordinance)
Invitations	The office invites organizations which have concluded an agreement, along with those enterprises engaged in distribution and projection in the respective film region and which have not finalized an agreement concerning diversity in their offer, to submit their agreements in writing (Art. 5 I, Film Ordinance)
Wishes	The International Telecommunications Union formulate recommendations and opinions [...] concerning telecommunication matters (Art. 1 II h, ITU Constitution)

Incentive taxes in the context of the environment operate the same way (Oberson and Maraia 2010). Individuals are free to put vegetable peelings in their garbage bags, but if the bag itself is taxed, it serves as a financial encouragement or incentive for individuals to sort their waste a little more carefully.

Labeling or certification requirements (Article 43a, Environmental Protection Act or EPA) serve to guide the choices market actors make. They can certainly ignore the requirements, but may then find themselves at a competitive disadvantage in obtaining public contracts (Subilia-Rouge 2010: N. 73 et seq.), or find themselves in difficulties when monitoring or controlling procedures are carried out.

Awards and prizes to citizens from the authorities (Article 7, Film Act) are an indirect recommendation to follow the rewarded behavior. Training can also profoundly influence an individuals' behavior, at least over the longer term. What is taught acts like a recommendation for those who are taught when public authorities include this means in their toolkit (Delley 1991).

Depending on the context, even objectively presented information or description may have an incentive effect. The scientific observation that 'smoking kills', when affixed to a cigarette package, can be interpreted as a recommendation not to smoke.

However, unilateral, non-obligatory acts are not exhausted by recommendations alone. A series of special cases attests to this.

7.2.1.2 Special Cases

Many special cases demonstrate that non-obligatory acts take a different form than recommendations. Thus, in areas where international relations are strongly intertwined, foreign law can have a place in national law like that of soft law. Switzerland's adoption of EU law provides an illustration. As a non-EU member, Switzerland is not obligated to follow EU law. Nevertheless, it behooves—and helps—the Swiss to follow EU law, as appropriate. The same could be said of domestic draft law: it can exert real influence in helping interpret a rule, justify a litigious legal basis, or anticipate potential implementation issues (Flückiger 2004: 205 et seq.). These are not examples of recommendations, as neither a foreign law nor a domestic draft law in itself has a recommendatory purpose.

Swiss law also produces administrative orders, which encompass circulars, directives, instructions, guides, and similar material. These are not binding on the administered but are binding on those who administer (Moor et al. 2012: 420 et. seq.). The former may be interested in complying almost by reflex, particularly when such orders affect their legal situation.

In urban planning, certain actions are obligatory, the best known of which are land allocation plans (Section 21, Land Use Planning Act). Many other actions are only partly required, or not required at all, and in this case, they bind only the authorities (Moor and Poltier 2011: 578 et seq.).

7.2.2 Concerted Non-obligatory Acts

The soft law toolkit includes concerted acts, referred to here as arrangements. This notion of concerted non-obligatory acts is also known in international public law, and are called gentlemen's agreements, non-binding agreements, joint statements, charters, arrangements, codes of conduct, and the like (Daillier et al. 2009: 422 et seq.; Pauwelyn et al. 2012; on codes of conduct specifically, see Keller 2008). Such acts unite flexibility with cooperation, two typical features of governance. They are the favored expressions of self-regulation but should not be confounded with it. Numerous classifications are imaginable, but we focus here on concerted acts which have a degree of linkage to legal acts.

7.2.2.1 Preparing a Legal Act

Certain arrangements may be made in conjunction with preparing a legal act. We can mention (Flückiger 2004: 207 et seq.):

- a declaration of intent describing reciprocal concessions;
- an agreement on a draft decision;
- a consultation charter intended to frame the negotiations in construction procedures;
- informal arrangements in the context of legislative consultation procedures.

Such arrangements may also be concluded between public authorities (see Article 31a EPA, which provides for a mediation procedure if the cantons cannot agree).

7.2.2.2 Implementing a Legal Act

Other arrangements are meant to help implement the legal rules, such as those for environmental audits in which the state agrees to reduce the intensity of surveillance in return for commitments by a company to implement an audit and certification system (Subilia-Rouge 2010: N. 51).

7.2.2.3 Preventing a Legal Act

Some gentlemen's agreements are concluded with the aim of preventing the state from carrying out a legal act. In return, individuals provide a service which makes it possible to respond more appropriately to the problem that the legal act was meant to resolve. In legal terms, if the renunciation of the power to legislate does not rest on a legal basis, the state can always intervene. In this situation, individuals could not avail themselves of this renunciation should the state nevertheless decide to legislate (Decision of the Federal Supreme Court of 7 July 1992: ATF 118 lb. 367, 380, § 9b and d). This type of arrangement is therefore based on a dual relationship. On the one hand, it is a relationship—in the nature of a recommendation—between the state and private individuals. On the other hand, it is a link—at times obligatory—between individuals that makes it possible to implement the substituted mechanism (Errass 2010: 62 et seq.).

One should note here that codes of professional ethics are very informal precursors of this type of arrangement. They make it possible to avoid having public authorities themselves adopting rules to monitor the profession. The Swiss National Bank used such informal arrangements as early as the 1930s, and they were gradually integrated into ordinary law and thus lost their initial informality. More recently, public authorities have concluded many gentlemen's agreements (Brunner 2004).

Swiss law provides several examples of the gradual formalization of the vertical relationship between the state and individuals:

- In environmental matters, the law now requires the public authorities to work with private sector organizations to enforce the law. The public authorities are free to encourage sectoral agreements by indicating targets and timelines. However, before issuing implementation requirements, they must examine voluntary private sector measures. Wherever possible and necessary, sectoral agreements are to be incorporated into the implementing regulations, in whole or in part (Art. 41a, EPA).
- 'Damoclean' laws institutionalize the vertical relationship of an agreement by specifying the objectives to be attained, the state's commitment to not legislate pending finding a self-regulating solution, and its substitution mechanism should the specified objectives not be reached. The CO_2 Emissions Reduction Act was designed in this manner (other examples can be found in Flückiger 2005). There are other cases which are simply meant to keep the state from making a decision in a particular case.
- The most questionable, in a legal sense, are those agreements in which the public authorities tolerate an activity in exchange for specific actions to be carried out by the citizens. To try to frame such practices in the most sensitive areas, legislators have formalized the question. This is the case when relief is granted by the public authorities when the remediation of an ecologically non-compliant installation is disproportionate (Article 17 (1), EPA).
- By contrast, there are agreements to nullify illegal situations, such as informal agreements reached to clean up contaminated sites. The public authorities should try to reach an agreement with the persons directly affected and may renounce making a formal decision if enforcement of the measures can be otherwise assured (Article 23, Contaminated Sites Ordinance).

7.2.3 Material Acts

Among non-obligatory state acts, one can also speak of material acts in the narrow sense. Their common point is their use of concrete measures. Examples include building traffic obstructions to mitigate traffic flows, installing gates or barriers to prevent trespassing, installing mechanisms which keep vehicles from starting until the cars' seat belts have been fastened, or regulating the Internet by using its technical architecture.

Such material acts in the narrow sense are not legally binding but are instead concrete actions. Unlike mandatory or voluntary norms, acts of this kind influence behavior through facts rather than declarations. One can therefore say this type of state action is neither 'law' nor even 'soft'. Transgression, when it is possible, provokes consequences at the level of facts. Still, depending on the case, such a transgression can be more penalizing than the transgression of a legal act. For example, repairing shock absorbers damaged by driving too quickly over a speed bump meant to slow cars down may ultimately prove more expensive than paying a fine for speeding.

7.3 Legal Effects of Non-obligatory State Acts

Although state actions under soft law are in principle not legally binding, they are nonetheless legally relevant (Moor et al. 2012: 410 et seq.). Indeed, they can infringe on rights, fundamental or not. Article 35 (2) of the Swiss Constitution, in fact, states that 'whoever acts on behalf of the state is bound by fundamental rights and is under an obligation to contribute to their implementation'. This ensures that material acts, in a broad sense, are subject to concrete legal control (Decision of the Federal Supreme Court of 13 November 2006: ATF 133 I 49, 56). In this case, examining non-obligatory state acts makes it possible to detect a specific normativity, one staggered in several steps.

Thus, in some very particular cases, non-obligatory state acts may become mandatory. For example, the Federal Food Act empowered the Federal Council to order that certain sections of the Food Manual are binding, even though the manual itself was a recommendation (Articles 22 (2) and (3)). Another example is provided by the Competition Commission. Indeed, given 'good faith' principles (noted in both Art. 5 and Art. 9 of the Swiss Constitution), this Commission is obliged to apply the criteria it adopts and publishes in documents called 'general notices' (see Art. 6 (1) of the Cartel Act), which are without binding force.

Legislation may also include special clauses which indirectly confer a binding force on a non-obligatory act, such as when a law states that decision X must be consistent with recommendation Y, which means there is no choice but to comply with the recommendation. Thus, in constructing high-current electrical equipment, the technical recommendations of the association of Swiss electric power stations 'must be followed' (Article 7 (2), High Current Ordinance).

Less frequent are the cases in which a recommendation is included in a normative act. Here the recommendation has no direct effect on individuals. It can however bind other public authorities, especially those in a hierarchical or supervisory relationship. For example, according to the Federal Road Traffic Ordinance, car lights 'should' be on even during daylight hours (Article 31, FRTO). The Federal Office of Energy, for example, no longer has the right to make a recommendation to the contrary, on the grounds that compliance with such a measure would increase fuel consumption and increase pollution.

A governmental recommendation may also have a permissive effect, in that it legitimizes the action of those who follow it. In this case, its recipients do not commit an offense by acting in a manner which is recommended. If it was to be considered that they committed one, it would mean that the act itself is contrary to the law. This implies that such acts can be controlled by a judicial body in case of doubt as to their compatibility with legal norms.

Finally, the public authorities may define, using a legal standard or norm, the jurisdiction for adopting a non-obligatory act. Here again, such a rule does not bind the addressees. However, it has a legal effect since the public authorities still must act within the framework thus drawn. It is the same when the law incorporates such an act into a more general procedural framework. The enactment of the recommendation is then a preliminary step in a process which leads to adopting a legal act. The result is a legal effect, since the failure to enact may constitute a procedural defect. In this case, the non-obligatory act constitutes a prerequisite for the adoption of the obligatory act. For example, Article 14 of the Price Surveillance Act requires the public authority in charge to obtain a ruling from the Price Regulator when required by law.

7.4 The Implementation of Non-obligatory State Acts

When the authority resorts to governance mechanisms which are not binding, one can legitimately wonder whether these have a useful effect on society. To answer this, one needs to address the more general issue of the effectiveness of soft law (Sect. 7.4.1) and then examine the techniques which have been developed to strengthen it (Sect. 7.4.2).

7.4.1 The Effectiveness of Soft Law

The addressees of acts of soft law are not legally bound to follow them. Nevertheless, such acts are recognized as having a concrete effect of varying intensity (Moor et al. 2012: 415 et seq.)—and many non-binding state acts do not need to be legally binding to be regarded as politically imperative. Obedience obviously does not depend on attractiveness or fear, consequences classically sought by the law. They instead depend on moral, ethical, political, economic, or psychological considerations.

Some examples serve to illustrate the power and influence of acts of soft law. Thus, the 1999 Bologna Declaration has led to a rapid and profound reform of the practices in institutions of higher education throughout Europe even though the Declaration itself is devoid of legal force. Public administration offices or courts are also likely to use soft law to interpret legal rules, though here the effect is indirect. For example, the European Court of Human Rights has condemned Romania for violating the right everyone has 'to respect for his private and family life and his home' (Article 8, European Convention on Human Rights) on the grounds that Romania has not stopped mining for gold ore, despite the precautionary principle enshrined in the Rio Declaration, a non-obligatory act (Tatar vs. Romania, 27 January 2009, vs. 120; Ailincai 2017).

Fear of civil or criminal liability can act as a strong incentive to comply with a recommendation. Following a drowning, the head of a water park was convicted of negligent homicide, on the grounds that a CCTV camera placed underwater, as recommended by the Swiss Accident Prevention Bureau, could have prevented this death (Federal Supreme Court, Decision 6S.358/2004 of 10 November 2004, paragraphs 5.3 and 7.2).

In some cases, the effects of soft law may be even more severe. The classic example is provided by alerts issued against defective products. Due to the potential damage to the image of the company, the publicity generated by issuing a warning (a non-obligatory act) carries greater weight than a simple notification prohibiting the distribution of a defective product (an obligatory act).

7.4.2 *Techniques for Reinforcing Effectiveness*

The state can resort to various mechanisms, both psychological and legal, to increase the effectiveness of the actions it takes. Techniques from social psychology or affective science can be particularly effective; they make tactical use of the emotions of addressees of an act by evoking feelings of fear, guilt, or desire. The use of such techniques, however, is clearly an issue in a society predicated on freedom and individual autonomy. They must therefore be justified, all the more so because of the weaker democratic legitimacy of soft law (Flückiger 2009).

Mechanisms of a legal nature can also strengthen the respect for soft law. Those to whom such soft law is directed remain free to follow them or not, but the de facto constraint can be strong, and in terms of its effects, may be indistinguishable from a legal constraint. Take the example of financial or regulatory pressure. The behavior an incentive tax or a subsidy suggests is only a recommended path, but not following it may be expensive or even jeopardize the existing system.

Legislation may also require that a recommendation be used simply as a basis for making a decision or that exemption from a recommendation be motivated (non-binding imperative clauses). Public authorities are not obliged to scrupulously follow the provisions contained in such a soft law act, but must instead use it as a basis in the decision-making process. Thus, the Federal Veterinary Office, in preparing and publishing statistics, takes international recommendations 'into account' (Article 147 II, Animal Protection Ordinance). Finally, legislators can insert a retrospective evaluation clause regarding the implementation of a non-obligatory act. Under Swiss law, for example, the federal government must 'inform' the Aircraft Accident Investigation Bureau of actions taken as a result of safety recommendations, or the reasons measures are not being taken (Art. 32 Directive on investigating aviation accidents and serious incidents).

7.5 Conclusion: Legitimizing Soft Law, Beyond Efficiency

Implementing the goals of public policy is no longer conceivable today without the use of soft law, as the Swiss case amply demonstrates. Indeed, the flexibility in adopting such instruments, combined with the effects they are likely to have, makes them indispensable in terms of efficiency.

However, as noted in the introduction, such soft law tools are problematic inasmuch as they do not enjoy the same democratic legitimacy as ordinary acts of law. If soft law had no effect, this would not pose particular problems, but as we have shown, this is not the case. Faced with this situation, it is necessary that public authorities adopt legitimization measures adapted to the particularities of soft law. One can suggest the following: the more non-obligatory acts by the state infringe on a right (at whatever level), and/or the more important their effects, the more one must ensure they are treated as equivalent to ordinary legal acts.

Specifically, a non-imperative act must be treated by the legal system almost the same way a legal act is when its effects are virtually obligatory (or very binding in fact), and when it affects a right extensively. Conversely, a non-imperative act which is devoid of effect and does not encroach on a right can have a quiet existence far from the legal constraints of the state.

In this perspective, the public authorities then need to become creative in finding ways to legitimize soft law. On the one hand, they must respect the values underlying basic principles of the rule of law: legality, public interest, proportionality, equality, and prohibiting arbitrariness. On the other hand, they must avoid codifying acts of soft law to the point of sacrificing their effectiveness.

Analysis needs to be carried out on a case-by-case basis, according to the different types of acts and the contexts in which they occur. For example, we can cite the requirement that recommendations be carried out in a way that respects the principles of objectivity and transparency, or the need for a consultation in order to guarantee an open, consensual, and participatory process when it comes to non-obligatory urban planning acts. It is also conceivable that procedural guarantees be increased (establishing a consultation process, providing a right to be heard before a recommendation is adopted, or publishing charters).

Finally, one needs to ensure soft law acts can be reviewed. Long limited to liability law, Swiss law has now been extended to allow for the judicial review of non-obligatory acts. Thus, any person with an interest worthy of protection can request that the public authorities refrain from illicit acts, cease trying to carry them out (or even revoke them), eliminate their consequences, or recognize their illegality. The responsible public authorities then reach a decision on this demand, one subject to appeal (Article 25a of the Federal Act on Administrative Procedure). In the case of an infringement of a fundamental right, at least one which is sufficiently grave, Article 35 (2) of the Swiss Constitution cited above imposes legal control (see also Decision of the Federal Supreme Court of 13 November 2006: ATF 133 I 49, 56).

It is not always possible to have a judge intervene, and in such cases, it is preferable to develop alternative control mechanisms, such as mediation bodies, an evaluation of public policies, or reporting to the relevant supervisory authority.

References

Abi-Saab, G. (1997). Cours général de droit international public. *Recueil des cours de l'Académie de droit international*, tome 207.

Ailincai, M. (2017). La soft law est-elle l'avenir des droits fondamentaux? *Revue des Droits et Libertés Fondamentaux, 20.*

Brunner, U. (2004). Regulierung, Deregulierung und Selbstregulierung im Umweltrecht. *Revue de droit suisse, II*, 307–370.

Cassese, S. (2005). Administrative Law without the state? The challenge of global regulation. *New York University Journal of International Law and Politics, 37*, 663–694.

Conseil d'Etat. (2013). *Le droit souple: Etude annuelle 2013.* Paris.

Daillier, P., Forteau, M., & Pellet, A. (2009). *Droit international public.* Paris: LGDJ.

Delley, J.-D. (1991). L'action par la formation. In C.-A. Morand (Ed.), *Les instruments d'action de l'Etat* (pp. 89–112). Basel/Frankfurt: Helbing & Lichtenhahn.

Errass, C. (2010). *Kooperative Rechtssetzung.* Zurich/St. Gallen: Dike.

Flückiger, A. (2004). Régulation, dérégulation, autorégulation: l'émergence des actes étatiques non obligatoires. *Revue de droit suisse, 2*, 159–303.

Flückiger, A. (2005). La loi Damoclès. In B. Bovay & M. S. Nguyen (Eds.), *Mélanges Pierre Moor* (pp. 233–248). Bern: Stämpfli.

Flückiger, A. (2009). Pourquoi respectons-nous la soft law? Le rôle des émotions et des techniques de manipulation. *Revue européenne des sciences sociales, XLVII-144*, 73–103.

Guzman, A., & Meyer, T. (2010). International soft law. *Journal of Legal Analysis, 2*(1), 171–225.

Hachez, I., et al. (Eds.). (2013). *Les sources du droit revisitées: Théorie des sources du droit* (Vol. 4). Limal: Anthemis, Chap. II.

Keller, H. (2008). Codes of conduct and their implementation: The question of legitimacy. In W. Rüdiger & R. Volker (Eds.), *Legitimacy in international law* (pp. 219–298). Berlin: Springer.
Mader, L., & Rütsche, B. (2004). Regulierung, Deregulierung, Selbstregulierung: Anmerkungen aus legistischer Sicht. *Revue de droit suisse, 2*, 3–156.
Manfrini, P.-L. (1991). Les contrats de marchés publics mis au service de la poursuite d'une politique publique. In C.-A. Morand (Ed.), *Les instruments d'action et l'Etat* (pp. 127–146). Basel/Frankfurt: Helbing & Lichtenhahn.
Moor, P., & Poltier, E. (2011). *Droit administratif* (Vol. II). Bern: Stämpfli.
Moor, P., Flückiger, A., & Martenet, V. (2012). *Droit administratif.* Bern: Stämpfli.
Morand, C.-A. (1999). *Le droit néo-moderne des politiques publiques.* Paris: LGDJ.
Nowak, C. (2011). *Europarecht nach Lissabon.* Baden-Baden: Nomos.
Oberson, X., & Maraia, J.-F. (2010). Remarques liminaires ad art. 35a-35c LPE, Problèmes juridiques posés par l'utilisation de taxes d'incitation. In P. Moor, A.-C. Favre, & A. Flückiger (Eds.), *Loi sur la protection de l'environnement (LPE)*. Bern: Stämpfli.
Pauwelyn, J., Ramses, W., & Wouters, J. (Eds.). (2012). *Informal international law-making.* Oxford: Oxford University Press.
Peters, A. (2011). Soft law as a new mode of governance. In U. Diedrichs, W. Reiners, & W. Wessels (Eds.), *The dynamics of change in EZ governance* (pp. 21–51). Cheltenham/Northampton: Edward Elgar Publishing.
Rodondi, O. (2001). Les critères d'aptitude et les critères d'adjudication dans les procédures de marchés publics. *RDAF I, 57*, 387–413.
Shelton, D. (2008). Soft law. In D. Amstrong (Ed.), *Handbook of international law* (pp. 68–80). London/New York: Routledge Press.
Subilia-Rouge, L. (2010). Art. 43a LPE. In P. Moor, A.-C. Favre, & A. Flückiger (Eds.), *Loi sur la protection de l'environnement (LPE)*. Bern: Stämpfli.

CHAPTER 8

Judicial Federalism and Constitutional Review in the Swiss Judiciary

Pascal Mahon

8.1 Introduction

This chapter deals with the Swiss judicial system. Its aim is to succinctly present the judicial system and to highlight its main features, though length constraints limit this overview to the essential characteristics of the system and what makes it unique. The focus is on two elements: the federalized manner in which the judiciary is organized (Sect. 8.2), and the particularities of Swiss constitutional justice (also called constitutional jurisdiction) (Sect. 8.3).

The chapter first describes the organization of the judicial system, which is strongly marked by the federal character of Switzerland (so there is a pronounced judicial federalism). The philosophy of the system at the federal level is presented, and judicial organization of the cantons is briefly described. The chapter then describes the Swiss system of judicial review (control of the constitutionality of the laws and other state acts), a system which is relatively complete and extended, but, at the same time, has a notable exception in international comparison: Switzerland lacks judicial review of federal laws (and international law).

P. Mahon (✉)
Faculty of Law, University of Neuchâtel, Neuchâtel, Switzerland
e-mail: pascal.mahon@unine.ch

A. Ladner et al. (eds.), *Swiss Public Administration*, Governance and Public Management,
https://doi.org/10.1007/978-3-319-92381-9_8

8.2 Judicial Organization in General: A Pronounced Judicial Federalism

8.2.1 Judicial Federalism and 'Reforming the Judiciary'

Swiss judicial organization remains very marked by federalism. The application of cantonal law naturally lies with the cantonal judicial authorities. Less naturally, the application of federal law is to a great extent also in the hands of the cantonal judicial authorities. This is generally true for nearly all civil law and practically all criminal law (Art. 122 and 123, respectively, of the Swiss Federal Constitution, abbreviated Const.). Hence, divorces are finalized and murderers prosecuted and punished under material federal law (following the Civil or the Penal Code), by cantonal and not federal prosecuting authorities and courts.

This very pronounced judicial federalism differs from other systems, such as the American, in which two complete, but separate, judicial organizations coexist and yet are superimposed. Put simply, US federal courts deal with federal and inter-state matters while state courts deal with cases arising within their respective states. This is not the case in Switzerland, other than in a few rare cases recently introduced in the context of what is called 'the reform of the judiciary', which is discussed later in this chapter.

Since modern Switzerland began, which is to say since the advent of the modern federal state in 1848, each of the cantons has had a complete judicial organization. Today, their mission, in matters of civil and criminal, and to some extent administrative, is to apply federal law in the same manner as the application of cantonal law. In return, the constituent power in 1848 dispensed with creating an entire federal judicial apparatus. It left to the cantonal judicial authorities, as subordinate bodies, the task of guaranteeing the application of federal law. The federal *power* limited itself for a long time to only establishing a single higher instance, the Federal Supreme Court, which itself was made permanent only in 1874.

This sharing of organizational and judicial competencies has been somewhat modified in recent years as the result of a constitutional amendment to reform the judiciary approved by the voters and the cantons on 12 March 2000. Its purpose was to give the Confederation the power to legislate in procedural matters in civil and criminal domains (through amendments to Art. 122 and 123 Const.), though the organization of the judiciary and the administration of justice were to remain, in principle, in the hands of the cantons (Haller 2016: 80).

In addition, Articles 188 et seq. of the Federal Constitution were modified to permit a complete revision of the Federal Judicial Organization Act intended to introduce a single appeal to the Federal Supreme Court and to regulate—meaning limit—access to this tribunal (Federal Council 2001: 4000). The creation of two new federal courts of first instance, a Federal Criminal Court and a Federal Administrative Court, followed by a Federal Patent Court, was also provided for (Art. 191a Const.).

On 1 January 2007, the new Federal Supreme Court Act (FSCA) of 17 June 2005, which replaced the old Federal Judicial Organization Act of 1943, entered into force. To unify criminal and civil procedures, the Federal Parliament adopted a new Criminal Procedure Code on 5 October 2007 and a new Civil Procedure Code on 19 December 2008. These codes, which entered into force on 1 January 2011, replaced the 26 cantonal codes of criminal procedure and of civil procedure.

As part of the revision of the Swiss Constitution in 1999, a number of new statutes were adopted concerning the two new Federal Courts of First Instance; the Federal Criminal Court Act (of 4 October 2002), later replaced by the Federal Criminal Law Justice Authorities Act of 19 March 2010, in force as of 1 January 2011; the Federal Administrative Court Act of 17 June 2005, in force as of 1 January 2007; and the Federal Patent Court Act of 20 March 2009, in force as of 1 March 2010. We will return briefly below to these different federal courts of first instance. First, however, the Federal Supreme Court, Switzerland's highest court of law, will be presented.

8.2.2 The Federal Supreme Court

8.2.2.1 The Dual Role of the Federal Supreme Court

The Federal Supreme Court is 'the supreme judicial authority of the Confederation' (Art. 188 (1) Const.).

The Federal Supreme Court has a dual role. On the one hand, it must ensure that national law is interpreted and applied in a uniform manner, whether these are legislative acts, regulations, or international law (where it plays the role of supreme judge). On the other hand, it needs to guarantee that both federal and cantonal constitutions are respected, including protecting the constitutional rights of individuals (where it plays the role of constitutional judge). It is therefore one and the same court which, as supreme authority, performs the functions of ordinary judge (in civil, criminal, and administrative matters) as well as constitutional judge of the Confederation. As compared with the French judicial system, the

Swiss Federal Supreme Court combines the roles of the *Cour de cassation* (the highest court in civil and criminal matters), the *Conseil d'Etat* (the highest court for administrative justice), and the *Conseil constitutionnel* (the highest constitutional review authority). In German terms, it combines the roles of the *Bundesgerichtshof*, *Bundesverwaltungsgericht*, *Bundesfinanzhof*, *Bundesarbeitsgericht*, *Bundessozialgericht*, as well as that of the *Bundesverfassungsgericht*.

Consequently, it generally only intervenes as a last resort. As already noted, the control over the application of cantonal law is not only the business of the cantonal courts, but is largely true in the application of federal law—at least at the lower levels—as well. The cantons all have complete, multi-level judicial organizations, but with exceptions for specific areas, the Swiss Confederation has few lower instances. So for the most part, the Federal Supreme Court only acts once the cantonal courts have done their work, and then as a court of appeals against their judgments, whether in civil (Art. 72 et seq. FSCA) or criminal matters (Arts. 78 et seq. FSCA), and in public law (Art. 82 et seq. FSCA). Only in exceptional cases does it judge certain cases as the sole instance, for example, when jurisdictional disputes arise between federal and cantonal authorities, or between cantons (Art. 120 (1) (a) and (b) FSCA).

The law provides for various means of legal redress in bringing a case to the Federal Supreme Court: three ordinary (civil law, criminal law, and public law appeals) and one extraordinary (a subsidiary constitutional appeal). As conditions for admissibility, it also places certain limitations on access, such as setting minimum values in civil or administrative litigation or even restricting access entirely. The FSCA (Art. 83), for example, gives a long list [from a. to x.] of areas where a public law appeal is not admissible, for example.

8.2.2.2 The Composition of the Federal Supreme Court and the Appointment of Judges

By law, the Federal Supreme Court is composed of 35 to 45 ordinary judges (Art. 1 (3), FSCA); the number of deputy judges may not exceed two-thirds of the number of ordinary judges (Art. 1 (4) FSCA). Through a regulation, it is in fact the Federal Assembly which determines the number of judges (Art. 1 (5), FSCA). As of 30 September 2011, this was set at 38 ordinary judges and 19 deputy judges. It is also the Federal Assembly, meaning both houses of Parliament, which elects the federal judges (Arts. 168 (1) and 157 (1) a) Const.).

In practice, Parliament tries to adhere to a proportional representation of the different linguistic regions, the two Christian denominations and, above all, the main political parties represented in the Federal Assembly. As a result, federal judges are always associated with a (major) political party (Lienhard et al. 2017: 417–419). When a vacancy occurs, it is the political party of the retiring judge which, in principle, selects and presents replacement candidates to the Judicial Committee of the Federal Assembly. The National Council (lower house) is re-elected every four years; if a significant modification in the equilibrium of the political forces takes place, the new power balance can be taken into account when one or more vacancies appear in the Federal Supreme Court, whence the composition of the latter can be adapted to the new order. Ordinary judges and deputies are elected for a six-year period and can be re-elected (Art. 145 Const. and Art. 9 (1) FSCA).

It is a peculiarity of the Swiss judiciary system that federal judges are elected on a partisan basis, and for a limited time period, by Parliament. Cantons follow suit: some even provide for the popular election of judges, and the terms can vary from one to as many as ten years, depending on the canton.[1] Such a judicial system is often little understood abroad, given the principle of an independent judiciary. This process is rarely strongly contested in theory and is fairly widely accepted in Switzerland, as it is seen to guarantee to the citizens that judges will represent the existing, and differing, political tendencies or sensitivities in society, at least as represented in Parliament.

According to many authors and even some magistrates, it can give the third power—as with the other two—the democratic legitimacy and the transparency it needs. Added to this argument is the fact that this system is the result of a long tradition and reflects the Swiss conception of democracy. However, the democratic argument loses force with regard to re-election, as judges in most cantons and at the federal level are subject to re-election at regular intervals (Mahon and Schaller 2013a, b). It is theoretically possible that a judge will not be re-elected, and that at the discretion of politicians and without reasons given; this can pose problems in terms of judicial independence. One cannot rule out the potential influence which could be exerted and which could threaten a re-election.

However, while there is no right to be re-elected, in practice, at least thus far, re-election has always been the rule and non-re-election the exception. Judges are virtually never removed for political reasons. The rare cases of a failure to reelect were due to a dysfunction, not politics. Thus, despite the theoretical risk to the independence of the magistrates

[1] The only exception is the canton of Fribourg where judges are elected by the cantonal Parliament, but since 1 January 2008, for an unlimited period.

which the system suggests, in practice such independence has been relatively well ensured until now. In Switzerland, the risks to an independent judiciary are also linked to the small size of the (cantonal, especially in the first instance) territories in which magistrates exercise their office. The 'cantonalisation' of the judicial system, and in the cantons, its organization into districts, results in an almost complete absence of mobility.

Another peculiarity in recruitment is the absence of initial vocational training for becoming a judge in Switzerland, in contrast to the relatively extensive training which exists, and is required, abroad. However, for federal judgeships, Parliament only selects experienced and eminent jurists from the ranks of the cantonal judges, though they sometimes also choose lawyers or university professors (Lienhard et al. 2017: 418).

Finally, at the cantonal level, cantonal laws sometimes require that judges be domiciled in the canton where they exercise their office.

8.2.2.3 The Structure of the Federal Supreme Court

The headquarters of the Federal Supreme Court are in Lausanne (Art. 4 (1) FSCA), and the work of the court is organized by the domains of law they address. The two divisions which address social law are located in Lucerne (Art. 4 (2) FSCA). Currently, there are two public law divisions (each with six judges), two civil law divisions (one with five, the other with six judges), one criminal law division (five judges), and two social law courts (each with five members). They serve as appeals courts to challenge the judgments of lower cantonal and federal authorities. Other bodies also exist, with their member judges who belong to one of the seven divisions. They include an Appeals Commission, composed of three ordinary judges, which decides in particular about personnel and transparency issues, and two administrative bodies, the Conference of Presidents and the Administrative Commission.

With the exception of the powers—essentially administrative—for which the law requires plenary sessions, the Federal Supreme Court exercises its judicial powers through its divisions, which deliberate alone, unless one of them proposes to derogate from the case law of one or more other divisions, in which case an agreement of that (or those) divisions is necessary (Art. 23 FSCA). The law provides that the divisions are constituted for two years, and as a rule, sit as a three-judge court which is assisted by a law clerk (Haller 2016: 154, 155; Lienhard et al. 2017: 415, 416). If a case concerns a legal question of principle or if a judge so requests, this can be raised to five. A five-judge court is also necessary for appeals against a cantonal act which can be subjected to a referendum, as well as cantonal decisions about the admissibility of an initiative or the requirements of a referendum (Art. 18 et seq. FSCA).

In principle, court sessions are open; remarkably, this is also true for the deliberations as well as voting. However, the law provides for the possibility of ordering a closed session (Art. 57 et seq. FSCA) (Haller 2016: 155). In practice, it is possible to choose a simplified procedure, specifically when the decision is to not consider a case (Art. 108 and 109 FSCA), in which judges decide unanimously and by circulating material (Art. 58 FSCA). Open or public deliberations have become rare or very rare.

8.2.3 *The Other Federal Courts*

As noted earlier, as part of the 'reforming the judiciary', and in particular to relieve the Federal Supreme Court, the Federal Assembly created new federal courts of first instance which had not previously existed: the Federal Criminal Court, the Federal Administrative Court, and the Federal Patent Court.

8.2.3.1 The Federal Criminal Court

If the application of the federal criminal law is largely in the hands of the cantonal judicial authorities, in the sense that crimes and offenses are in principle prosecuted and judged by the cantonal prosecuting authorities and courts, there are still certain categories of infractions whose prosecution and adjudication are the responsibility of the federal authorities (namely, the Federal Public Prosecutor and Federal Criminal Court). These include crimes committed against federal authorities or members of foreign states, offenses related to the use of explosives or toxic gases, and crimes and offenses related to forging money. They also include falsifying watermarks, stamps, or official titles used by the Confederation, genocide and crimes against humanity, war crimes, crimes against the state and national defense, crimes which go against the will of the people and the public authorities, and other matters (see the list of offenses listed in Art. 23 and 24 Criminal Procedure Code).

As the first instance, the Federal Criminal Court therefore judges criminal cases which fall within the purview and competence of the Confederation; its decisions can then be appealed to the Federal Supreme Court.

The Federal Criminal Court has its seat in Bellinzona and is composed of 15–35 ordinary judges who are elected by the Federal Assembly. As per a parliamentary order of 13 December 2013, there are currently 16 ordinary judges and three deputies serving on this court.

8.2.3.2 The Federal Administrative Court

On 1 January 2007, the Federal Administrative Court replaced the 30 or so federal administrative appeals boards that had previously existed. They had been responsible for reviewing, on appeal, the application of federal administrative law in their specific area of competence.

Generally speaking, it is the responsibility of the cantonal administrations to apply federal administrative law. Thus, to take the example of road traffic, cantonal offices are responsible for applying the federal laws regarding car registration. By having the cantons administer federal substantive law, the Confederation had thus been—and is—able to avoid setting up and maintaining a ponderous network of federal offices. In various domains, it has been satisfied with maintaining a relatively small administrative apparatus that in essence supervises the application of federal substantive law by the cantons.

In some areas, however, the federal legislature has chosen to entrust the application of federal administrative law not to the cantons but to a specific federal administrative unit which is created and set up to this end. This is the case, for example, in asylum law, where the decisions about applying the federal laws on asylum are taken by a federal entity, the State Secretariat for Migration (SEM, formerly the Federal Office for Refugees and then the Federal Office for Migration). This is also the case in a number of other, quite disparate domains, including applying customs, nuclear energy, and organ transplantation laws and regulations.

However, in matters of federal administrative law, litigation is organized following a distinction related to competencies. Thus, when federal administrative law is applied in a given field by a cantonal instance, then recourse is first sought in that canton's administrative court. Only then, insofar as a further appeal is admissible, does it go to the Federal Supreme Court. But if federal administrative law is implemented through an administrative authority of the Confederation, then the appeal is to a federal judicial authority, which since 2007, is the Federal Administrative Court. In this new Court, competencies previously scattered among specialized appeals boards have been concentrated in a single appellate authority of first instance.

As long as the law does not preclude the possibility, decisions of the Federal Administrative Court may be appealed to the Federal Supreme Court (Art. 1 (2) FACA). The Federal Administrative Court has its seat in St. Gallen, and is composed of 50–70 judges who are elected by the Federal Assembly. As per a parliamentary order of 17 June 2005, there are currently 65 judges serving on this court.

8.2.3.3 The Federal Patent Court

The Federal Patent Court Law came into force on 1 March 2010. This Court rules as the first instance of the Confederation in matters of patents, replacing the cantonal courts which previously had competence in this area.

The Federal Patent Court has its seat at the Federal Administrative Court. It is composed of two ordinary judges and 41 deputy judges who must have technical training, meaning that 28 non-permanent judges possess technical training and 13 have legal training. All of them have proven knowledge of patent law, and all are elected by the Federal Assembly.

8.2.4 Judicial Organization in the Cantons

The cantons have a great deal of autonomy in terms of judicial organization. With the exception of the federal courts just discussed, all Swiss judicial authorities do indeed proceed from cantonal law.[2] However, what characterizes this cantonal judiciary organization is its extreme diversity from canton to canton. This is not only a horizontal diversity between cantons but also vertical: one has to distinguish, in each canton, between the civil, criminal, and administrative jurisdictions.

The Swiss Constitution expressly states that the cantons 'are responsible for the organization of the courts and the administration of justice in civil matters' (Art. 122 (2) Const.), and the same is true for jurisdiction in criminal cases (Art. 123 (2) Const.). The Swiss Constitution does not expressly state the same for administrative matters, but jurisdiction here is based similarly on the organizational autonomy of the cantons. The organization of the cantonal judicial authorities includes the questions of territorial jurisdiction, the conditions of appointments and remunerations of the judges, and the finances and the overseeing of the management of courts (Tophinke 2013: 273, 274; Lienhard et al. 2017: 419).

For civil and criminal matters, cantons generally have two authorities at their disposal in their judicial organization. The judicial system is often organized into lower courts, constituted by district or region, depending on the canton, and a single superior instance, usually called the Cantonal Court. In administrative matters, the application of cantonal administrative law is generally the responsibility of the cantonal administration and its departments. Their activities and decisions are usually overseen by the

[2] One should also note the exception of military courts and military jurisdiction, both under federal law; they are not addressed further here.

higher cantonal administrative court, which is the final cantonal instance before appealing to the Federal Supreme Court.

8.3 Constitutional Jurisdiction: An Extensive Review with a Notable Exception

The so-called in Switzerland 'constitutional jurisdiction' (constitutional justice) is well developed and combines different types of constitutional review (Auer 1983).

Different types of constitutional review are generally identified. It is either centralized in the hands of a (supreme or constitutional) court or decentralized (Cappelleti 1970). It should also be noted that an abstract constitutional review occurs in the absence of a concrete case of application. The Court simply reviews the constitutionality of norms and these will either not come into force or be repealed. By contrast, concrete constitutional review takes place when an individual decision is based on potentially unconstitutional legislation and the court conducts a preliminary review of the legal norm.

Paradoxically, and despite the worldwide enlargement of constitutional justice (Hertig Randall 2010: 221 et seq.), there has been a notable exception in Swiss law with respect to a category of legal norms: federal laws. Indeed, even if they are unconstitutional, federal laws must be applied by courts and authorities. With the exception of this limitation, all state acts (promulgated in the form either of federal statutes, ordinances, and decrees or decisions), whether adopted by federal, cantonal, or municipal authorities, are subject to constitutional review.

To outline the main aspects of constitutional justice in Switzerland, we therefore first examine it from the perspective of legal instruments (Sect. 8.3.1). Then we will examine the peculiarity of having an absence of review of federal laws (Sect. 8.3.2).

8.3.1 Legal Instruments Subject to Constitutional Review

As mentioned, other than federal laws (Art. 190 Const.), all legal instruments are subject to constitutional control. Nevertheless, the type of review is not always the same. Two forms of instruments must be distinguished. First, there are 'legal rules' which express binding, abstract, and general norms. Such legal rules can be adopted by the Parliament (statutes or ordinances) or by the Executive (ordinances or decrees) at the federal or cantonal level. These legal acts form the legislation. Second, the scope of some legal instruments can be limited to individual and concrete cases, which are then the 'decisions'. Public authorities, such as public administration or the judiciary, can adopt decisions. To look more precisely at consequences on the question of constitutional justice, we will start with the federal regulations. After that, we will consider the cantonal law and finally we will briefly look at decisions.

8.3.1.1 Federal Regulations

Federal legal rules can be adopted in the form of statutes and federal ordinances, which are adopted by the Parliament (statutes and ordinances), the Executive (ordinances), or the department and offices of the federal public administration (ordinances). The sources of review are the Federal Constitution but also international law. However, not all appellants have the possibility of invoking all the provisions of the Federal Constitution, as will be seen.

A concrete constitutional review of federal legal acts is undertaken only when they are applied. This means that when the Federal Council or another federal authority adopts an ordinance contrary to the Constitution, individuals can only challenge the unconstitutional act in the framework of a specific case. In other words, other than in cases of action taken by cantons (see below), there is no 'abstract constitutional review' for federal legal rules, at least not one at the disposal of individuals.

Such a conception of constitutional review was adopted in 1874 in the first Federal Judicial Organization Act, and remained unquestioned. This option was not questioned either when a new Federal Judicial Organization Act was adopted in 1943, or in the latter's replacing FSCA of 2005. However, as already mentioned, there is an exception to this absence of abstract review of federal (non-statutory) acts. Cantons can appeal to the Federal Supreme Court (the formerly so-called public law claim) by claiming that a non-statutory act violates the Federal Constitution, in particular that it violates the division of powers between the Confederation and the cantons, thus encroaching on cantonal competencies. Through this form of appeal can cantons trigger an abstract constitutional review of federal acts by the Federal Court (Art. 189 (2) Const.). In this framework, the Federal Supreme Court does verify the constitutionality (and legality) of federal ordinances. In such cases, the Federal Supreme Court generally shows considerable restraint. If the ordinance is based on legislative delegation, the Federal Court limits itself to verifying that the author of the ordinance remained within the framework and limits of the delegation. Furthermore, insofar as the law does not authorize the delegate to derogate from the Constitution, the Federal Supreme Court reviews the constitutionality of the ordinance (for the formula generally used by the Federal Supreme Court see, e.g., the Decision of the Federal Supreme Court of 22 December 1978: ATF 104 Ib 412, 420, 421).

Let us add here that the constitutional review is not only concentrated in the hands of the Federal Supreme Court but also decentralized, meaning that any federal or cantonal authority which is responsible for applying federal legislation in a given case must—or at least may—refuse to apply it if they consider it contrary to the Federal Constitution. The question of constitutionality may thus be raised at any stage when applying the legal rules and before any authority. In the end, this question can even be brought to the Federal Supreme Court in principle by ordinary means of appeal (whether in civil, criminal or public law matters).

8.3.1.2 Cantonal Law

The review of cantonal legislation is significantly more extensive than for federal legal rules in two respects. The review can be abstract as well as concrete and, in both cases, is available to individuals. It should be emphasized, however, that the Federal Supreme Court refuses to review—in principle—the cantonal constitutions, on the grounds that these have already been controlled by the Federal Assembly (Art. 172 (2) Const.) (Mahon 2014: 110, 111).

Concerning the sources of the review, it is first of all based on the Federal Constitution and on international law as well. There is also a conformity control with cantonal constitutional law or at least with certain parts of cantonal constitutional law. It must be added that the cantonal norms have to be in conformity with the federal law (see below).

The constitutional review of cantonal norms is decentralized, meaning it applies to all the procedures applying these norms. When applying a cantonal norm in a concrete case, all authorities, administrative or judicial, must—or at least can—refuse its application if they consider it contrary to the Federal Constitution. For example, an administrative court of a canton will thus refuse to apply a tax law if it considers it contrary to the principle of equality (Art. 8 (1) Const.) or refuse to apply a cantonal law on trade if it deems it contrary to economic freedom (Art. 27 Const.).

The constitutional review of cantonal norms can also be abstract. Indeed, unlike federal acts, a cantonal or municipal act enforced can be appealed for violation of the Constitution outside any cases. In such a hypothesis, the appeal is brought directly before the Federal Court, which judges in principle as the sole and unique body. The review is therefore 'concentrated'. However, the cantons are also free to establish a constitutional court which can review all the laws and ordinances of the canton (Bolkensteyn 2014). Some cantons have done so, including the canton of Jura (Art. 104 Constitution of Jura), the canton of Vaud (Art. 136 Constitution of Vaud), the canton of Graubünden (Art. 55 Constitution of Graubünden), and the canton of Geneva (Art. 124 Constitution of Geneva). The cantons of Nidwalden and Zurich provide such review to a more limited extent (without control of the laws). In such cases, the individuals must first appeal to the cantonal authority and then, on review, take the case to the Federal Supreme Court. An appeal against a cantonal law must be sent to the Federal Supreme Court within 30 days of publishing the cantonal act. Once this period has elapsed, the legal norms can no longer be reviewed in an abstract manner, but it can still be controlled in an application case (concrete control). However, the abstract control does not prevent—with exceptions—the entry into force of the norm.

As cantonal law is applied by the cantons, there is a general right of review in the cantonal judiciary. The remedy must be appealed to in the framework of the application of the norm. Indeed, in concrete cases, when two legal norms are in conflict, the judiciary must determine which one prevails and apply it. Such a power has been derived from the principle that federal laws break cantonal law (Art. 49 Const.) (Mahon 2014: 141–143). Cantons are obliged by federal law to have courts of second instance, meaning cantonal courts or upper courts, and decisions they take can be brought to the Federal Supreme Court if they apply a cantonal norm that violates the Federal Constitution or a constitutional right, by an ordinary means of appeal (*appeal in civil matters* and *appeal in criminal matters* will however be rather rarer than *appeal in matters of public law* insofar as there are none or only few cantonal statutes in these fields). If none of these ordinary appeals are possible, the legislator has created a subsidiary constitutional appeal (Art. 113 FSCA) for which three conditions must been fulfilled: the decision emanates from a cantonal authority of last instance, the appellant invokes a 'violation of constitutional rights', and the appellant must prove a 'legal interest' (Art. 113 to 116 FSCA).

The means of appeal to review a cantonal legal act by the Federal Supreme Court, without any application, is always the public law remedy (Art. 82b (b) FSCA).

8.3.1.3 Decisions Taken by Federal or Cantonal Authorities

Administrative authorities and the judiciary make decisions in which legal rules are applied. Their common feature is that they concern an individual and specific case, and all levels—federal, cantonal, and local authorities—can make such decisions. They are the last category to be considered under this section.

Such legal instruments are subject to reviews of their constitutionality regardless of the legal norm on which they are based. It is alleged that the decision itself is violating the Constitution. In other words, it is how the law is applied which is—supposedly—contrary to the Constitution and not the legal norm on which the decision is based. Unlike the decision, the legal norm can be entirely in accordance with the Constitution.

The remedies for the constitutionality review against such acts are those applied in general. As far as the Federal Supreme Court is concerned, as the last instance, the remedies (civil matters, criminal matters, public law matters or subsidiary constitutional appeal) depend on the subject. Appeals are directed either against the cantonal court, the Federal Administrative Court, the Federal Criminal Court or another federal authority (Haller 2016: 153). Nevertheless, individual decisions taken by the Federal Assembly (e.g. concerning the validity of a popular initiative) are excluded from the constitutional review despite the fact that it creates a conflict with the guarantee of access to the courts guaranteed by the Swiss constitution in Article 29 (Haller 2016: 263).

8.3.2 A Breach of the Rule of Law: The Case of Federal Laws (and of International Law)

Article 190 of the Federal Constitution provides that 'the Federal Supreme Court and the other judicial authorities must apply the federal acts and international law'. Known as the 'immunity clause' of federal laws, the constitutional provision limits the constitutional review of legal norms in Switzerland. It implies that federal statutes adopted by the Federal Assembly, having found the endorsement—explicit or tacit—of the Swiss people, have to be applied even when they have no constitutional basis or are in conflict with the Federal Constitution. That being said, the Federal

Assembly must respect the Federal Constitution when adopting laws. To understand better the scope of such a limitation, we will briefly evoke the reasons behind it and question this breach in the Swiss constitutional justice. We will thereafter describe the extent of the notion of 'immunity' and will finish by presenting its mitigated effect due to international law.

8.3.2.1 Reasons and Questions on the Breach

This rule also applies to international laws. In this case, it is motivated by the concern of ensuring the international credibility of Switzerland. To put it another way, once an international law has been validly adopted, the binding rules resulting from international obligations must be respected.

The reason for limiting the constitutional review in Article 190 Const. is founded in concepts of separation of powers and direct democracy. The constituent power of 1874 made these two principles prevail over the idea of complete judicial control of legal norms. In short, the idea was that a federal law should rarely be contrary to the Constitution. Most often, it is the opinion of the sense of the Constitution which varies according to interpretations. Finally, there was also no reason to prefer the interpretation of a court to that of Parliament. Such a vision of the constituent power in 1848 occurs at a time where there were very few legislative powers and therefore federal laws.

Nevertheless, the immunity of federal laws has always been debated, and the question of whether it (still) has a *raison d'être* remains controversial today. While many legal scholars advocate to enlarge the constitutional review to federal laws, the political authorities have always been opposed to it, at least in their majority. Two motions in 1923 and 1924 and a popular initiative in 1939 were rejected. At the time of the total revision of the Swiss Constitution, the Federal Council proposed—in the project on the 'reform of the justice system' (Federal Council 1997: 652)—to abrogate, at least partially, such a rule of immunity of the federal laws but the Federal Assembly did not agree. The Federal Council once again proposed a partial lifting of the immunity of federal laws in the framework of the reform of financial equalization and division of powers between the Confederation and the cantons (the so-called "RPT reform" (for "Réforme de la péréquation et de la répartition des tâches"), Federal Council 2002: 2155). The cantons, and only they, would have had the opportunity to challenge federal laws affecting their sphere of jurisdiction, but this proposal too was rejected by Parliament. Two more recent parliamentary interventions proposing the repeal of Article 190 Const. have also suffered a similar fate (Report of the National Council's Legal Affairs Committee 2011: 6707–6724; Federal Council 2011: 6995–7000).

This notable exception inside the constitutional justice seems thus deeply entrenched in the Swiss constitutional beliefs and shows a certain contradiction with the idea of constitutional state, in which all legal norms must absolutely be adopted in conformity with the constitution and be reviewed by an independent court. It is now appropriate to consider more specifically the scope of this concept of 'immunity'.

8.3.2.2 The Scope of the Notion of 'Immunized' Legal Norms

As stated in Article 190 Const., it is federal laws and international law which are immunized. Considering federal laws, this applies to both ordinary and urgent laws (Art. 165 Const.; Mahon 2014: 275). Other legislative instruments are not open to review by the Federal Supreme Court.

Indeed, as already mentioned, the cantonal constitutions are also immune against the (federal) constitutional review. Such an interpretation has been developed in the case law of the Federal Supreme Court, which often argued that cantonal constitutions are guaranteed by the Federal Assembly (Art. 51 (2) Const.). This Supreme Court jurisprudence is often criticized by legal scholars (Grisel 1996; Töndury 2004). They consider that the review exercised by the Federal Assembly is too summary to bind the courts. The Federal Court has remained unmoved by this critique and continues to refrain from checking whether cantonal constitutions are in conformity with federal law. However, it must be noted that the Court has exceptionally agreed to check the conformity of the cantonal constitution with the rules of federal law that were adopted after the granting of the Federal Parliament's guarantee. In such a case, it is not likely to disavow the Federal Assembly (see Decision of the Federal Supreme Court of 18 Mai 2004: ATF 131 I 126, 130, where the Federal Court notes, despite the almost unanimous criticism among Swiss legal scholars, that there is no need to change the case law).

In addition, when a legal norm inferior (e.g. an ordinance or a cantonal decree) to a federal law, in the hierarchy of norms, repeats or applies an unconstitutional legal rule found in an immunized act (e.g. federal law), the former is also covered by this immunity clause. It is therefore an indirect effect—a reaction, in a way—of this immunity. Indeed, the Federal Court has considered that such a norm is not controllable, because here the review would relate, indirectly, to the immunized act and would come up against the immunity clause. Such is the case of a federal ordinance, adopted by the Federal Council or the Assembly, which repeats or executes the solution chosen by the federal legislators (Mahon 2014: 329, 330; Haller 2016: 261).

8.3.2.3 The Mitigated Effects of the 'Immunity Clause' and the Relationship Between National and International Law

If the immunity clause of federal laws is not ready to be questioned by the political authorities, it has been, however, subject to various attenuations.

The first of these temperaments is that the enforcement authority can, while applying the law, criticize it and even invite the legislator to modify the provision in question. In other words, to use the German adage often used to illustrate this aspect, Article 190 provides an *Anwendungsgebot* but not a *Prüfungsverbot*—an application directive but not a prohibition on scrutinizing it (see Decision of the Federal Supreme Court of 11 December 1996: ATF 123 II 9).

Another form of mitigation of the rule of immunity of federal laws is related to the principle called 'interpretation in conformity with the Constitution'. Concretely, when a law is open to more than one interpretation, the implementing authority gives the preference to the one compatible with the Constitution. Such a margin of discretion can only go so far in an attempt to give a norm a constitutional content, as the authority cannot deviate from the clear text of a legal norm (see Decision of the Federal Supreme Court of 12 July 1993: ATF 119 Ia 241).

Third temperament to the rule of immunity is the fact that a new constitutional provision prevails, if it is sufficiently precise, over an earlier statute. This is logical, as far as prevails the subsequent decision of an organ endowed with a greater legitimacy (the constituent) than that of the legislator.

To conclude on the question of the immunity rule, it must be noted that Article. 190 Const. does not answer the question of which rule prevails in the event of a conflict between a provision of a federal—immunized—law and that of an international treaty—which benefits from the immunity clause provided in Article 190 Const. as well. On this question, Article 5 (4) Const. entrenches the principle of the primacy of international law. It means that a provision of an international treaty prevails on a domestic law provision. This rule must be underlined. Indeed, the Federal Supreme Court has admitted, in some cases, to review federal laws in light of the international law of the European Convention of Human Rights or the UN Covenants (Hertig Randall 2010: 248 et seq.). Such a test is known as the 'control of conventionality', skirting around the limit of the constitutional review of Swiss laws.

References

Auer, A. (1983). *La juridiction constitutionnelle en Suisse*. Basel: Helbing & Lichtenhahn.

Bolkensteyn, A. (2014). *Le contrôle des normes, spécialement par les cours constitutionnelles cantonales*. Bern: Staempfli.

Cappelletti, M. (1970). Judicial review in comparative perspective. *California Law Review, 58*, 1017–1053.

Federal Council. (1997). Message du Conseil fédéral du 20 novembre 1996 relatif à la nouvelle constitution fédérale. *Feuille fédérale I*, 1–653.

Federal Council. (2001). Message du Conseil fédéral du 28 février 2001 concernant la révision totale de l'organisation judiciaire fédérale. *Feuille fédérale*, 4000–4280.

Federal Council. (2002). Message du Conseil fédéral du 14 novembre 2001 concernant la Réforme de la péréquation financière et de la répartition des tâches entre la Confédération et les cantons (RPT). *Feuille fédérale*, 2155–2414.

Federal Council. (2011). Avis du Conseil fédéral du 30 Septembre 2011 sur la Juridiction constitutionnelle. *Feuille fédérale*, 6995–7000.

Grisel, E. (1996). La garantie des constitutions cantonales: une procédure politique ou une procédure judiciaire? In J.-M. Rapp & M. Jacquard (Eds.), *Le droit en action*. Lausanne: Faculté de droit.

Haller, W. (2016). *The Swiss constitution in a comparative context*. Dike: Zurich/ St Gall.

Hertig Randall, M. (2010). L'internationalisation de la juridiction constitutionnelle: défis et perspectives. *Revue de droit suisse, 129*(2), 221–380.

Lienhard, A., Kettiger, D., Bühler, J., Mérillat, L., & Winkler, D. (2017). The federal supreme court of Switzerland: Judicial balancing of federalism without judicial review. In N. Aroney & J. Kincaid (Eds.), *Courts in federal countries: Federalists or unitarists?* (pp. 404–430). Toronto: University of Toronto Press.

Mahon, P. (2014). *Droit Constitutionnel. Institutions, juridiction constitutionnelle et procédure* (Vol. 1). Bâle: Helbing Lichtenhahn.

Mahon, P., & Schaller, R. (2013a). L'élection des juges entre tradition démocratique et exigences de l'Etat de droit. *Parlament – Parlement – Parlamento, 2*, 1–17.

Mahon, P., & Schaller, R. (2013b). Le système de réélection des juges: évidence démocratique ou épée de Damoclès? *Justice-Justiz-Giustizia, 1*, 1–13.

National Council's Legal Affairs Committee. (2011). Parliamentary initiatives, constitutional jurisdiction: Making the constitution workable for the law enforcement authorities. *Feuille fédérale*, 6707–6724.

Töndury, A. (2004). *Bundesstaatliche Einheit und kantonale Demokratie – Die Gewährleistung der Kantonsverfassungen nach Art. 51 BV*. Zürich: Zürcher Studien zum öffentlichen Recht Bd. 160.

Tophinke, E. (2013). Tribunaux et jurisprudence. In A. Ladner, J.-L. Chappelet, Y. Emery, P. Knoepfel, L. Mader, N. Soguel, & F. Varone (Eds.), *Manuel d'administration publique Suisse* (pp. 267–282). Lausanne: Presses polytechniques et universitaires romandes.

PART III

The Management of Tasks and Services

CHAPTER 9

The New Model of Swiss Public Management

Jean-Loup Chappelet

9.1 Introduction

During the 1980s, the need for academic research and teaching in public administration was fully recognized in Switzerland. The response was the creation of the Swiss Graduate School of Public Administration (IDHEAP) in 1981, interestingly, by the same visionary, Enrico Bignami, who had created a similar institution (the IMEDE, today the International Institute for Management Development or IMD) for the needs of private industry—a sector in which Bignami worked as CEO of Nestlé (Marion 2004).

New public management (NPM) emerged in Switzerland, as in many other countries, in the 1990s. One could even say that Switzerland is one of the main loci, at local, cantonal and federal levels, for experimenting with the many managerial approaches it has inspired (Steiner et al. 2014). The management of Swiss public organizations has evolved considerably under the influence of these new approaches, though not all of these evolutions have been successful (Emery and Giauque 2008).

In 2017, the Swiss Confederation introduced a new management model (known as NMG) to better manage the federal administration and "increase transparency and facilitate steering at all levels" (FFA 2017).

J.-L. Chappelet (✉)
IDHEAP, University of Lausanne, Lausanne, Switzerland
e-mail: jean-loup.chappelet@unil.ch

A. Ladner et al. (eds.), *Swiss Public Administration*, Governance and Public Management,
https://doi.org/10.1007/978-3-319-92381-9_9

The goal is to apply this model to all administrative units at the federal level. It is worth exploring this model better, to understand how it is applied in practice, and to consider whether it can inspire new ways of managing not just at the national but also at the cantonal and local levels, much as when NPM was introduced (and when it seemed ubiquitous). Will the NMG become the "Swiss way of management" in the public sector, to borrow the title of a well-known book about the Swiss private sector (Bergmann 2000)?

To answer this question, we first look at the history of NPM-inspired approaches adopted by the federal government, in particular the GMEB (in German, FLAG) model, a precursor to the NMG. We then describe the peculiarities of the NMG, and in what manner it is "new" compared with other Swiss and foreign approaches. Finally, we examine the case of the Federal Office of Topography, known as swisstopo, an office which was both a pioneer in adopting the GMEB model and one of the first to use the new NMG mode.

9.2 The GMEB Model and NPM-Inspired Approaches

The first applications (and proliferation) of NPM approaches took place in Switzerland at the local and cantonal levels (e.g., see Delley 1994 or Schedler 1995). In 1997, meaning soon thereafter, the Swiss federal government launched the GMEB, the Management by Performance Mandate and Global Budget program. Its focus was on measurable performance in the federal administration, and on results. After a pilot phase, the GMEB was introduced in about 20 administrative units by 2002 (see FFA 2006 for a program overview and list of the units which used this program at the time).

In 2009, the federal government published a generally positive evaluation of this large-scale experiment. This accorded with commitments made to Parliament during the institutionalization of the model, in turn part of the 2004 revision of LOGA, the Government and Administration Organization Act (in German, RVOG) and the LFC, the Federal Finance Act (in German, FHG). Twelve years later, about one-third of the units in the federal administration were using GMEB, including the Federal Office of Sports, the Federal Roads Office, and swisstopo, the Federal Office of Topography. A total of 23 units used GMEB, about one-sixth of the federal administration and accounting for 30% of its expenditures.

GMEB is based on having each administrative unit involved develop a performance mandate specifying the objectives to be achieved by that unit in the coming years, together with the criteria for attaining those objectives. After the Federal Council and Parliament approve the strategic objectives, the performance objectives and the budget, the mandate is entrusted to the administrative unit. It is to be carried out operationally in the form of an annual performance agreement or a service-level agreement.

Figure 9.1 illustrates how the GMEB model is operationalized. It is inspired by the Schedler model (Schedler and Eicher 2013: 380) which summarizes a series of NPM approaches used in Switzerland. It combines political and administrative management by converting political and strategic objectives into administrative objectives geared to the provision of benefits.

This model allows the department to which an administrative unit belongs, and its head (one of the seven Swiss cabinet members who form the Federal Council, the federal executive), to regularly receive the information needed for judging the extent to which stated objectives have been achieved. If necessary, the department can correct the unit's performance. At the end of the mandate, usually after four years, the department reviews the mandate and objectives, together with the administrative unit. Swiss cabinet members in fact are formally the administrative heads of the ten or so units in the department they are responsible for.

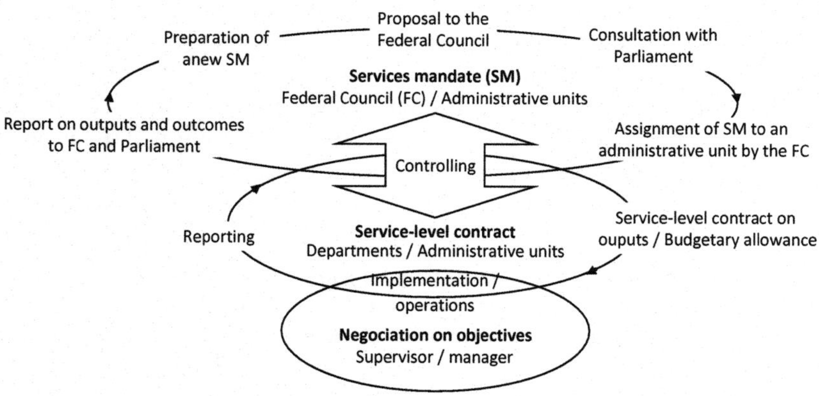

Fig. 9.1 The GMEB model. (Source: www.flag.admin.ch/f/themen/1-3-1modell.php)

The transformation of political into administrative rationality which the GMEB (Fig. 9.1) provided nevertheless reached its limits when it came to performance. The GMEB did not go so far as to evaluate the results achieved; we will examine how well the NMG, in place since 2017 (and presented below), is tackling this task.

According to the GMEB website, the following four principles were put into practice (www.flag.admin.ch/e/themen/1-1-4entstehung.php):

- Separating strategic management from operational management; implementing management tools;
- Transforming resource-based (input) into service-based (output) management;
- Transforming administrative units into service centers which assume greater responsibility for results (they benefit from greater autonomy in their operations);
- Introducing elements of marketplace competition.

A self-assessment conducted in 2009 by the Federal Council (2009: 7152) concluded that units in which the GMEB had been introduced were satisfied and did not want to return to the earlier model. The GMEB allowed them to have a more integrated planning with respect to available resources and tasks, allowing the relevant bodies to carry out controlling.[1] The departments responsible for the administrative units were also satisfied and found the GMEB facilitated political management. A new accounting system for the federal government was introduced the same year. The departments found "there was still significant room for improvement" in linking GMEB managed using the new accounting system.

A substantial majority of parliamentarians were also satisfied, though some (Rey 2005) found the GMEB "strengthens the position of the Federal Council and the national administration at the expense of the sovereignty of Parliament over the budget". To better control expenses, the parliamentar-

[1] According to the Glossary of Terms of Evaluation issued by the Federal Office of Public Health (FOPH) in 2005 (page 5), "Controlling is a central management task which is intended to provide a solid basis of information to assist in decision-making. It guides the entire planning process and management of an organization. It includes the selection, collection, analysis and interpretation of data relevant to the goals and objectives of the organization as well as the procedures put in place to achieve these ends. The analysis takes into account the quantitative and qualitative indicators defined to measure the achievement of the different sets of objectives. 'Controlling' in Switzerland is taken as synonymous with 'performance management'".

ians insisted that the principles of annuity and of specialty[2] in the budget lines should be strictly respected. The socialist group in parliament, however, proposed intensifying the use of the GMEB model, in particular to better take into account outcomes expected beyond the outputs themselves. The self-assessment (Federal Council 2009) noted in particular that, beyond cost efficiency, efficacy and economizing/economy in the federal administration were better taken into account, thanks to the GMEB:

> Setting targets based on efficiency models has a motivating effect on employees because it allows them to better measure the importance of their contribution to their office's performance. Developing an orientation towards results and objectives is an ongoing task in managing staff and administering, beyond the GMEB model:
>
> - Relevance or economy: employees in GMEB units felt they were more aware of costs than those in non-GMEB units. However, a review of resource use showed no significant differences between the units. This is why more attention needs to be paid to the specific indicators used to assess the relevance of objectives;
> - Global budget: the flexibility administrative units have in operational management is one of the major advantages of the GMEB. This room for maneuver is a result of the principle of a global budget itself, as it encourages administrative units to perform their tasks in a cost-efficient manner. A global budget, however, can only fully deploy its effects when it is combined with indicators one can measure.

In this quote, and in the GMEB approach, we find the well-known trio of efficiency, efficacy and economy, the "triangle of management control" (DIRE 2002) which link objectives, resources (or inputs) and services (or outputs, achievements) (see Fig. 9.2).

The GMEB reflects a general trend observed in integrated models of public management at the turn of the century; they link these three peaks/vertices of the management control triangle. Service-oriented and output-oriented models are now widely used in Swiss cantonal administration (*wirkungsorientierte Verwaltung* in German), and they are used abroad. They are very similar to management models in the private sector, except

[2] "Budgetary specialty" is one of the main public finance principles (along with annuity, unity, universality and sincerity). It consists of ensuring that each budget line item has a clear purpose; the executive or the administration cannot modify it without legislative approval.

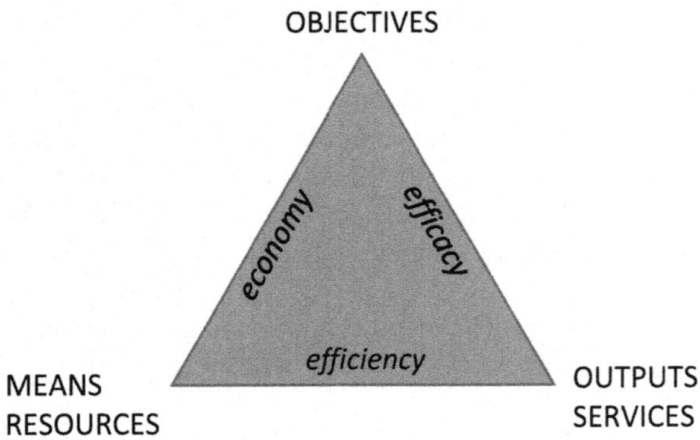

Fig. 9.2 The triangle of performance control

that in private companies, managers do not have to share responsibility with executives and legislators, or even with citizens (see the "Public Management Tetrahedron" (Chappelet 2013) which links the four sides of this solid to the four main stakeholders of public management: public managers, executives, MPs, citizens).

The GMEB five main characteristics can be summarized as follows:

- An orientation toward the tasks and services to be performed in an efficacious manner by the administration
- The coordination of tasks and means or resources (through budgets)
- Global budgets to give more autonomy and responsibility to administrative units in carrying out their objectives-based tasks
- The assignment of performance mandates by the administration
- Performance measurement through management control and evaluation

Following the self-assessment of the GMEB in 2009, Parliament agreed with the Federal Council in 2010 that the GMEB model should be used in the entire federal administration. It would be recast as a new model more focused on results and performance, and be better linked to globally allocated financial means or resources. "From this perspective, planning and reporting will be redefined from the ground up to conform to an integrated, results-based approach. Financial means (resources) and performance will be brought together in a visible manner, with global appropriations for the particular domain of the administration. The political leadership will focus more on medium-term objectives; the annual budget will remain the decisive financial benchmark" (Federal Council 2013a).

9.3 The New NMG Model

Following the introduction of a new model for accounting at the national level, it was felt necessary to improve budgetary management by reorienting it not just to deliver services and assess efficiency and efficacy but to provide services or benefits according to the political objectives to be achieved. In other words, the idea was to engage in performance-oriented budgeting (and auditing) in the manner increasingly practiced in private companies. This approach, called the new management model for the Federal Administration (in French NMG and in German, *Neues Führungsmodell für die Bundesverwaltung* or NFB), was introduced in 2017.

It is based on the GMEB and augments the scope of the performance contract and of the traditional budget by adding a PITF, an Integrated Task and Financing Plan. This is a new way of presenting the budget of a given unit according to groups of services that the administrative unit provides or produces, along with a global budget for each group of services. It also states the political objectives to be achieved, as well as the indicators and target values for the next four years. A department and the administrative units that comprise it then agree on a performance contract. This contract sets out the operational objectives for projects, defines the groups of services to be provided or produced (in principal, from one to maximum of five), and these are accompanied by two global budgets, one for outlays, the other for income.

In other words, the strategic/political aspect of the services provided is included in the budget through a PITF—which allows for better control by Parliament—while the operational aspect is included in the annual performance contract agreed upon between a given unit and its department—which allows for better control by the (political) head of the department. Under the GMEB, the performance mandate combined information about political and operational steering; the NMG separates them better.

The NMG approach is based on five documents or instruments (Federal Council 2013b):

- At the beginning of a parliamentary term, the Federal Council sets priorities for the next decade or so. In light of this proposed political program, the legislature, which is elected for a five-year term, establishes a financial plan, paying particular attention to the foreseeable budgetary expenditures in doing so.
- The annual federal budget includes a PITF for each administrative unit. It describes the ongoing multi-year projects, along with their objectives and target values, and identifies the groups which will benefit. This document is submitted to Parliament, which may amend it following to the rules given in the Parliament Act or in the Finance Act.
- A performance contract is drawn up for each administrative unit. It is the result of the agreement reached annually between the head of the department (who sets policy) and the head of the unit (who lays out the administrative guidelines). It also establishes the annual objectives to achieve relative to the service groups, and it discusses the projects mentioned in the PITF.
- Global budgets and the rules which make it possible to build reserves and/or transfer credits from one group which benefits to another (as in the GMEB).
- An analysis of accounting practices in the federal administration to ensure that the costs of the services are known; this makes it possible to control expenditures.

Figure 9.3 summarizes the relationship between these different NMG management and planning instruments (FFA 2017: 2). The NMG insists that operational tasks be politically steered through the annual budgetary process.

> As a basis, the NMG needs a catalog of the services provided by all administrative units. The achievements can be described on the basis of quantity, quality, timeliness, cost, or how satisfied the recipients of a service are. Each administrative unit should identify one to five groups it serves; the federal administration thus will have about 140 such groups in all. This level of detail is to ensure that political actors will not get lost in too long lists of articles and services, and to ensure that administrative managers can still recognize their activities and effectively implement the directives of the political actors. (Federal Council 2013b)

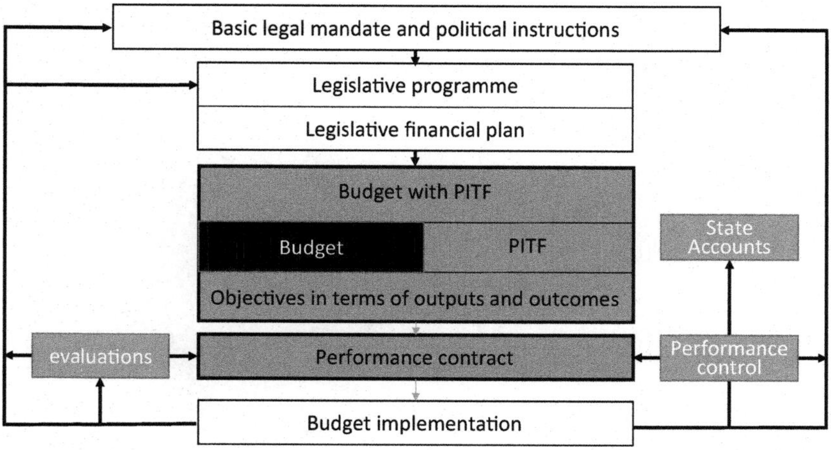

Fig. 9.3 Relationship between NMG management and planning instruments

Introducing the NMG was an objective of the legislative session of 2011–15. To facilitate its implementation in 2016–17, the Federal Finance Administration (FFA) made online training available, based on what was learned from introducing PITFs or global budgets at the cantonal level in the Aargau, Bern, Graubünden, Lucerne, Solothurn, Zug and Zurich.

The NMG model should make it possible to abandon the running of two systems in parallel (the new GMEB in 20 units and the old/traditional system in all the other units) and create an identical, homogeneous management model throughout the federal administration. It should improve the units' room for maneuver and improve transparency. In terms of savings, under certain conditions, the units will be authorized to accumulate financial reserves, as in the GMEB model. Ultimately, this will be a shift from a management culture based on resources (e.g., GMEB) to a culture based on goals and results (e.g., NMG).

This evolution can be schematically represented by a "performance diamond" (see Fig. 9.4) where two new dimensions of performance appear: effectiveness and allocative efficiency.

Effectiveness, which is to say the relationship between services and outcomes, measures the real effects, or the results a public policy actually has on the societal problem to be solved (Pollitt and Bouckaert 2004: 17). Allocative efficiency, which is to say the ratio between inputs and outcomes (Knoepfel et al. 2006: 256), is about optimally allocating means or

Fig. 9.4 The public performance diamond

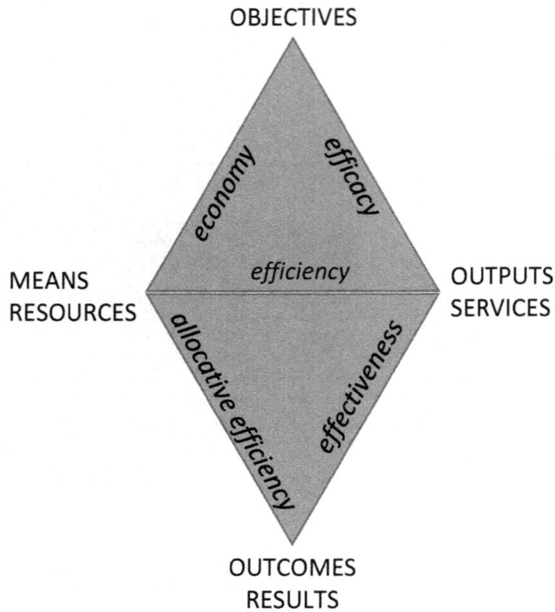

resources to obtain desired results. Efficiency (sometimes called "technical efficiency" or "productive efficiency"), by contrast, focuses on the unit cost of services (if possible, kept as low as possible). The diamond represents the two dimensions of public performance: output management (top triangle) and outcome management (bottom triangle).

The NMG model is the apex of a number of reforms (NGP, NPM) introduced at the federal level since the late 1990s to better monitor administrative objectives, performance and outcomes. At the beginning of the twenty-first century, and after LOGA was adopted in 2004, the GMEB model was a first step in this direction, tried in a few federal units.

Other changes were also taking place at about the same time. A "debt brake"[3] was enacted. A new model of accounting introduced in 2009 transformed the management of the federal budget management. IT management, as part of an evolving technology, has also been profoundly

[3] The debt brake is a budgetary device intended to guarantee balanced accounts over a complete business cycle. Adopted in 2000 in Switzerland at the national level and implemented as of 2003, it serves as a model for Germany as of 2009. It aims to curb the growth in debt as well as curb structural budget deficits.

changed. Finally, by abolishing the status of federal civil servant and introducing salary elements related to benefits, the formal status of federal employees has also been altered (see the chapter by Yves Emery).

The efficiency and efficacy objectives highlighted in GMEB have also been pursued through reforms such as clearly separating federal from cantonal tasks, or by transferring federal tasks to private sector companies or more autonomous para-public agencies. The result-oriented NMG model should allow greater progress to be made in managing the federal "household". Since 1999, Art. 170 of the Swiss Constitution has called on the Parliament "to ensure that federal measures are evaluated with regard to their effectiveness".

9.4 The Case of Swisstopo

The Swiss Federal Office of Topography (swisstopo) is responsible for the description, representation and long-term availability of spatial geodata, including national maps, altitude and landscape models, satellite images and orthophotos[4] of the Swiss territory. Swisstopo is a unit (office) of the Federal Department of Defense, Population Protection and Sports (DDPS). It was selected as a pilot project office for trying out the GMEB model when it was first launched in 1997. In 2017, it was also one of the first federal offices to use NMG.

As compared to the GMEB, the application of the NMG in swisstopo introduces new elements. It comments on contextual factors and the results to be achieved globally (e.g., to guarantee the provision of Swiss geodata), provides indicators with deadlines, has a section on the strategy and important projects conducted by swisstopo and provides a new level of detail about services, staff and IT. The part of the 2018 Swiss national budget relevant to swisstopo, which includes a PITF, begins with a list of current projects. It then provides an "overview of the profit and loss statement and of the investment account (including benefit entitlements)" for 2016 and 2017, together with the budget for 2018 and financial plan projections for 2019–21, accompanied by a commentary (FFA n.d.). Swisstopo sells various services and thus has significant income (more than 23 million CHF in 2017, with costs of nearly 90 million), though investments have been very low in 2017.

[4] An orthophoto is an aerial digital image, in color, of a landscape taken so as to neutralize the influences of camera inclination and terrain relief.

A number of pages in the budget are dedicated to the groups of services (outputs) which are produced by swisstopo. For 2018, as in 2017, swisstopo lists three groups of services:

1. Topography and cartography
2. Measurement and geo-coordination
3. National Geological Service

A page in the PIFT describes each of these, giving the basic mandate along with comments relevant to the group of services. It is followed by a commented table of operating and investment income and expenses, a table of objectives (broken down by services) with the criteria to be achieved, accompanied by contextual information with financial figures. Figure 9.5, as an example, gives all the objectives set in the 2018 PIFT, including information about criteria and performance by unit of measurement for the first group of services (topography and cartography).

The PIFT document concludes with the items relevant to the federal budget, namely income and expenditure. These are explained and compared to the previous three years. Projections for the 2018–21 period are also provided, which allows for planning over four years. In the depart-

OBJECTIFS

	C 2016	B 2017	B 2018	PF 2019	PF 2020	PF 2021
Mensuration nationale topographique: les données sont régulièrement mises à jour et adaptées aux nouveaux besoins des utilisateurs						
- Orthophotos: surface de la Suisse mesurée par an (%, min.)	34	30	30	30	30	30
- Modèles altimétriques: surface de la Suisse mesurée par an (%, min.)	19	15	15	15	15	15
- Modèle topographique du paysage: surface de la Suisse mesurée par an (%, min.)	21	15	15	15	15	15
- Élaboration d'un modèle de surface de l'ensemble du périmètre (%)	-	22	34	44	57	67
Mensuration nationale cartographique: les données sont régulièrement mises à jour et la production est convertie à la forme numérique						
- Cartes nationales: surface de la Suisse mesurée (%, min.)	18	15	15	15	15	15
- Mise en œuvre du modèle cartographique numérique MCN 1:25 000: surface de la Suisse numérisée par an (%, min.)	34	49	66	83	100	-
Satisfaction de la clientèle: les clients considèrent que ces prestations sont de très bonne qualité						
- Satisfaction des clients en termes d'offre/de qualité (échelle 1 à 5)	-	-	-	4,15	-	-

INFORMATIONS CONTEXTUELLES

	2011	2012	2013	2014	2015	2016
Géodonnées livrées (nombre)	3 125	3 325	3 837	4 309	4 148	3 560
Mégapixels fournis par l'infrastructure fédérale de données géographiques (nombre, mio)	86,600	162,000	225,400	321,500	329,600	509,400
Impressions PDF sur la base des services de l'IFGD (nombre, mio)	1,294	1,602	1,879	2,238	2,531	3,393
Cartes imprimées vendues (nombre, milliers)	698	581	603	513	408	494
Satisfaction de la clientèle (échelle 1 à 5)	-	-	-	-	4,14	-

(C = accounts, B = budget, PF = financial plan)

Fig. 9.5 Swisstopo group of services 1: objectives and contextual data. (C = accounts, B = budget, PF = financial plan)

ment of defense—where swisstopo was formally placed—performance contracts remain on an annual basis. As swisstopo makes specific products or services (such as maps, models or orthophotos) available, these products or services can be more readily quantified and enumerated for the purposes of the budgetary process. A qualitative indicator (customer satisfaction) is also measured.

The financial data come from SAP accounting software. Reporting is done annually, as part of the federal budgeting process, and quarterly within the department. Parliamentary committees (Finance Committee, Management Committee, and the specialized Committee, which in the case of swisstopo is the Committee on Education, Science and Culture) provide political guidance. Meeting—or not meeting—the stated objectives do not (yet) carry the practical consequences as in other countries where incentives are offered—or sanctions levied—in case the stated criteria are exceeded—or not met.

The NMG model emerged from the strong desire to better link the federal budget with the services or benefits provided and with the final results obtained by the administrative units. Output needed to be linked to outcome. It is reminiscent of the objectives set out in the 2001 French constitutional bylaw on budget acts (known as LOLF) which wanted to modernize the management of the French administration and set quantified objectives for the various ministries. The goal was to move from a budget based on resources to a public administration managed based on results, even if this goal was difficult to achieve (Rochet 2010; Petitbon and Ledenvic 2011).

9.5 Conclusion

This chapter has looked at the NMG model in the Swiss federal administration, from its origins to its introduction across all federal-level administrative units in 2017, including in swisstopo. Beyond the public services to be provided, the NMG emphasizes the results to be achieved. This emphasis is both operational and political (or strategic), and stands in relation to the main mode of governmental action, namely its budget. That budget also determines the number of posts which can be funded to achieve the stated objectives, both through services and by specifying expected results.

In addition to the classic criteria of efficiency, efficacy and economy, an analysis of the NMG indicates the importance of effectiveness and allocative efficiency (see Fig. 9.4), aspects which should more often be taken into account by managers in public administration positions.

Though it is not wholly original, the NMG has the merit of being implemented on a large scale throughout the entire Swiss federal administration. It is a practical way of combining operational management with strategic or political management. The former is the responsibility of managers in the public administrative units as well as of the heads of their departments—who in Switzerland form the federal executive. The latter is provided by Parliament, and, at times, also by the people through the referendums and initiatives they can launch. The exception here is finances: this remains the responsibility of Parliament, whose power and oversight is now reinforced through PITFs. We therefore have a new and genuinely "Swiss Way of Public Management" (at least at the federal level), and how it will be implemented, given recent changes to the system of national public administration, will be followed with interest in the years to come.

References

Bergmann, A. (2000). *Swiss way of management ou les évidences cachées des entreprises suisses*. Paris: ESKA.

Chappelet, J.-L. (2013). Le tétraèdre du management public. In A. Ladner, J.-L. Chappelet, Y. Emery, P. Knoepfel, L. Mader, N. Soguel, & F. Varone (Eds.), *Manuel d'administration publique suisse* (pp. 321–344). Lausanne: PPUR.

Delley, J.-D. (1994). *Quand l'esprit d'entreprise vient à l'Etat, pour une réforme du service public*. Lausanne: Domaine public.

DIRE. (2002). *Le contrôle de gestion dans les administrations de l'Etat, éléments de méthodologie*. Paris: Délégation interministérielle à la réforme de l'Etat.

Emery, Y., & Giauque, D. (2008). *Repenser la gestion publique: bilan et perspectives en Suisse*. Lausanne: PPUR.

Federal Council. (2009). Rapport sur la gestion par mandat de prestations et enveloppe budgétaire – Evaluation et suite de la procédure (Rapport d'évaluation GMEB 2009). *Message du Conseil fédéral au Parlement*, Bern.

Federal Council. (2013a). *Federal council press release of 20 November 2013*, Retrieved from www.efd.admin.ch/efd/en/home/dokumentation/nsb-news_list.msg-id-51039.html. Accessed 22 Nov 2017.

Federal Council. (2013b). *Documentation de base: le nouveau modèle de gestion de l'administration fédérale (NMG)*. Bern: Federal Council.

FFA (Federal Finance Administration). (2006). *Les bons chemins réduisent les distances*. Berne: Programme GMEB, Federal Finance Administration.

FFA. (2017). *Nouveau modèle de gestion NGM*. www.efd.admin.ch/efd/fr/home/themen/finanzpolitik/nouveau-modele-de-gestion-de-ladministration-federale--nmg-/fb-neues_fuehrungsmodell_bv.html. Accessed 30 Sept 2017.

FFA. (n.d.). *Budget 2018 avec plan intégré de taches et des finances 2018–2021 des unités administratives A+T, DFAE, DFI, DFJP, DDPS* (Vol. 2A, pp. 335–342).

Knoepfel, P., Larrue, C., & Varone, F. (2006). *Analyse et pilotage des politiques publiques.* Zürich: Ruegger Verlag.

Marion, G. (2004). Bignami, Enrico. *Dictionnaire historique de la Suisse.* Bern.

Petitbon, F., & Ledenvic, P. (2011). *Manager public: vos solutions au quotidien.* Paris: Editions d'organisation.

Pollitt, C., & Bouckaert, G. (2004). *Public management reform.* Oxford: Oxford University Press.

Rey, J.-N. (2005). Bulletin officiel – Parlement CH, Conseil national, Session de printemps 2005 Quatorzième séance, 16 Mars 2005. Retrieved from www.parlament.ch/fr/ratsbetrieb/amtliches-bulletin/amtliches-bulletin-die-verhandlungen?SubjectId=8576

Rochet, C. (2010). *Politiques publiques: de la stratégie aux résultats.* Bruxelles: DeBoeck.

Schedler, K. (1995). *Ansätze einer wirkungsorientierten Verwaltungsführung.* Bern: Haupt.

Schedler, K., & Eicher, A. (2013). Rapport entre l'administration et politique. In A. Ladner, J.-L. Chappelet, Y. Emery, P. Knoepfel, L. Mader, N. Soguel, & F. Varone (Eds.), *Manuel d'administration publique suisse* (pp. 369–385). Lausanne: PPUR.

Steiner, R., Ladner, A., & Reist, P. (Eds.). (2014). *Reformen in Kantonen und Gemeinden.* Bern: Haupt.

CHAPTER 10

The Road to Digital and Smart Government in Switzerland

Tobias Mettler

10.1 The Beginnings of E-government in Switzerland

With the advent of the Internet, low-priced computing devices, and the increasing availability of broadband access in offices and households in the late 1990s, governments all over the world started to discuss how to harness information and communication technology (ICT) to enhance governmental operations and transform public services, and thus their relationship to citizens and businesses. Emulating the preceding radical revolution in banking and commerce, which led to an 'e-everything' phenomenon across all sectors of the economy (Cronin 2000), the new catchword 'e-government' emerged at the turn of the millennium to characterize the onset of digitalizing governments, as well as to describe a new mindset of technology-inspired, forward-looking, and entrepreneurial civil servants.

At about this time, the European Commission (EC) set out the *Lisbon Strategy 2000*—later succeeded by the *Europe 2020* strategy in 2010—which formulated the first strategic objectives related to the use of

T. Mettler (✉)
IDHEAP, University of Lausanne, Lausanne, Switzerland
e-mail: tobias.mettler@unil.ch

A. Ladner et al. (eds.), *Swiss Public Administration*, Governance and Public Management,
https://doi.org/10.1007/978-3-319-92381-9_10

innovation in general and ICT in particular for boosting economic progress throughout Europe. This strategic memorandum also paved the way for more detailed e-government action plans—known under different designations over the years, such as the eEurope (Europe Commission 2001), i2010 (Europe Commission 2006), or simply the e-government action plan—the first of which was published only a year later (see Fig. 10.1).

Though not a member of the European Union (EU), the Swiss government's strategic objectives related to e-government have been very much aligned with the EC's strategy. As it was confronted with rapid technological and societal changes at the end of the millennium, the Swiss Federal Council launched a working group in 1997. The goal was to devise a strategic plan and establish priorities with respect to the emerging information society, as well as reallocate the responsibilities for overseeing and coordinating ICT efforts at the federal level.

Based on these working group discussions, the Federal Council mandated a complete reorganization of federal ICT efforts, which led to establishing a new federal steering unit (FITSU)[1] in 1999. It was responsible for overall ICT program management, and a first federal ICT strategy was set out in 2000. This strategy included preparing two 'lighthouse' projects, an online platform for citizens and businesses known as a 'virtual counter', which went live in 2005,[2] and a multi-site 'e-voting' project. The latter was set up in 2003 in the cantons of Geneva, Neuchâtel, and Zurich to experiment and obtain experience with electronic voting systems, though access to it was limited to Swiss expatriates.

FITSU launched two additional initiatives in 2002. The first was meant to increase interoperability and foster collaboration between the Confederation, the cantons, and the communities. To this end, the non-profit eCH association[3] was founded. Consisting of volunteers from all levels of government, industry, and academia, organized in dedicated chapters or sections, and run on a militia basis—a principle and notion firmly rooted in Swiss identity and mentality—eCH defines technical and non-technical standards and promulgates exemplary process models as well as data to make the implementation of e-government services easier. The second, the *eVanti* project (Didisheim and Belle 2004) (from the

[1] Swiss Confederation, Federal IT Steering Unit, https://www.isb.admin.ch/isb/en/home.html

[2] Swiss Confederation, https://www.ch.ch/en/

[3] eCH Association, https://www.ech.ch

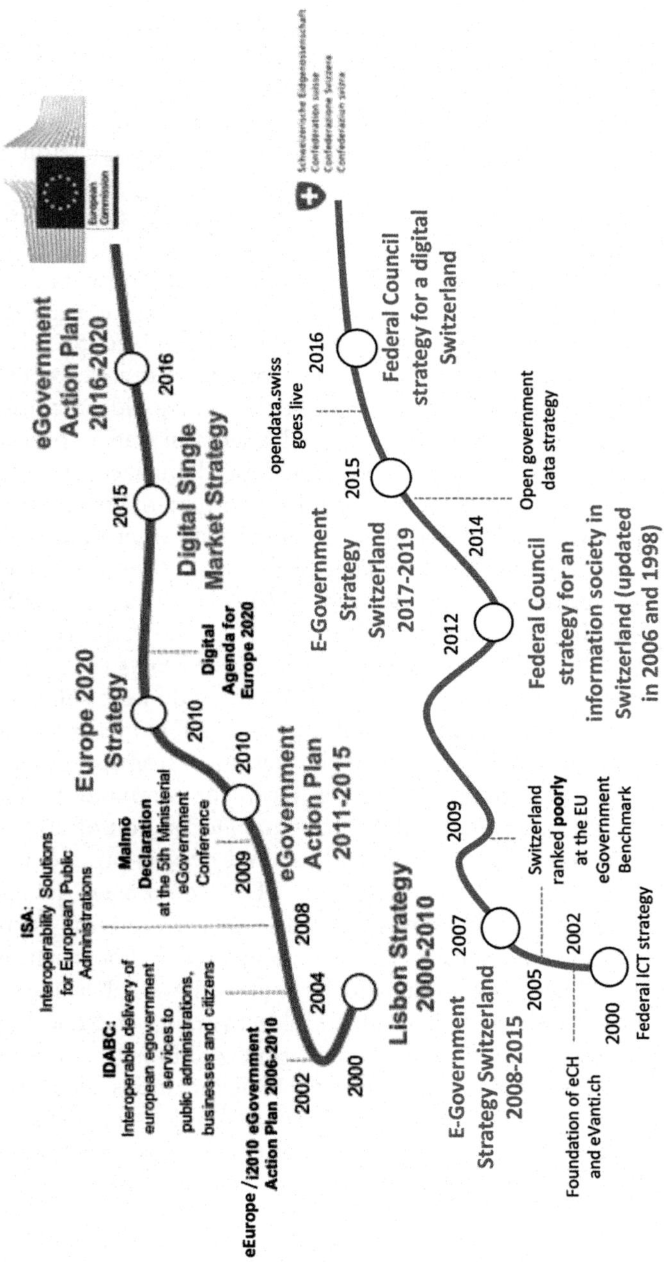

Fig. 10.1 A brief history of e-government in the EU and Switzerland

Italian word "avanti", meaning "forward") sought to create a common platform for information exchange between stakeholders, to increase the visibility of successful e-government projects, and to measure how far along existing digital services were. This effort bore some similarity to the *Good practice framework for e-government* (European Commission 2007) established in 2002 by the EC.

Despite these early efforts and an above-average broadband Internet availability, Switzerland ranked at the bottom of the list of countries assessed in the 2005 EU e-government benchmark. This low ranking led to a reconsideration of strategic objectives several years later and led to crafting a new *E-government Strategy Switzerland 2007–2015*. This strategy had three goals: first, the most important administrative procedures between businesses and the authorities henceforth should be conducted electronically; second, frequent or complex administrative procedures between citizens and the authorities should be digitalized as well; and lastly, all governmental authorities should modernize their business processes and deal with each other using contemporary electronic channels. To advance the last of these, the Federal Council created a framework agreement on e-government cooperation in 2008 (Federal Council 2007), which clarified the financing, organization, tasks, and responsibilities of the different bodies within the Swiss e-government ecosystem.

While the Swiss authorities at the end of the decade were still occupied with projects such as GEschäftsVERwaltung (GEVER),[4] meant to re-engineer internal processes and managing the transition from paper-based to electronic styles of working, the EU e-government community—inspired by the targets defined at the Malmö Ministerial Declaration of 2009—had shifted its focus toward a more citizen-centered design, production, and delivery of online services. Accordingly, the EU *e-Government Action Plan (2011–2015)* (European Commission 2010) emphasized the increased mobility of citizens and their need for empowerment. For instance, the accessibility of public information could be improved by establishing a more user-friendly service delivery through social networking and collaborative tools. Open standards and a service-orientation could further improve the interoperability of existing services and initiate deliberations about the necessary legal and technical preconditions for cross-border services.

Yet because the country neglected to emphasize the central place of the citizen, along with the inward-looking orientation of Swiss governmental

[4] Federal Chancellery, "GEVER", https://www.bk.admin.ch/bk/de/home/dokumentation/gever-bund.html

authorities, the Swiss e-government community was dealt a fresh shock in 2009, when Switzerland was again ranked at the bottom end in the EU e-government benchmark.

10.2 The Transition Years: From E-government to Digital Government

Confronted with yet another poor ranking in the EU's e-government benchmark, and given that the last major strategy update had been in 2006, the Swiss Federal Council realized that it needed to engage in a major revision and recalibrate its strategic objectives. The updated *Strategy of the Federal Council for an Information Society* published in early 2012 (Federal Council 2012) included several new areas of activity under sub-headings such as Internet governance, high-performance computing, open networks, and the role of ICT as a tool for optimizing energy and resource efficiency.

Three new initiatives were also launched. As a result of an Internet Corporation for Assigned Names and Numbers' decision to abolish most restrictions on the names of generic top-level domains, the first initiative dealt with developing appropriate instruments to preserve Switzerland's public interest in view of the imminent liberalization of the domain name market. On account of the missing citizen-centricity in the previous years, a second priority initiative was to improve and extend barrier-free and equal opportunity access to online information as well as to improve the communications services and transactions of and with the government and the federal administration. The third initiative aimed to enhance the range and availability of statistical data in order to be able to compare the attractiveness of Switzerland with other countries.

As part of this third initiative, the Federal Council devised an open government data (OGD) strategy in 2014, one of whose goals was to increase the availability and reuse of, as well as the access to, public data in machine-readable and open formats. A further goal was to establish an open-data culture in the federal civil service through free, uniform, and understandable terms of use (standardization) and by providing additional information about individual data sets (metadata).

To realize this objective, the Federal Council envisaged building a central infrastructure to replace the pilot portal *opendata.admin.ch*, which had never been fully operational. It was a major milestone for the Swiss

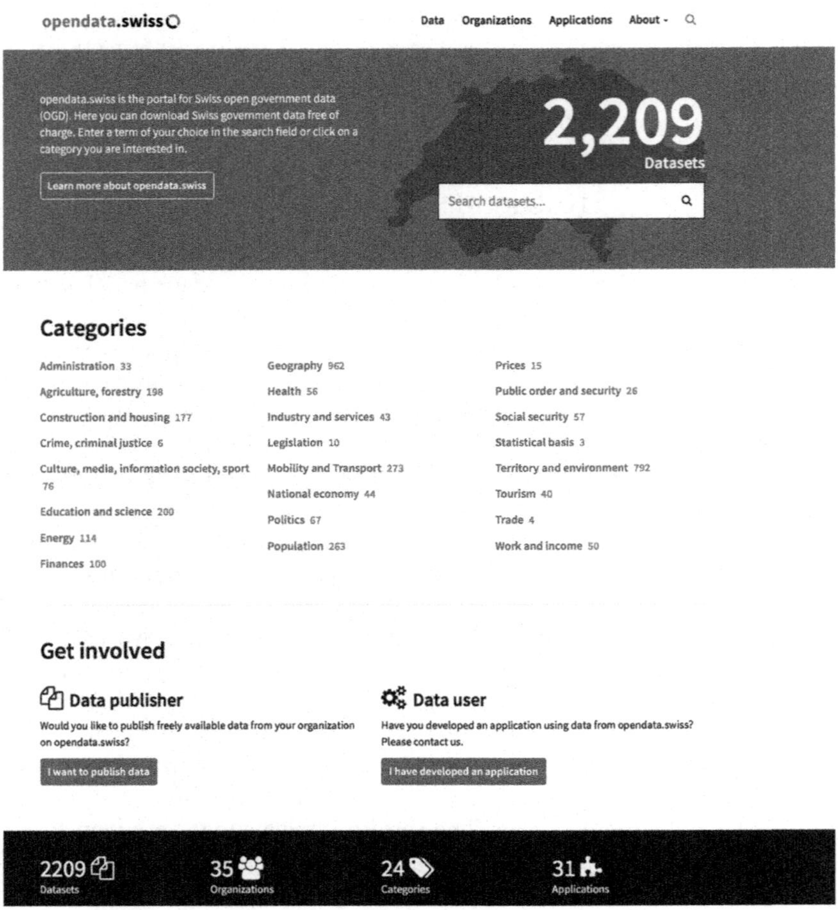

Fig. 10.2 Opendata.swiss—Switzerland's open government data portal

e-government community when the new OGD portal *opendata.swiss* was launched on February 2016. It held about 500 unique datasets originating from 17 different public organizations, including the Swiss Federal Railways and the Federal Roads Office, and it covers a wide range of topics in the Swiss public sector (see Fig. 10.2). It is hosted and maintained by the Swiss Federal Archive[5].

[5] Swiss Federal Archive, https://opendata.swiss/

10.3 The Vision for a New Digital Switzerland

In many ways, 2015 marked an important turning point for the European e-government community. Jean-Claude Junker's election as President of the EC in late 2014 ushered in a new orientation to, and prioritization of, digital initiatives. The previous *Europe 2020* strategy had focused strongly on the transition to a digital society; the new *Digital Single Market Strategy* envisioned establishing a business-friendly environment for the European economy with the goal of fostering innovation and creating hundreds of new jobs in the technology and service sector. There are plans to emend the rules for online cross-border sales, improve cross-border parcel delivery, abolish geo-blocking, reform European copyright law, review the rules for audiovisual media, assess the role of big corporate online platforms, define priorities for e-government standards and interoperability, and to address issues of ownership, usability, and access to large data collections (European Commission 2015).

In keeping with this shift in European e-government priorities, there is now a new *Federal Council strategy for a digital Switzerland* (Federal Office of Communictions 2016) and a redefined Swiss *e-Government Strategy 2017–2019* (Swiss Confederation 2016).

The goals of the Federal Council's new strategy include the following:

- Improving the general conditions of Switzerland's digital economy and monitoring developments, anticipating challenges and addressing regulatory issues related to the sharing economy
- Defining coherent and future-oriented national data policies and further developing the national data infrastructure based on the existing OGD platform
- Extending access to high-speed broadband to all Swiss municipalities by 2020
- Increasing the use of innovative technology to reduce energy consumption and CO_2 emissions as well as enhancing the attractiveness of domestic online trade
- Ensuring multiple uses of different solutions and implementing a secure digital identity to create seamless interactions with civil society and the private sector

- Introducing electronic patient files to improve both quality and efficiency in health care, facilitating health reforms, and enhancing information exchange with European health organizations
- Expanding the use of ICT for democratic decision-making and opinion-formation
- Increasing the availability of new opportunities for education and training as well as intensifying Switzerland's role in research and innovation related to the digital society and the digital economy
- Establishing digital cultural production and providing universal access to cultural heritage facilitated by the Internet

As before, and in keeping with the Federal Council's strategy and with the strategic objective to support the innovative potential of the Swiss economy, as well as strengthen standardization and the economic viability of governmental digital initiatives, the Swiss e-Government Strategy 2017–2019 also identified a number of 'lighthouse' projects[6] that are meant to have a short-term impact and pave the way for a new digital Switzerland. The Swiss Confederation, cantons, and communities agree to collaborate on realizing the following goals and projects:

- A joint organization to be established by 2018 for procuring, operating, and maintaining e-government solutions
- Having a seamless electronic change of residence registration system throughout Switzerland by the end of 2018
- Establishing a uniform registration procedure for e-government services on various government portals by 2019
- Integrating the ten electronic public services most frequently requested by the general public and by businesses into the national e-government portals by the end of 2019
- Introducing an electronic identity (eID) that is valid nationally and internationally, as well as assigning data to a specific person as part of the electronic exchange between information systems to be established by 2019
- Developing an electronic transmission procedure for reporting value added tax (VAT), to be effective by 2019
- Extending electronic voting to more voters, with the aim of seeing two-thirds of the cantons use electronic voting by 2019

[6] Swiss Confederation, "Strategic projects and services", https://www.egovernment.ch/en/umsetzung/schwerpunktplan/

10.4 The Path Yet to Go to Create a Smart Government…

Aside from the actions coordinated from the top that have been noted, there are many promising bottom-up developments at the local and cantonal levels, including hospitals or universities that have experimented with new service delivery models facilitated by the Internet of Things (IoT) (Wortmann and Flüchter 2015). These 'smart government initiatives' use emerging technologies such as sensor-based systems or artificial intelligence in conjunction with various social innovation strategies. The goal is to improve a public authority's understanding of its community and constituency in order to enhance the accuracy of their decision-making and response efficiency, not at least in case there are unexpected or seriously adverse events (Gil-Garcia et al. 2014). In doing so, physical components and devices (e.g. intelligent energy controllers, parking lot systems, web cams, motion sensors) are connected with extant public digital platforms and private infrastructures, creating unprecedented ways for both passive and active interaction between a public administration and citizens (see Fig. 10.3).

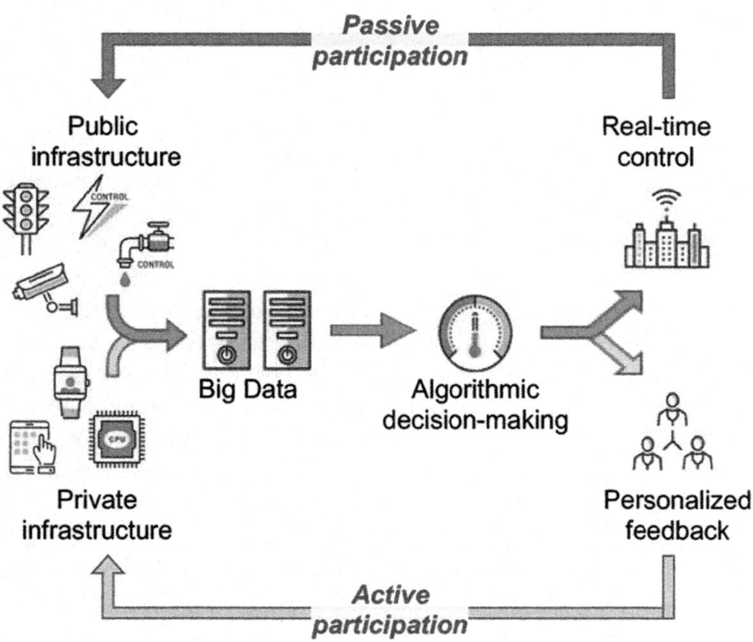

Fig. 10.3 Smart government lifecycle Guenduez et al. (2017)

Thus, the city of Lausanne is developing a centralized management system that is able to control all 14,000 of its street lights. The city of St. Gallen has recently implemented several smart appliances, including intelligent power-charging stations which can inform electric car owners where to find free spots for charging their batteries in the city or sensor-based waste containers that can notify citizens and municipal garbage collectors alike about how full the containers currently are. Based on combining sensor data with open data, the city of Zurich has introduced online services and mobile apps such as *AirCHeck* (which issues real-time information about the city's air quality) and *ParkenDD* (which shows where the free parking spaces are in the city). Given that smart appliances and services frequently raise privacy concerns, at Lausanne's Swiss Graduate School of Public Administration (IDHEAP) we are also experimenting with privacy-aware alternatives to 24 × 7 monitoring, including in the search and rescue of people with disabilities[7].

Such examples are only the first steps toward smarter governance, sustainability, and increased citizen experience. But there is still a long way to go until smart government projects can create value beyond the local habitat which nurtured them.

10.5 Conclusion

Digital initiatives in Switzerland involve various stakeholders at different government levels, but unlike countries which are ruled from the center, Switzerland's approach to digitalization has required finding political consensus. That has both advantages and disadvantages.

On the one hand, important top-down decisions concerning the basic direction and prioritization of digitalization endeavors are more broadly supported in this consensus-oriented polity, resulting in targeted and collaborative efforts among and across different levels of government. Moreover, positive and dynamic change has resulted from bottom-up initiatives driven by local communities, cities, non-profit organizations, and businesses. This combined approach—coordinated political and policy actions together with grassroots movements—is characteristic of Switzerland and is a continual driver of innovation as well as modernization.

On the other hand, Switzerland's decentral form of governance significantly increases the complexity of the country's digital transformation and

[7] T. Mettler, "iCare Research project website", http://unil.ch/icare/

ultimately negatively influences the pace at which emerging technologies are introduced. To a certain extent, it also means tolerating inefficiencies, as when various rival systems co-exist. In this context, the Swiss e-government community needs to find more efficient and effective ways of overcoming issues concerning legal and organizational boundaries. Suitable ways to align top-down and bottom-up initiatives or competing innovation strategies will also need to be developed.

From an international perspective, it would be nice to see a more layered, contextual monitoring and benchmarking of technological, political, economic, and social aspects of the country's digital transformation. Many attempts to somehow 'quantify' the effects of digitalization favor centralist countries, often disregarding the inequalities or ignoring the 'digital divide', which separates regions, urban from rural areas, differing cultures, or population segments in the country. In this regard, Switzerland is an interesting case, as digitalization is promoted both centrally and locally, yet with a view to balance needs, power, and responsibilities among the many distinct actors in Swiss society.

References

Cronin, M. J. (2000). *Unchained value: The new logic of digital business.* Boston: Harvard Business School Press.

Didisheim, J.-J. & Belle, L. (2004). *eVanti.ch – eine Initiative zur Förderung des eGovernments.* http://www.visit.isb.admin.ch/2004/programm/referate/07_didisheim_belle.pdf

European Commission. (2001). *eEurope 2002.* http://eur-lex.europa.eu/legal-content/EN/TXT/?uri=uriserv:l24226a. Accessed 26 Mar 2018.

European Commission. (2006). *i2010 eGovernment Action Plan.* http://eur-lex.europa.eu/legal-content/EN/TXT/?uri=URISERV%3Al24226j. Accessed 26 Mar 2018.

European Commission. (2007). *Good practice framework for eGovernment – Final report.* https://bookshop.europa.eu/en/good-practice-framework-for-egovernment-pbKK0414484/

European Commission. (2010). *European eGovernment action plan 2011–2015.* http://eur-lex.europa.eu/legal-content/EN/TXT/?uri=CELEX%3A52010DC0743

European Commission. (2015). *A digital single market strategy for Europe.* http://eur-lex.europa.eu/legal-content/EN/TXT/?qid=1447773803386&uri=CELEX%3A52015DC0192

Federal Council. (2007). *Framework agreement under public law on e-government cooperation in Switzerland.* https://www.admin.ch/opc/de/federal-gazette/2008/3391.pdf
Federal Council. (2012). *Federal strategy for Switzerland's digital future.* https://www.admin.ch/gov/en/start/dokumentation/medienmitteilungen.msg-id-43694.html
Federal Office of Communictions. (2016). *Federal council strategy for a digital Switzerland.* https://www.bakom.admin.ch/bakom/en/homepage/digital-switzerland-and-internet/strategie-digitale-schweiz/strategy.html
Gil-Garcia, J. R., Helbig, N., & Ojo, A. (2014). Being smart: Emerging technologies and innovation in the public sector. *Government Information Quarterly, 31,* I1–I8.
Guenduez, A. A., Mettler, T., & Schedler, K. (2017). Smart Government – Partizipation und Empowerment der Bürger im Zeitalter von Big Data und personalisierter Algorithmen. *HMD – Praxis der Wirtschaftsinformatik, 54,* 477–487.
Swiss Confederation. (2016). *eGovernment Strategy 2017–2019.* https://www.egovernment.ch/de/umsetzung/schwerpunktplan1
Wortmann, F., & Flüchter, K. (2015). Internet of things: Technology and value added. *Business & Information Systems Engineering, 57*(3), 221–224.

CHAPTER 11

Public-Private Partnerships: A Swiss Perspective

Laure Athias, Moudo Macina, and Pascal Wicht

11.1 Introduction

Since the first implementation of the Private Finance Initiative in the United Kingdom in 1992, the last decades have seen a spectacular development of public-private partnerships (PPPs) in many developed as well as developing countries. It has meant an increased participation of the private sector in providing a service itself as well as its accompanying infrastructure.

Interestingly, while most countries have adopted PPPs, the prevalence of such arrangements differs widely across countries, and the differences have persisted. In particular, while 722 PPP projects were launched in the United Kingdom between 1994 and 2016, Switzerland only had two during the same period. In Europe, Switzerland exhibits one of the lowest numbers of PPPs.

What could explain this low number, and is this a good or a bad thing? What is the right number of PPPs? In answer, we first define what PPPs are and what they are not (Sect. 11.1). We then develop a theoretical framework establishing the conditions under which PPP arrangements are

L. Athias (✉) • M. Macina • P. Wicht
IDHEAP, University of Lausanne, Lausanne, Switzerland
e-mail: laure.athias@unil.ch; elhadjimoudo.macina@unil.ch; pascal.wicht@unil.ch

A. Ladner et al. (eds.), *Swiss Public Administration*, Governance and Public Management,
https://doi.org/10.1007/978-3-319-92381-9_11

optimal, or more optimal than other possible modes of provision (Sect. 11.2). This normative analysis highlights that the choice to use a PPP should be driven by the characteristics of the public service considered. As we expect public services to be quite similar across countries at a similar level of economic development, only cultural and institutional differences can explain the differences in the PPPs which are actually implemented. We then consider the bad reasons to use and not to use PPPs which might differ across countries. We point out that while there are probably too few PPPs in Switzerland, there are clearly too many of them in some other countries (Sect. 11.3). We conclude with some policy recommendations.

11.2 What Is a Public-Private Partnership?

11.2.1 Public-Private Partnerships Within the Myriad Ways of Providing Public Services

Once a public service has to be provided, public authorities can choose between a large number of modes of provision. To distinguish between these possibilities, it is useful to divide the life cycle of a project or an infrastructure into four main tasks: designing, building, financing and operating or maintaining. The allocation of these tasks between one and several agents (public and/or private) determines the mode of provision. The most frequent modes of provision are presented in Table 11.1.

Under traditional procurement, the public authorities remain in charge of all four stages, except for building, which is often contracted to a private firm through a procurement contract. This means that the public authority keeps control over the infrastructure and the service provided, and that it also bears all the risks except for construction risks. The public authority may give some autonomy to the public provider of the service by creating specific public entities. These entities can be either autonomous public entities (e.g., the Geneva Airport) or state-owned limited companies under public law (e.g., the Swiss Federal Railways and the Swiss Post) or under private law (e.g., the air navigation service provider Skyguide). The relationship between the authority and the autonomous entity can either be based on a law or on a contract (as in FORS, the Swiss national centre of expertise in the social sciences; see Athias 2013 for details). All these arrangements correspond to a public provision of a public service.

Table 11.1 Overview of the possible modes of provision of public services

Tasks / *Modes of provision*	*Designing*	*Building*	*Financing*	*Operating*	*Ownership of the infrastructure*
Traditional procurement	Public	Private	Public	Public	Public
Private financing	Public (possibly with private)	Private	Private (possibly with public)	Public	Public
Service contract (lease/ management contracts)	Public	Private	Public	Private (≠ building)	Public
PPP	Private (possibly with public)	Private	Private (possibly with public)	Private	Public
		The same private provider is involved in all stages			
Regulated market	Private	Private	Private	Private	Private

Another way to provide a public service, quite specific to Switzerland,[1] is when a private operator builds and finances all or part of a public infrastructure in exchange for the opportunity to exploit the premises for commercial purposes unrelated to the public service (e.g., shopping malls or office buildings). This is made possible by granting a distinct and permanent leasehold right,[2] whose duration is typically between 30 and 100 years. This gives the private partner the right to build and own a distinct asset on ground whose ownership remains in the hands of the public authority. An example is the Tissot Arena, the new sport complex inaugurated in 2015 in Biel, which encompasses football, ice-hockey and curling fields, as well as a shopping mall. While these arrangements are often considered as PPPs due to the private financing of the public infrastructure, they are not PPPs as there is no involvement of the (same) private partner in the service provision.

When the provision of a public service does not require physical assets or when the public authority owns an infrastructure but wants to delegate

[1] Among the projects considered as PPPs by the Association PPP-Switzerland, 11 projects actually correspond to private financing schemes.

[2] Known in French as *Droit distinct et permanent (DDP)*, and in German as *Selbständiges und dauerndes Recht (SDR)*.

only its operation to a private entity, the private party involvement is mostly based on service contracts, such as for child day-care centres or for services provided to migrants. Within such contracts, we can distinguish between lease contracts, where the private firm is paid by the users of the service, and management contracts, where the private operator receives a fixed-price payment from the public authority.

The provision of the public service can also be outsourced through PPPs. PPPs can be defined as long-term arrangements between a public authority and a private partner, chosen after a competitive tendering, in order to design, build, finance and operate an infrastructure that is used to provide the public service.[3] This infrastructure can be either a new one or an already existing that needs to be renovated. The peculiarity of PPPs lies in the bundling of building and operation stages. As highlighted by HM Treasury, *"Private sector expertise and experience has always been used in public sector procurement, but, where in traditional procurement, private companies built and then walked away, PPP seeks to ensure that the private sector takes responsibility for the quality of design and construction it undertakes, and for long term maintenance on an asset, so that value-for-money is achieved"* (HM Treasury 2003).

PPPs can be either *contractual* or *institutionalized*. In the first case, the public authority concludes a contract with the project company (which can be a consortium) without being part of it. By contrast, in institutionalized PPPs, the public authority is a (minority or majority) shareholder of the project company. Boxes 11.1 and 11.2 below provide Swiss examples of both types of PPPs. Among PPPs, we can further distinguish *availability* and *concession* schemes. Whereas both are fixed-price, long-term arrangements to design, build, finance and operate a public infrastructure, the main difference relies in the sharing of risks between the public and private partners. In availability schemes, the public authority pays a fixed price to the project company according to performance criteria (demand risk is hence borne by the public sector). By contrast, in a concession scheme, the project company is remunerated according to the demand for the service (either directly by the users or indirectly by the

[3] Maskin and Tirole (2008) define a public-private partnership as *"A long-term development and service contract between government and private partner. The government typically engages its partner both to develop the project and to operate and service it. The partner may bear substantial risk and even raise private finance. Its revenue derives from some combination of government payments and user fees"*.

public authority via shadow tolls) and hence bears the demand risk. In Switzerland, the term concession is used to describe the right to pursue economic activities that are regulated by the state, mainly because of the monopolistic nature of the market (e.g., local public transportation) or because this activity needs an access to a limited public resource (e.g., water, as in the case of dams or run-of-river facilities, or radio frequencies) or the use of the public domain (e.g., to build and operate a gas network) or due to the sensitive nature of the regulated activity (e.g., casinos) or to increased risks (e.g., airports or the storage of dangerous substances). Swiss "concessions" must then be distinguished from PPP concessions as they can be awarded to public or private service providers, and under all kinds of governance structures. For instance, the Federal Office of Civil Aviation (FOCA) can award concessions to operate airports to public authorities or to private firms. Although no such example curently exists in Switzerland, it would also be possible to award an airport concession to a PPP.

Finally, a public service can be provided through a regulated market. In this case, an authorization to provide the service is required, subject to compliance with some minimum requirements to ensure the quality of the service provided. Unlike PPPs, which are dedicated to specific projects, the requirements in regulated markets apply to all the firms in a sector; they are based either on federal, cantonal or municipal legislation, or on specific guidelines issued by a public authority. This is, for example, the case for nursing homes, which are more or less strictly regulated by the cantons (Athias and Wicht 2018a). This regulation can, in some cases, be the counterpart of public subsidies.

Box 11.1: The Administrative Centre Neumatt, the Only Contractual PPP in Switzerland

The first and only example of a contractual PPP in Switzerland is the administrative complex Neumatt, in the town of Burgdorf (BE). The availability contract was signed in 2009 between the Canton of Bern and the project company Zeughaus PPP AG, formed by the construction groups Marti AG and Royal BAM AG, as well as Hälg Facility Management AG. This contract covers a period of 25 years, starting in 2012, and includes designing, building, financing and operating a new complex which includes a regional prison for 110 inmates, four administrative buildings, a workshop for the canton's Road and Civil Engineering Services, as well as an underground car park. The project company was chosen from among five companies, after three rounds of competitive tendering, and the total value of the project is 150 million CHF.

The operator of the complex is in charge of all tasks except those related to the custody and care of inmates. The services provided by the private partner encompass, among others, building facility management, the management of the car parks, refuse management, internal mail service, the staff restaurant, the signage, the management of the keys and the management of the office supplies. The private company is also in charge of the security and the surveillance of the complex, with the exception of the prison, which remains in the hands of the public authority.

Box 11.2: Cadiom, an Institutionalized PPP to Provide Distance Heating in the Canton of Geneva

Cadiom is an institutionalized PPP created in 1999 between the *Services Industriels de Genève* (SIG, an autonomous state company) and the consortium Vulcain, composed by CGC Energie, two engineering companies, and the construction group Zschokke (now Implenia). The public authority holds a majority (51%) in the project company Cadiom SA. The goal of this company is to design, build and operate a distance heating network in order to use the surplus heat coming from the incineration plant of Les Cheneviers in Aire-la-Ville. This network provides heating to more than 10,000 homes in five municipalities in the Canton of Geneva. The company Cadiom is paid directly by the clients (homeowners), hence corresponding to a concession scheme. The canton grants Cadiom the right to use the public domain and monitors the price and the quality of the service. The private partner was chosen after a competitive tendering process.

11.2.2 PPPs in the World and the Swiss Position

Between 1994 and 2016, 1458 PPPs were created in Europe (see Fig. 11.1), with a total value of 428.2 billion Euros. Among these projects,

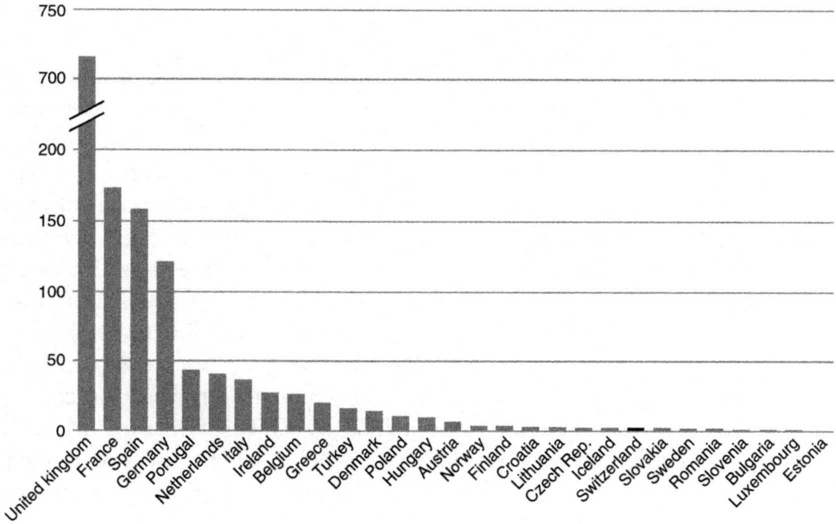

Fig. 11.1 Number of PPPs in European Countries (1994–2016)

almost half were realized in the United Kingdom (49.1%), far ahead of France (11.9%) and Spain (10.9%).

Switzerland has a very low number of PPPs. Indeed, though many projects are incorrectly described as PPPs by the authorities, only two genuine PPP projects have been realized in Switzerland so far: the administrative centre Neumatt in BE (a contractual PPP, see Box 11.1), and the distance heating network Cadiom in the Canton of Geneva (an institutionalized PPP, see Box 11.2).

11.3 When Should Governments Resort to PPPs?

This question is related to the more general question of optimal organizational choices, addressed in the work of the economists Ronald Coase ("Nobel Prize" 1991) and Oliver Williamson ("Nobel Prize" 2009).

11.3.1 Make or Buy for Public Services: The General Framework

A broad distinction can be drawn between the in-house provision of public services ("make"), such as through traditional procurement and private financing schemes and by outsourcing to the private sector ("buy"), either through service contracts or PPPs or regulated markets.

Ronald Coase posed the fundamental question of what the difference is between "make" and "buy", in other words, why firms (or more generally public and private organizations) exist alongside the traditional market governance structure. He distinguishes between the hierarchy (the firm/organization) as a governance structure, where the coordination mechanism is the authority and hierarchy of the entrepreneur (through the labour/subordination contract),[4] and the market, where it is the price mechanism that ensures the coordination of different players. As Coase (1937, p. 390) wrote: "The main reason why it is profitable to establish a firm would seem to be that there is a cost of using the price mechanism". The concept of a cost of using the price mechanism—a transaction cost—was further developed in the early 1970s by Oliver Williamson,[5] who developed the transaction cost theory (hereafter TCT) and formulated precise propositions on the nature of transactions costs, their measurement and the trade-off between "make" and "buy".

According to the TCT, the market has a productive efficiency advantage due to stronger incentives related to the private ownership of profit and the competitive pressure that allows for disciplining and sanctioning the poor performance of agents. In some cases, the market governance structure might also achieve cost efficiency through economies of scale associated with high fixed costs services. That is the case, for instance, when the private partner has many clients and is present in many markets, which enables it to spread the average costs across a larger area of production, which is not possible for a single geographically limited public administration entity. Finally, the market governance structure might lead to productive efficiency gains when it allows an optimal allocation of risks. In particular, the market solution makes it possible for the public authority to transfer some risks to the private provider, who has a better ability to manage these risks (due to greater experience), such as risks associated with demand, availability and construction. By contrast, a public authority is better able to manage other risks, including the political and the environmental, and should bear such risks.

[4] As Coase (1937) points out, when the firm's employees switch from one department to another, this is not because they are responding to changes in the wage but because they are ordered to do so.

[5] In particular Williamson (1975, 1985).

There is nevertheless a cost in using the market, because contracts are incomplete per se due to the assumption of the bounded rationality of agents. Agents are assumed to be rational, but they face cognitive limits in processing all the available information to design a complete contract. This contractual incompleteness leads to transaction costs that can manifest themselves *ex ante* (costs of redaction and negotiation, guarantees) and, above all, *ex post* (costs of contract maladaptation, renegotiation, contract enforcement, as well as the costs of breaching the contract). While the most important transaction costs are not observable, the very important contribution of the TCT is to highlight that their magnitude can be nevertheless assessed according to the characteristics of the transaction in terms of asset specificity, uncertainty and complexity.

Asset specificity is defined as the extent to which the investments made to support a particular transaction have a higher value to that transaction than they would have if they were redeployed for any other purpose (this difference of value constitutes a quasi rent). For example, if an individual learns Navajo, a language only spoken by a specific Amerindian community in the southwestern United States, he is making a very specific investment compared to those learning English, as the knowledge of Navajo is nearly without value outside this community. As a result, the presence of specific assets leads to the apparition of the so-called quasi rent (the difference of value of the investments for the transaction and outside the transaction). Asset specificity can be of different types such as physical specificity involving specific equipment, human capital specificity associated to the specific knowledge valuable to the transaction or site specificity involving specific geographical localization and other types. Asset specificity leads to transaction costs because it locks-in contracting parties into a situation of bilateral dependence, increasing the likelihood of occurrence of opportunistic behaviours to appropriate the quasi rent from both contracting parties, knowing that contracts are incomplete.[6]

In addition to asset specificity, uncertainty regarding the conditions that will prevail during the execution of the contract is another important determinant of transaction costs. As agents are supposedly rationally bounded, they might be unable to forecast all future contingencies during the life cycle of the contract. Thus, uncertainty often calls for welfare

[6] It is important to note that asset specificity, if it generates transaction costs, has important advantages in terms of production costs reduction or product differentiation, leading to higher revenues.

enhancing adaptation *ex post* by renegotiating the initial contractual terms, opening the door to potential opportunistic behaviour, and hence, overall, transaction costs.

Finally, transactions might be intrinsically complex in their object. The contractual difficulty generated by complexity can manifest itself either *ex ante* or *ex post. Ex ante*, it comes from the difficulty in specifying in the contract the expected service and the quality requirements, whereas *ex post,* it comes from the difficulty of observing and measuring the quality of the service provided. It might also be the case that even if the quality can be measured, it may be difficult to prove to third parties (e.g., a court) that an observed insufficient quality is attributable to the provider and not to exogenous causes. As a consequence, private providers can reduce costs to the expense of the quality of the public service. This is what Hart et al. (1997) observe in the particular case of US prisons. When operated by private operators, they observe that wardens are under-qualified, leading to an increase in violence and escapes. This would explain why, according to them, prisons delegated to private providers in the United States are prisons for those under 18 and not for dangerous prisoners.

Thus, the magnitude of potential transaction costs is determined at the transaction level, according to the above-mentioned transaction characteristics. This magnitude, in turn, drives the choice of the governance structure. Considering the respective advantages and drawbacks of the governance structures, the main theoretical proposition from the TCT is as follows: the higher the expected transaction costs, the more hierarchical the chosen governance structure should be. The optimality of the choice depends then on the adaptation of the governance structures to the characteristics of the transactions that they have to frame, defining the alignment principle.

11.3.2 Relative Optimality of PPPs

The trade-off developed above applies to the particular case of PPPs. As described in the first section of this chapter, PPPs correspond to a "buy" solution and hence exhibit advantages in terms of productive efficiency but drawbacks in terms of transaction costs, which will be more or less important according to the public service considered. Nevertheless, PPPs also have specific potential advantages and drawbacks.

First, a specific benefit of PPPs derives from bundling different phases of a project. In particular, bundling the design, build, operate and maintenance phases leads to life cycle cost savings. The private partner responsible for building a certain infrastructure has a stronger incentive to provide better quality when she also has to manage the maintenance of this infrastructure, in order to reduce her total costs. In other words, bundling induces the private partner to internalize, at the building stage, possible externalities during the operating phase, and thus to exploit the complementarities and synergies between the different phases of the project. This could lead to innovations at the building stage. The higher the externalities between different project phases, the higher the productive efficiency gains associated with PPPs. This bundling also allows for an improvement in global cost transparency.[7] Bundling hence increases the alignment of incentives between public and private partners.

However, bundling involves a certain number of disadvantages in terms of transaction costs. In particular, bundling leads to a longer procurement process and to higher costs associated with bidding than traditional procurement processes (see Athias and Chever, 2018). Bundling different phases also increases the complexity and uncertainty of the project, and hence may increase transaction costs due to contract maladaptation and/or renegotiation. As a consequence, problems of adverse selection might arise; these are certainly the main source of transaction costs. More specifically, the winning private provider might not always be the most efficient one. Instead, this provider might be either the most opportunistic one (i.e., who best anticipates the future renegotiation of the contract) or the most optimistic one (regarding future demand or costs). It leads to the "winner's curse" (see Athias and Nuñez 2008, 2015).

Thus, the specificities of PPPs increase both productive efficiency gains and transaction costs associated with the market solution. The alignment principle mentioned above would then call for a hierarchical PPP structure to minimize total costs. Athias and Saussier (2018) highlight that contractualized PPPs, more specifically concession contracts, might indeed be very hierarchical, with, for instance, contractual clauses that foresee not

[7] PPPs reduce the leeway to "salami-slice" a project, that is, to break the project into a number of distinct sub-projects (which could consist in dividing the construction and operation stages of the project), so as to favour legislative project approval. A good example is given by the concert hall of Fribourg. In 2006, a budget of 35 million CHF for its construction was approved. In 2010 (one year before the inauguration), the local parliament voted an additional five million CHF in order to complete the construction, in particular to improve the quality of the technical infrastructure, but also to finish equipping the office spaces (e.g., air conditioning as well as heating and electric installations).

only that partners will have to renegotiate the contract every three or five years but also how renegotiations should take place. They also highlight that PPP contracts exhibit heterogeneity in terms of hierarchical structure, a function of the degree of uncertainty surrounding the transaction, as predicted by the theory. In addition, within PPPs, the features of institutionalized PPPs make them more hierarchical than contractual PPPs.

We expect then that institutionalized PPPs would more likely be chosen for public services which are potentially prone to significant contractual hazards. This is in line with the two case studies presented in Boxes 11.1 and 11.2. In the case of the Cadiom, the project involved the design, building and operation of a distance heating network with high uncertainty over the source of energy to be used. This uncertainty led to the choice of a more hierarchical form of PPP, which allowed for more coordination and mutual adaptation. By contrast, the Neumatt project involved simpler tasks, thus leading to a less hierarchical form of PPP, the availability contract.

As a result, the question of when governments should use PPPs, and which form of PPPs, depends on the characteristics of the service(s) to be delivered. It is hence possible to explain variations in the propensity to use PPPs across services, but not across countries at similar levels of economic development.

11.4 Why Is Switzerland Different?

Efficiency considerations should drive the use (or non-use) of PPPs, and that in turn depends on the type of service which is to be provided. To explain the low number of PPPs in Switzerland, one needs to look at institutional and cultural considerations that lead public authorities to use (or not use) PPPs.

11.4.1 Bad Reasons for Using PPPs

PPPs are frequently perceived by policy makers as a good way for a public authority to realize an infrastructure project when the financial means are constrained. While PPPs make it possible to avoid, or at least limit, an initial investment and hence the future interest and amortization of the debt, the counterpart is that the public authority will have to pay a contribution to the private provider (in the case of an availability contract) or to forego earnings from user fees (in the case of a concession), and this throughout the operation stage of the project. This boils down to the Ricardian Equivalence: the resources saved by the government by not paying the upfront investment under a PPP should be equal, in present value, to fees paid or user fee revenue foregone to the private provider. In addition, this leads to shifting the cost of a project to future generations. Thus, PPPs must not be considered as a means to get a "free lunch".

In practice, choosing a PPP only because a public authority cannot bear the initial investment is often a means of circumventing a debt constraint imposed by law or upper tiers of government. As The Economist (2009) notes: *"Cynics suspect that the government remains keen on PFI not because of the efficiencies it allegedly offers, but because it allows ministers to perform a useful accounting trick"*. This also happened in the administrative centre Neumatt. The Canton of Berne decided the project did not fall under the debt brake, as the investment was borne by the private partner rather than the canton. However, the canton's auditing office required the project be treated as a standard investment. The minister in charge of cantonal infrastructure then explained that the canton subsequently became less interested in engaging in new PPPs because, despite the success of the project, *the goal of this approach, that is, alleviating the burden on the investment budget, has not been reached* (Neue Zürcher Zeitung 2013, translation). This window-dressing of budget deficits as a way to get around the law is obviously not an acceptable, valid economic reason to justify using PPPs. Accounting rules for PPPs have been revised in order to avoid such behaviour from governments.[8]

In Switzerland nevertheless, another way to circumvent debt constraints is through the private financing project scheme, as highlighted in the first section of the chapter. Since the private provider finances the construction of the infrastructure associated with the particular public service being provided, no debt to the public authority is incurred. As with PPPs, it gives the authorities the illusion of a "free lunch", and the opportunity cost associated with the alternative use of the ground is not assessed, even if it is potentially important. Thus, private financing is used in Switzerland as a substitute for PPPs to circumvent debt constraints. Privately financed projects can also be used by Swiss public authorities to

[8] In particular, the IPSAS 32 standard, whose application is also recommended by the Swiss Public Sector Financial Reporting Advisory Committee as part of the Harmonized Accounting Model for the Cantons and Municipalities (HAM2), requires that the assets and liabilities related to a PPP are included in the balance sheet of the public authority.

avoid facing a referendum, which may become mandatory if proposed spending exceeds a specified amount. As private financing projects makes it possible to avoid the initial public investment, this could lead public authorities to use private financing schemes as a means to circumvent the semi-direct democratic instrument of the referendum.

PPPs are also often used in order to circumvent weaknesses in the traditional procurement process. In particular, a public authority might use a PPP to force itself to evaluate the *overall* costs of a project, by locking itself into a contractual or institutionalized relationship. In other words, PPPs could be used as a commitment device by public authorities. Although this might at first glance lead to better efficiency, it would be more appropriate to correct the organizational problems within the administration rather than turning to a PPP when it is not efficient. PPPs are not the quick-fix solution to the inefficiencies and bad practices of the public sector.

This would in turn explain why the use of PPPs is less frequent in countries where the public sector is considered to be more efficient, as in Switzerland. For instance, Afonso et al. (2005) constructed a Public Sector Efficiency indicator that measures the quality of the administration in terms of corruption, red tape, quality of judiciary and shadow economy. According to this indicator, Switzerland ranks well above all the other advanced OECD countries (see Fig. 11.2).

11.4.2 Bad Reasons for NOT Using PPPs

However, if there are bad reasons to use PPPs, there are also bad reasons NOT to do so.

Public choice theory tells us there are private benefits for politicians to keep the provision of public services within the public sector. It allows policy makers to award jobs to their relatives, friends or political colleagues, though one should quickly add that Transparency International considers Switzerland one of the least corrupt countries in the world. Switzerland does have some forms of hidden corruption in its public service hiring and public procurement practices. This cronyism (referred to as the "*B vitamins*" in Switzerland, where B stands for the German word *Beziehungen*, i.e., Relationships) is widespread in Swiss administrations, especially at the local and cantonal levels. The high degree of decentralization gives substantial power to local politicians who, due to the militia

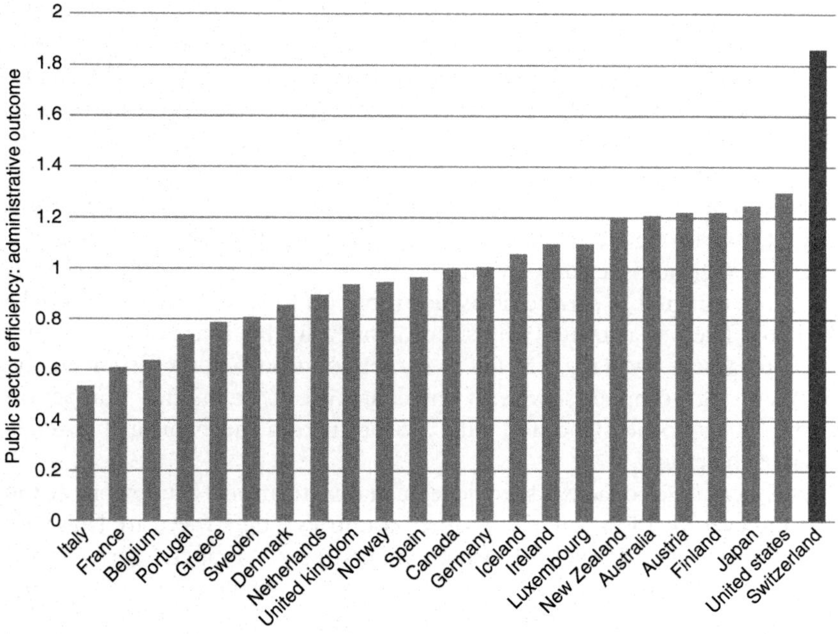

Fig. 11.2 Comparative public sector efficiency

system (meaning that most politicians are non-professional: less than 2% of local executive board members serve full time (Ladner 2011; Geser et al. 2012)), have closer connections with private interests (Meinhardt et al. 2014) and are hence more likely to make biased choices. In the same vein, at a higher level, it is a fact that the interest groups and lobbies have an effective influence on the militia members of the cantonal and federal parliaments. Their willingness and practices to advance their private interests which are often detrimental to the public interest are easier to hide in non-PPP projects for which it is easier to adapt the project in order to circumvent the obligation to use competitive tendering that applies to PPPs.[9] This would also help explain why Swiss public authorities are biased against PPPs.

[9] In accordance with the general rules of procurement law (i.e., the Federal Law and Ordinance on Government Procurement and the World Trade Organisation Agreement on Government Procurement), competitive tendering is compulsory for PPPs in Switzerland (Brahier 2017). See also Athias and Chever (2018) for an analysis of the pros and cons of competitive tendering.

There are also "bad reasons" to avoid PPPs on the private sector side. Indeed, while PPPs allow the private sector to be involved in providing public services, the private sector may be sceptical about the rather hierarchical nature of most PPPs. In such a governance structure, the mission orientation of a public authority may conflict with the profit orientation of the private provider.

As a matter of fact, in Switzerland, the degree of mission orientation strongly varies between cultural groups, in particular between language areas, as German-speakers are more prone to consider that public firms must be managed as private firms (for more on this, see Athias and Wicht 2018b). There is a cultural reluctance, from a sizable share of the population, to accept the fact that for a market solution to be efficient in the provision of complex services (which are prone to higher transaction costs), it has to be associated with a coordination mechanism that tends towards hierarchy.

Switzerland also lacks a specific legal and institutional framework at the federal level for PPPs. Unlike in other countries where there are laws specifically designed for PPP arrangements (e.g., France, the United Kingdom), PPPs in Switzerland are based on the general rules of contract and procurement laws. Thus, the legal environment in Switzerland is weaker than in other countries, leading market solutions through PPPs likely to be less efficient in this country than elsewhere. In addition, whereas some countries have specific institutions to support the implementation of PPPs (e.g., the *FIN INFRA* in France), this is not the case in Switzerland. As a consequence, local decision makers might not have developed the skills and expertise to implement PPPs.

11.5 Conclusion

PPPs are not a panacea for providing public services, and they are optimal solutions only in very specific cases. There is thus no advocacy in Switzerland to systematically use PPPs, as has been the case, for example, in the United Kingdom. This might appear to be good news.

However, Swiss public authorities have shown a tendency to privately finance projects as a way to circumvent both debt and the constraints of a semi-direct democratic political system. Even when PPPs might be optimal solution, this tendency often biases the choice to not use PPPs. However, one could change the accounting rules for the private financing of projects by imposing competitive tendering for all projects, whether privately financed or as PPPs. Legislation should also be strengthened to provide a strong framework for implementing PPPs, and specific institutions should be developed to help the public authorities in implementing such arrangements and providing them with the required skills. Finally, the conception of the market might gain from evolving in Switzerland. Even in a competitive market, the existence of transaction costs implies that the provision of public services has to be regulated.

References

Afonso, A., Schuknecht, L., & Tanzi, V. (2005). Public sector efficiency: An international comparison. *Public Choice, 123*(3–4), 321–347.

Athias, L. (2013). La contractualisation de service public: une analyse économique. In A. Ladner, J.-L. Chappelet, Y. Emery, P. Knoepfel, L. Mader, N. Soguel, & F. Varone (Eds.), *Manuel d'administration publique suisse* (pp. 679–697). Lausanne: PPUR.

Athias, L., & Nuñez, A. (2008). Winner's curse in toll road concessions. *Economics Letters, 101*(3), 172–174.

Athias, L., & Nuñez, A. (2015). Effects of uncertainty and opportunistic renegotiations on bidding behaviour: Evidence from toll road concessions. In A. Picot, M. Florio, N. Grove, & L. Kranz (Eds.), *The economics of infrastructure provisioning: The changing role of the state* (pp. 285–314). Cambridge, MA: MIT Press.

Athias, L., & Saussier, S. (2018). Are public private partnerships that rigid? And why? Evidence from price provisions in French toll road concession contracts. *Transportation Research Part A: Policy and Practice, 111*, 174–186.

Athias, L., & Wicht P. (2018a). *Institutional environment and organizational choices: The impact of state-level norms within Switzerland on the prevalence of for-profit nursing homes* (Working paper).

Athias, L., & Wicht, P. (2018b). *Using differences in the salience of public sector's mission-orientation across neighbor cultures to uncover its impacts on public service delivery productivity* (Working paper).

Brahier, J.-M. (2017). Partenariat public-privé et concession de travaux – Proposition de systématisation et réflexions sur la soumission au droit des marchés publics des partenariats publics-privés et des concessions de travaux. *Journées suisses du droit de la construction.*

Coase, R. H. (1937). The nature of the firm. *Economica, 4*(16), 386–405.

Geser, H., Meuli, U., Horber-Papazian, K., Ladner, A., & Steiner, R. (2012). *Les membres des exécutifs dans les communes suisses.* Glarus/Chur: Rüegger.

Hart, O., Shleifer, A., & Vishny, R. (1997). The proper scope of government: Theory and an application to prisons. *The Quarterly Journal of Economics, 112*(4), 1127–1161.

HM Treasury. (2003). *PFI: Meeting the investment challenge*. London: HM Treasury.

Ladner, A. (2011). *Die Schweizer Gemeinden im Wandel: Politische Institutionen und lokale Politik* (p. 237). Lausanne: Cahiers de l'IDHEAP.

Maskin, E., & Tirole, J. (2008). Public–private partnerships and government spending limits. *International Journal of Industrial Organization, 26*(2), 412–420.

Meinhardt, M., Lenggenhager, F., & Labhart, O. (2014). Switzerland. In J. Pickworth & D. Williams (Eds.), *Bribery & corruption*. London: Global Legal Group Ltd.

Neue Zürcher Zeitung. (2013). *Wenn Private den Staat zu mittelfristigem Denken zwingen* (p. 13), 12.09.2013. Neue Zürcher Zeitung.

The Economist. (2009, July 2). Singing the blues: Recession is heaping problems on a controversial form of public investment. *The Economist*.

Williamson, O. E. (1975). *Markets and hierarchies: Analysis and antitrust implications*. New York: Free Press.

Williamson, O. E. (1985). *The economic institutions of capitalism*. New York: Free Press.

CHAPTER 12

In-Depth Modernization of HRM in the Public Sector: The Swiss Way

Yves Emery

12.1 Introduction

Human resources management (HRM) is undoubtedly the area in the public sector which has evolved the most in the last 25 years, especially in Switzerland. Those in positions of political responsibility in parliaments and executives have realized that a modernization of the public sector cannot be achieved without profoundly reforming HRM statutes and processes; the need was already highlighted quite some time ago (OECD 1997a). Public managers have also often argued that they needed more room for maneuver in managing their staff (Hablützel 2013). Even the voting population has supported reforms. In 2000, following a referendum, nearly two-thirds of the voters approved a new status for federal civil servants (now called *public employees*) by accepting the Swiss Federal Personnel Act (Federal Chancellery 2000). Starting from the simple management of personnel files, HRM in the public sector has become increasingly oriented to strategically managing human

Y. Emery (✉)
IDHEAP, University of Lausanne, Lausanne, Switzerland
e-mail: yves.emery@unil.ch

A. Ladner et al. (eds.), *Swiss Public Administration*, Governance and Public Management,
https://doi.org/10.1007/978-3-319-92381-9_12

capital (Emery and Chassot 2009). However, this remains a road many public administrations in Switzerland are still traveling; HRM projects continue to converge on this vision.

12.2 The Progressive Maturation of Human Resource Management in Swiss Public Administration

The Swiss reforms in human resources are not the result of sudden radical changes. In keeping with Switzerland's tradition of incremental reform (Giauque 2013), they have gradually gathered momentum. A brief look at the genesis of "personnel services"[1] shows that in most cases, such units were first created in the 1970s (Germann 1996). Centralized personnel units gave significant impetus to professionalizing HRM in the public sector. In fact, their primary task was to administer personnel statutes by creating regulations and tools—such as grids for classifying jobs and grading systems—which were meant to be applied to all employees. The processes were essentially imposed, meaning mandatory practices were introduced from the top down. The mission was to formulate a set of HRM standards that would establish a basis for treating civil servants equally, to have these standards approved by the political authorities in charge—principally by executives, but on occasion also by parliament in passing statutes governing personnel—and then to implement and *control* the application of these legal standards.

The idea that human resources are a decisive factor in organizations generally, and in public services in particular, is gradually gaining ground. By the early 1990s, personnel offices began to become interested in the *people* being managed and not just in their *files and data* (Emery and Gonin 2009). A parallel can be drawn with changes in operational services to increase their customer-orientation[2]. Specifically, this evolution involves defining and developing the skills, competencies, and behavior of civil servants, in accordance with the expectations of the administration, explicit *job specifications*, and sometimes *competencies frameworks*. Personnel recruitment, work evaluations, and training and development are increasingly important, and have benefitted from increased resources. In the

[1] Often called "personnel offices" to highlight the physical space where employees came to discuss their affairs, and at times, to collect their pay.

[2] Or *Bürgerorientierung* [citizen-oriented] in German; see, for example, Schedler and Proeller (2000).

wake of such reforms, personnel units are often renamed as *human resource departments* to highlight their new focus on *people* rather than just on their files or records.

All such people-centered practices have inevitably led to devolving centralized human resource (HR) services and to move toward a greater *decentralization* as well as to greater responsibility and accountability by public managers at all levels. Yet the fact that more interest is taken in individuals will not be credible if it is done remotely by human resource specialists who never actually meet with employees themselves. Therefore, a strong emphasis is placed on selecting and training managers in leadership skills and leadership styles, which are designed to develop and motivate public servants. This role of HRM managers, now essential, is illustrated by the orientation taken in publications of the Federal Office of Personnel (2002); they highlight administrative management qualities as a key axis of modernization. This argument is widely found in other European countries as well with well-developed training programs for managers (Kuperus and Rode 2008). The creation of "HR respondents" (see below) directly subordinate to operational departments and to those who are meant to work as *business partners* (Ulrich et al. 2009) contributes to achieving such decentralization.

The final stage of the maturation of Swiss public HRM is, for the most part, yet to come. It is linked to an important vein in the HRM literature which highlights the added value and strategic impact that HRM practices can have on the performance of an organization (Saridakis et al. 2017). This evolution implies the transition from a process orientation to a results orientation, as well as aligning HRM practices with the strategy and objectives pursued by the administration (Barrette 2005). This evolution is doubtless one of the key challenges public sector HRM will face in the next few years, though recent studies tend to highlight more specific challenges, for example, demographic changes or talent management (Giauque et al. 2012a). The fact that there are more and more *HR strategies* in the administration is an indicator of this evolution to come (see below).

12.3 Public Sector HRM in Switzerland: The Essential Axes of Modernization

The metamorphosis in public management resulting from the large-scale introduction of New Public Management (NPM) principles has profoundly modified how civil servants do their work (see Chappelet in this volume). At the very least, and for the sake of coherence between management systems, HRM should be adapted to meet the new expectations which have arisen from NPM. It calls on training civil servants in new skills and competencies and to rethink the way their performance is evaluated and rewarded. Many analysts even think HRM has been the cornerstone of modernization in many countries (OECD 1997b), as it is an essential lever in bringing about organizational change: it directly affects the profile and behavior of public officials on a daily basis. We think that this has also been true in Switzerland, and so it is worth examining the typical levers for modernizing public HRM in Switzerland.

12.3.1 Hybrid Public Statutes

New public sector HRM practices are based on official statutes, often in the form of a law voted on by Parliament; these statutes have evolved considerably. Internationally, public employment conditions have become increasingly aligned with those in the private sector, other than in countries with a long tradition of a *career-based system* of civil service such as France, Germany, or Austria (Demmke and Moilanen 2010). Most European Union (EU) countries have retained some form of job security for their civil servants, but Switzerland has gone a long way in transforming its statutes, both at federal and cantonal levels, bringing civil service employment conditions closer in line with those found in the private sector (Bellanger and Roy 2013; Wisard 2007). It is also a question of remaining competitive in a labor market where specialized skills and "talents" remain rare. Because of the "open entry" or *position-based system* of the Swiss civil service, it is crucial that the public employment sector be concerned with how competitive its jobs and compensation packages are.

The deeper evolution of the relevant legal framework illustrates the hybrid nature of what we call the "post-civil service"[3], since this framework usually provides a *public law contract* as the legal form of employment (Koller et al. 2011). This was long considered heresy, as it juxtaposed a *public law* logic (with its basic in legality, equal treatment, proportionality, etc.) with *contractual principles.* However, it also made it possible for employer and employee *together* to agree on specific employment arrangements, albeit within the framework of personnel statutes which continues to define the main rights and duties of public employees. It was a very pragmatic Swiss solution, permitting flexibility while maintaining a well-defined legal framework.

[3] In line with the post-bureaucratic approach, very popular in the literature.

Moreover, and also a hallmark of Swiss modernization, public employers enjoy considerable autonomy in setting the conditions for their personnel, and as a result, also of their HR processes and tools. Thus, the federal administration, the 26 cantons, and the 2200-odd municipalities (and in existing public enterprises, where employers have a less formal role), can largely determine their own conditions of employment. This creates a remarkable heterogeneity in what counts as being a "public employee" (Bellanger and Roy 2013; Ladner 2013). It reflects local needs as well as political relations as reflected in the parliaments and at all three governmental levels. In other words, it is a system diametrically opposed to having a unified career civil servant system governed by a single legal framework applying to every public official.

12.3.2 The Introduction of HR Policies and Strategies

Legislators increasingly require that civil service statutes include the formulation of an HR policy (Emery and Lambelet-Rossi 2000; Thom and Ritz 2013). It is then up to the government to formulate, and ensure, the implementation of this policy; this complements or completes the juridical-administrative logic of the civil service, giving it a more strategic orientation. Human resource policy can be defined as a strategy for reaching defined goals in the coming years, with the needed actions correspondingly planned[4]. Sometimes, this strategy even forms a part of the master plan of the larger administrative unit, thus creating a link to a more general strategy being pursued.[5] Thus, the federal administration's new "HR Strategy" for 2016–2019 clearly states that one objective is to be competitive on the labor market: "Thanks to working conditions for personnel which are competitive, the federal government as employer offers interesting and attractive jobs not only for persons of all generations, as well as from the regions and linguistic communities of the country, but also for those who are disabled, and that irrespective of the sex of the persons concerned".[6]

[4] See, for example, http://www.pa.zh.ch/internet/finanzdirektion/personalamt/de/ueber_uns/was_wir_tun/personalmanagement-strategie.html Accessed 14 Sept 2017.

[5] HUG, Strategic axes of the Geneva University Hospitals.
http://www.hug-ge.ch/vision-2020/projets-strategiques

[6] Office fédéral du personnel, Stratégie concernant le personnel 2016–2019 https://www.epa.admin.ch/epa/fr/home/themes/politique-du-personnel/personalstrategie_2016_2019.html Accessed 29 Aug. 2017.

Defining a human resources policy permits the administration to position itself in a clearer, more offensive, and positive way in the labor market. This makes public service employers more attractive in an increasingly competitive market, one in which potential candidates may not necessarily consider working for government as their top priority (Widmer 2010). A study carried out by the author more than 15 years ago indicated that the public administrations of most cantons and larger cities did not have a formalized HR policy (Emery and Lambelet-Rossi 2000). This has changed considerably, though in the absence of empirical data, it is difficult to know precisely how much HR policies in Swiss public administration have developed. Public administrations have become more and more active on their internet sites, as well as in social networks, and take an "employer branding" approach in promoting their distinctive assets, as shown by a recent analysis (Emery and Kouadio 2017). What is evident from this research is that in addition to stressing the legal and material conditions of employment (most notably job security, but including other aspects such as ergonomics), the use of modern HRM practices and leadership, and the many opportunities for personal and professional development, emphasis is given to the value and meaning of the public mission, in conjunction with a so-called *public service motivation* (Giauque et al. 2012b).

12.3.3 The Development of a Decentralized Network of HR Professionals

Although HR services have long handled personnel in a very centralized and even centralizing manner (see above), this situation has changed considerably in the past decade or so. Indeed, so much so that some analysts have begun criticizing what they see as the fragmentation of human resource management in public administration. In doing so, they echo the critique of private enterprises made some 20 years ago, so much had decentralization been pushed there. The rationale in this evolution is linked to a *contextualist* vision which emphasizes the importance of making decisions at a level "close to the shop floor" so as to better understand the needs, constraints, and challenges of each operational unit concerned (Pichault and Nizet 2013).

In Switzerland, this development has been quite marked. It is not just a matter of a transfer of power between the HR department and the line managers, but also a gradual delegation of competencies between parliament and government, which itself delegates certain responsibilities to the public managers as the heads of units. This tendency of having HR decisions being made "closer to the shop floor" is reinforced by the decentralization of HR units as such. To this end, many Swiss administrations have created the role of "HR respondent", a function corresponding to that of a *business partner*, as the literature puts it (Ulrich 1998). This is a decentralized function, ordinarily dependent on the departmental hierarchy, but—following a functional logic—reporting to the centralized HR department. For instance, in the city of Lausanne, HR respondents were established in 2004 in each of the 45 or so administrative services, at an initial ratio of 1 full-time HR respondent for 400 people (Ospel 2011). Such decentralized HR roles are highly developed in the federal administration, most cantonal administrations, and in the larger cities.

12.3.4 The Professionalization of Recruitment

A public administration based on merit and professional expertise is one of the defining characteristics of a bureaucratized civil service, according to Max Weber. Yet this does not mean that the skills or competencies required to perform the jobs entrusted to civil servants have been defined and evaluated in a professional manner (Guérard and Pailot 2007). The determination of specific competency profiles, to assess the *degree of fit* between the position (and its environment) and the person, is a relatively new practice and one that has improved significantly in Swiss public administration. It is the starting point of a professional hiring process which allows one to recruit those with the best skills, for public administration posts that anyone can apply for.

The techniques for evaluating applications which are used in Swiss public administration employ reliable and sophisticated assessment tools which look not only at competencies but also at the professional interests and personality of the candidates (Emery and Gonin 2009). This tendency is attributable to human resource departments which generally have expertise in occupational psychology. Furthermore, these departments are more systematically involved as experts in recruitment processes led by public managers. For a long time, it was entirely up to the political and administrative hierarchy to select personnel, though without always having the necessary expertise. Nowadays, it is not uncommon to have recruitment processes, particularly for executive managers, which involve two or three successive interviews along with the involvement of an assessment center, all of which can last more than a day. This does not include soliciting references or conducting other analyses, depending on the post to be occupied; this is especially true for senior management positions.

Finally, public administrations have increasingly resorted to using internal internet portals and both public and private internet job recruitment sites. These promote or accelerate recruitment and help improve the image of the public employer in the labor market—but it is often undertaken without developing a proper marketing strategy (Sivertzen et al. 2013). A presence at recruiting fairs, for example, on university campuses, is now common, though this was not true even 15 years ago.

12.3.5 Performance Management Is Universalizing

In line with the NPM's performance orientation, performance management for public employees has been a major topic of modernization in the last 20 years (Gerrish 2016). Numerous analyses have addressed the problem of properly defining the performance of public employees, as well as objectives and criteria for their assessment. The methods implemented in public administrations take into account the specificity of public action and reflect this orientation toward results.

It is the responsibility of line managers at all levels to set goals and assess the performance of their subordinates, while at the same time trying to provide a more participatory, less *transactional*, and more *transformational* leadership (van Wart 2013). Performance assessment practices have a long tradition in the private sector, though even there they are not universally accepted (Reyge 2007). In the public sector, these practices are subjected to even greater criticism, even if their introduction is now nearly universal (OECD 2005).

Now widely introduced in Switzerland, the performance management of public employees thus appears as an indispensable practice, one that is basically complementary to mechanisms aiming to introduce performance-related pay, a theme that is dealt with in the following section. Most current personnel statutes specify that public employees are subject to an annual assessment of their work. And this practice is well accepted, even though it does not always proceed in an optimal fashion, as it is a complex process both from a technical and a human point of view (Vidaillet 2012).

12.3.6 *Well-Established Performance-Related Pay*

The OECD reported that the 1990s were an era in which, internationally, pay for performance was actively promoted in the public sector (OECD/PUMA 1997). Such practices were also introduced in Switzerland (Schedler 1993). The experience and the reflection on such practices were very important, not least because it was possible to make needed corrections: the practice of *performance-related pay* is not self-evident in public organizations (Atkinson et al. 2014).

Today most cantons, as well as the Confederation, have adopted this practice (Bellanger and Roy 2013). An analysis conducted a few years ago by the author in a dozen cantons across Switzerland[7], however, revealed a country divided between two politico-administrative cultures. German-speaking Switzerland is closer to the Anglo-saxon English tradition, which is open to the new principles of public management, while French-speaking Switzerland is closer to the French tradition, corroborating wider findings related to NPM (Giauque and Emery 2008). Apparently, salary increases are near-automatic in French-speaking cantons, though they are subject to budget decisions in parliament, and these may limit or block the increases granted to civil servants. By contrast, the non-payment of the annual salary increase is regarded as a form of sanction for the employee concerned. In German-speaking cantons and in the Confederation, however, pay increases only depend on the performance of the employee, which is evaluated by his or her line manager during the annual evaluation interviews (see above).

The recognition of civil servants through remuneration is a cornerstone of the Swiss modernization of HRM, even when the available budget to do so has not always been up to the expectations of staff members or does not reach the levels theory recommends (Thériault and St-Onge 2006). There are, though, additional forms of financial reward such as bonuses for extraordinary performance, for complex project management, or for suggestions which lead to savings. That is, the available repertoire for this type of reward is often broad, even if its amplitude (meaning the amounts awarded) is limited by internal directives (they rarely exceed 5% of ordinary pay).

12.3.7 *The Development of Career Paths*

The traditional bureaucratized career system, with its programmed and near-automatic progression up through the ranks, has largely disappeared

[7] Confidential commissioned report. The cantons included Geneva, Vaud, Neuchatel, Fribourg, Bern, Jura, Basel-Stadt, Zurich, Lucerne, and the federal administration.

in Switzerland, with the exception of a few bodies, such as the police. The current arrangement structures career progression around acquiring new skills and competencies or completing training modules—*certification* is required in order to assume a higher level of responsibility or to perform more specialized tasks. Such training, or the acquisition of technical, social, and management skills, has been considerably expanded in the last 15 years, making Swiss public administration organizations genuinely *qualifying* organizations, which further develop the employability of their staff. In most public administrations, training for basic, middle, and senior management is the subject of specific and compulsory seminars, as is true in the federal administration[8].

In line with international findings (Demmke and Moilanen 2010), civil service careers in Switzerland today are less linear than in the past. That is, they are based less on a kind of automatic and incremental path, independent of the current level of performance, previously largely linked to seniority. They are also less vertical, this classic version of the civil service career having been supplanted by many alternate career paths. In particular, due to internal schemes to increase mobility, the option of moving transversally has been emphasized; it is an effort to decompartmentalize services, offices, and organizational entities more generally. But resistance to this remains significant. The Description des emplois et classification des fonctions (DECFO) project in Vaud's cantonal administration goes in this direction[9], in a manner similar to the general tools developed in the French interministerial Directorate of Administration and Civil Service (DGAFP 2010).

12.3.8 The Facilitated Termination of Employment

In the classic Weberian system, civil servants were sheltered from political pressure through their security of employment and appointment. This special protection has been considerably loosened in Switzerland in recent years, but with respect to employment security, public sector employment remains clearly superior to private sector employment. For this reason, it remains an important (extrinsic) source of motivation for job candidates, and even a competitive advantage, one which can be decisive in a tough labor market.

[8] Office fédéral du personnel, Développement du personnel et des cadres https://www.epa.admin.ch/epa/fr/home/themes/developpement-du-personnel-et-formation/developpement-du-personnel-et-des-cadres.html Accessed 1 Oct 2017.

[9] Canton of Vaud, DECFO-SYSREM http://www.vd.ch/index.php?id=25244 Accessed 2 Oct 2017.

As for termination, the Swiss tendency has been to facilitate it *without prejudice*. Therefore, it also lacks the administrative inquiry process (*enquête administrative*) that was once part of dismissing civil servants from their posts (Emery and Grund 2017). The message is clear, and it concerns as much the legal contract binding civil servant to an employer as the psychological contract involved. Public employment in Switzerland is not guaranteed and an employee can be terminated for economic reasons (e.g., during a restructuring of the administration which results in job cuts), for inadequate performance, or for unacceptable behavior. If a position is eliminated, a comparable position must be offered by the employer in the administration concerned, but should a comparable position not exist, or the employee refuse to take it, then he or she can be dismissed. Similarly, if poor performance or unacceptable behavior is involved, then mandatory objectives are set and evaluated, and a formal warning is sent to the person concerned. If the problem persists, a dismissal can be pronounced.

As far as we are informed, dismissal for unacceptable behavior is relatively rare—contrary to the fears civil service unions expressed when this possibility was introduced. But accurate figures on this are not available and central statistics are lacking, which is, to say the least, surprising.

12.4 Other Factors Accounting for the Success of the Swiss HRM Model

The HRM processes mentioned previously are at the heart of the modernization of Swiss public sector HRM. However, other conditions have also favored this modernization:

- The comparatively high level of remuneration paid to Swiss public employees. However, this is not true of senior management positions, where the attractiveness of the private sector is greater, given its freedom to set its own remuneration schemes.[10] The evidence from the Federal Statistical Office is clear: average salaries in the public sector

[10] And that despite the Swiss population approving the "Minder" initiative (named after its initiator) in 2013 which was (https://www.admin.ch/ch/f/pore/vi/vis348t.html Accessed 2 Oct 2017) aimed at limiting the salaries of senior executives in the private sector. According to the latest analyses, it does not seem to have produced the desired effects (http://www.bilan.ch/tag/initiative-minder Accessed 2 Oct 2017).

are higher than in the private sector (Federal Statistical Office 2014). It is not uncommon that, for basic jobs requiring a vocational training qualification (such as the Federal Diploma of Vocational Education and Training) or for jobs requiring a lower level of qualifications, public sector pay is 20% or 30% higher than what is offered in the private sector. This salary attractiveness contributes to the evolution of the existing public sector HRM system, in concert with the other fields of modernization noted.

- A fairly pragmatic "social partnership" especially in the German-speaking part of Switzerland, where all public management modernization efforts, including those involving HRM, have not led to much political mobilization. This is not the case in French-speaking Switzerland, particularly in Geneva, where reforms to the statutes governing public servants remain the object of strong opposition, particularly from the trade unions. It is exemplified by the Système compétence, rémunération, évaluation (SCORE) project, which tried to reassess remuneration throughout the civil service of the Canton of Geneva.[11] Launched in 2011, this project is yet to be completed. Still, this example is not representative of the social partnership within the Swiss civil service, where the unions (external to the administration) and the staff committees (internal to the administration) have shown a broad openness to modernization.
- Finally, one should mention the other key players: the political leaders, members of executive bodies, who are open to reforms. Their openness reflects a Swiss culture in which the principles of good organization and generic management (often mistaken for private management) are often welcomed. It should be remembered that many Swiss women and men in politics are career professionals who hold only part-time positions in the various political executives in the country. At the federal level, this particular political career profile of the "militia politician" is changing (Bühlmann et al. 2015). But that many Swiss politicians have experience in the private sector means modernization and innovation in public administration can proceed—even if it is often at an incremental pace (Giauque and Emery 2016).

[11] Canton of Geneva, SCORE, le nouveau système d'évaluation des emplois et des rémunérations http://ge.ch/etat-employeur/service-public/score-nouveau-systeme-devaluation-emplois Accessed 2 Oct 2017.

12.5 In Conclusion

All these public HRM modernization initiatives were made possible in Switzerland by an evolution in the legal framework (statutes)-governing civil servants. They also came about due to a managerialization of public administration, as well as a political context receptive to this type of evolution. It has led to a convergence, in the area of employment, between public and private sectors. It should be remembered, however, that Swiss public sector HRM practices are infinitely more diverse than this brief overview can capture, reflecting the multitude of statutes in force.

References

Atkinson, M. M., Fulton, M., & Kim, B. (2014). Why do governments use pay for performance? Contrasting theories and interview evidence. *Canadian Public Administration, 57*(3), 436–458.

Barrette, J. (2005). Architecture de ressources humaines: Perspectives théoriques et pistes de recherche. *Relations Industrielles, 60*(2), 213–243.

Bellanger, F., & Roy, C. (2013). Evolution du cadre légal et réglementaire de la fonction publique suisse. In A. Ladner, Y. Emery, J.-L. Chappelet, P. Knoepfel, L. Mader, N. Soguel, & F. Varone (Eds.), *Hanbuch öffentliche Verwaltung* (pp. 461–480). Zürich: Neue Zürcher Zeitung libro.

Bühlmann, F., Beetschen, M., David, T., Ginalski, S., & Mach, A. (2015). Transformation des élites en Suisse. *Social Change in Switzerland, 1*. Retrieved from http://socialchangeswitzerland.ch

Demmke, C., & Moilanen, T. (2010). *Civil service in the EU of 27: Reform outcomes and the future of the civil service*. Berlin: Peter Lang.

DGAFP. (2010). *Répertoire interministériel des métiers de l'Etat Politiques d'emploi publiques*. Paris: Ministère du Budget, des Comptes publics, de la Fonction publique et de la Réforme de l'État.

Emery, Y., & Chassot, F. (2009). Evolution de la politique institutionnelle de gestion des ressources humaines: quelles valeurs ajoutées pour la mise en oeuvre des politiques publiques substantielles ? In P. Knoepfel (Ed.), *Réforme de politique institutionnelle de gestion des ressources de l'action publique* (pp. 137–164). Lausanne: PPUR.

Emery, Y., & Gonin, F. (2009). *Gérer les ressources humaines*. Lausanne: PPUR.

Emery, Y., & Grund, F. (2017). La fonction publique avec ou sans droit disciplinaire. In F. Bellanger & T. Tanquerel (Eds.), *Le droit disciplinaire: instrument nécessaire de l'efficacité administrative ou relique d'une époque révolue ?* Genève: Schulthess.

Emery, Y., & Kouadio, A. B. (2017). Marque employeur et stratégies RH pour les employeurs publics. Le cas du bassin d'emploi Franco-Valdo-Genevois. *Management International, 21*(2), 47–59.

Emery, Y., & Lambelet-Rossi, L. (2000). *Les politiques du personnel: conception, analyse et recommandations* (Vol. 192). Chavannes-près-Renens: IDHEAP.

Federal Chancellery. (2000). *Votation no 473, Tableau récapitulatif*. https://www.admin.ch/ch/f/pore/va/20001126/det473.html. Accessed 11 Sept 2017.

Federal Statistical Office. (2014). *Wage levels—Private and public sectors*. https://www.bfs.admin.ch/bfs/fr/home/statistiques/travail-remuneration/salaires-revenus-cout-travail/niveau-salaires-suisse/secteurs.prive-public.html. Accessed 21 Nov 2017.

Germann, R. E. (1996). *Administration publique en Suisse*. Berne: Haupt.

Gerrish, E. (2016). The impact of performance management on performance in public organizations: A meta-analysis. *Public Administration Review, 76*(1), 48–66.

Giauque, D. (2013). L'administration publique fédérale suisse en comparaison internationale: à la recherche d'une tradition administrative. In A. Ladner, J.-L. Chappelet, Y. Emery, P. Knoepfel, L. Mader, N. Soguel, & F. Varone (Eds.), *Manuel d'administration publique suisse* (pp. 31–45). Lausanne: PPUR.

Giauque, D., & Emery, Y. (2008). *Repenser la gestion publique*. Lausanne: PPUR.

Giauque, D., & Emery, Y. (2016). Les acteurs de l'administration publique au coeur du changement et de l'innovation. In D. Giauque & Y. Emery (Eds.), *L'acteur et la bureaucratie au XXIème siècle* (pp. 353–384). Laval/Québec: PUL.

Giauque, D., Anderfuhren-Biget, S., & Varone, F. (2012a). HRM practices, intrinsic motivators and organizational performance in the public sector. *Public Personnel Management, 42*(2), 123–150.

Giauque, D., Anderfuhren-Biget, S., & Varone, F. (2012b). La «guerre des talents» est-elle perdue d'avance? Attirer et fidéliser les salariés par les valeurs du service public. Pyramides. *Revue du Centre d'études et de recherches en administration publique, 23*, 21–48.

Guérard, S., & Pailot, P. (2007). Entre concours d'entrée et évaluations des compétences: Recrutement renouvelé des agents publics. In Y. Emery & D. Giauque (Eds.), *Dilemmes de la GRH publique* (pp. 109–137). Lausanne: LEP.

Hablützel, P. (2013). Bureaucrates, managers ou concepteurs de systèmes ? L'administration suisse et la direction de l'administration en pleine évolution. In A. Ladner, J.-L. Chappelet, Y. Emery, P. Knoepfel, L. Mader, N. Soguel, & F. Varone (Eds.), *Manuel d'administration publique suisse* (pp. 83–97). Lausanne: PPUR.

Koller, C., Heuberger, N., & Rolland, A.-C. (2011). Monitoring de l'état. Indicateurs pour la mesure comparative des administrations publiques et des autorités cantonales. In *Working Paper de l'IDHEAP 2* (pp. 1–97). Lausanne: IDHEAP.

Kuperus, H., & Rode, A. (2008). *Hauts fonctionnaires en Europe*. Maastricht: EIPA.

Ladner, A. (2013). Etat, système politique et accomplissement de tâches. In A. Ladner, J.-L. Chappelet, Y. Emery, P. Knoepfel, L. Mader, N. Soguel, & F. Varone (Eds.), *Manuel d'administration publique suisse* (pp. 7–30). Lausanne: PPUR.

OECD (Organisation for Economic Co-operation and Development). (1997a). *En quête de résultats. Pratiques de gestion des performances*. Paris: PUMA/OECD.

OECD (Organisation for Economic Co-operation and Development). (1997b). *Questions et évolution dans la gestion publique*. Paris: PUMA/OECD.

OECD (Organisation for Economic Co-operation and Development). (2005). *Performance-related pay for government employees*. Paris: OECD.

OECD/PUMA. (1997). *La rémunération à la performance pour les cadres de la fonction publique* (Vol. 15). Paris: OECD.

Office fédéral du personnel (Ed.). (2002). *Führen lehren—Führen lernen* (Vol. 15). Berne.

Ospel, L. (2011). *Partenaires RH—Perceptions croisées, Ville de Lausanne*. (Master Thesis). Geneva: Geneva University.

Pichault, F., & Nizet, J. (2013). *Les pratiques de gestion des ressources humaines: conventions, contextes et jeux d'acteurs*. Paris: Points.

Reyge, G. (2007). *Evaluation du personnel. Histoire d'une mal-posture*. Paris: L'Harmattan.

Saridakis, G., Lai, Y., & Cooper, C. L. (2017). Exploring the relationship between HRM and firm performance: A meta-analysis of longitudinal studies. *Human Resource Management Review, 27*(1), 87–96.

Schedler, K. (1993). *Anreizsysteme in der öffentlichen Verwaltung*. Berne: Haupt.

Schedler, K., & Proeller, I. (2000). *New public management*. Berne: Haupt.

Sivertzen, A. M., Nilsen, E. R., & Olafsen, A. H. (2013). Employer branding: Employer attractiveness and the use of social media. *Journal of Product & Brand Management, 22*(7), 473–483.

Thériault, R., & St-Onge, S. (2006). *Gestion de la rémunération: Théorie et pratique*. Montreal: Gaëtan Morin.

Thom, N., & Ritz, A. (2013). *Le management public. Concepts innovants dans le secteur public*. Lausanne: PPUR.

Ulrich, D. (Ed.). (1998). *Delivering results*. Boston: Harvard Business Review Book.

Ulrich, D., Allen, N. J., Brockbank, W., Younger, J., & Nyman, M. (2009). *HR transformation. Building HR from the outside in*. New York: McGraw Hill.

van Wart, M. (2013). Lessons from leadership theory and the contemporary challenges of leaders. *Public Administration Review, 73*(4), 553–565.
Vidaillet, B. (2012). *Evaluez-moi ! Evaluation au travail: les ressorts d'une fascination*. Paris: Seuil.
Widmer, P. (2010). *Dans quelle mesure l'administration fédérale est-elle compétitive sur le marché du travail ? Perspective des étudiants et jeunes professionnels du droit*. Lausanne: IDHEAP.
Wisard, N. (2007). Le statut de la fonction publique en mutation: contrat de droit public et individualisation des conditions de travail. In Y. Emery & D. Giauque (Eds.), *Dilemmes de la GRH publique*. Lausanne: Editions Loisirs et Pédagogie.

CHAPTER 13

Communication and Transparency

Martial Pasquier

13.1 Introduction

The management of public organisations has undergone considerable change over the past three or four decades as a result of increased pressure on results, greater autonomy in using resources and setting priorities, heightened accountability requirements and interest from citizens and the media in public decisions and action. Management tools—some from the private sector and others developed specifically for the public sector—have been added to the range of instruments available to public managers. Among these tools, communication—within organisations, with all the partners, with the community as a whole—plays an important role. Increasingly, those responsible for public action must present the issues involved in public policies, explain decisions that are taken, provide justification for the ensuing measures and respond to the needs of, and requests made by, the beneficiaries of services.

A number of factors account for the development of public communication over the past two decades. Among the most important are the following:

M. Pasquier (✉)
IDHEAP, University of Lausanne, Lausanne, Switzerland
e-mail: martial.pasquier@unil.ch

A. Ladner et al. (eds.), *Swiss Public Administration*, Governance and Public Management,
https://doi.org/10.1007/978-3-319-92381-9_13

- Growing autonomy in public administration and the desire of agencies to forge a distinct profile.
- Citizens' need for information to enable them to participate in democratic life.
- The mediatization of society, especially with respect to government and politics, together with the rising expectations of citizens regarding the capacity of public administrative bodies to account for their decisions and activities.

This chapter is divided into three parts. The first presents the various functions fulfilled by public communication in a modern democracy. The second sets out the principles of active communication, specifically communication organised by public administrations. The third and final part discusses the principles of transparency—also called passive communication, meaning communication issued in response to access to information (ATI) requests.

13.2 The Functions of Public Communication in Our Society

Public communication, unlike that in private organisations (whose primary goal is to persuade people to acquire goods or services), often has to fulfil a number of very different functions at the same time. Although it is difficult to rank these functions in the order of priority (any may be important, depending on the type of organisation, the field of public policy or the particular situation), core functions can be distinguished from complementary functions on the basis of legal requirements. Some tasks, such as informing the public or promoting values, are enshrined in laws. Other tasks, such as highlighting the activities of an organisation or receiving citizens, are generally accepted and recognised but not mentioned in laws, except perhaps indirectly.

13.2.1 Core Functions

Core functions normally arise out of a legal obligation placed on a public institution or organisation. Core functions can be divided into four main categories: information, explanation, promotion of values and dialogue.

13.2.1.1 Public Information

This is the most important function in a democracy and stems from the principle of publicity[1]. If a democracy is to function correctly, debates and decisions must be transparent and known to all. Democracies therefore oblige their governments to publish all laws, by laws and orders in publicly available documents and to transcribe and publish parliamentary proceedings. Similarly, trials and judicial decisions must be public[2].

The publicity principle applies to all decisions and actions of institutions and the administration, which have a responsibility to provide regular, comprehensive information on their activities and decisions, ranging from the publication of the appointment books of ministers and senior civil servants, to announcements of public appointments and detailed activity reports. This function is vital because, with increased demands from citizens, the complex institutional framework and "legislative inflation" (growth of legal norms), clear and accurate information must be readily accessible to those concerned.

13.2.1.2 Explanations and Complementary Information on Decisions

The complexity of public policies—as regards both their content and their implementation—together with a wider application of the accountability principle requires public institutions and organisations to provide explanations of the issues and scope of the decisions made and to accompany these decisions with communications measures. This function goes beyond information, since it involves anticipating questions that may be raised by those concerned and requires pedagogical skills to convey information that is often complex for non-professionals. For example, following the passage of a law in Switzerland that clamped down on undeclared work, the federal government instituted a series of measures to provide information and raise awareness, including a communication campaign targeting the general public. The primary aims of the campaign were to make people aware of the problem (including private households that hire domestic staff), to invite them to visit a website and to thank those who observed the rules.

[1] Kant (1795) considered the publicity principle to be fundamental for a democracy: "Every legal claim *must* be capable of publicity." Bentham (1830) held that general sittings of the legislature must be open to the public and that publicity is "the very soul of justice" (Gérard et al. 1987).

[2] The European Union has many portals for information access, such as EUR-Lex, the European law portal (http://eur-lex.europa.eu), the European e-Justice Portal (https://e-justice.europa.eu) and the Open Data portal (https://open-data.europa.eu).

13.2.1.3 Promotion of Values and Responsible Conduct

One of the tasks of the state is to protect and promote human rights and the basic values of the rule of law (equality, fair treatment, individual freedoms, etc.), as well as values recognised by society and institutions (e.g. the integration of people with disabilities) and responsible civic conduct (respect for the environment).

First, these values and behaviours must be exhibited by public institutions and organisations, taking care to avoid inconsistencies that are often detected by interest groups and the media (such as a minister with responsibility for social solidarity who has undeclared domestic staff). Second, they must be conveyed to the population through organised events (women's rights day, mobility day, etc.), awareness campaigns aimed at target groups (children regarding nutrition, the elderly for flu shots, etc.) or public discussion. This function goes beyond the promotion of values; to guarantee a lasting effect, it must increasingly include support for those who observe these values.

13.2.1.4 Dialogue Between Institutions and Citizens

A notable feature of democratic life is citizen participation in institutions and debates. The development of multilevel governance with an increase in the number of political decision levels (European, regional, conurbation and inter-community) and the complexity of a great many public policies mean that both institutions and the administration have a responsibility to maintain an ongoing dialogue with citizens. Many organisations communicate only when they have information to convey. People cannot be expected to take in and process information if the organisation conveying the information is unknown and has little credibility. In a modern society, communication is an ongoing and interactive process.

13.2.2 Complementary Functions

Complementary functions differ from core functions not because they are less important in communications terms but because very often they have no explicit legal foundation. They arise out of a modern conception of public organisations.

13.2.2.1 Service Delivery

Very few laws address the manner in which citizens should be received by an administration, the information that is made available in advance, the physical comfort of the reception provided, the manner in which staff answer the telephone or attitudes displayed during personal interactions.

And yet the initial contact with an organisation, waiting time and comfort, the friendliness and empathy of staff and the ease with which contact is made with someone using appropriate attitudes and language are essential components in the evaluation of a public service. Signage, office layout, urban furniture and people's attitudes and behaviours are all part of an organisation's identity; public organisation managers are thus placing growing importance on establishing a distinct identity for their organisations and facilitating relations with the recipients of services, especially in cases where managers enjoy some administrative autonomy.

The office of a department dealing with personal bankruptcies pronounced by a judge (inventory of assets, liquidation of assets, etc.) was housed in a building showing all the classic stereotypes associated with bureaucratic administration: an anonymous, overheated reception area, personnel separated from the public by a narrow counter topped with opaque glass, manually opened counter windows and so on. Relations with administrative personnel were often tinged with aggression (no privacy and an insufficient number of—uncomfortable—seats). The managers of the department took the opportunity afforded by a move to consider how their clients could be received and played an active part in the interior architectural design of the reception area, which featured a waiting room that was comfortable but not luxurious, spaces for discussion with tables and chairs, low partitions to provide a minimum of privacy while protecting employees' safety and so on. Managers reported that relations with clients improved considerably following the introduction of these changes.

13.2.2.2 Responsiveness

Responding to the public goes further than simply interacting with citizens because it requires an organisation to have specific processes and instruments. Responsiveness does not refer to an individual official's ability to comprehend a person's needs and make an appropriate response, but rather an administration's aptitude for gathering information from users in an organised manner, synthesising it and making sense of it so that a political or administrative response can be made when necessary. Some traditional tools for accomplishing this are claims management, symposia for recording and discussing criticisms, discussions with organised user groups and other forms of citizen participation.

Surveys are very widespread in government and administrative spheres and are sometimes the subject of an official communications mission. They may be qualitative or quantitative and are used to assess the extent to which members of the public are informed about and comprehend various topics, to sound out public opinion on a subject at a given time or to take note of as yet unidentified needs or expectations.

13.2.2.3 Organisational Legitimacy and Public Actions

Many public organisations are little known to the public. There are a variety of reasons for this: they only affect small groups of the population (prisons), deal with highly complex subjects (research centres) or are very rarely on the political agenda (legal metrology departments in charge of units of measurement, measuring instruments and methods).

Public organisations can accomplish their missions more easily if they are known to the public, recognised as legitimate and provide clearly identified services. Communication measures can therefore serve to raise public awareness, inform those concerned of their rights and obligations and the possibility of calling on the organisation's services and make it easier for the organisation itself to recruit staff.

13.2.2.4 Maintenance of Social Cohesion

While all the functions mentioned hitherto may be the subject of targeted measures and sometimes even purely ad hoc measures, the final function, maintenance of social cohesion, is more general and more difficult to pin down. It is nevertheless of vital importance, because a society's vitality depends on the bonds linking members to one another. Although well-integrated urban populations rarely experience problems with social cohesion, it is often difficult for those who are marginalised physically, geographically or socially to feel that they are full members of the community, to develop in the community and contribute to its development in their own way. Public authorities can also use communication to help forge and maintain social bonds among people who would like to do so. Support for local media and even the creation of such media (regional press, web TV solutions, etc.), the organisation of lectures and discussions and online forums are all examples of measures that contribute to social cohesion.

13.3 The Principles of Active Communication

A number of rules are found in almost every case, each of particular significance depending on the political system, cultural diversity and medium used.

13.3.1 *Legal Bases*

Although legal bases differ considerably from one country to another, a distinction can be drawn between general and specific legal bases (Barrelet and Werly 2011):

- General legal bases: legal bases vary between countries. In Switzerland, the provision of information is a duty defined in section 180 of the 1999 Constitution[3]. Details of this duty are set out in sections 10 and 10a of the Government and Administration Organization Act. Although a legal basis for public communication exists in most countries, there is wide variation in the formal level of this duty and especially in its material content. Perhaps on account of this very general nature—which is of little use in differentiating public communication from political communication—a number of countries have formulated internal guidelines to frame all such activities[4].
- Specific legal bases: numerous specific provisions are found in laws, rulings, decrees, orders and guidelines, some concerning a field of public policy and others a specific institution. In Switzerland, for example, section 10 of the Energy Law of 16 June 1998 stipulates that "The federal energy board and the cantons provide the public and authorities with information and advice on the conditions of economic and ecological energy supply, the possibilities for using energy efficiently and rationally, and the use of renewable energies [...] and that [...] the Confederation and the cantons may, as part of such activities and in collaboration with individuals, set up organizations tasked with providing information and advice to the public."

13.3.2 *Identification of the Source*

The first criterion is that the source, or issuer, should be clearly identified. It is very important that all those to whom a communication is addressed are able to identify promptly and without any doubt that the issuer is a public institution or organisation. The legitimacy of a message is first and

[3] Paragraph 2: "It informs the public about its activity in a timely and detailed manner, provided that this is not precluded by any preponderant public or private interest."

[4] Switzerland: *Information et communication du Conseil fédéral et de l'administration fédérale. Ligne directrices de la Conférence des services d'information de la Confédération* (2003).

foremost a function of the quality of its source. If the issuer is not known or not identifiable, there is a risk that the information will be given no more consideration than information released by any organisation without particular legitimacy.

The necessity for a clearly and easily identifiable source to some extent precludes the use of certain communications techniques, for example, those of viral marketing. Tools that enable messages to be transmitted quickly by directly asking all the members of a community or network to forward information must be handled with care in order to prevent any loss of control over the content or a biased interpretation due to the bearer's lack of legitimacy.

13.3.3 Maintaining Arm's Length from Electoral Issues or Referenda

The most sensitive criterion in the discussion over the use of public money for political purposes is the proximity of communications activities to election or referendum dates. A party in power or an elected representative may be strongly tempted to use government services to promote their political record or defend political choices that they have made when the public is called upon to cast their votes.

Although rules to counter such behaviour can be introduced with relative ease in countries with a representative democracy, the situation is very different in countries where citizens are called to the ballot box regularly. This is the case in Switzerland, where use of instruments such as the popular initiative and referenda can result in citizens' having to vote as many as four times per year at the federal, cantonal and communal levels. While the administration must show great restraint in communication activities connected with the subject of the vote, it is not excluded from the debate, since its members can participate, provided that they observe the principles of neutrality and proportionality. Often, the administration will publish reports and civil servants will take part in the debate, but such communications must remain technical in nature or help to explain the government's position. Taking a position could appear to be partisan and is thus prohibited[5].

[5] A senior civil servant was criticised for having authorised publication of a paid advertisement in which his photograph was shown next to remarks he had made. In answer to a question from a member of parliament, the minister stated: "[…] it is proper for a senior civil

So delicate is this subject, however, that such government or administration involvement is frequently the subject of political debate or court rulings. In 2008, the administrative court of the canton of Geneva annulled a referendum on the grounds that the government's summary of its position and opposing arguments in the official pamphlet mailed to citizens was "schematic" and "peremptory" and asserted a "partisan position" (ATA/583/2008 of 18.11.2008). In 2003, a group of citizens launched a popular initiative entitled "Popular sovereignty without political propaganda" demanding that both government and administration abstain from political debate concerning referenda (only an information brochure and a short position statement in the media would be authorised). Although the initiative was soundly rejected by over 75% of voters in a referendum on 1 June 2008, it highlighted the delicate balance that has to be maintained between the duty to inform, promoting a government project and political debate. Very recently (2017), the president of the city of Geneva was sanctioned for producing an imbalanced referendum brochure, leading to the referendum's cancellation.

13.3.4 Continuity

While private organisations and political parties are free to choose whether or not to communicate about a given subject, the same does not apply to political and administrative authorities. The two elements that must be taken into account are continuity in communication and timely transmission of information.

Continuity in communication means that organisations cannot wait until the end of a process or until they have all the relevant information before communicating. Thus partial results, variants and intermediate stages must also be presented to the public even though definitive answers cannot be given at the time. This implies that authorities cannot keep important information hidden for tactical reasons or to avoid embarrassment.

Information must also be passed on in a timely manner in order to fuel democratic debate and facilitate the work of elected representatives and the media. Generally speaking, information is of value only at certain times

servant to explain the technical reasons that support the Federal Council's point of view; his photo may even accompany his statements, but he should not appear in the visuals of a paid advertisement" (Bulletin officiel du Conseil national, 11.06.07, AB 2007 N 766/BO 2007 N 766).

and information that is released too early or, more problematically, too late is in many cases useless. For example, authorities frequently time the release of information to coincide with holiday periods or school holidays, with the aim of avoiding extensive media coverage.

13.3.5 Transparency of Funding

The financing of communications activities must be transparent with regard to both the amounts and origins of the sums spent. If public communication is directly or indirectly funded other than out of the public purse, this information must be clearly conveyed so that the receiver can, if applicable, take into account the relationship between the issuer and the source of funds when interpreting the message.

13.3.6 No Favourable Treatment for Recipients

Although a communication may be addressed for objective reasons to certain target groups, it must not discriminate against members of these groups. Public communication must therefore refrain from favouring particular journalists or particular elected representatives by informing them pre-emptively or more fully and thus ensure that all recipients of the message are treated the same way. This guideline is not always easy to follow, particularly in view of media needs and expectations. Given the competition between media and their different publishing or broadcasting schedules, the timing of the release of information may favour certain media to the detriment of others.

13.3.7 Objective and Comprehensive Content Tailored to the Target Audience

Most internal guidelines within an administration specify that messages must be objective and thorough. Although total objectivity in communication is impossible, and all the information available often cannot be released for reasons of time and space, public communication must strive to be objective by not suppressing criticism and by providing balanced information.

Adapting the content of communication to target groups is also very important. While specialists may be familiar with technical terms and acronyms, non-experts and the general public are not. In fact, the challenge in formulating a comprehensible message is not only to avoid the use of technical language but to consider whether people who are not proficient in the national language(s) are able to take in and understand official information. When one takes into account residents from foreign cultures and those who lack the ability or skills to read (the visually impaired and people of low literacy[6]), one can assume that a significant part of the populace is unable to understand typical messages disseminated by public authorities (the police, schools, administrative authorities, etc.). When formulating any important communication, administrations must consider the information needs of potentially marginalised populations and tailor the message accordingly.

13.3.8 Consistent and Coordinated Communication Between Administrative Departments and Levels of Government

In matters involving public policies affecting several departments of an administration, administrative departments at different institutional levels, and sometimes private stakeholders as well, those responsible for communication must coordinate the messages issued by all actors involved and ensure their consistency. This is particularly important in conflict or crisis situations where there is a high risk that even minor differences in content and a lack of coordination in the timing of messages could cause confusion that is difficult to remedy subsequently. In their communications activities, public institutions and organisations must make it a priority to coordinate messages and see that they are consistent—a delicate task, especially if the theme of the communication is a subject of much political controversy.

13.3.9 Communication Proportionate to Objectives and Target Audiences

A very useful criterion for differentiating public communication from political communication is proportionality with regard to objectives and target audiences. Although some political parties or elected representatives focus a significant share of their communications on a very small number of subjects, public communication must cover all subjects and

[6] According to the *Association lire et écrire*, one in six adults in Switzerland does not have the expected reading and writing skills. Source: https://www.lire-et-ecrire.ch/ressources-et-outils/lillettrisme-en-bref (retrieved on 4 January 2018).

deal with them in a proportionate manner. While public institutions and organisations are rarely criticised for failing to cover certain subjects, extensive media coverage of other subjects can be seen as politically significant.

13.3.10 Communication Focused on Dialogue

Because of the functions it must perform, public communication must stimulate dialogue and favour media that allow interaction between the organisation and the recipients of the message. It is often much easier to purchase advertising space to publish an announcement than it is to take on the task of organising and participating in debates and facing criticism. For many governments, the concept of dialogue is broader still and includes taking note of citizens' opinions through studies and surveys.

13.4 Passive Communication (Transparency)

Passive communication involves information issued by the administration in response to a request from a person under ATI rights. These rights are generally enshrined in freedom of information (FOI) laws, also known as transparency laws (Pasquier and Villeneuve 2007; Pasquier and Meilland 2009).

Historically, the foundations of the principle of access to government information were laid in Sweden, with the Freedom of the Press Act of 1766. In recent history, Finland in 1951 was the first country to protect citizens' right to information in its laws. Since then, many other countries have followed suit: the United States in 1966, France and the Netherlands in 1978 and Canada in 1983. In the early 1990s, it was the turn of southern European countries to pass transparency laws: Spain in 1992 and Greece and Portugal in 1993. More recently, similar legislation came into force in the United Kingdom in 2005 and in Germany and Switzerland in 2006.

FOI laws are similar from country to country and often have the same characteristics:

- Information that can be consulted: the basis of any FOI legislation is the possibility for citizens to request information, or a document containing the desired information, without having to give reasons for the request. The documents in question can be very varied in nature:

reports, notes, minutes of meetings, letters, emails and even unwritten documents such as telephone conversations. FOI laws must thus explicitly state what information is available and what is not.
- Exceptions: generally, these laws apply to all government and administrative bodies. However, exceptions are provided for on grounds of higher interests of the State (international relations and security services) or protection of citizens (courts and privacy).
- Assistance provided by the state in the search for information: given the complexity of government operations, citizens cannot be expected to know about all the documents that exist and are thus available to them. Depending on the country or the institution concerned, mechanisms are provided to inform citizens of the type of documents produced by the government.
- Time required for delivery of information: laws and regulations generally stipulate the time frame within which the government or body concerned must respond to an ATI request. Governments cannot therefore keep citizens waiting unduly. This is a vital point, considering that information often loses its value over time (subject no longer topical, important vote taken, etc.).
- Search costs and fees: generally, access requests are free or carry a nominal charge that will not create a significant obstacle. If search costs exceed a certain threshold (high number of photocopies, research time, etc.), they may be billed. However, the amounts in question must be reasonable, so as not to put access rights beyond the reach of some citizens.
- Remedy procedures: generally, a distinction is drawn between levels of remedy within the administration and the right to go to court to defend ATI rights when the administration refuses to comply, exceeds the permitted time frame or bills unreasonable charges.

Even though FOI legislation varies in the different countries that have adopted such legislation and processes can take diverse forms, the main objectives often present similarities. Governments claim that the public can obtain information and use it to verify that they work in the citizens' interests. From a philosophical point of view, Bentham directly connects secrecy with conspiracy and thus affirms that public officials will be less tempted to misuse power because of external monitoring (Hood 2006). Despite such support from both governments and citizens, it should be noted that, in some countries, there has been relatively low use of the new legislative instruments so far. Although the capacity to obtain more information about government through legal processes intuitively implies more transparency, two limitations remain. First, ATI requests in certain countries are mainly submitted by journalists, lawyers and interest groups. Second, low usage of ATI may reflect either a lack of interest or complex procedures for obtaining access. Consequently, greater access to governmental and administrative information may create a more transparent environment, but a real increase of transparency would probably involve more citizen participation. Figure 13.1 shows how requests have evolved over the last few years.

The number of ATI requests depicted above excludes requests made by phone, email and so on and those submitted at subnational levels. In Switzerland, cantons adopted transparency laws at different times. Bern was the first to legislate on the matter (the law was adopted in 1995), followed by 14 cantons between 2001 and 2011. A transparency law at the federal level (Ltrans) was voted in 2004 and enforced two years later.

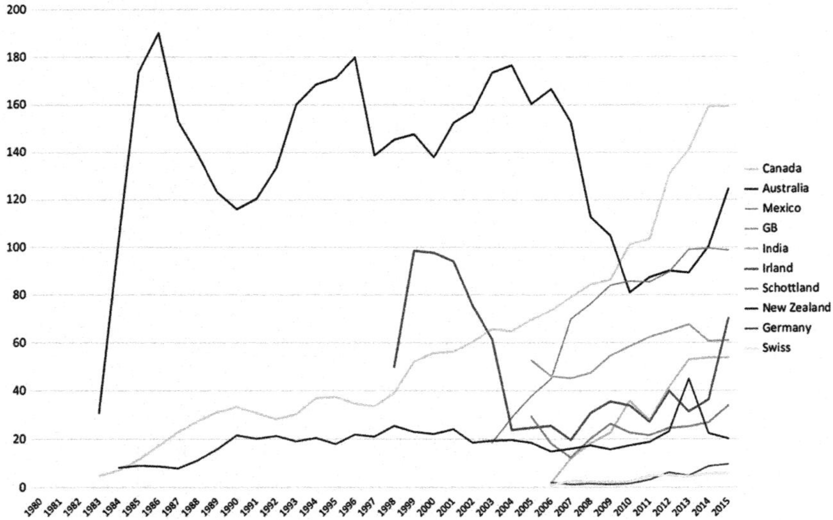

Fig. 13.1 Changes in the number of requests since FOI legislation was introduced in various countries (number of requests per one million inhabitants). (In Canada and India, requests are based on the fiscal year, running from April 1 to March 31, and in New Zealand and Australia, from July 1 to June 30. All other collected data are calendar year based)

Explanations given for the low number of ATI requests vary. One issue is how much awareness is there of the right to information among the population and certain specific groups, such as journalists. Since the right was granted relatively recently in Switzerland, it appears not to be well known to the public.

The country's communications policy, its ability and its willingness to disclose information proactively—mainly through making it available in a structured manner on websites—undoubtedly have a very great impact on the number of requests recorded. If information is freely accessible through directories, most people with access to a computer can easily download documents without the administration being able to count such downloads as access requests. One can assume, therefore, that a high number of officially filed requests correlate negatively with the possibility of accessing available information directly and freely.

Another reason often mentioned in the literature is the level of trust that citizens place in the government and authorities. The higher the trust, the lower the number of access requests should be, since one of the reasons put forward to account for the development of ATI rights is the possibility of holding the administration accountable and establishing a relationship of trust. The level of trust in the government is higher in Switzerland than in any other European country. A low level of trust may therefore account for a high number of requests.

Because the countries being compared have very different political systems, the information needs of certain groups and of the population as a whole at a given time may vary considerably. In a system with a governing majority and a minority in opposition, numerous requests are made by the opposition parties. They ordinarily receive limited information and as opposition, seek to counter the plans of the party in power. But in a system where the main parties are in power and have direct ATI held by the administration, as is the case in Switzerland, this need is significantly reduced.

The last reason concerns the level of government in charge of public policies. Citizens need information that affects their daily lives (schools, roads, land use, health, various authorisations, etc.) and the corresponding public policies fall within the purview of different levels of government in different countries. In the United States, Canada and Switzerland, many requests are not addressed to the federal government because the matters at issue fall under the jurisdiction of a region or municipality. This being so, all requests filed at all levels of government would have to be recorded in order to establish an accurate picture of the use of the right of ATI.

Naturally, the number of requests filed is not a sufficient indicator to determine the level of openness of any government but, combined with other indicators and interpreted in the light of the characteristics of the political system, it does provide evidence of citizens' interest in information held by the administration.

13.5 Conclusion

Public communication in Switzerland is characterised by two essential components of the country's political system: federalism and popular rights.

With three levels of government (Confederation, cantons and communes) and a large number of institutions working through networks (inter-cantonal conferences, urban areas, inter-communal organisations, etc.), the number of actors involved in communication is very high. In addition, most are very close to residents because public services are offered or managed by the lower levels of government (cantons and communes). Communication is thus highly decentralised, with strong proximity between the transmitter (administration) and receiver (citizens).

The second important characteristic, which is very specific to Switzerland, is popular rights, particularly referenda and popular initiatives. Because laws enacted by parliaments may be subject to a referendum, the way that information is managed by the administration and the needs of political parties differ from those in other countries. Often, it is not in the administration's interest to conceal information when preparing a parliamentary debate, because doing so could rebound against the government when a referendum is held, which may be several years later. Conversely, political parties and lobbyists do not necessarily need to access information ahead of parliamentary proceedings, because they know that they still have the referendum as a means of getting their ideas across, which is clearly not the case in countries where a government can push a law through parliament in a matter of months, with no possibility of a referendum.

References

Barrelet, D., & Werly, S. (2011). *Droit de la communication*. Berne: Stämpfli.

Gérard, Ph., Ost, F., & Van de Kerchove, M. (1987). *Actualité de la pensée juridique de Jeremy Bentham*. Bruxelles: Publication des Facultés universitaires Saint-Louis.

Hood, C. (2006). Transparency in historical perspective. In C. Hood & D. Heald (Eds.), *Transparency: The key to better governance? Proceedings of the british academy* (pp. 3–23). Oxford: Oxford University Press.

Pasquier, M., & Meilland, P. (2009). L'introduction du principe de la transparence dans l'administration fédérale. In P. Knoepfel (Ed.), *Réformes de politiques institutionnelles et action publique* (pp. 209–229). Lausanne: PPUR.

Pasquier, M., & Villeneuve, J.-P. (2007). Organizational barriers to transparency: A typology and analysis of organizational behaviour tending to prevent or restrict access to information. *International Review of Administrative Sciences, 73*(1), 147–162.

PART IV

Fiscal and Financial Management

CHAPTER 14

Financial Management System, Legislation and Stakeholders

Nils Soguel

14.1 Introduction

This chapter briefly depicts how financial management at the various Swiss government levels is governed by legislation and organized in practice. It presents the legal framework, the main institutional settings and the actors involved[1]. Within the Swiss federalist system, the cantons exercise considerable autonomy in financial management; each canton has designed its own way to manage its public finances. The 'standard'

[1] Here we use 'government' in the way it is used by the International Monetary Fund (IMF 2014): a unique legal entity established by political processes that has legislative, judicial or executive authority over other institutional units (households, corporations and non-profit institutions) within a given area (p. 14). Therefore, a government is an organization that includes several branches: a legislature (parliament), an executive branch with its administration and a judiciary, either at the federal, the cantonal or the municipal level.

The author is grateful to Aurélia Buchs and Ramon Christen for their contribution to this chapter.

N. Soguel (✉)
IDHEAP, University of Lausanne, Lausanne, Switzerland
e-mail: nils.soguel@unil.ch

A. Ladner et al. (eds.), *Swiss Public Administration*, Governance and Public Management,
https://doi.org/10.1007/978-3-319-92381-9_14

financial management both at the level of the Confederation (the upper tier) and at the cantonal level is summarized here, and while their financial system is similar, municipalities are not explicitly addressed.

The following section presents the legal foundations and guiding principles of financial management at the national and cantonal levels. Section 14.3 addresses the implications the legal foundations have for preparing and implementing the budget, detailing the role the different bodies play at each stage of the process. Section 14.4 is dedicated to two specifically Swiss institutions meant to ensure the government's fiscal sustainability, the fiscal rules[2] and the financial referendum together with the right of initiative.

14.2 Legal Foundations

The legal foundation governing financial management is provided by the Constitution and the Financial Management Act of Parliament (FMAP). The same legal architecture prevails at the level of the Confederation and in each of the 26 cantons. Each canton is free to decide upon the procedures for managing its budget. Therefore, each canton also has its own FMAP. Cantonal FMAPs have similarities, as do their processes of financial management.

The legal foundation—Constitution and FMAP—generally governs the budgetary principles, the appropriations, the financial budgeting and reporting and the financial management at the operational level. It regulates the parliament (either at the federal or at the cantonal level), the executive branch and the various public administration units. It also defines the financial management abilities of these bodies.

Most of the legally binding budgetary principles are standard. For instance, the principle of legality demands that there be a legal base for all expenditures and revenues. Expenditures and revenues must be balanced, at least in the long run. The principles of efficiency and effectiveness should guide spending behavior and contribute to balancing the budget. The principle of urgency also helps to prioritize expenditures and guarantee project necessity and feasibility. Earmarking main taxes and pre-appropriating them for specific types of expenditures are in principle prohibited. The user-pays principle is relatively uncommon, though it is mentioned in the FMAP of several cantons. It postulates that, wherever possible, beneficiaries of public services must bear the costs of these services.

[2] Fiscal rule is also often referred to as budget constraint or financial rule.

In general, a typical cantonal FMAP is fairly detailed regarding the regulation of appropriations (i.e., the regulation of credits called *Kreditrecht* or *droit des credits*). Apart from complying with the principle of legality, every expenditure item must be based on a credit appropriated by the Parliament. An FMAP usually typically specifies four kinds of appropriations: budgetary, supplementary, contingent and ancillary.

The budgetary appropriation (*Budgetkredit*, *crédit budgétaire*) is the most straightforward, since the budget formally approved by the Parliament for the next fiscal year (i.e., the beginning-of-the-year budget) is largely the sum of the budgetary appropriations requested by the executive branch. Once approved, the budgetary appropriation counts as an authorization to spend for the specific and corresponding purpose.

The supplementary appropriation (*Nachtragskredit, crédit supplémentaire*) is a further 'authorization to spend'. This type of credit is requested by the executive branch during the fiscal year when the existing budgetary appropriation proves insufficient. Both budgetary and supplementary appropriations are valid only for the fiscal year at hand. Should these appropriations not be spent by the end of the year, the executive branch is not authorized to later spend what remains.

The two remaining kinds of appropriations are meant for projects lasting more than a fiscal year and that typically entail capital expenditures for infrastructure such as school or hospital buildings. To commit itself to such projects, the council of the executive branch (hereafter the Executive Council) must be reasonably confident that once it requests funds from Parliament via a budget appropriation that Parliament will agree to appropriate the necessary amount. To obtain this assurance, the Executive Council submits a contingent appropriation (*Verpflichtungskredit, crédit d'engagement*) for parliamentary approval. The request may be submitted at any time during the year and, in principle, is outside of the usual procedure for drafting and adopting the budget. A contingent appropriation authorizes the Executive Council to make commitments to the various stakeholders in the corresponding project, but does not count as an authorization to spend. For that, the executive branch must ask Parliament to transform the contingent appropriation into a budgetary appropriation for the portion that corresponds to the work to be carried out during the coming fiscal year. In case the amount of a contingent appropriation is not enough to complete the project, the executive branch may request an ancillary appropriation (Zusatzkredit, crédit complémentaire), meaning a supplementary contingent appropriation. These four kinds of appropriations require majority approval by Parliament.

14.3 Financial Process and Main Actors

The financial process may vary between cantons. Figure 14.1 shows the sequence of a typical process with its respective outcome documents: the mission statement, the financial plan, the contingent appropriations, the budget, the financial statements, the audit report and the financial statistics. The fiscal year in question is designated as year t, and Fig. 14.1 shows when each step takes place relative to it. The Swiss fiscal year is the same as the calendar year, running from January 1 to December 31.

Figure 14.1 underscores the decision-making power of the different participating bodies: the Executive Council, the Parliament and, in some cases, the citizens. The process may appear to be like that in other countries, but there are Swiss particularities, including the instruments of direct democracy, the preeminence of legislative over the executive branch and the fact that citizens directly elect the members of Executive Councils (*Regierungsrat, Conseil d'Etat*). This last characteristic contrasts with other countries in which executive members are not elected but appointed by a prime minister or president. In Swiss cantons, the member of the executive responsible for financial management (the finance minister) and other members responsible for thematic issues like education or health (the spending ministers) have additional incentives to play their typical roles in the financial process if they intend to run for re-election and want to present a positive record of their accomplishments. This creates checks and balances between the 'spending ministers' on the one side and the finance minister on the other side.

14.3.1 Mission Statement and Financial Plan

The financial process begins before the debate about allocating financial resources commences. In fact, the FMAP requires a newly elected Executive Council to immediately draw up a joint mission statement for Parliament covering the four- to five-year electoral term (if the executive has a longer-term vision, this time horizon sometimes can be extended). To ensure that the mission statement remains specific, the departments (the cantonal equivalent of national-level ministries) are required to design and cost out the projects which will fulfill this vision of the executive. These projects are then collected and subsumed within a multi-year financial plan (*Finanzplan; plan financier*) accompanying the mission statement.

	Earlier years	Year t-1	Year t	Year t+1	Beyond Year t+1
Mission statment and financial plan	Council of the executive branch				
Planning of major projects and contingent appropriations	Council of the executive branch				
Decision over contingent appropriations	Parliament or citizens				
Change in the tax law		Parliament or citizens			
Budget preparation		Council of the executive branch			
Budget adoption and budgetary appropriations		Parliament			
Budget execution			Council of the executive branch		
Supplementary appropriations			Parliament		
Preparation of the financial statements				Council of the executive branch	
Financial and compliance audit				Audit office	
Approval of the financial statements				Parliament	
Elaboration of the financial statistics				Federal Department of Finance	

Fig. 14.1 Typical financial process and the decision-making bodies

14.3.2 Planning of Major Projects and Contingent Appropriation Requests

Careful planning is necessary if a mission statement, or existing legislation, calls for implementing major projects, because the FMAP lays out special features before any spending can occur. As already mentioned, a contingent appropriation is necessary for multi-year projects. Additionally, should the amount requested exceed a predetermined amount (see below), the FMAP requires that a referendum be held on the contingent appropriation which has been approved by parliament.

To illustrate this process, consider a department with a project that requires a contingent appropriation. The department must prepare a report justifying the project and planning for its finances (expected capital expenditure and receipt and recurring expenses and revenues). The report is submitted to other departments which are potentially affected, inviting them to express their views. As most projects have financial consequences, the department of finance (DoF) also offers its comments. In its report, the DoF evaluates whether the project meets the budgetary principles (efficiently, effectively, etc.). Next, the Executive Council considers the comments and debates about the project. Provided the expenditure level does not exceed its financial mandate, the Executive Council decides, definitively, whether to accept it or not. Otherwise it must pass the request on to the Parliament.

14.3.3 Decision over Contingent Appropriation Requests

Once the executive branch passes the request to Parliament, the relevant parliamentary commissions (financial or thematic) analyze the project and forward their opinion to the plenum. Depending on the amount involved, Parliament's decision is enforceable or may be challenged by popular referendum. Once the project and the corresponding contingent appropriation are accepted, be it by the Executive Council, the parliament or the citizens after a referendum, it must then be translated into annual installments, in the form of budgetary appropriations in the next budget and beyond that in the annual forecasts of the multi-year financial plan.

14.3.4 Budget Preparation

In Switzerland, the budget reflects the existing legal foundations, including the tax provisions. Due to time constraints associated with launching a referendum against a law, the possibilities of adapting laws when preparing the budget are limited. In countries without this right, the government is freer to amend its laws, including tax laws, when creating its budget. In Switzerland, the decisions surrounding public policies and their execution therefore come into play well before the creation of the budget.

That being said, the annual budget (for year t) is prepared simultaneously with updating the financial plan for the following years. The usual time horizon for the plan is three years (t + 1 to t + 3). Accordingly, the previous plan is considered when elaborating a budget and updating the financial plan. However, this is not binding, and an Executive Council will issue fresh guidelines to the various departments which are based on the DoF forecasts of expected revenues and projected tax revenue.

The finance ministers, as heads of the respective DoFs, are usually very cautious in their tax revenue forecasts, often underestimating them in an attempt to rein in the appetite for budgetary appropriations before the fact (Chatagny and Soguel 2012). Once the DoF receives the various departmental claims for budgetary appropriations and consolidates them, the total usually exceeds the guidelines or the expected revenues, or fails to meet the target imposed by a canton's FMAP fiscal rule (see below). It typically takes several rounds of negotiations between the DoF and the spending departments (typically education, social welfare or health) to finalize the budget. The Executive Council intervenes when administrative departments cannot agree. The budget is prepared according to the standards for presentation provided in the FMAP, standards which also apply to presenting the financial statements at year's end.

The above depiction of executive-level budget preparation suggests that this preparation is a bottom-up and incremental process. It is certainly still so in many cantons where the budgetary appropriation claims for year t are based on budgetary appropriations approved by Parliament for the previous year (t – 1). Only large efficiency distortions, the need to finance new projects, or fiscal stress might force the government to systematically review existing programs. According to Aschwanden and Gerny (2013), this happened in 2013 when 16 cantons experienced unusual difficulties in balancing their budgets and had to adjust them.

With the onset of the New Public Management, performance-based budgeting has been implemented in some cantons. In this case, Parliament no longer governs the executive exclusively in an input-oriented manner but also specifies the expected qualitative or quantitative characteristics of the public service to be provided. Along with these specifications come the corresponding budgetary appropriations. This makes the budget process more output-oriented. For instance, in the canton of Aargau, Parliament sets the health department goals for school-based immunization.

In line with strengthening the fiscal rules, many cantons have also adopted a more top-down budgeting process. Fiscal rules straitjacket the government's budget and it becomes legally virtually impossible to run deficits. Therefore, the forecasts of expected revenues made by a DoF at the outset of the process are more binding than when the fiscal rules were softer. To make sure the fiscal rule requirement is fulfilled, the Executive Council, sometimes with the approval of the Parliament's standing committee on finance, undertakes the initial budgetary appropriation and allocates the forecasted revenues between the departments. This approach enables a better match between the council's mission statement and the budget. Every department then is required to allocate the granted appropriation—but not more—to the various tasks it must carry out.

14.3.5 Budget Adoption

Most cantonal parliaments must only take note of the updated financial plan referred to it by the executive branch in early autumn. Parliamentary budget debate thus focuses on the budget for the next fiscal year, with preliminary discussions taking place in several parliamentary commissions. The financial commission usually takes a defensive position, trying to maintain the balance proposed by the Executive Council, while each thematic commission tries to expand its own public services by advocating for more expenditures, whether for education, health or culture. Eventually, the budget is accepted by Parliament in December.

In principle, Parliament has the final say in the budget, giving it more power than the Executive Council. However, the tight schedule prevents Parliament from initiating fundamental changes once the budget has been submitted to it (Pfäffli 2011), which means power actually resides in the Executive Council and the public administration. Nevertheless, when a tax law change is proposed while the budget is in preparation, the proposal can be subject either to a mandatory or optional referendum, giving the final say to the citizens.

For instance, in late 2016, voters in the canton of Lucerne rejected the tax rate increase proposed by Parliament and thus rejected the proposed 2017 budget. Consequently, the government had to start the 2017 fiscal year without a valid budget until the Parliament agreed over the necessary spending cuts that enabled compliance with the fiscal rule without increasing the tax rate. The agreement was reached in mid-September 2017 only. In the meantime, the executive branch had to limit itself to necessary spending related to contracts already signed (von Däniken 2017).

The threat of a referendum gives both the Executive Council and the administration incentives to initially propose an acceptable budget. However, a power gap still exists between the government and the citizens because the latter by and large face a tie-in sale as they cannot decide upon individual budgetary appropriations. Yet two mechanisms are available which allow citizens to directly influence the budget allocation: (1) using a financial referendum to fight a contingent appropriation proposal or (2) launching a popular initiative (petition) requiring a change in legislation that would then increase or decrease expenditures (see below).

14.3.6 Budget Execution and Supplementary Appropriations

The executive branch executes the budget once it has been approved by Parliament. The executive branch applies the budget. Indeed, the budget appropriations give the executive branch the right to spend monies, up to the appropriated limit and for the prescribed purposes, between 1 January and 31 December of Year t.

Budget implementation usually does not go as planned. The cost of some inputs or the demand for certain public services may increase, and so initial budgetary appropriations may not suffice. The Executive Council has some leeway in reallocating initial appropriations, but the need may be greater than what has been already appropriated. In that case, the executive branch submits a request to Parliament for a supplementary appropriation.

14.3.7 Preparation of the Financial Statements

The fiscal year-end period rings in the preparation of the annual financial statements. The DoF prepares them under the accrual basis of accounting according to the FMAP. This involves the faithful representation of the effects of transactions, as well as other events and conditions, in accordance with the definitions and recognition criteria for assets, liabilities, revenue and expenses. It also involves some book entries that satisfy secondary interests rather than present the financial situation as it is. Insofar as these entries are within the limits of the FMAP, the literature calls them creative accounting or political finessing techniques (Clémenceau and Soguel 2018)[3].

Indeed, the finance ministers have incentives to exploit the opportunities for political finessing provided by the FMAP. First, techniques can directly help fulfill the fiscal rule, especially if the rule is stringent. Second, an excessive deficit, but also a large surplus, may place the finance minister in an awkward position. In case of a deficit, citizens may judge that the minister has lost control of the public finances. In case of a surplus, they may feel they are paying too much in tax and demand either greater public spending or a reduction of the tax burden (e.g., using a popular initiative). If these claims are successful, the long-term fiscal balance is at risk, especially if the surplus was triggered by a favorable business cycle. The prospect endangers compliance with existing fiscal rule as well as the finance minister's re-election chances (Clémenceau and Soguel 2017).

14.3.8 Financial and Compliance Audit of the Financial Statements

The FMAP requires the auditing of the financial statements and sets the reference terms for the auditor. It explicitly requires a financial and compliance audit, in order to investigate the legality of expenditures, the proper recording of receipts and the correct operation of receipts and expenditures controls. The auditor must certify the absence of fraud and whether reports follow the law. It is worth noting that in most cantons, this does not require the auditor to certify whether the reports actually provide a true and fair presentation. That paradox is worth mentioning, since the FMAP often allows the aforementioned political finessing. The auditor's report is sent to Parliament together with the financial statements.

Each canton has an audit office (*Finanzkontrolle; Contrôle des finances*), governed by a cantonal law that is usually distinct from the FMAP. Depending on the canton, the head of the audit office is appointed by the Executive Council or by Parliament. The audit office is usually administra-

[3] The most common possibility—but not the obligation—offered by FMAPs for political finessing is to discretionarily inflate operating expenses with a book entry called 'additional depreciation charges'. The aim is to accrually and artificially lower the reported surplus. This book entry must not be confused with the true depreciation charges representing actual wear and tear or the obsolescence of assets.

tively attached to the finance minister. However, it is only in the law's debt and is therefore functionally independent when it acts as external auditor of the financial statements for the benefit of Parliament. Aside from its function as external auditor, it supervises the entire government during the fiscal year with respect to the principles noted above (legality, urgency, economy, etc.). In this capacity, it acts as an internal auditor for the benefit of the Executive Council, in a manner like that found in the private sector[4].

14.3.9 Approval of the Financial Statements

Once the financial statements are audited, the Executive Council submits them to the Parliament for approval, which is a mere formality.

14.3.10 Elaboration of the Financial Statistics

The last step of the financial process consists in making the information contained in the financial statements of the 26 cantons—but also of the municipalities and of the central government—comparable and available for further analysis. This takes place in the years that follow the presentation of the financial statements by the various governments at all three levels.

The presentation of the financial statements is supposed to be harmonized between all these entities, but in reality, this is far from being the case. The central government's DoF has the unenviable task of overseeing financial statistics for the entire country, and along with the variation in what is reported. Notably, the scope of the financial statements must be harmonized, since some cantons, for instance, include hospitals in their accounts while others do not; the same prevails for universities or for job centers. Dealing with all these difficulties, ensuring that financial statistics satisfy quality requirements and comply with international guidelines (IMF Statistics Department 2014) thus takes a lot of effort and time. This is the price to be paid in a system as decentralized as the Swiss one.

[4] Anachronistically, two cantons (Geneva and Vaud) have decided to install a court of auditors (*Rechnungshof; Cour des comptes*) in addition to the audit office they already have. The idea was to have a more independent authority to supervise the government's work. The members of this court are elected by direct universal suffrage in Geneva and by Parliament in Vaud. Strangely enough, in Vaud, the court of auditor's main task is performance auditing rather than compliance auditing.

14.4 Two Specific Institutions Constraining the Public Finances

The economic literature gives various reasons for the existence of deficits or surpluses (Krishnakumar et al. 2010). When it comes to Switzerland, it is worth focusing on two institutions which are particularly significant for the management of the different tiers of Swiss government: the fiscal rules and the financial referendum.

Switzerland experienced an economic depression in the 1990s, with a resulting increase in its sovereign debt attributed to two asymmetries. First, governments behave asymmetrically by tolerating or engaging in deficit spending when the economy is in recession without securing surpluses when the economy is booming. The second asymmetry is that decision-making competency for expenditures is not granted at the same institutional level as it is for receipts. Parliament can often decide autonomously to spend, but a tax increase proposal must be put to a popular referendum (Lienhard and Marti Locher 2015).

14.4.1 Fiscal Rules

Fiscal rules and financial referenda have long been implemented to mitigate both asymmetries: The canton of St. Gallen implemented a so-called debt brake (debt containment rule) already in 1929. It was (anecdotally) reported that its debt level began decreasing two years after the debt brake was introduced, whereas it continued to rise in the other cantons. By now, all cantons but one (the small half-canton of Appenzell Innerrhoden) have introduced a fiscal rule, but the design and stringency of the fiscal rule varies widely. Some cantons anchored it in their constitution and others only in their FMAP, where it is easier to modify. The rule sometimes applies to the budget (beginning-of-the-year), sometimes to the annual account (end-of-the-year) and sometimes to both. In general, rules require balancing the budget, but this may apply to all transactions or only those entered in the operating account (i.e., excluding capital expenditure and receipts). Sometimes, a time period by which a fiscal balance must be obtained is explicitly required, as well as a sanction mechanism in case of missed targets, for example, a compulsory tax increase (Yerly 2014). Empirical evidence shows that cantons with stricter rules have significantly lower budget deficits and debt (Feld and Kirchgässner 2008).

As for the central government, 85% of Swiss voters supported the implementation of a debt brake. The mechanism is thus anchored in the Federal Constitution and has been applied since 2003. The rule requires balancing the budget over the course of a business cycle. To achieve that goal, expenditures are capped each year with a ceiling that depends on the annual receipts, adjusted for the economic situation. The adjustment is calculated using a cyclical factor—the ratio of potential gross domestic product (GDP) to actual GDP—with which the receipts are multiplied. When the economy is depressed and the output gap negative, the factor is greater than one. In this way, the ceiling for expenditures is higher than the actual receipts, allowing for a deficit. When the economy is booming and the output gap positive, the factor is less than one. The ceiling for expenditures is then lower than the actual receipts, requiring a surplus. In exceptional circumstances, a qualified majority in parliament can raise the expenditure ceiling. By considering the business cycle in a mechanical way, the federal fiscal rule offers the automatic stabilizers the room they need to function, and even offers the government some flexibility in taking counter-cyclical measures.

14.4.2 Financial Referendum and the Right of Initiative

The financial referendum is an instrument a majority of cantons have adopted; it can be optional or mandatory. It applies if a one-time or recurring expenditure exceeds a defined threshold. The threshold varies significantly among the cantons: between 250,000 and 25 million CHF for non-recurring expenditures and from 50,000 to 400,000 CHF for recurring expenditures. When the possibility of an optional referendum exists, meaning that the population must petition to have an expenditure put to a popular vote, the required number of petitioners (i.e., the number of signatures to collect) also varies from 100 to 10,000 citizens, depending on the canton. Empirical evidence shows that where mandatory financial referenda exist, expenditures are significantly lower (Funk and Gathmann 2011). For instance, in the alpine canton of Graubünden, the instrument was successfully used in 2017 to combat the Executive Council's request for a contingent appropriation to organize the 2022 Olympic Winter Games.

The introduction of a financial referendum at the central level has been discussed for some time, but such proposals have never been able to appeal to a majority in Parliament. Opponents fear possible delays in the political process. They also think it is useless, since a large portion of central government expenditures are annual transfer payments to other public entities, notably the cantons.

Swiss citizens also can make use of their right to launch popular initiatives to influence public finances; since government budgets as such are legally beyond the control of the referendum. A striking example was provided by the 'redistribution initiative' launched in 1997 by the Social Democratic party. It called for a popular vote on a proposal to amend the Federal Constitution and oblige the central government to cut military expenditures in half over ten years and invest one-third of the savings into international peace efforts. The initiative was rejected by 62% of the voters, although it was accepted in four French-speaking cantons.

14.5 Conclusion

The various Swiss financial management systems have some unique features, both due to the interplay of the instruments for direct democracy and with Parliament not being under the Executive Council's thumb. Considered together, these elements build systems of checks and balances that have led—particularly in the last two decades—to sound public budgets with relatively low debt levels.

Having said that, the system could be improved, for as in almost every country, Parliament is granted only a limited time to scrutinize proposed budgets. The result is to have the approved budget that strongly resembles the Executive Council's proposed budget. Additionally, since the finance minister acts within the Executive Council as one among equals, there is an inherent risk of finding all the 'spending ministers' arrayed against the sole 'budget minister'. Financial concerns become demoted through this situation, though thus far, the conservative stance of finance ministers has helped control this risk.

The finance minister sometimes also has recourse to political finessing, for instance, by underestimating tax receivables when preparing the budget or by artificially inflating some accrued expenses. This has proven useful for guaranteeing sound public financing—though it is detrimental to the fair view one expects from a governments' financial statements. Accurately reporting the financial situation will not expose Swiss governments unduly, especially if the instruments of direct democracy are in place and working. In that respect, those cantons that do not have a financial referendum, or that have eliminated this possibility, might want to reconsider. Cantons where the fiscal rule is not stringent enough should reinforce this constraint, as long as it is adjusted to the business cycle in the manner of the federal debt break.

References

Aschwanden, E., & Gerny, D. (2013, August 15). Kantone sparen über 1 Milliarde. *Neue Zürcher Zeitung*, p. 13.

Chatagny, F., & Soguel, N. (2012). The effect of tax revenue budgeting errors on fiscal balance: Evidence from the Swiss cantons. *International Tax and Public Finance, 19*(3), 319–337.

Clémenceau, M., & Soguel, N. (2017). Does personal background influence a finance minister to cook the books? An investigation of creative accounting in Swiss cantons. *Applied Economics, 49*(10), 941–953.

Clémenceau, M., & Soguel, N. (2018). How does depreciations management affect subsequent fiscal performance? The case of the Swiss cantons. *Swiss Journal of Economics and Statistics, 154*(7), 1–15.

Feld, L., & Kirchgässner, G. (2008). On the effectiveness of debt brakes: The Swiss experience. In R. Neck & J.-E. Sturm (Eds.), *Sustainability of public debt* (pp. 223–255). Cambridge: MIT Press.

Funk, P., & Gathmann, C. (2011). Does direct democracy reduce the size of government? New evidence from historical data 1890–2000. *The Economic Journal, 121*(557), 1252–1280.

IMF (International Monetary Fund) Statistics Department. (2014). *Government finance statistics manual*. Washington, DC: International Monetary Fund.

Krishnakumar, J., Martin, M.-J., & Soguel, N. (2010). Explaining fiscal balances with a simultaneous equation model of revenue and expenditure: A case study of Swiss cantons using panel data. *Public Budgeting and Finance, 30*(2), 69–94.

Lienhard, A., & Marti Locher, F. (2015). Art. 126. In B. Waldmann, E. M. Belser, & A. Epiney (Eds.), *Bundesverfassung, Basler Kommentar* (pp. 2025–2038). Basel: Helbing Lichtenhahn Verlag.

Pfäffli, S. (2011). *Budgetierung im öffentlichen Sektor: ein Handbuch für Studium und Praxis aus finanzwissenschaftlicher Sicht*. Berne: Haupt Verlag AG.

Von Däniken, A. (2017, May 26). Budget: Es geht um alles oder nichts. *Luzerner Zeitung*. Retrieved from http://www.luzernerzeitung.ch

Yerly, N. (2014). Les règles budgétaires entre souplesse et rigidité: la situation des cantons suisses. *La Vie économique, 6*, 38–40.

CHAPTER 15

The Swiss Way of Presenting the Governments' Financial Statements

Nils Soguel

15.1 Introduction

The goal of this chapter is to give the reader the keys to understanding the financial statements and budget plans as they are prepared and presented by Swiss governments at the three different levels.[1] This means presenting the main statements and their purpose, as well as how the statements are interrelated.

In Switzerland, as elsewhere, financial statements are a major element of governmental information systems and must be organized so as to respond to the various expectations interested parties have of the government. These expectations have evolved over time as the country's internal

[1] Here we use 'government' in the way it is used by the International Monetary Fund (IMF 2014): a unique legal entity established by political processes that has legislative, judicial, or executive authority over other institutional units (households, corporations, and non-profit institutions) within a given area (p. 14). Therefore, a government is an organization that includes several branches: a legislature (parliament), an executive branch with its administration, and a judiciary, either at the federal, the cantonal, or the municipal level.

The author is grateful to Evelyn Munier for her contribution to this chapter.

N. Soguel (✉)
IDHEAP, University of Lausanne, Lausanne, Switzerland
e-mail: nils.soguel@unil.ch

A. Ladner et al. (eds.), *Swiss Public Administration*, Governance and Public Management,
https://doi.org/10.1007/978-3-319-92381-9_15

institutions have transformed, as well as due to technical, accounting and computing changes.

Therefore, the two following sections retrace the historical evolution of public accounting in Switzerland and the requirements for the accounting model. Section 15.4 presents the overarching structure of financial statements, while Sect. 15.5 is dedicated to two specific features of financial reporting: internal service pricing (ISP) and political finessing.

15.2 The History of Switzerland's Governmental Accounting System

The history of governmental accounting in Switzerland is marked by repeated attempts to harmonize policies both horizontally—between cantons—and vertically—between municipalities, cantons and the Confederation. The first attempts at harmonization date from the nineteenth century.

The federalist organization of Switzerland for many years doomed these attempts to failure. Each canton sets out, in its own Financial Management Act of Parliament (FMAP), how it will organize itself financially, including what system it will use to prepare and present its financial statements. This explains why, until the mid-1960s, virtually every canton used a different system. Some cantons, like most Swiss municipalities, used a system inspired by the private sector, namely double-entry accounting with an income statement and a balance sheet. But other cantons used cash-basis accounting, like the central government.

Nonetheless, the modernization of the state slowly increased the need for harmonization of accounting systems. This came out of increased expectations in transparency, comparability and accountability. In a federalist system like Switzerland's, harmonization is particularly necessary to provide the consistent information required by the fiscal equalization system. It is also necessary to guarantee fiscal policy coordination.

It still took until the late 1970s for movement toward harmonization both between the cantons and the municipalities to begin. This movement was initiated by the intercantonal Conference of the Cantonal Finance Ministers (CFM) (*Konferenz der kantonalen Finanzdirektorinnen und Finanzdirektoren, Conférence des directrices et directeurs cantonaux des finances*). This Conference brings ministers together with the goal of coordinating the cantonal policy in fiscal matters when cantons decide that coordination is necessary. Nevertheless, the CFM cannot force the cantons to act; it can only formulate recommendations. Thus, it was only able to recommend the cantons to implement, for themselves and for their municipalities, the first Harmonized Accounting Model (HAM1) (see CFM 1981). The heart of HAM1 consisted of a detailed chart of accounts to be used both for the budget plan (beginning-of-the-year) and for the financial statements (end-of-the-year), but also for the multi-year financial plan. The chart of accounts is designed around a statement of financial performance, a statement of capital expenditure, a statement of financial position, and an embryonic cash flow statement.[2]

It would only be by the mid-1990s that most cantons and municipalities took the first step toward harmonization. However, they applied the HAM1 in highly variable ways (and rigor), while the central government continued to use a cash-based accounting system.

Eventually the central government's position became more and more untenable. Several factors finally forced it, in 2007, to switch to an accrual accounting system in order to provide a more faithful representation of its financial condition. This change came about partly in response to New Public Management (NPM) pressures, but it was also due to the development of the International Public Sector Accounting Standards (IPSASs), to the need for more robust financial statistics at the national and international levels, and for lenders to be more readily able to understand the central governments' financial statements.

Certain cantons were also confronted with the same demands as the Confederation. This was particularly true for Geneva and Zurich, cantons frequently present on the capital market due to the size of their debt burdens. In response to their particular needs, the CFM created a second-generation Harmonized Accounting Model (HAM2; see CFM 2008). The heart of HAM2 remained the chart of accounts, but in the modified or evolved form. The HAM2 also proposes 20 standards that are essentially recommendations since the cantons remain free to include them or not into their FMAPs.

The HAM2 is an evolution of the HAM1 which is compatible with the 2007 central government's accounting system and with the IPSASs. It offers governments, in ten or so cases, alternative accounting policies (e.g. linear or degressive depreciation; the possibility but not the obligation to

[2] Note that the terminology used in the text is that provided by the IPSASs (International Public Sector Accounting Standards). When necessary the German and French equivalent, as used in the Swiss governments, is given.

restate their administrative assets when introducing the HAM2; and the opportunity that their FMAP provides for the possibility of some forms of political finessing when preparing the financial statements). With these alternatives, all cantons found their way: both those that want their financial statements to provide a faithful representation of economic and other phenomena,[3] and those cantons adept at a more political approach to public finance which place a much greater emphasis on the prudence concept.

When it published its 2008 Manual, the CFM recommended the cantons implement the HAM2 within a maximum period of ten years. By 2018, all cantons will have introduced this new model, and the municipalities, will do so by 2021 or 2022. So far, the proposed chart of accounts has been uniformly implemented. However, the cantons do take advantage of the alternatives offered by HAM2. As a result, policies are becoming harmonized, but remain far from uniform (Soguel and Munier 2017).

15.3 Requirements for the Accounting Model and Principles for the Recognition of Transactions

Both HAM1 (1981) and HAM2 (2008) were designed to serve various functions as follows:

- Make it possible to implement the legal framework for financial management (*Finanzrecht, Droit budgétaire*) and specifically to regulate appropriations and the granting of credits (*Kreditrecht, Droit des crédits*)
- Serve as the basis for financial management, notably to establish and control financial plans, service provision agreements, fiscal rules, or financial indicators
- Link performance-focused and fiscal management in order to stimulate the managerial conduct within and between the various governmental units

[3] As stated in the IPSASB Conceptual Framework (2015, p. 49), 'faithful representation is attained when the depiction of the phenomenon is complete, neutral, and free from material error. Information that faithfully represents an economic or other phenomenon depicts the substance of the underlying transaction, other event, activity or circumstance——which is not necessarily always the same as its legal form'.

- Enable macroeconomic analysis so as to be able to implement a sensible fiscal policy
- Support the creation of financial statistics
- Facilitate the protection of creditor interests

To fulfill these functions and to ensure that the information provided in the financial statements are as faithful as possible, the HAM2 explicitly outlines several basic rules:

- accrual principle (*Periodenabgrenzung; Comptabilité d'exercice*);
- going concern principle (*Fortführung; Continuité*);
- materiality principle (*Wesentlichkeit; Importance*);
- gross recognition principle (*Bruttodarstellung; Produit brut*);
- reliability principle (*Zuverlässigkeit; Fiabilité*);
- comparability and consistency principles (*Vergleichbarkeit und Stetigkeit; Comparabilité et permanence des méthodes*);
- understandability principle (*Verständlichkeit; Clareté*). This last principle is particularly important in a system like Switzerland's, in which parliamentarians are part-time, and in which direct democracy requires that citizens understand their governments' financial condition.

15.4 Overarching Structure of the Financial Statements

The financial statements give a structured representation of a government's financial condition. They provide information about revenue and expenses, current and capital expenditure and receipts, cash flow, and assets and liabilities. The set of financial statements recommended by the HAM2 comprises a statement of financial performance (SoPERF), of capital expenditure (SoCAPEX), of financial position (SoPOS), and of cash flow, along with notes providing additional financial and non-financial explanations.

Taken together, the SoPERF and the SoCAPEX form the 'administrative statement' in HAM1. This designation demonstrates that all current or capital expenditure granted by a budgetary appropriation must be recorded in this dedicated group of statements. It also demonstrates that all spending items recorded in the 'administrative statement' are accordingly submitted to the political supervision of the council of the executive branch and of the Parliament.

15.4.1 Statement of Financial Performance

The SoPERF (i.e. income statement, *Erfolgsrechnung, Compte de résultats*) provides information about the government's operating costs and the degree to which revenue covers the charges. It indicates whether revenue—notably tax revenue—is sufficient to cover the costs of the services provided. Ideally, the income statement must be balanced, if not annually, then at least in the medium term.

The SoPERF also lists the budgetary appropriations for current expenditures granted by a Parliament when it approves a budget plan. In the (end-of-the-year) financial statements, this makes it possible to control the level of use of these credits.

This makes the SoPERF a key element of the government's financial management system. Indeed, its total is targeted by the fiscal rules in all cantons and in most municipalities, which is why SoPERF is usually located at the beginning of the report on the budget plan and the financial statements. Furthermore, in both documents most of the pages are dedicated to the SoPERF.

The HAM2 introduced a three-level structure in the SoPERF, replacing what had been only a single level statement (see Fig. 15.1).

The first level isolates operating revenue and operating expenses to show the operating result (*Ergebnis aus betrieblicher Tätigkeit; Résultat d'exploitation*). Operating revenue includes tax revenue, royalties and

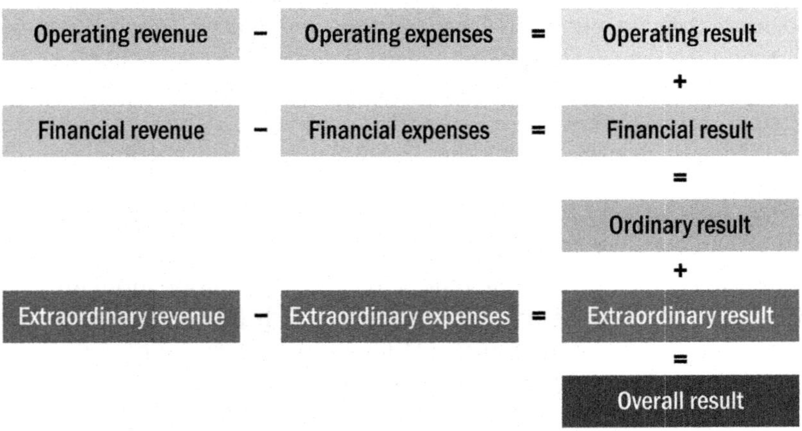

Fig. 15.1 The three-step statement of financial performance

concessions, revenue from exchange transactions, or transfer revenue. Operating expenses include notably personnel expenses, purchases of goods and services, depreciations of administrative assets, or transfer expenses.

The second level isolates financial revenue (e.g. interest income) and expenses (e.g. interest expense) to show the financial result (*Ergebnis aus Finanzierung; Résultat financier*). Together the operating result and the financial result form the ordinary result (*Operatives Ergebnis; Résultat opérationnel*).

The third level isolates extraordinary revenue and extraordinary expenses to show the extraordinary result (*Ausserordentliches Ergebnis; Résultat extraordinaire*). Extraordinary items correspond to unpredictable and beyond-anyone's-control events, like natural catastrophes. They also include various political finessing operations (see below).

The overall result is obtained by summing the ordinary result and the extraordinary result, or in other words, shows the difference between all revenues and all expenses. A surplus increases the net worth in the SoPOS, while a deficit reduces the net worth. The ordinary result is that which best reflects financial performance since it excludes the extraordinary elements and those relevant to political finessing.[4]

Revenue and expenses must be registered and classified according to their nature, meaning following an economic classification. In addition, they must be classified by functional purpose, such as health, education or social protection. Both classifications are standardized in the HAM2 chart of accounts, easing inter-government comparisons. The functional classification is compatible with the UN's Classification of Functions of Government (COFOG). Governments may use a third classification reflecting how their organization is designed, which is essential for monitoring how budgetary appropriations are used by various ministries or departments. However, since governmental organizations differ, this classification cannot be standardized.

[4] IPSAS do not explicitly preclude the presentation of items as extraordinary items (IPSASB 2015, p. 206). However, given the IPSAS requirement for faithful representation, the IPSAS understanding of the concept of extraordinary expenses or revenues does not encompass political finessing.

15.4.2 Statement of Capital Expenditure

The SoCAPEX (*Investitionsrechnung, Compte des investissements*) is a particular characteristic of the HAM. It comes in addition to the statement required by the IPSASs and is nonetheless compatible with them.

Any expenditure that creates an asset used by the government over several years in providing legally required public services must be recorded in the SoCAPEX, together with the corresponding receipts (e.g. capital grants). Such assets are labeled administrative assets (*Verwaltungsvermögen, Patrimoine administratif*).

Some expenditures do not create administrative assets. For instance, the government may use an asset as a yield-producing investment vehicle (e.g. by-to-let properties or securities; *Geldanlage, Placements*). Such yield-producing expenditure creates non-administrative assets (*Finanzvermögen, Patrimoine financier*). These assets are directly recorded in the SoPOS. All other expenditures are current expenditures and do not create any assets. These latter are registered in the SoPERF instead.

The distinction between the three kinds of expenditures (current, capital, and yield-producing) is important from a legal perspective. Current and capital expenditures depend on budgetary appropriation and thus on parliamentary decisions. Yield-producing expenditures, on the other hand, are in principle the prerogative of the executive branch council and are exempt from parliamentary approval.

In this way, the SoCAPEX provides information on the government's equipment and infrastructure efforts. On average, capital expenditures are equivalent to about 10% of current expenditures. The balance of the SoCAPEX shows net capital expenditures after deducting capital receipts. Expenditures are usually larger than receipts except when grants are not received in the same accounting period when expenditure are recognized. When closing the account, the administrative assets created are recognized as such in the SoPOS.

Capital expenditures can take various forms. They include expenditures to buy, build, or improve tangible and intangible fixed assets, like land, civil engineering work, building construction, plant and equipment, software or patents. They also include contributions or loans provided to other entities or governments, which are meant to create assets for the provision of public services required by law.

15.4.3 Statement of Financial Position

The SoPOS (*Bilanz, Bilan*) is less important in the financial statements of Swiss governments than it is in the statements of private companies. In the private sector it comes first, but in the public sector, it typically comes at the end of the financial statements. Nevertheless, the purpose is similar: the SoPOS offers an inventory of assets and shows to what extent they have been financed by borrowing (i.e. liabilities) or through equity (i.e. accumulated surpluses). The statement is a static picture of the financial condition, typically on 1 January or 31 December. It is thus unlike the other statements, which give information about flows throughout the year showing the flow of expenses and revenue, of capital expenditure and receipts, and of cash.

In the inventory, the HAM2 distinguishes between administrative assets stemming from capital expenditure and non-administrative assets stemming from yield-producing investment vehicles. The distinction is not required by the IPSASs nor is it encountered in the private sector. It is based upon the alienability principle, a notion introduced in HAM1 but no longer included in HAM2. Besides being justified by the regulation of appropriations, the distinction makes it possible to figure out which assets may not be sold (e.g. administrative assets without which a legally required public service could not be provided) and which assets can be sold without endangering existing public services (i.e. non-administrative assets).

Non-administrative assets are split between current and fixed assets (Fig. 15.2). The HAM2 requires that they be measured and reported at their fair value and, if available, at their market value. By providing governments with a common measurement basis and a unified principle to separate them from administrative assets, the HAM2 dramatically increases the comparability of net debt between governments. The government's net debt is defined as the difference between liabilities and non-administrative assets, since the latter can be sold freely and converted into cash to pay back the debt. Although a comparison of Swiss governments based on net debt is thereby made possible, this is not the case between countries, which is why international comparisons are almost always based on gross debt. This approach involves a risk of bias. Indeed, a variable part of the public debt can be contracted to finance yield-producing investment vehicles. Yet contracting a debt for this reason should be analyzed from a fundamentally different perspective compared to when the debt is contracted to finance administrative assets that the law forbids from selling.

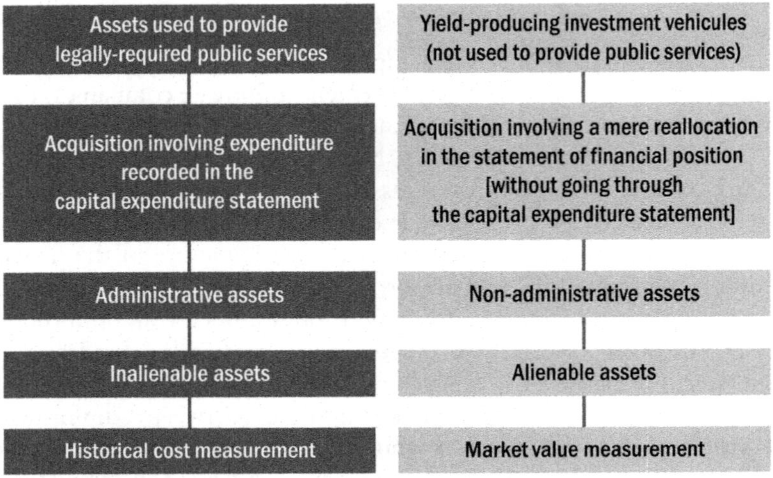

Fig. 15.2 Assets in the statement of financial position

In terms of administrative assets, HAM2 stipulates that they should be measured and reported at their depreciated historical cost, meaning at the cost incurred upon their acquisition and subsequent enhancement less a reduction for depreciation to date. Year after year, over their useful life, their reported amount is gradually reduced by recognizing the depreciation that represents their wear and tear and obsolescence. For each accounting period, depreciation is recorded in the SoPERF.

The liability side is structured in the same way as in the private sector, with a subdivision between liabilities and net worth (Fig. 15.3). Liabilities are measured at their fair value and classified according to their nature and time period (short or long term). Net worth is split between various components, including the accumulated annual surpluses and deficits and various types of reserves (dedicated to the financing of future capital projects or future fiscal policy measures).

15.4.4 Interactions Between the Three Statements: Financial Performance, Capital Expenditure and Financial Position

The amounts presented in the SoPOS vary between the beginning and the end of the year because of transactions recognized in the SoCAPEX and in the SoPERF. As shown in Fig. 15.4, capital expenditures increase the

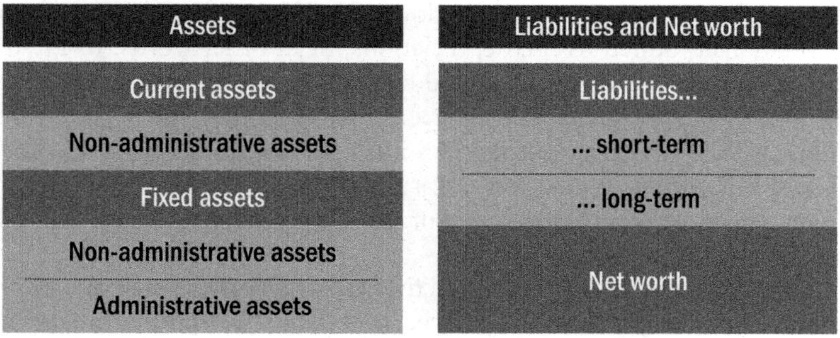

Fig. 15.3 Structure of the statement of financial position

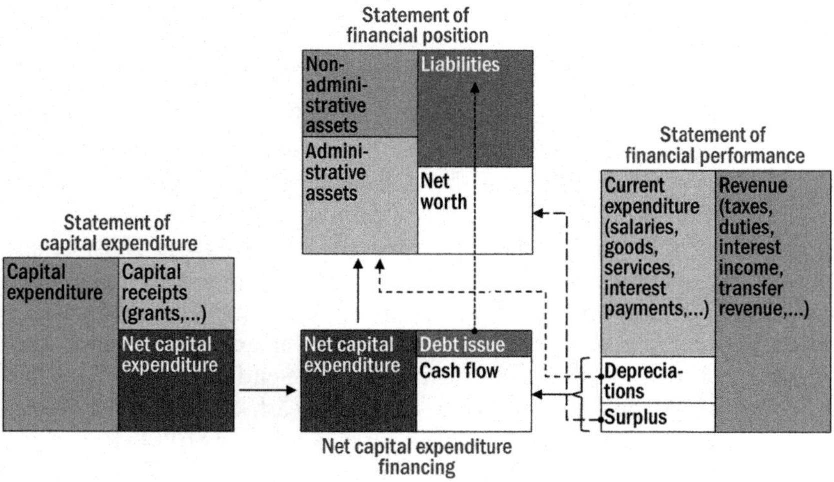

Fig. 15.4 Interactions between the statements and the simplified cash flow statement

overall amount of the administrative assets, while depreciations reduce this amount. The net worth increases or decreases depending on whether the SoPERF reports a surplus or a deficit.

Figure 15.4 also shows the embryonic cash flow statement introduced by the HAM1. Net capital expenditure, the cash drain from the difference between capital expenditure and receipts, may be financed either with the cash flow originating in the transactions recorded in the SoPERF, or by issuing debt. To simplify, this cash flow is considered equal to the surplus (or the deficit) added to the depreciations, or in other words, to the difference between cash flow generated by revenue and cash drain generated by expense. It is the difference between current receipts and expenditures. A depreciation expense typically does not involve cash. Instead, it reduces the surplus without reducing the cash account in the SoPOS. Thus the difference between expense and current expenditure is mainly due to depreciation.

There are other scenarios. In case the cash flow is larger than net capital expenditure, the government pays back its debt (liabilities). In case the deficit is larger than the depreciations, the cash flow becomes negative and debt must be issued not only to finance capital expenditure but also to cover current expenditure.

15.4.5 Cash Flow Statement

The HAM2 introduced a fully fledged cash flow statement (*Geldflussrechnung, Tableau des flux de trésorerie*), providing information on how the government raises the cash required to finance its activities over the reporting period and how this cash was used. The information is classified according to the various activities, following the IPSASs, and thus listing operating, investing and financing activities. The only specifically Swiss element here is that within investment activities, a distinction is made between the activities triggered by capital expenditure and those triggered by yield-producing investments. In the end, the statement sheds light on the reasons for changes in cash (and cash equivalents) between the beginning and the end of the year, as shown in the SoPOS.

15.4.6 Notes to the Financial Statements

The notes (*Anhang, Annexe*) give information about the accounting policy. A government whose financial statements do not comply with all HAM2 requirements must explicitly mention in which manner they diverge. The notes must also provide additional information regarding changes in equity, provision, equity participation, guarantees, and tangible assets. Finally, the notes must include any additional information explaining the development of net assets, financial position, and the result of operations. The requirements regarding the content of the notes are similar to those contained in the IPSASs.

15.5 Two Specific Features

15.5.1 Internal Service Pricing

Internal service pricing (ISP) was heralded as an important feature of the HAM1. The aim was to explicitly promote a cost-based way of thinking. The equivalent of the service is credited as revenue in the department providing the service; it is debited as an expense in the department receiving the service. Such ISP entries are purely book entries and as such neither generate nor drain cash.

ISP was implicitly expected to raise the level of cost transparency in public management, in order to increase public managers' accountability for the costs they incur and to enhance competition between internal suppliers and external competitors. So far empirical evidence shows that the target was not met at the cantonal level: the volume of ISP does not significantly and negatively correlate with that of government expenditure (Clémenceau and Soguel 2014).

This may have been because the ISP amounts were too small to influence management practices; on average among cantons, they amount to only 6% of total expenditures. The ISP is mainly used in areas where it is necessary to decide over the price to be paid by external users, meaning where the full cost must be charged to citizens (fees) or shared with other jurisdictions (transfers). One can also legitimately ask whether ISP reflects a faithful view of internally provided services. ISP is mainly the result of allocating centrally borne costs (depreciation, interest payments, information technology (IT), etc.), and so most of the costs allocated as ISP are only marginally the result of a rational decision over the goods and services to be internally purchased. As a result, they may not reflect a self-defined consumption, and public managers may even have less flexibility to cut internally charged services. This suggests that the lack of impact of the ISPs could mainly be due to how they are computed.

15.5.2 Political Finessing

Although the FMAP differs from canton to canton, all 26 FMAPs share a common and conservative fiscal stance. Thus, it does not come as a surprise that the Conference of CFM explicitly embedded several modes of political finessing into the HAM2. Many cantons have decided to adopt one or more of these possibilities into their own FMAPs. These are meant to artificially inflate expenses in the SoPERF, and include 'cookie-jar' reserves, reporting capital expenditure as operating expenditures, pre-funding, and 'additional depreciation charges'.

This last goes beyond depreciation charges that arise from actual wear and tear or the obsolescence of administrative assets. Depending on the canton and year, such 'additional depreciation charges' can amount to more than 2% of 'true' expenses. Managing depreciations seems to produce a significant and positive impact on a cantons' future financial performance (Clémenceau and Soguel 2018). Political finessing fosters the flexibility to ensure structural surpluses, prevent structural deficits, and facilitate meeting fiscal rule requirements. Admittedly, these operations must be reported as extraordinary expenses and thus do not impact the ordinary result. Nevertheless, they have an impact on the overall result and prevent 'true' performance from being reported with full transparency. Ultimately, when translating the HAM2 into their FMAP, cantons must make a tradeoff between conflicting wishes for fiscal soundness and faithful financial reporting.

15.6 Conclusion

The downsides concerning the possibilities of political finessing and the fact that ISP is not better used should not make us forget that Swiss governments have achieved a high standard of quality in their financial statements. The central government is close to fulfilling all the requirements formulated in the IPSASs. This also holds for several cantons, including Basel-Stadt, Bern, Geneva, Lucerne, and Zurich. Other cantons and municipalities are gradually improving the quality of the information provided in their financial statements.

This is remarkable when considering the great autonomy the cantons have in this area and remarkable in the absence of legal strictures obligating cantonal governments to use the proposed harmonized accounting model. Improvements are also being made possible by the Swiss Public Sector Financial Reporting Advisory Committee, a committee established by the intercantonal Conference of the CFM. It has become a de facto standard-setter for how accounting is conducted in the three tiers of Swiss government.

References

CFM (Conference of Cantonal Finance Ministers/Konferenz der kantonalen Finanzdirektoren). (1981). *Government accounting manual/Handbuch des Rechnungswesens der öffentlichen Haushalte [HAM1]*. Bern: Verlag Paul Haupt.

CFM (Conference of Cantonal Finance Ministers/Konferenz der kantonalen Finanzdirektorinnen und Finanzdirektoren). (2008). *Manual – Harmonised accounting model for cantons and municipalities/Handbuch – Harmonisiertes Rechnungsmodell für die Kantone und Gemeinden [HAM2]*. Bern: CFM.

Clémenceau, M., & Soguel, N. (2014). Impact des imputations internes sur le niveau des déficits publics: Le cas des cantons suisses. In M. Djouldem, G. Tellier, & C. de Visscher (Eds.), *Les réformes des finances publiques: Enjeux politiques et gestionnaires* (pp. 187–216). Bruxelles: Ed. Bruylant.

Clémenceau, M., & Soguel, N. (2018). How does depreciations management affect subsequent fiscal performance? The case of the Swiss Cantons. *Swiss Journal of Economics and Statistics, 154*(7), 1–13.

IMF (International Monetary Fund) Statistics Department. (2014). *Government finance statistics manual 2014*. Washington, DC: International Monetary Fund.

IPSASB (International Public Sector Accounting Standards Board). (2015). *Handbook of international public sector accounting pronouncements*. New York: International Federation of Accountants-IFAC.

Soguel, N., & Munier, E. (2017). Harmonisierung der Rechnungslegung in den Kantonen und Gemeinden. *Rechnungswesen & Controlling, 2*, 2–4.

CHAPTER 16

Tax Power and Tax Competition

Nils Soguel

16.1 Introduction

There are few domains as suited as taxation at expressing the particularities of the Swiss system. Various elements combine here: the smallness of the country and of its states, thus their exposure to external political and economic context, the federal system, the country's decentralization, and the Swiss system of direct democracy. The current tax system is the result of a historical evolution, which is why it so often departs from being a rational, systematic, or even theoretical construction.

Swiss fiscality offers a diversity that likely does not exist anywhere else. Over time, each of Switzerland's 26 cantons established its own tax laws and they then evolved in response to various global and local circumstances. This explains why tax bases like revenue, wealth, profit, capital, and even inheritances are taxed differently depending on the canton. In addition to this, the municipalities, like the cantons, can also choose the taxes they wish to levy and the tax rate. At the same time, the

N. Soguel (✉)
IDHEAP, University of Lausanne, Lausanne, Switzerland
e-mail: nils.soguel@unil.ch

A. Ladner et al. (eds.), *Swiss Public Administration*, Governance and Public Management,
https://doi.org/10.1007/978-3-319-92381-9_16

Confederation (the federal level) also taxes income and profit, though a large part of the federal taxes are indirect.[1]

This chapter focuses on the essential characteristics of Swiss taxation. The following section discusses the legal foundation upon which taxes are based. Section 16.3 quantifies the importance of the various types of taxes for each institutional level (Confederation, cantons, and municipalities). Here the Swiss context is compared to that of the member countries of the Organisation for Economic Co-operation and Development (OECD). Section 16.4 offers an analysis of the tax burden on businesses and households, by comparing their situation in Switzerland to those of other OECD countries and by comparing the situation that exists in the different cantons. Sections 16.5 and 16.6 are dedicated to two key elements of the Swiss tax system: tax competition and the particular balance between direct and indirect taxes.

16.2 The Legal Basis for Taxes

The Swiss Constitution states that "The Cantons are sovereign except to the extent that their sovereignty is limited by the Federal Constitution. They exercise all rights that are not vested in the Confederation" (Art. 3). This general provision also applies to taxation, and so cantons are in principle free to select the taxes they intend to levy. However, the Constitution reserves certain indirect taxes (value added and certain consumption taxes, stamp duty, and withholding tax) to the Confederation and forbids the cantons or municipalities from raising such taxes (Art. 134). In fact, the Confederation can only levy taxes the Swiss Constitution permits it to levy, which is the case for the direct tax on the income of private individuals, and on the net profit of legal entities (Art. 128). However, the Confederation does not have an exclusive right to levy direct taxes, and as a result, the cantons levy direct taxes as well.

[1] A tax is considered indirect when collected by an intermediary—rather than by the government—from the person (legal or natural) who bears the ultimate economic burden of the tax. Examples are value added tax (VAT), tobacco tax, or custom duties. The legal taxpayer pays the tax to the government, but the burden is eventually passed on to the taxbearer. Thus the legal and the economic taxpayer (the taxbearer) are not the same person. When the tax is a direct tax, both the legal and the economic taxpayer are the same person. Examples are personal income tax or profit tax, which are collected directly by the government from the person on whom they are imposed.

In terms of indirect taxes, the Constitution gives the Confederation an exclusive right to levy a value added tax (VAT), as well as to tax tobacco, beer, distilled spirits, automobiles, and mineral oil taxes, as well as to levy stamp duties (on some commercial transactions), customs duties, and a withholding tax on capital assets, lottery winnings, and insurance benefits (Art. 130–133) The 1999 Constitution even stipulates a maximum VAT rate the Confederation may levy: 6.5%, with an additional 1.5% to contribute to financing social insurance and railway infrastructure (Art. 130 and Art. 196). Thus, in 2017, Switzerland's normal VAT was 8%. By way of comparison, the (unweighted) VAT average in OECD countries was 19.2%.

Each canton's constitution determines if the canton's municipalities have the right to levy taxes. Cantonal legislation, and thus the canton's legislative body, guarantees this right. As a result, like the cantons, the municipalities also have genuine fiscal and tax autonomy, which goes hand-in-hand with their functional autonomy. In addition to taxes, the municipalities can or must finance their local public services (water, sewage, garbage collection, etc.) through user fees.

Switzerland uses a 'piggy-back' system for taxing income and profit, which means the same tax base is tapped by all three levels of government. In most cantons, the law on direct taxation establishes tax schedules, meaning the range of applicable tax rates depending on the level of taxable income or profit. In most cantons, as in the Confederation, the income tax schedule is progressive, but the degree of progressivity varies due to cantonal tax autonomy. It is for that reason that two small cantons, Uri and Obwalden, have nonetheless adopted a flat-rate tax system (based on a proportional tax scale; FTA 2017).

A given cantonal tax schedule applies both at the cantonal and at the municipal level; the canton and each municipality define a coefficient that multiplies the tax due by the legal tax scale.

To illustrate how this works, consider a single taxpayer who is without dependents, lives in the city of Bern, and who has no religious affiliation (Switzerland has church taxes). In 2016, this taxpayer has an income, as a professional, of 70,000 CHF, and once all deductions have been taken, is left with a taxable income of 50,000 CHF. The tax scale in the tax law gives the tax as 1973 CHF, to which the canton of Bern applies a 3.06 coefficient. So the cantonal tax is 6038 CHF. The city of Bern, by contrast, uses a coefficient of 1.54, and so the local tax is 3039 CHF. In addition, our taxpayer must pay 445 CHF in federal income tax. So together, on gross income of 70,000 CHF and net income of

50,000 CHF, our resident of Bern pays a total of 9522 CHF in local, cantonal, and federal tax—19.0% of net income (or 13.6% of gross income).

This freedom in selecting tax scales, rates, and allowances is protected by the Swiss Constitution—which explicitly says these are "matters excluded from harmonization" (Art. 129). The Confederation can only standardize the tax system in a formal way, inasmuch as it sets out tax liability and the object of a tax and its assessment. The only constitutional limitation to cantonal tax autonomy regarding the choice of tax scale is that the tax burden should be commensurate with the taxpayer's ability to pay, provided the nature of the tax permits it (Art. 127). On this basis, the Federal Supreme Court in 2015 declared that a regressive personal income tax system with a decreasing tax scale, which one canton (Obwalden) attempted to implement, violated this basic redistributive principle.

The fact that legislation authorizes all three levels of government to decide over their own taxes is a distinctive feature of the Swiss tax system. Also distinctive is that Swiss citizens can decide whether they want the state to be able to levy a tax, and if so, at what rate. This is because the tools of direct democracy also function in the area of taxation. Any constitutional amendment, including those related to taxation, is subject to a mandatory referendum at both federal and cantonal levels. Modifications of laws, no matter what the type, can trigger optional—and in some cantons, even mandatory—referendums. Citizens can also use their right to launch an initiative to request a modification of the (constitutional or legal) tax provisions. In other words, the tools of direct democracy give the citizens the opportunity and the means to oppose the introduction of a new tax or to suppress an existing tax.

16.3 The Importance of Taxes

Looking at all three levels of government, in 2015, more than 80% of their revenue comes from taxes, with 59.0% from direct taxation and 22.4% from indirect taxation (Table 16.1). These proportions differ significantly between the levels of government. Because indirect taxes are nearly nonexistent in the cantons and municipalities (accounting for only 2.4% and 0.2%, respectively), direct taxes count for that much more. Revenue from exchange transactions and fiscal equalization are all the more significant. Fiscal equalization represents 30.6% of cantonal income (their second largest source of financing) and 11.9% of municipal income (their third largest source of financing). Given that most utilities are municipally

Table 16.1 Swiss government receipts, 2015

	Total[(1)]		Confederation		Cantons		Municipalities	
	CHF bn	%	CHF bn	%	CHF bn	%	CHF bn	%
Direct taxes	**94.9**	**59.0**	**30.2**	**43.9**	**42.1**	**48.9**	**27.5**	**58.7**
Personal income tax	54.4	33.8	10.4	15.1	27.3	31.7	18.8	40.1
Personal wealth tax	6.3	3.9	–	–	4.0	4.7	2.6	5.5
Corporate tax[(2)]	19.8	12.3	9.7	14.2	7.3	8.5	4.2	8.9
Withholding tax	5.5	3.4	6.5	9.5	–	–	–	–
Other direct taxes[(3)]	8.8	5.5	3.5	5.1	3.5	4.0	2.0	4.2
Indirect taxes	**36.0**	**22.4**	**33.8**	**49.1**	**2.3**	**2.6**	**0.1**	**0.2**
Value added tax	22.6	14.0	22.4	32.6	–	–	–	–
Mineral oil tax	5.0	3.1	4.7	6.9	–	–	–	–
Stamp duties	2.1	1.3	2.4	3.5	–	–	–	–
Motor vehicle tax	2.1	1.3	0.0	0.0	2.2	2.5	–	–
Other indirect taxes	4.2	2.6	4.3	6.2	0.1	0.1	0.1	0.2
Receipts from exchange transactions[(4)]	**19.6**	**12.2**	**3.0**	**4.3**	**10.1**	**11.7**	**8.9**	**18.9**
Financial receipts	**7.1**	**4.4**	**1.3**	**2.0**	**2.8**	**3.2**	**3.2**	**6.9**
Transfer receipts	**1.1**	**0.7**	**0.2**	**0.4**	**26.3**	**30.6**	**5.6**	**11.9**
Investment receipts[(5)]	**2.3**	**1.4**	**0.2**	**0.4**	**2.5**	**2.9**	**1.6**	**3.4**
Total[(5)]	160.9	100.0	68.8	100.0	86.1	100.0	46.8	100.0

[a]After consolidation between government units
[b]Profit and capital
[c]Property related, death and gift duties
[d]Including royalties, concessions and miscellaneous receipts
[e]Excluding extraordinary receipts
Source: Federal Finance Administration (2017). *Switzerland's Financial Statistics for 2015. FS Model.* Berne. According to national consolidation based on the Swiss governments' harmonized chart of accounts (FS Model)

owned, municipalities also have wide discretion over fees and user charges, and thus revenue from exchange transactions are particularly high (18.9%).

The Confederation is almost wholly financed through taxes, 49.1% from indirect taxes among which 32.6% comes from VAT, and 43.9% from direct taxes. It is the Confederation which benefits from indirect taxes and from the withholding tax, not the other levels. Overall, its taxes are also the largest, at 64 billion CHF (10% of gross domestic product (GDP)), followed by the cantons at 44 billion CHF (7% of GDP) and the municipalities at 28 billion CHF (4%). But because the Confederation redistributes a large part of its tax revenue through transfers to the cantons, this kind of comparison is a little misleading.

In terms of individual categories of direct tax, and regardless of the level, the tax on individual income is the largest, followed by the corporate tax. Together, these two taxes generate nearly half of all cantonal and municipal tax revenue.

Overall, the tax share at the sub-central level in Switzerland is close to 52%, one of the highest degrees of tax decentralization among industrialized democratic countries (OECD 2002). Canada is "the only country with a similarly high degree of tax decentralization" (Schmidheiny 2017, p. 74).

In Switzerland, the tax-to-GDP ratio is weak compared to the level recorded in other OECD countries (Fig. 16.1). In 2015, Swiss government units collected taxes equal to 21% of GDP. Social security contributions (which include mandatory contributions for old-age and survivors' insurance, disability insurance, compensation for loss of earnings and unemployment insurance, agriculture family allowances, and maternity insurance in the canton of Geneva) represent an additional 7%. Although mandatory, health insurance, accident insurance, and pension fund contributions are not taken into account. According to the sectoring principles of the European System of Accounts, these go to enterprises (either public or private) and thus do not belong to the general government sector. Therefore, the Swiss tax-to-GDP ratio is not to be understood as the ratio of compulsory payments. Nevertheless, the 28% Swiss tax-to-GDP ratio can still be compared to the OECD (unweighted) average of 34%. It means that Tax Freedom Day was April 12, 2015, in Switzerland, compared to May 4, 2015, on average in the OECD countries.

The OECD (2000) stresses that there are important limitations when using the tax-to-GDP ratio as a comparative measure of tax burdens. However, ranking seventh out of 35 OECD countries still indicates that comparatively speaking, the Swiss government overall uses a significantly lower proportion of GDP to finance its tasks using taxes and contributions, than many other countries. This correlates with its comparatively low government expenditure-to-GDP ratio.

16.4 Tax Burden Linked to Direct Tax

Measured by the tax-to-GDP ratio, the tax burden in Switzerland is thus lighter than elsewhere. The same conclusion can be reached when looking at households and companies.

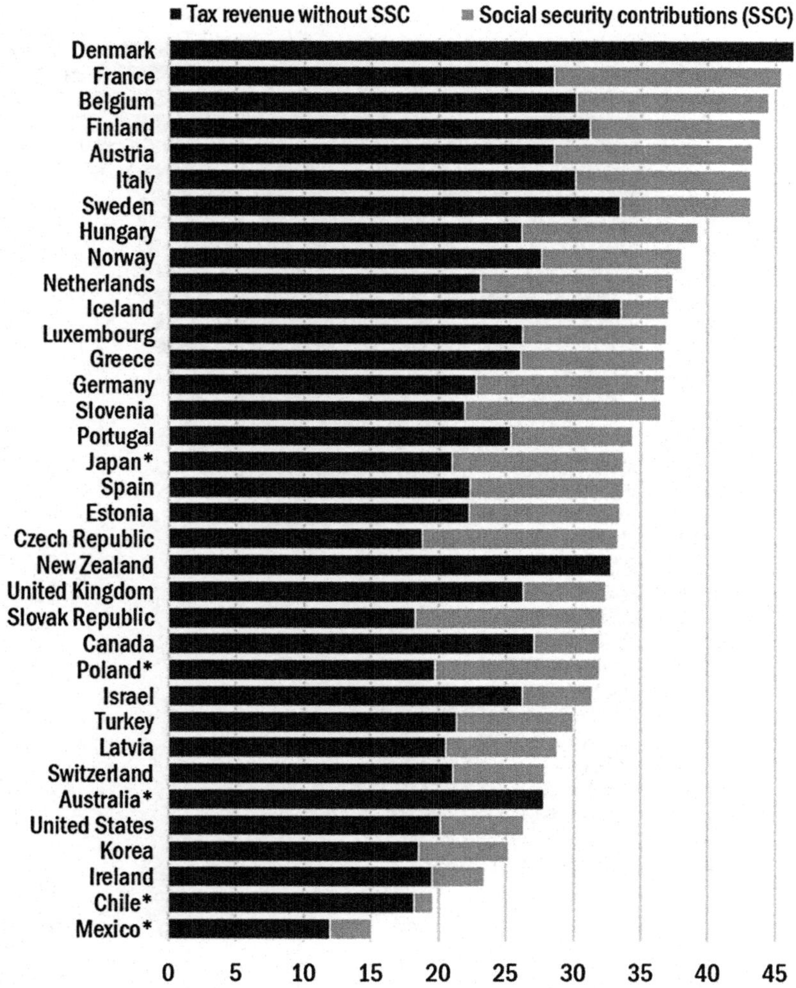

Fig. 16.1 Comparative government tax-to-GDP ratios in the OECD countries, 2015. (Source: OECD. Stat. Revenue Statistics. Revenue as % of GDP. * 2014 figures)

Figure 16.2, based on OECD (2017), presents the situation of a single taxpayer without dependents whose income is that of an average employee, defined as the average full-time adult gross wage earnings in each OECD economy (it corresponds to 86,000 CHF in the city of Zurich, the city used in OECD data for Switzerland). The figure indicates, with respect to

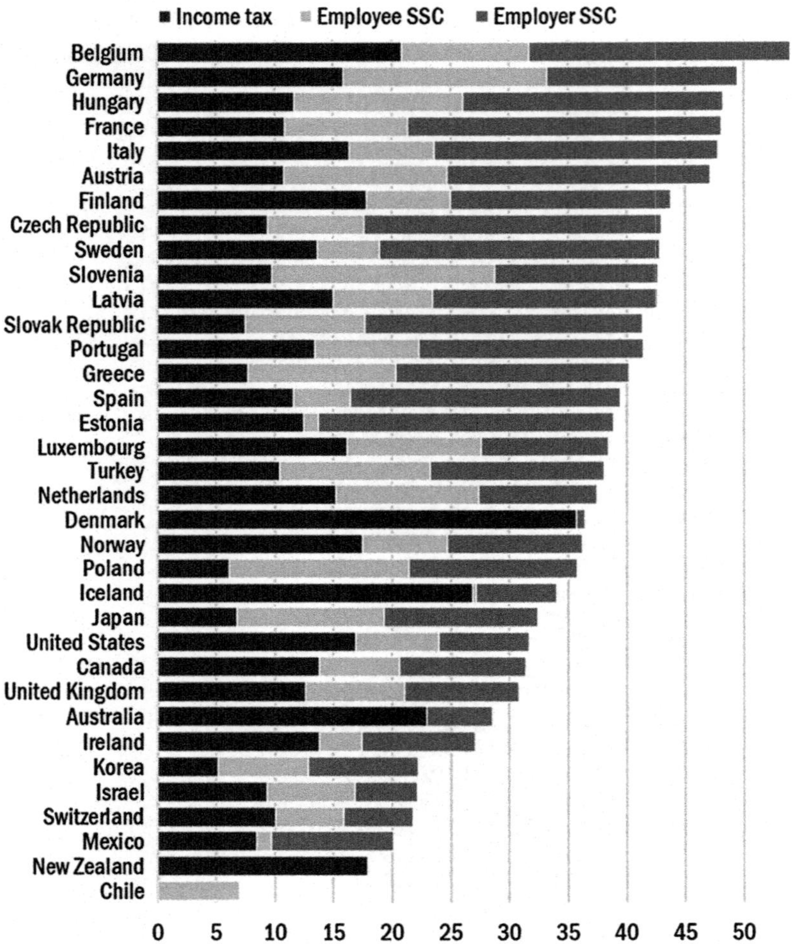

Fig. 16.2 Tax wedge as % of labor costs in the OECD countries, 2016. (Source: OECD. Stat. Tax wedge decomposition. Income tax plus employee and employer social security contributions (SSC) as % of labor costs. Single individual without children at the income level of the average worker)

the labor costs to the employer, the corresponding net take-home pay of the employee. Differences stem from personal income tax, social security payments, other contributions, and payroll taxes (aggregated with employer social contributions), and correspond to how the OECD defines the 'tax wedge'. Other taxes (corporate income, net wealth, and consumption) are not taken into consideration.

Income tax cuts into a Swiss taxpayer's income by 10%. Though this is higher than what prevails in about ten other OECD countries, it is less than what taxpayers face in France (11%), Germany, or Italy (16%), or the OECD average (13%). Including social security contributions into the comparison only reinforces these findings: in Switzerland, the tax wedge is one of the lowest, with 22% compared to an average of 36% in other OECD countries. This remains true even if we modify the composition of the household or the income level.

Figure 16.3 looks at the situation of companies and presents the statutory corporate tax rate. In this way, it only offers a simplified vision of the reality given the fact that the effective situation of companies varies considerably[2] and that the tax rate can vary within a single country. Thus, for Switzerland, the table indicates that a company based in the city of Zurich can be subject to a rate of 21.15% (of which 8.5% goes to the Confederation). Even if this is one of the highest rates in Switzerland (see the following), this tax burden remains lower than what is seen in the majority of OECD countries.

These aggregated figures obscure the vast differences between cantons, a direct result of cantonal tax autonomy. Figure 16.4 presents the statutory tax rate for companies operating in each of the principal cities of the 26 Swiss cantons. A Zurich-based company is subject to a statutory rate of 21.15%. This rate is one of the highest, though a company in Geneva is subject to the highest at over 24% while a Lucerne company pays only a little more than 12%.

The rates given in Fig. 16.4 do not even reflect the extremes, inasmuch as municipalities can impose lower or higher coefficients than the principal cities of the canton.

The strong tax autonomy Swiss municipalities have creases of significant differences in tax burdens from canton to canton as well as between municipalities in the same canton. The effects of municipal autonomy in the choice of a tax coefficient are well-illustrated in Fig. 16.5, in this case for personal income tax. As shown before, the case shown is of a single taxpayer without children, with a gross income from labor of 80,000 CHF. The tax burden is the overall amount levied by all three levels of government.

[2] We prefer to present here the statutory tax rate, that is, rates which are specified in law, since the estimation of effective tax rate is sensitive to several analytical choices.

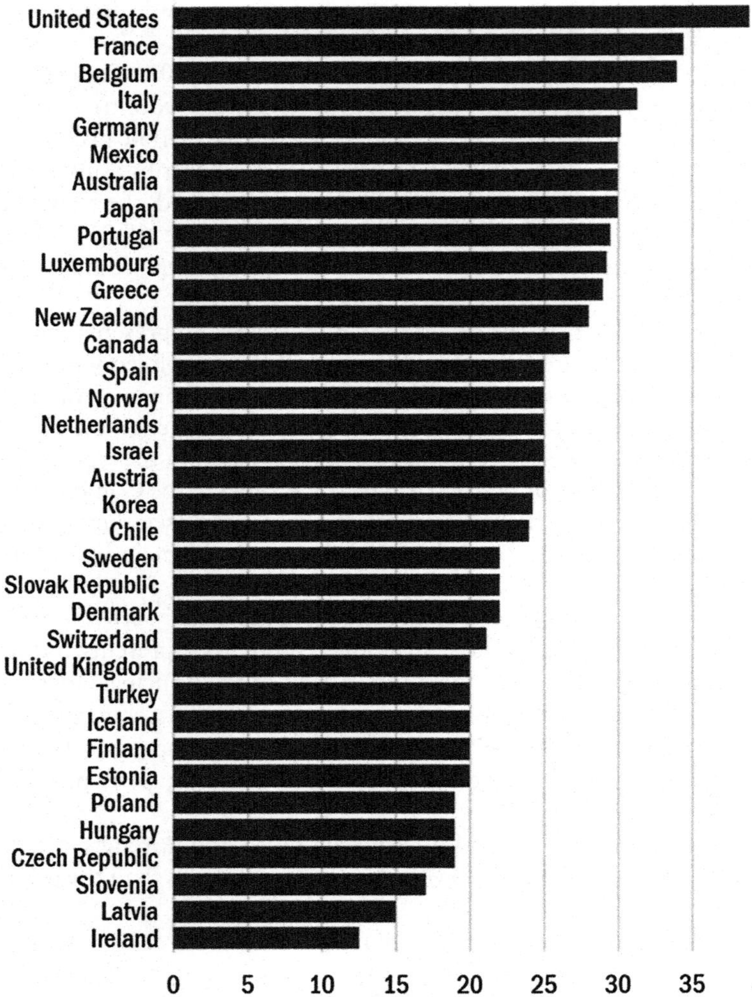

Fig. 16.3 Switzerland statutory corporate tax rate compared to the other OECD countries, 2016. (Source: OECD. Stat. Statutory corporate income tax rate)

The cantons are listed in increasing order, based on the tax burden imposed by the median commune. To take the example of the canton of Zurich again, if the taxpayer lives in the city of Zurich, she pays an income tax equivalent to 10.7% of her gross income. This is more than if she lived

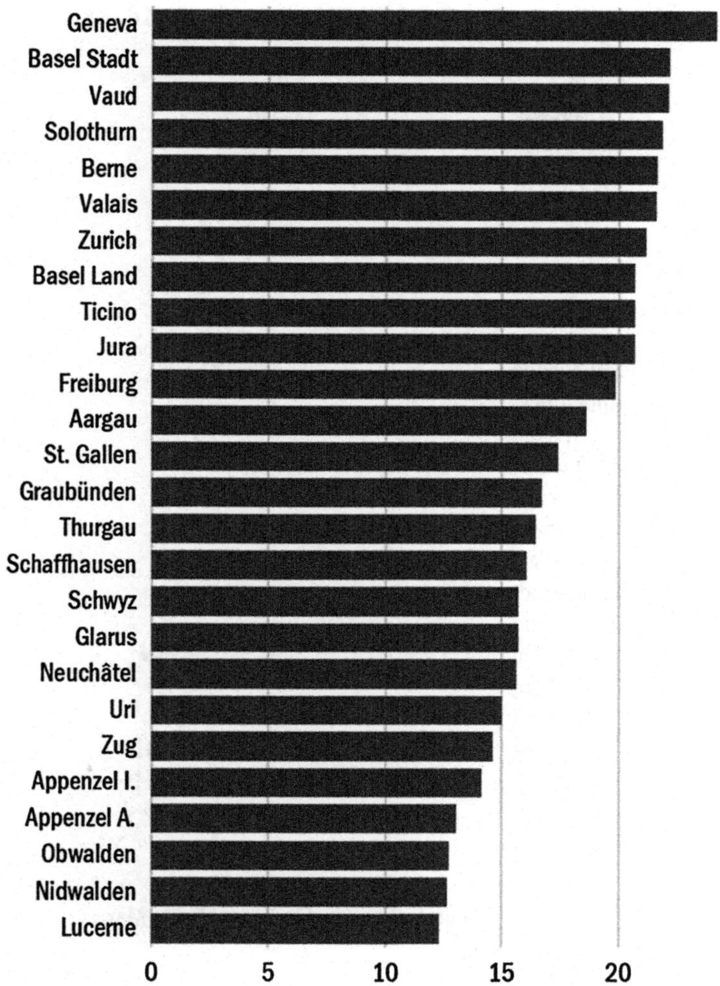

Fig. 16.4 Cantonal statutory corporate tax rate, January 2016. (Sources: PwC (June 2016). Corporate Tax Reform III)

in the cantonal municipality with the lowest burden (8.9%) or even the median burden (10.4%), but less than where the burden is the highest (11.5%). The Swiss municipality with the lowest burden (5.6%) is located in the canton of Zug, while the one with the highest (18.4%) is in the

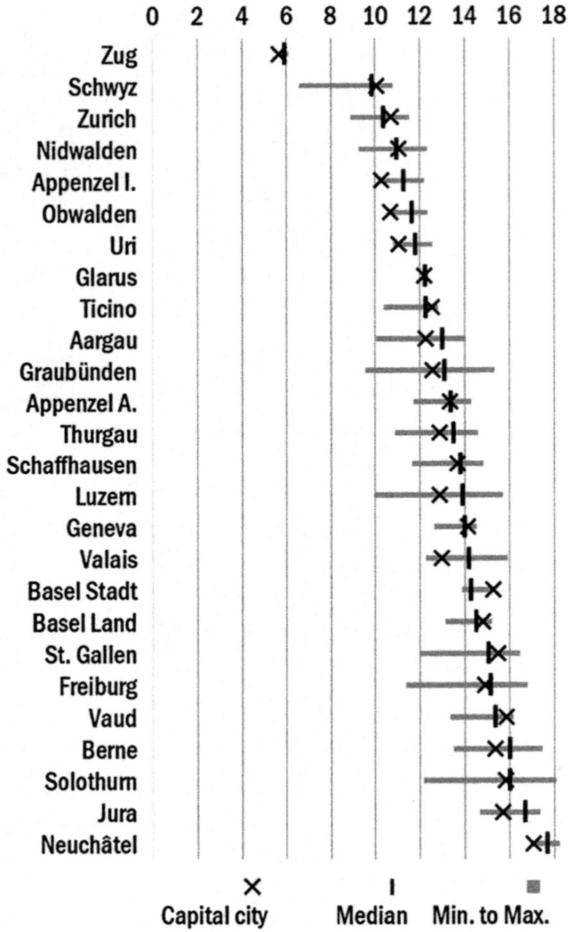

Fig. 16.5 Tax burden by canton and variation between municipalities as % of gross labor income, 2016. (Source: Federal Tax Administration. Single individual with gross income of 80,000 CHF)

canton of Neuchatel. In other words, as for Tax Freedom Day, depending on whether a taxpayer lives in the most fiscally advantageous municipality or the most expensive, he will have fulfilled his income tax requirement either by January 20 or not until March 18, 2016.

16.5 Tax Competition

Tax competition can be defined as a public policy to attract a mobile tax base and companies to boost economic development, employment, and output growth within the jurisdiction implementing it. This can be done by setting tax rates at a relatively low level, by allowing more generous tax deductions, or by introducing tax breaks or tax holidays in order to enlarge the tax base at the expense of other jurisdictions. Tax competition between countries has long existed, and Switzerland clearly participates, as demonstrated.

Furthermore, and together with the United States and Canada, Switzerland is one of the rare countries in which subnational jurisdictions take advantage of a fiscal autonomy that is large enough to allow them to engage in tax competition (OECD 2002, p. 59). The small size of cantons and municipalities makes it possible for private and corporate taxpayers to move to areas with weaker tax burdens. Tax competition has increased because of the well-developed infrastructure in the country which allows for considerably labor mobility and commuting.

Schmidheiny (2017) demonstrates that taxes have been falling in most cantons since the mid-1980s. Of course, it is not enough to observe differences or modifications of the tax burden to conclude that tax competition exists. In order to conclude this, the targeted tax base must be mobile and react to tax incentives. Feld and Kirchgässner (2001) showed that competition is stronger between municipalities than between cantons, due to the lower transaction costs of moving between neighboring towns. For these two authors, corporate and personal income taxation are an important factor in understanding the regional distribution of companies and regional employment differences, even if location-based decisions depend on many factors. A higher proportion of high taxable income is observed in cantons with a low tax burden than in cantons with a high tax burden.

Eugster and Parchet (2013) analyze the situation in bilingual cantons and show that the tax rates in French-speaking municipalities are higher than in German-speaking municipalities in the same bilingual canton. However, the difference vanishes in municipalities close or right on the language border. This spatial convergence of tax rates indicates the presence of tax competition, at least between neighboring jurisdictions. Feld and Reulier (2009) also find that cantons set their income tax rates strategically, depending on the tax rates of other cantons.

Other authors look at corporate fiscality. For example, Rossi and Dafflon (2004) show that tax competition between cantons which is meant to attract companies does not much occur at the level of the business sector, taken as a whole, since all jurisdictions will lose part of their revenues from openly lowering taxation.

The competition takes place at a more micro-level, with particular companies being granted ad hoc advantages (at the time of writing, such arrangements are still permitted although Switzerland is under international pressure to limit or even to suppress them). A further micro-level for tax competition is when cantons or municipalities offer particular tax arrangements, not to corporate taxpayers but to a company's managers—in the form of a somewhat negotiable tax base.

Tax competition between cantons has intensified in the last 15 years. A favorable economic climate brought cyclical budget surpluses, and several cantons took advantage of this situation to reduce their tax rate in the hope of attracting high-income individuals and companies.

This raised fears of a 'race to the bottom', since it is legally possible for cantons and communes to fiscally compete with one another. Earlier, an analysis by Kirchgässner and Pommerehne (1996) had concluded that tax competition between cantons had no harmful effects on the provision of public services. But the recent disappearance of cyclical budget surpluses make it no longer possible to compensate for the cyclical budget deficits brought on by lowered taxes, in particular when the new taxpayers are not as numerous as expected. Faced with this situation, the hard budget constraints introduced make fiscal consolidation packages inevitable. Several cantons have been affected, at different levels, but the cantonal population frequently opposes, via referendum, an increase in the tax rate in order to balance the budget. The only solution remaining to the government is to reduce the provision of public services, that is, unless substantial efficiency gains can be achieved within the government.

These recent developments seem to support the idea that tax competition may be detrimental, at least in terms of public service provision. Tax competition is also seen as harmful by the OECD, since it leads to "fiscal externalities among subnational entities, to a distortion of corporate and residential location choices, to fiscal unfairness and to a race to the bottom with respect to social or environmental standards" (OECD 2002, p. 58).

Many years ago, Brennan and Buchanan (1977) used the 'Leviathan argument' to object: the state has a tendency to excessive taxation, and tax competition applies a downward pressure which enhances efficiency. From this perspective, fiscal decentralization and the tax autonomy of Swiss municipalities, as well as the tax competition they allow, should be judged positively. That being said, Feld and Kirchgässner (2001) or Krishnakumar et al. (2010) demonstrated that direct democracy itself was probably a more effective restraint on 'Leviathan', because popular approval, by referendum, is needed to increase tax rates and in deciding to engage in large public expenditures.

The effects of tax competition should also be put in context. The research noted (Feld and Kirchgässner 2001; Eugster and Parchet 2013) certainly shows that competition exists, but it also shows that this competition is geographically limited. This explains that the differences in Figs. 16.4 and 16.5 persist despite the tendency of the tax burden to diminish. As the OECD suggested, "a tax equilibrium affecting location-based choices might have been achieved. One explanation could be that tax rates and public services are in line with the preferences of the population [...]. Another explanation could be that locational decisions may be affected by factors other than tax rate differentials. This might partially offset competition on tax rates..." (2002, p. 59).

16.6 The Balance Between Direct and Indirect Taxation

A repeated criticism of the Swiss tax system is that it uses direct taxation too much and indirect taxation too little, notably with the VAT. The OECD (2012) thus recommends that Switzerland shift taxation from direct to indirect taxes to reduce economic distortion and boost economic activity. To do this, the OECD suggests reducing the personal income tax since this tax discourages entrepreneurial activity and investment. It suggests instead that the base of the VAT be widened and the standard VAT rate be increased. It is true that the VAT represents 17% of the tax receipts of all Swiss government units (Table 16.1), while the average of the OECD countries is well above it (at 27% in 2014). While tax receipts from personal income tax are 41% of Swiss governmental tax receipts, this is rather lower (33%) in OECD countries.

If, in theory, VAT engenders fewer tax distortions compared to other taxes, it is also important to consider the institutional context. Studies like that of Keen and Lockwood (2010) show empirically that an increase in VAT receipts is not linked to a decrease in other tax receipts, and that as a result, the tax-to-GDP ratio increases.

In Switzerland's case, and no matter what the OECD says, the fact that personal income tax dominates compared to VAT should be seen positively. In Switzerland, personal income tax, unlike VAT, is a tax mostly levied by the cantons and the municipalities, making it one of the drivers of fiscal federalism and tax competition. To reduce its predominance would weaken both of these advantages of Swiss institutions.

Direct democracy is another advantage of the Swiss system, and its proper functioning is conditioned by the fact that voters pay more direct than indirect taxes. In essence, direct taxation requires taxpayers to fill out a self-assessed tax return, receive notification of tax assessment, and see to it that their tax bill gets paid. This process gives voters a better price signal regarding the cost of public services and the cost of their decision in a referendum or an initiative. The signal is more perceptible than the one indirect taxation sends: it affects, in an intransparent way and at homeopathic dose levels, the many transactions in which a taxpayer participates.

Finally, one should not ignore the role progressive scales for personal income tax play in terms of redistribution and macroeconomic stabilization. Because of these tax scales, the tax system contributes to the state's mission of redistribution, not only between individuals but also between cantons and different regions. This element of spatial and automatic redistribution of wealth should not be underestimated in terms of its effect on the sustainability the Swiss federalist system. Progressive tax scales also contribute more effectively to macroeconomic stabilization, more than if the tax system relied more heavily on indirect taxation. Essentially, the effect of cyclical variations of the tax bases (contraction during economic downturns and expansion during economic boomtimes) on income tax is amplified when the tax scale is progressive. As a result, the effect on overall demand is also amplified. In other words, the more the tax system relies on direct taxation with progressive tax rates, the greater are the automatic stabilizers, thus facilitating the smoothing out of economic business cycles.

16.7 Conclusion

The Swiss tax system offers genuine advantages. Those advantages, however, are intricately linked to and dependent on the country's institutional characteristics. Having said that, it remains perfectable, both in terms of its overall design and in the subtleties of its execution. We hope that there could soon be an end to the special cantonal tax regimes for companies that carry out limited commercial activities in the country and whose income from foreign sources is taxed less than Swiss-source income. This would allow Switzerland to reduce the possibilities for corporate profit-shifting.

The OECD has also provided some recommendations regarding the Swiss tax system (2015). For instance, individual as opposed to family taxation should be introduced to promote women's participation in the work force; the deductibility of mortgage interest and maintenance outlays for property owners should be limited so as not to exceed the amount of declared imputed rent.

Nonetheless, these changes will not help in reducing the differences in the cantonal and municipal tax burdens. Initiatives have been launched on several occasions to harmonize tax burden, either between cantons or between municipalities within the same canton. Each time, however, these initiatives were overruled through popular vote either nationally or cantonally. This demonstrates how important cantonal and municipal tax autonomy is to the Swiss population—or at least to those who vote. It also demonstrates the need for fiscal equalization to prevent tax burden difference between rich and poor jurisdictions from becoming too big. The next chapter will take up this issue.

References

Brennan, G., & Buchanan, J. M. (1977). Towards a tax constitution for Leviathan. *Journal of Public Economics, 8*(3), 255–273.

Eugster, B., & Parchet, R. (2013). *Culture and Taxes. Towards Identifying Tax Competition*. University of St. Gallen, Discussion Paper, 2013–2039.

Feld, L. P., & Kirchgässner, G. (2001). Income tax competition at the state and local level in Switzerland. *Regional Science and Urban Economics, 31*(2–3), 181–213.

Feld, L. P., & Reulier, E. (2009). Strategic tax competition in Switzerland: Evidence from a panel of the Swiss cantons. *German Economic Review, 10*(1), 91–114.

FTA (Federal Tax Administration). (2017). *The Swiss tax system*. Bern: Swiss Tax Conference Information Committee.

Keen, M., & Lockwood, B. (2010). The value added tax: Its causes and consequences. *Journal of Development Economics, 92*(2), 138–115.

Kirchgässner, G., & Pommerehne, W. W. (1996). Tax harmonization and tax competition in the European Union: Lessons from Switzerland. *Journal of Public Economics, 60*(3), 351–371.

Krishnakumar, J., Martin, M.-J., & Soguel, N. (2010). Explaining fiscal balances with a simultaneous equation model of revenue and expenditure: A case study of Swiss cantons using panel data. *Public Budgeting & Finance, 30*(2), 69–94.

OECD (Organisation for Economic Co-operation and Development). (2000). *Tax burden: Alternative measures*. Paris: OECD Publishing.

OECD. (2002). *OECD territorial reviews: Switzerland*. Paris: OECD Publishing.

OECD. (2012). *OECD economic surveys: Switzerland 2011*. Paris: OECD Publishing.

OECD. (2015). *OECD economic surveys: Switzerland 2015*. Paris: OECD Publishing.

OECD. (2017). *Taxing wages 2017*. Paris: OECD Publishing.

Rossi, S., & Dafflon, B. (2004). Tax competition between subnational governments: Theoretical and regional policy issues with reference to Switzerland. In E. Hein, A. Heise, & A. Truger (Eds.), *Finanzpolitik in der Kontroverse* (pp. 227–250). Marburg: Metropolis.

Schmidheiny, K. (2017). Emerging lessons from half a century of fiscal federalism in Switzerland. *Swiss Journal of Economics and Statistics, 153*(2), 73–101.

CHAPTER 17

Intergovernmental Fiscal Transfers and Equalization

Nils Soguel

17.1 Introduction

It is extremely rare for Swiss institutions to undergo a revolution. And yet for the last ten years, the fiscal transfer and equalization system (*Finanzausgleich; péréquation financière*) between the Confederation and the cantons have been reformed so much that it can rightly be considered a revolution. And even more so, because most cantons followed suit and transformed their own fiscal transfer and equalization systems with their municipalities based on the federal model.

These changes came about in a context in which certain elements of Swiss federalism were, and still are, being debated: the elements include the degree of decentralization that is desired, the prevention of negative incentives in economic development, and adverse selection phenomena in the jurisdictions where redistribution is the most generous.

The author is grateful to Yves Ammann for his contribution to this chapter.

N. Soguel (✉)
IDHEAP, University of Lausanne, Lausanne, Switzerland
e-mail: nils.soguel@unil.ch

A. Ladner et al. (eds.), *Swiss Public Administration*, Governance and Public Management,
https://doi.org/10.1007/978-3-319-92381-9_17

This chapter briefly surveys how the transfer systems are organized, and describes their benefits and shortcomings.[1] Though fiscal transfer and equalization reform generally include revising the division of tasks between fiscal tiers, this will not be discussed here. The following sections first discuss the design of the national fiscal equalization (Sect. 17.2) and then discuss where it can be improved (Sect. 17.3). Section 17.4 focuses on the financial dependence of the Swiss cantons on transfers which largely come from the central government. Sections 17.5 and 17.6, respectively, briefly present the design of the different cantonal fiscal equalization systems, and where there is room for improvement.

17.2 Design of the National Fiscal Transfers and Equalization

The revised national fiscal transfer and equalization system, and the division of tasks between the Confederation and the cantons, came into effect in 2008. To the extent that the revision necessitated modifying laws and the Constitution, Switzerland's method of direct democracy required that these be approved by both the majority of Swiss citizens and by a majority of the cantons. The modifications were subjected to popular referendum on November 28, 2004, and were approved by nearly 65% of the voters and 23 of the 26 cantons. The three which rejected the project were all cantons which would become net payers (Nidwalden, Schwyz, Zug).

The new system corrects several weaknesses in the previous system. The previous system was designed to achieve two goals when the Confederation made a financial transfer to a canton. One goal was to at least partly compensate a canton for the costs it had to bear when carrying out tasks that benefitted the Confederation (cost compensation; *Lastenausgleich; compensation des charges*). But transfers were simultaneously also intended to make additional financial resources available to cantons considered financially weak (resource equalization; *Ressourcenausgleich; péréquation des ressources*).

[1] Financial transfers between governments fit the more general definition of transfers: "a transaction in which one institutional unit provides a good, service, or asset to another unit without receiving from the latter any good, service, or asset in return as a direct counterpart. This kind of transaction is also referred to as being unrequited, a 'something for nothing' transaction, or a transaction without a quid pro quo. Transfers can also arise where the value provided in return for an item is not economically significant or is much below its value" (IMF 2014, p. 41).

Transfers often were earmarked and came in the form of matching grants. For example, the Confederation gave grants to cantons for the construction and maintenance of highways. Financially stronger cantons were given grants at rates as low as 40% (of the corresponding costs), while the weakest cantons had rates of nearly 90%. Nevertheless, these kinds of equalizing supplements (which in this case could vary by as much as 50 % points) had not made it possible to reduce resource differences between the cantons. Additionally, in the previous system the cantonal tax burden was included in computing a cantons' fiscal capacity. Fiscal capacity was used to calibrate the equalizing supplement as well as federal revenue sharing with the cantons (notably 13% of the federal income and profit tax). Given the cantons' significant tax autonomy, it is not surprising that the cantons tried to manipulate their tax burden in order to maximize the grant they received from the central government.

The new scheme no longer attempts to kill two birds with one stone; one reason is that it is now based on two key pillars. In the first pillar, the main goal is to equalize financial resources across the cantons. The second pillar is meant to compensate cantons for the cost incurred in various areas.

The Federal Act on Fiscal Equalization and Cost Compensation (*Bundesgesetz über den Finanz- und Lastenausgleich; Loi fédérale sur la péréquation financière et la compensation des charges*) designates the relevant constitutional provisions. Its Article 2 states that the goals of the equalization scheme are to "strengthen the financial autonomy of the cantons" and "decrease differences in terms of fiscal capacity and tax burden" between them. Indeed, the 26 cantonal governments are far from being on equal footing in providing their respective populations with public services. They face quite different economic situations. As a result, the tax base differs substantially and obliges "poorer" cantons to place a higher tax burden on their citizens. Also, their respective population structures or geographic situation generates differing needs and costs in providing the requisite public services.

17.2.1 Resource Equalization

Resource equalization is the most important pillar of this scheme. It is specifically designed to help out the financially weaker cantons, that is, those that have a lower potential for fiscal resources stemming from their own local economy. Equalization relies on an estimate of the resource potential (*Ressourcenpotenzial; potentiel de ressources*) per capita for each canton. The potential is determined by an aggregation of the tax bases of the different taxes levied by the cantons. Essentially, it means adding together the effective taxable resources, something which cannot be directly influenced by the cantons, at least in the short term.

Comparing the per capita cantonal potentials to the Swiss average creates a resource index (*Ressourcenindex; indice de ressources*). Cantons with a score higher than 100% of the average contribute to the equalization, while those with a score lower than 100% receive equalization funds. Figure 17.1 presents the index for 2018, which shows that three-fourths

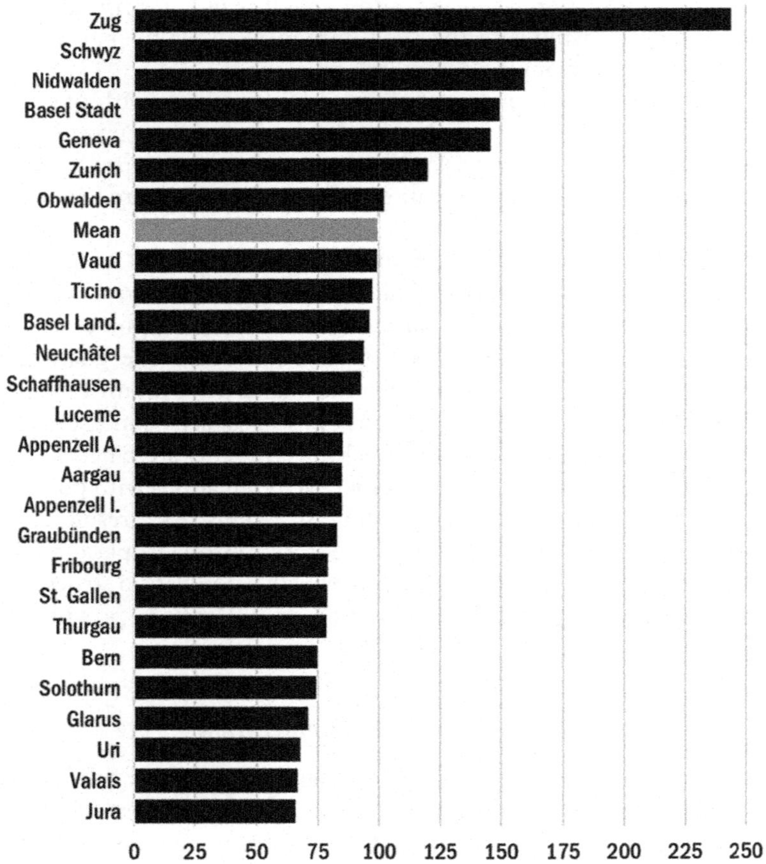

Fig. 17.1 Resource index, 2018. (Source: Federal Finance Administration)

of all the cantons have a lower score than the average. The weakest canton (Jura) has only 66% of the average; the strongest (Zug), 244%.

Figure 17.2 illustrates the significance of the redistribution effects national financial equalization creates by showing the polar cases: one in which equalization would have no redistributive effect and one in which the effect would make resources completely uniform across all the cantons.

In the Fig. 17.2, the resource index before equalization (i.e., corresponding to the canton's own potential) is shown on the horizontal axis; the index after equalization is shown on the vertical axis. Imagine that the

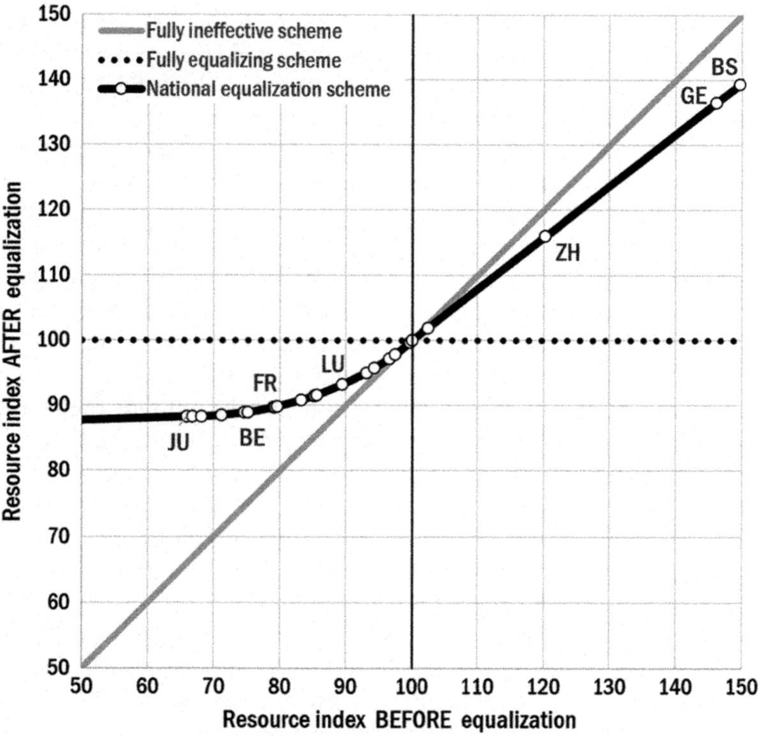

Fig. 17.2 National equalization scale, 2018. (Note: *JU*, Jura; *BE*, Bern; *FR*, Fribourg; *LU*, Lucerne; *ZH*, Zurich; *GE*, Geneva; and *BS*, Basel Stadt. In order to improve the readability of the chart, the values for the three financially richest cantons are not displayed: Nidwalden (Index was 160 before and 147 after equalization), Schwyz (172 and 157), and Zug (244 and 214). Source: Federal Finance Administration)

equalization scheme would be completely ineffective: the values would remain the same both before and after (gray line). No redistribution would take place, and the weaker cantons would remain weak (e.g., with an index of 80), whereas the "strong" would remain strong (e.g., at 120).

The opposite is depicted by the horizontal dotted line: a fully equalizing scheme where the resources of the strongest cantons are reduced to such an extent that after equalization, their resources would only amount to 100% of the national average. The weaker cantons would receive grants that would bring them up to the 100 mark after equalization. Regardless of the situation before equalization, all cantons would have the same resource levels per capita after equalization.

The national equalization system, represented by the dark solid curve, lies between these extremes: a few cantons are indicated for the sake of readability. The scheme guarantees a minimum allocation of about 85% after equalization (*Mindestausstattung; dotation minimale*), so that the canton with the lowest index (Jura, JU) before financial equalization receives enough transfer payments so that its index afterwards reaches 88%. Among cantons shown in the figure, the canton with the highest index before (Basel Stadt, BS), at 147%, is still at 137% after equalization. (Not displayed are the cantons that have even a higher index values, namely ZuG, Schwyz, and Nidwalden, all three cantons which voted against the reform) The equalization rate is thus regressive for the weakest cantons (i.e., an increase in their own potential corresponds to a decrease in the amount of transfer they receive) and becomes proportional for the strongest cantons: the amount they have to pay is a fixed percentage of the difference between their index and 100.

Fiscal equalization is not only financed by the fiscally strongest cantons. It is also financed by the central government. In 2018, the Confederation paid in 2.42 billion CHF (0.36% of gross domestic product (GDP)) and the seven financially strong cantons paid in 1.65 billion CHF (0.24%); and the 19 weakest cantons received 4.07 billion CHF.

Compared to the former equalization scheme, the reformed system incorporates horizontal transfers, although the vertical transfers are still larger. Also, grants are no longer earmarked, and the receiving cantons can freely allocate them as if they were their own resources.

17.2.2 Cost Compensation

The cost compensation scheme is meant to help the most urbanized cantons as well as the mountain cantons; each face—if for quite different reasons—structurally higher costs. Only costs necessary to provide the population with the public services for satisfying their basic needs are compensated, and in principle, only for the part of the cost that exceeds "normal" cost. Thus, public spending that goes beyond basic needs and reflects specific cantonal preferences are, in principle, not compensated. Spillover effects between jurisdictions also are not compensated within the national scheme.[2]

The compensation here involves two types of costs incurred by the cantons. Some cantons—especially the more urbanized—face higher needs, and thus costs, due to socio-demographic factors. Amounts allocated to these cantons are based on the incidence of poverty, age structure, integration of foreigners, and urbanization. Other cantons—especially the more mountainous and rural ones—face higher costs due to geo-topographical factors. Amounts allocated here are based on altitude, slope of the terrain, structure of the habitat, and population density.

This form of compensation is financed entirely by the central government, and so these transfers are uniquely vertical. In 2018, the Confederation paid in 0.72 billion CHF (0.11% of GDP), with half going to the first group of cantons (for socio-demographic reasons) and half to the second group (for geo-topographical reasons).

17.2.3 Compensation for Hardship Cases

Compensation for hardship cases rounds out the two pillars of the scheme (*Härteausgleich; compensation des cas de rigueur*). This was introduced to alleviate the financial loss experienced by the financially weaker cantons when the former fiscal equalization scheme was reformed. The compensation declines by 5% per year and is expected to expire completely by 2036. It is allocated exclusively to financially weak cantons, and the need for it is reviewed at regular intervals. In 2018, only six cantons qualified and 0.30 billion CHF (0.04% of GDP) was transferred; two-thirds of the money comes from the Confederation and one-third from the cantons.

[2] A canton that provides public services benefiting the population of other cantons can receive compensation for the corresponding costs in the specific context of an intercantonal collaboration and outside the national transfer system.

17.3 Room for Improvement in the National Equalization System

According to a recent evaluation by the Federal Council (2014), national fiscal equalization contributed to a notable reduction in intercantonal disparity, and it exhibited no serious flaws. Furthermore, as the Organization for Economic Co-operation and Development (OECD) (2015) pointed out, the established equalization system made it possible to significantly mitigate the effects of tax competition between the cantons.

But there is a downside. The current scheme reduces, or even obliterates, any incentive for the financially weakest cantons to develop their own resource potential. In essence, in the cantons in which the resource index is lower than 85%, each ten-franc increase in resource potential per capita is, on average, compensated by a decrease of eight CHF in equalization transfers (Federal council 2014). One proposal would then be to reduce this marginal clipping rate (*Grenzabschöpfungsquote; taux d'écrêtage marginaux*) of 80%.

A second problem comes from how the tax bases of the different taxes are aggregated to estimate the resource potential. A simple addition is not possible since the wealth tax base is much larger than the income tax base, for example, and the tax rates are markedly different. This makes it necessary to weight the tax bases to account for their respective contributions to the resource potential, but this involves an element of arbitrariness and reduces the transparency of the system. Additionally, it impacts the incentive given to the cantons to attract new companies. Putting a smaller weight on company profits when calculating resource potential should solve this problem while limiting the rise in revenue potential.

Third, vertical equalization is always much larger than horizontal equalization: 3.34 billion CHF currently, about two-thirds of the total. Yet vertical equalization is less effective at correcting inequalities because it benefits the financially weaker cantons without much affecting those cantons which are financially strong. Put differently, horizontal equalization has a positive effect on the weak and a negative effect on the strong.

Finally, only a small number of cantons contribute to horizontal resource equalization. The numbers mean that cantons which benefit have more political power to defend their gains or to demand an increase in equalization transfers. This certainly made it easier for referendum on the reform to be passed (as a majority of the cantons had to be in favor), but the contributing cantons increasingly feel that they are being subjected to the tyranny of the majority.

17.4 Cantonal Dependency on Transfers

In 2018, the national system involves transfers amounting to 5.09 billion CHF (4.07 billion CHF in resource equalization + 0.72 billion CHF in cost compensation + 0.30 billion CHF in hardship compensation). Although this amount seems large, it is only 0.75% of GDP. We can thus conclude that the cantons are not very financially dependent on this type of transfer, as Fig. 17.3 corroborates. Across all 26 cantons, equalization transfers are only 6% of all revenue. There is, however, a notable difference between cantons which receive next to nothing (e.g., Basel-Landschaft) and cantons in which the equalization transfers constitute more than 20% of their revenue (e.g., Uri).

The cantons can also count on transfers outside the national equalization scheme, especially vertical ones. In essence, the Confederation sends cantons compensation (*Entschädigungen; dédommagements*) when they provide public services for which the Confederation is legally responsible. In this case, the cantons are considered to be implementing agencies. The Confederation also provides contributions to cantons (*Beiträge; subventions* or *contributions*) to incentivize them to provide public services for which cantons are themselves responsible. Both compensations and contributions are specific grants, since the purposes for which they may be used is defined by the central government. These specific vertical transfers on average amount to some 13% of the revenue of the 26 cantons. Though this is double the amount of the equalization transfers, and though it may approach or exceed 20% of the total revenue in some cantons, it is still very small in international terms (Dafflon 2012).

Together, equalization and specific transfers (compensation and contributions) represent less than 20% of all cantonal revenue (6% and 13%). Indirectly, this demonstrates the cantons' strong fiscal autonomy, because their tax revenue must, on average, cover up to 80% of the fiscal consequences of their spending decisions. There are significant differences between cantons. Only two of them receive less than 10% from the Confederation (Geneva and Basel Stadt). At the other extreme, seven cantons exceed the 30% threshold.

The cantons also receive a share of federal tax revenue (*Ertragsanteile; parts de revenus*) amounting, in particular, to 17% of the income tax on private individuals and on the profit and capital of legal entities and 10% of withholding tax. This is only about 6% of the total revenue of the 26 cantons, and so cantons have limited dependency on these transfers. Furthermore, this dependency is financial rather than institutional. Indeed,

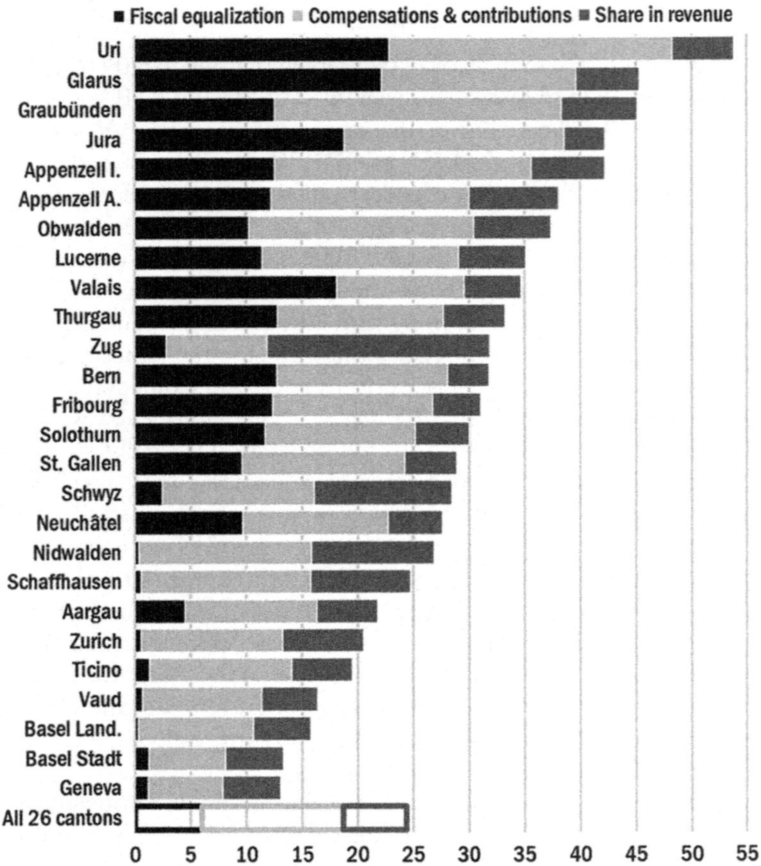

Fig. 17.3 Transfer dependency of Swiss cantons (transfers from the central government as a percentage of total cantonal revenue, 2015). (Note: Additional downloadable regular tables based on the Swiss governments' harmonized chart of accounts (FS Model). Fiscal equalization including cost compensation (account number 4620); compensations (4610) and contributions from the Confederation (4630); share in the tax revenue of the Confederation (4600); and total revenue (4) excluding extraordinary revenue (48). Source: Swiss Federal Finance Administration (2017). *Switzerland's financial statistics for 2015. FS Model.* Bern)

the cantons obtained the right to these shares of federal tax revenue in return for the power they have given the central government to encroach upon their tax prerogatives. The Confederation is therefore obligated to provide these shares. Like the equalization transfers, these revenue shares are general grants since they may be spent at each canton's discretion.

Figure 17.3 underscores the claim that all in all cantonal financial dependence on the Confederation is quite small. On average, only a quarter of cantonal revenue comes from the central government and only a third of the cantons depend on the Confederation for more than a third of their revenue. Generally, the urban cantons (or those close to a large city) are the least dependent. The mountain cantons (Alps and Jura) are more strongly dependent, especially because of the larger equalization transfers they receive.

17.5 Fiscal Equalization at the Cantonal Level

Cantons have also introduced internal fiscal transfer and equalization systems in order to reduce the inequalities between municipalities within the cantons. A further goal has been to guarantee that even the smallest communities are able to provide their citizens with at least a minimum level of public services. Here again, Swiss federalism and cantonal autonomy over finances means that cantons can themselves decide whether they want a system of fiscal equalization between their municipalities, and if so, how they want to design their system.

As a result, there are many different designs, although cantons all share the goal of reducing fiscal inequalities. Having said that, and inspired by the new national system, several cantons recently revised their fiscal equalization systems, the canton of Valais even adopted the entire design of the national system.

Transfers to the municipalities tend to be less earmarked so that the municipalities may spend the funds at their discretion. Furthermore, the ability of municipalities to influence the amounts they receive or that they must pay has been reduced or eradicated. Indeed, what they could previously put into play, such as their tax rates, has been removed from the calculation formulas used in establishing the levels of the transfers. Most cantons have also introduced a clear separation between the equalization of resources and the cost compensation. Kübler and Rochat (2016) note that while these equalizing systems reduce inequalities that exist between Swiss municipalities, they do not eliminate them completely.

This is because the equalization transfers are essentially horizontal (60% of the total). The amounts paid by the financially strong municipalities are redistributed to those which are financially weak, either directly or indirectly through a cantonal equalization fund. The cantons finance cost compensation for the benefit of those municipalities which face structurally higher costs than do other municipalities. The amounts redistributed each year from canton to municipality are quite large, reaching 5 billion CHF (0.8% of GDP) in 2013. The equalization effort is smaller in the French-speaking Swiss cantons than in the German-speaking ones (Rühli et al. 2013).

17.6 Room for Improvement in the Cantonal Equalization Systems

Rühli et al. (2013) evaluated the cantonal equalization systems according to various criteria: basic structure, extent of the redistribution, and the incentives contained in the transfers. The authors found shortcomings in several cantons, but especially in Graubünden, Solothurn, St. Gallen, and Ticino. The best practices were in Glarus and Fribourg. In general, the shortcomings at the cantonal level are similar to those at the national level.

One shortcoming stems from the minimum allocation guaranteed to the financially weaker municipalities; it corresponds to the horizontal portion to the left of the dark solid curve in Fig. 17.2. Basically, it involves a marginal clipping rate of 100% because in this zone, an increase in the resource potential of the municipalities is wholly canceled by the corresponding decrease in the equalization transfers received. Under these conditions, many financially weak municipalities have little incentive to improve their fiscal situation on their own. This is frequently also a reason municipalities do not merge, since even if they are financially weak, the equalization scheme provides them with enough resources to carry out their basic tasks. The largest problems arise in the German-speaking part of Switzerland where several cantons use high minimum allocations (e.g., the resource index after equalization is higher than 90).

A second shortcoming is that the tyranny of the majority is all the more nagging, as cantonal systems largely rely on solidarity between municipalities when it comes to the horizontal transfers. Yet the municipalities which benefit from equalization are often more numerous than the contributing municipalities. This problem exists because cantons are not infrequently made up of many rural municipalities with few resources and a handful of wealthy municipalities which inflate the resource indices. There is a resulting power imbalance: the larger group —the financially weak municipalities —directs decision-making to their profit (by obtaining, e.g., increased equalization transfers).

A third shortcoming stems from the existence of a "neutral zone" in the cantonal equalization scale. To reduce the solidarity efforts of the financially well-off municipalities, cantons have often introduced an interval in the resource index, usually between 80 and 100, and municipalities situated there no longer receive any equalization transfers. This neutral zone does not exist in the national equalization scale.

This zone, in Fig. 17.2, corresponds to a situation in which the dark solid curve of the equalization scale would merge with the line of the fully ineffective scheme. The effect of introducing this kind of zone is to reduce the number of municipalities benefitting from equalization transfers and re-calibrate the power balance. It also makes it possible to lower the total amount of the transfers, since municipalities located in the neutral zone do not receive equalization transfers. Nevertheless, introducing this zone creates an inconvenient break in the equalization scale, making it less transparent and less intelligible. Because of this break in the slope, transfers to the municipalities with an index that is close or within the neutral zone may be unstable and change from one year to the next. Furthermore, the municipalities below the neutral zone may have an incentive to avoid carrying out reforms so as not to enter it.

17.7 Conclusion

Opportunities to improve both the national and the cantonal transfer and equalization systems exist, and efforts at improvement vary depending on the fiscal situation of the governments. Economic crises, international competition over business taxes, migration, and the aging of the population are all factors which challenge the balance that, until now, has existed.

All the same, considerable progress has been made over the last decade. The contradictions between redistribution transfers and allocation transfers have greatly decreased, and governments can no longer directly influence the amounts they receive or must pay by, for example, manipulating their tax rates. Reforms to the equalization systems have also made it possible to decrease the effects of tax competition. They indirectly ensure that tax competition between both cantons and municipalities can continue to exist, but within acceptable and accepted limits.

These successes demonstrate that in Switzerland, notwithstanding the existence and the power of the tools of direct democracy, ambitious structural reforms involving numerous stakeholders remain possible. This obviously involves political strategizing, that is reflected in the introduction into the federal system—for a limited time—of compensation for hardship cases. And one must regard the recourse to a tyranny of the majority by governments which benefit from the transfers over the governments which finance the transfers as a necessary evil.

Despite, or thanks to, this tyranny, Switzerland has established rules meant to ensure fiscal equalization between its governments at all levels. These rules guarantee a certain automatism and a regularity to equalization flows, and by the same token, no discretionary decisions to give subsidy grants to decentralized municipalities—and no way for the wealthiest communities or cantons to ignore those political entities which are worse off than them.

References

Dafflon, B. (2012). Les transferts financiers entre collectivités publiques. In A. Ladner, J.-L. Chappelet, Y. Emery, P. Knoepfel, L. Mader, N. Soguel, & F. Varone (Eds.), *Manuel d'administration publique suisse* (pp. 661–678). Lausanne: PPUR.

Federal Council. (2014). *Wirksamkeitsbericht 2012–2015 des Finanzausgleichs zwischen Bund und Kantonen*. Bern: Schweizerische Eidgenossenschaft.

IMF (International Monetary Fund) Statistics Department. (2014). *Government finance statistics manual 2014*. Washington, DC: International Monetary Fund.

Kübler, D., & Rochat, P. E. (2016). 'Tamed Tieboutianism' and spatial inequalities in Swiss metropolitan areas. In J. M. Sellers, M. Arretche, D. Kübler, & E. Razin (Eds.), *Inequality and governance in the metropolis: Place equality regimes and fiscal choices in eleven countries* (pp. 107–124). London: Palgrave Macmillan.

OECD (The Organisation for Economic Co-operation and Development). (2015). *OECD economic surveys: Switzerland 2015*. Paris: OECD Publishing.

Rühli, L., Frey, M., & Frey, R. L. (2013). *Irrgarten Finanzausgleich. Wege zu mehr Effizienz bei der interkommunalen Solidarität*. Zürich: Avenir Suisse.

PART V

The Management of Public Policies

CHAPTER 18

Social Security Policy

Giuliano Bonoli

18.1 Main Objectives and Policy Instruments

As in other European countries, the social security system in Switzerland has a range of objectives[1]. These reflect the chronological and gradual development of the system. The system aims at providing a guaranteed minimum income for the entire resident population. The first schemes introduced at the national level, old age pensions in 1948 and disability insurance in 1960, clearly had this objective. They tried to achieve it by providing at least subsistence-level benefits to virtually all residents.

During the 1960s and early 1970s, the rise of the middle classes prompted the adoption of a more ambitious objective: an income guarantee aiming to give the recipients of benefits a standard of living close to the one they would have had—had they not been disabled, become unemployed, and so forth. Existing programmes were revised accordingly, and a compulsory second pillar of old age pension provision was introduced. In disability insurance, a system of benefit increases was introduced, which

[1] This chapter is based on research carried out in the context of the European Social Protection Network. It draws heavily on Bonoli and Trein (2017).

G. Bonoli (✉)
IDHEAP, University of Lausanne, Lausanne, Switzerland
e-mail: giuliano.bonoli@unil.ch

A. Ladner et al. (eds.), *Swiss Public Administration*, Governance and Public Management,
https://doi.org/10.1007/978-3-319-92381-9_18

was meant to reflect the wage increases workers typically experience during their careers. The new schemes, including unemployment insurance (introduced in 1978), had the goal of maintaining income levels from the start.

Towards the mid-1990s, with the rise in mass unemployment and permanent exclusion from the labour market for many, a new objective was added: activation. Over the last 20 years, the social security system has been gradually transformed, and the primary objective of all the relevant schemes is explicit to put "clients" back into the labour market. Several instruments are used to that effect: rehabilitation services for the disabled, active labour market policies for the long-term unemployed, vocational training, and wage subsidies.

In other words, over time, the Swiss welfare state has gone from being the provider of a minimum income to all to becoming an activation machine. Of course, this transformation concerns programmes providing coverage to working-age people. The old age pension system has not been affected by the "activation turn", also because Switzerland never really developed large-scale early retirement schemes.

With regard to the specific institutional architecture of the social security system for working-age individuals, there are three main schemes. First, Switzerland has a federal *unemployment insurance* programme. Contribution rates and benefit levels, as well as most other features, are set by the federal parliament, though the implementation is a cantonal responsibility. While cantons must implement federal law and must organize a public employment service (PES), they have a large degree of autonomy in many areas, including activation, coordination with other schemes, and managing their own PES. The federal government monitors the implementation and the performance of the cantonal PES, using somewhat controversial indicators and a benchmarking system.

Disability insurance is also a federal scheme implemented by the cantons. Such insurance provides earnings replacement benefits for individuals who cannot work because of a long-term or permanent medical impairment, but it also provides substantial rehabilitation and other activation-related services. In this case, too, cantons are relatively free with regard to how they choose to implement the programme, again within the terms and conditions set by federal law.

Finally, *social assistance* is entirely regulated and financed at the cantonal level. Federal-level involvement in social assistance is limited to an article in the federal constitution which entitles every resident to a minimum subsistence income and de facto forces cantons to run social assistance schemes (Swiss Constitution, Art. 115). As cantons give municipalities leeway, there is some variety in the approaches adopted in the different parts of the country. We lack a precise view of what actually goes on in terms of benefits and services across the 26 cantons and about 2200 municipalities that make up Switzerland.

Against the background of this high level of institutional fragmentation, a non-governmental body, the Swiss Conference for Social Welfare (CSIAS/SKOS), plays a very important role. CSIAS/SKOS is a private association with representatives of cantonal and municipal social services as well as from the main anti-poverty organizations such as Caritas. It has about 1000 individual and collective members. CSIAS/SKOS issues guidelines concerning benefit levels as well as the design and implementation of social assistance; its guidelines encompass several hundred pages of text (SKOS 2015). These guidelines are very precise and most cantons use them in defining social assistance rules and practices; they help reduce what would otherwise be a very high degree of variation across cantons and municipalities in social assistance practices and policy.

For the non-working-age population, Switzerland has developed an *old age pension system* based on three pillars. The first pillar covers the basic needs of retirees. It is moderately earnings-related and includes a means-tested pension supplement (*Ergänzungsleitungen/Prestations complémentaires*, EL-PC). The second pillar tries to ensure that retirees enjoy a standard of living close to the one they experienced while last employed and consists of mandatory occupational pensions for salaried employees. The third pillar makes it possible to tailor pension coverage to individual needs through non-compulsory personal pension payments which receive favourable tax treatment.

The first pillar provides universal coverage and is fairly redistributive. There is no contribution ceiling, but the amount of the benefit can vary between a floor and a ceiling twice as high as the floor. In 2018, the limits were set at CHF 1175 (€ 950) and CHF 2350 (€1900) per month, respectively, corresponding to approximately 20% and 40% of the average wage. Benefits are adjusted every two years using a "mixed index" derived from the arithmetic average of inflation and wage increases. A full pension is paid at age 64 for women and 65 for men.

The second pillar, occupational pensions, became compulsory in 1985 for all employees earning at least twice the minimum "first pillar" pension (Bonoli 2007; Leimgruber 2008). Coverage is near-universal among full-time employees, but some part-time and temporary workers are excluded. In fact, second pillar pensions are compulsory for workers earning more than 21,150 CHF per year (20,000 EUR). This threshold corresponds to about 30% of the average full-time wage. A full occupational pension is granted to employees who have contributed for 39 (women) or 40 (men) years. The law provides for a compulsory minimum level of provision (known as the Obligatorium) calculated on the basis of notional contributions. This gives existing pension funds a relatively high degree of autonomy over how to deliver and finance that minimum level of provision. It must be fully funded for private sector employers. Many pension funds, especially in the public sector, or those sponsored by large employers, offer better conditions than the Obligatorium (Bonoli and Gay-des-Combes 2003; Vontobel 2000). The occupational pension law also prescribes a government-set minimum nominal interest rate for second pillar pension funds covered by the Obligatorium. An important parameter defining second pillar pension benefits is the rate at which the accumulated capital is converted into an annuity (Umwandlungsatz/taux de conversion); that rate is set by law and currently stands at 6.8%.

The third pillar consists of voluntary private individual pensions which are tax-favoured. Employees can deduct payment into a third pillar pension account of up to CHF 6768 (€ 5547; figure for 2018) per year. The self-employed, who are not covered by compulsory occupational pensions, can deduct up to 20% of their earnings.

The Swiss multipillar pension scheme is seen as a rather successful example of a system that manages to address retirees' financial needs adequately without facing intractable financing problems. The division between the two main pillars, and the fact that the second pillar is fully funded, means that the ageing Swiss population will have less of an impact on the financing of pensions than countries in which the bulk of pension expenditure is financed on a pay-as-you-go basis.[2]

[2] In the literature on old age pensions, a distinction is made between pay-as-you-go schemes, in which current benefits are financed by current contributions, and funded schemes, in which current benefits are financed by past contribution. Funded systems are, in fact, compulsory savings schemes.

18.2 Main Actors and Structures

The social security schemes presented above are large governmental programmes that rely on a range of actors and structures which are located at different levels of the Swiss federal state.

18.2.1 Unemployment Insurance

The federal State Secretariat for Economic Affairs is in charge of the unemployment insurance scheme. It oversees the implementation of unemployment insurance by the cantons, signs a performance agreement with them, and runs an indicator and benchmarking system. At the cantonal level, the key role is played by cantonal PESs, which are responsible for managing benefits and activation. They have substantial autonomy in implementation.

Intercantonal associations also play a large role, including the association of cantonal PES. This association coordinates the implementation of unemployment insurance across cantons and represents their common interests at the federal level. Regional placement offices are key actors in implementation. They belong to the canton's PES and provide monitoring and activation services for job seekers. They have some autonomy in implementation, but it is limited by the given cantonal PES. There are some 100 such regional placement offices in the country.

The unemployment compensation funds are additional, significant, actors. They can be either cantonal or branch based, and administer contributions and benefit payments. They have little autonomy and can be considered as purely administrative actors.

Finally, there are non-governmental organizations (mostly NGOs and more rarely, for-profit private companies) which provide the activation services needed by the PES.

18.2.2 Disability Insurance

The federal social insurance office is the key actor in disability insurance. It coordinates and oversees implementation by the cantons and, more importantly, takes the lead in proposing national legislation.

Implementation is the responsibility of cantonal disability insurance offices, which are responsible for managing both benefits and activation measures. They have substantial autonomy.

As with unemployment insurance, intercantonal associations play a large role here. The most important one is arguably the intercantonal association of disability insurance agencies, which includes all cantonal disability insurance offices. It coordinates the implementation of unemployment insurance across cantons and represents their common interests at the federal level.

The regional medical services are another key actor; this provides the medical expertise needed in order to assess eligibility. There are ten regional medical services, each serving one or more cantonal disability offices.

In theory, they have little room for manoeuvre, as they have to strictly apply the law. In reality, medical assessments, especially of mental health, may fall into a grey area, giving a certain latitude to the regional medical services in how strictly they choose to implement the relevant laws. As with unemployment insurance, activation and rehabilitation services are provided mostly by non-state actors, including NGOs and for-profit private firms.

18.2.3 Social Assistance

Social assistance is a cantonal and municipal responsibility. As a result, there is no "social assistance office" or similar bureau at the federal level. As noted above, the only umbrella organization with a national scope is the Swiss Conference for Social Welfare, a private association.

Cantonal authorities (governments and parliaments), who are the most important actors, decide on cantonal social assistance laws. Given the absence of federal law in this area, they have substantial autonomy. Each canton has a social service, which is responsible for implementing social assistance laws, and regional or municipal social services deliver the benefits to clients. They are also in charge of the activation services, though their autonomy is limited by cantonal law. While big cities like Zurich, Basel, or Geneva can set up their own activation programmes (Duell et al. 2010, p. 101), smaller cities and municipalities lack the resources and capacities to do the same.

In some cantons, one still finds social commissions. These are made up of citizens designated by the municipal executive. They make formal decisions concerning eligibility and access to activation services. This is a premodern institution with a strong social control function; it has survived mostly in the German-speaking part of the country but been largely abolished in French- and Italian-speaking cantons. As in other branches of the social security system, one finds NGOs, or more rarely, for-profit private companies, which provide activation services needed by social assistance offices.

18.2.4 Old Age Pensions

Old age pensions are a federal responsibility. They are overseen by the federal social insurance office. With regard to implementation, a distinction needs to be made between the first pillar, which is public, and the second pillar, which is company or branch based. The first pillar is carried out by some 100 "compensation funds". Some are public (each canton has one) but most are branch-based. Some very large employers such as Coop, a large supermarket chain, have their own. Compensation funds collect contributions and distribute benefits, but they are all interconnected and under the umbrella of a central compensation fund based in Geneva; it keeps the records of every insured person.

For the second pillar, the key actors are around 2000 occupational pension funds. Large companies generally have their own, while a number of branch-based funds exist which companies are free to join. Finally, most insurance companies and banks also provide second pillar coverage to employers who do not have their own fund.

18.3 Policy Implementation and Outcomes

Switzerland has long had a low unemployment rate and relatively few social problems. The Swiss labour market also has been doing relatively well during the last few years. These are all not necessarily a result of the welfare state.

The employment rate has remained above the European Union (EU) 2020 target of 75% throughout the period covered in Table 18.1. It is intriguing to see that between 2010–2011 and 2014 both the employment and the unemployment rates increase. This may reflect an increasing level of competition in the labour market.

Against the background of this overall good labour market performance, some groups are experiencing more difficulties, in particular younger workers who lack a completed vocational or academic education. As Table 18.2 shows, the unemployment rate for the 15–24 age group is considerably higher than the general one.

Table 18.1 Key labour market indicators for the working-age (20–64) population

	2010	*2011*	*2012*	*2013*	*2014*	*2015*
Employment rate	81.1	81.8	82.0	82.1	82.3	82.8
Unemployment rate	4.2	3.8	3.9	4.2	4.5	4.5
Female employment rate	74.6	75.4	76.0	76.6	77.4	78.2

Source: Employment rates: Eurostat, unemployment rate, OECD

Table 18.2 Labour market position of younger people (aged 15–24 years)

	2010	*2011*	*2012*	*2013*	*2014*	*2015*
Employment	62.5	62.9	61.7	61.9	61.6	61.0
Unemployment	7.2	5.9	6.1	7.0	7.7	6.4

Source: Employment, Eurostat; Unemployment, Swiss statistical office (2nd quarter)

Non-European migrants are another group that is relatively disadvantaged in the Swiss labour market, with an employment rate lower than that of Swiss nationals and EU/EFTA (European Free Trade Association) migrants. Partly this has to do with the channel through which different migrants arrive in Switzerland. EU/EFTA nationals come most often in order to take up employment, and since the adoption of the agreement on the free movement of workers, their employment rate has increased. It is interesting to note that over the same period of time, the employment rate of Swiss has also increased, though to a smaller extent. Non-European migrants instead come to Switzerland mostly from other channels, often as asylum seekers. This is related to the lower employment rate of this group. It should also be noted that non-European migrants are the only group which has not taken advantage of the expansion of employment since the early 2000; Table 18.3 shows how invariant their employment rates have remained.

The overall poverty rate puts Switzerland in the same category as Germany, with AROP[3] rates around 15%. The very high AROP rate reported for

[3] AROP, the "at risk of poverty" rate, refers to the percentage of the population living in households with income below 60% of equivalent disposable income. This definition is used by the EU Commission and has become relatively widely accepted among poverty researchers.

Table 18.3 Employment rates by nationality (aged 15–64 years)

	2010	*2011*	*2012*	*2013*	*2014*	*2015*	*2016*
Swiss	82.5	82.9	82.6	83.3	83.7	83.7	84.9
EU or EFTA	84.7	85.7	86.0	86.0	86.7	86.5	87.2
Other country	74.4	73.2	74.0	73.7	74.7	73.4	74.8

Source: Bundesamt fuer Statistik, ESPA, data refer to second trimester

Table 18.4 Poverty statistics (percentages)

	2010	*2011*	*2012*	*2013*	*2014*
At risk of poverty, total	15.0	15.0	15.9	14.5	13.8
At risk of poverty, aged 65 years and over	27.6	28.1	29.9	29.5	25.7[a]

Source: Eurostat (based on SILC data) Data not available for 2015

[a]Change in series

older people by Eurostat is somewhat misleading, however. Swiss pensioners can choose to receive their second pillar pension as a lump sum, and many do because it is more convenient from a fiscal point of view. As a result, many income-poor seniors are in fact asset-rich. Swiss data therefore suggest that the actual economic situation of elderly people is not as unfavourable as suggested by Eurostat figures. Swiss perceptions are also that the pension system is fairly successful in guaranteed a decent standard of living to retirees—a perception that is clearly at odds with the very high reported AROP rate shown in Table 18.4.

The incidence of poverty can also be evaluated with reference to the proportion of the population that must rely on social assistance. Over the last few years, that proportion has remained constant at around 3%, but this stability in the percentage is also misleading. In fact, as can be seen in Table 18.5, between 2009 and 2015, a period of good labour market performance, the absolute number of social assistance recipients consistently increased, reflecting an increase in population size due to in-migration.

In fact, the increase in the number of social assistance recipients has been fairly constant since the early 1990s (Bonoli and Champion 2014), even during a recent period when employment was increasing. This indicates that the labour market has become more competitive, possibly because of the free movement of labour agreement with the European

Table 18.5 Social assistance caseload

	2009	*2010*	*2011*	*2012*	*2013*	*2014*	*2015*
Total number of recipients	230,019	231,046	236,133	250,333	257,192	261,983	265,626
As a percentage of the resident population	3.0	3.0	3.0	3.1	3.2	3.2	3.2

Source: Swiss Federal Statistical Office

Union, and less productive individuals are finding it more difficult to enter and remain in the labour market.

With regard to child poverty, a recent report by the Swiss Federal Statistical Office found that overall, children in Switzerland fare relatively well, particularly in comparison with other European countries. Only the Nordic countries and the Netherlands have indicators of child welfare which are as good or slightly better (FSO 2016, p. 26). Nevertheless, there are some groups which remain of concern, including children living in single-parent households, children living in households with three or more children, and children of non-Swiss parents. In these groups, poverty and deprivation rates are higher than the norm and more worrisome.

Overall, the Swiss social security system seems capable of delivering reasonably good levels of economic security to the resident population. However, the fact that social indicators remain rather favourable does not necessarily constitute proof that the Swiss welfare state is particularly well calibrated to the needs of society. It may well be that the good performance is due more to the country's overall economic competitiveness rather than to its welfare state schemes. In simpler terms, it is relatively easy to build an effective welfare state in a country with a buoyant labour market and a consistently low unemployment rate.

In reality, each of the four main schemes has strengths and weaknesses. In addition, the fragmentation of the system along federalist lines makes internal coordination of, and in, the Swiss social security system difficult.

The Swiss welfare state is a rather diverse construct with some programmes, such as the basic pension scheme, which are highly centralized, and others, such as social assistance, which are extremely decentralized. Between them, one finds schemes that rely on a division of labour between federal and cantonal levels. Unemployment and disability insurance are governed by the federal authorities but are implemented at the cantonal level, sometimes with substantial variations from canton to canton. This raises issues about the equality of treatment across cantons, creates difficulties in coordination, and more abstractly, principal–agent problems.

The current trend is to increasingly use quantitative indicators and benchmarking to try to ensure some coherence in how policies are implemented and to try to maximize their efficacy. Federal authorities also use benchmarking in an effort to "control" the cantons, as well as to avoid the potential problems of principal and agent that can emerge if financing and implementation are performed by two different levels of government.

Coordination strategies are pursued through intercantonal associations such as SKOS/CSIAS or other intercantonal bodies, which formally represent the relevant department and offices at the cantonal level. There seems to be an instinctive preference in Switzerland to resolve coordination problems through voluntary agreements between cantons rather than by centralizing systems.

Coordination problems are further compounded by the involvement of private actors in the system. This is most clearly the case in old age pensions, where private occupational pensions have developed into an industry, one with substantial interests at stake. The objectives of such private actors are not always compatible with the social policy goals set by the public authorities, so that substantial coordination work is needed on this front as well.

So though social indicators remain rather favourable, the institutional contours of the Swiss social security system also remain highly fragmented. The result is that public authorities need to invest substantial efforts in coordinating the welfare state system, and the fragmentation may prove a liability in the future.

18.4 Prospective Thinking

The Swiss social security system faces challenges like those faced by other European countries. They include:

- Financing the pension system over the longer term
- Containing the rise in the number of benefit recipients
- Improving the effectiveness of re-employment services
- Facilitating the work–life balance particularly for parents of young children

- Promoting the integration of migrants and their communities
- Enhancing social inclusion

Overall, the Swiss welfare state is relatively well equipped to deal with these challenges, and this task is facilitated by the overall favourable economic situation. Nonetheless, some issues will need to be resolved if the challenges above are to be dealt effectively.

First, though the pension system is regarded as rather efficient, it needs to be made more financially viable for the next few decades. The first pillar pension scheme has been running small deficits for several years, and owing to an ageing population, its financial situation will begin to become critical by around 2030. If no measures are taken, its reserve fund will be used up even before then.

Second, the conversion rate (of 6.8%, see above) applied to the assets of occupational pensions is not sustainable in the current low interest rates/low returns environment. The result is that a small proportion of current contributions are being used to pay for current benefits instead of being set aside for future pensions. Any extra returns obtained tend to be used to finance current pensions instead of being distributed across the whole pool of insured persons.

The long-term financing of the basic pension and the reduction of the conversion rate for second pillar pensions are thorny political issues. A high-profile reform which tried to deal with both problems without reducing the overall level of benefits was turned down by the voters in September 2017. It is unclear how these issues will be resolved. Pension policy has clearly become an object of political competition among parties, and it is difficult to find a consensus over unpopular measures.

Third, the social security system has been modernized and it now oriented towards the promotion of labour market re-entry. This reflects, at least in part, the "social investment approach" (Hemerijck 2017; Morel et al. 2012). Unemployment and disability insurance provide extensive labour market and rehabilitation programmes for non-working "clients".

However, the same is not true of social assistance. This "last resort" safety net is within the competence of the cantons, and in many cantons, of the municipalities. Here, the turn to activation or social investment has been much more uneven, with some cantons having clearly embraced the new paradigm while others lag behind. This may be one reason why social assistance caseloads keep increasing even in buoyant labour markets and an expanding economy. It will be a challenge in the next few years how the activation dimension in social assistance can be reinforced—and how to caseloads from increasing.

Fourth, the Swiss welfare state is highly fragmented, a broad but also a quite specific problem. There is evidence, for example, that cantonal or municipal social assistance programmes and federal social insurance schemes shift "clients" to one another, because there are structural incentives (including those associated with costs) to do so (Bonoli and Champion 2014; Bonoli and Trein 2016).

Finally, as in other countries, a major policy challenge for Switzerland remains improving the work–life balance, especially for families with young children. Switzerland provides only 14 weeks of maternity leave and has no parental leave. In addition, there are simply not enough childcare centres, as one can see from the long waiting lists in many urban areas. Furthermore, the cost of childcare for parents is among the highest of all the Organization for Economic Co-operation and Development (OECD) countries (OECD 2011, p. 150). This situation also results in a very strong social bias against certain migrant communities and low-income families; their access to childcare services is even more limited than for citizens (Bonoli and Vuille 2013; Schlanser 2011). This is unfortunate, because Switzerland is missing out on an important opportunity to promote social inclusion and the integration of migrant families.

References

Bonoli, G. (2007). Switzerland: Development and crisis of a multipillar pension system. In K. M. Anderson, E. M. Immergut, & I. Schulze (Eds.), *Oxford handbook of West European pension politics*. Oxford: Oxford University Press.

Bonoli, G., & Champion, C. (2014). Federalism and welfare to work in Switzerland – The development of active social policies in a fragmented welfare state. *Publius the Journal of Federalism, 45*(1), 77–98.

Bonoli, G., & Gay-des-Combes, B. (2003). *Evolution de prestations vieillesse dans le long terme: une simulation prospective de la couverture retraite à l'horizon 2040*. Bern: Office fédéral des assurances sociales, Rapport de recherche No. 3/03.

Bonoli, G., & Trein, P. (2016). Cost-shifting in multitiered welfare states: Responding to rising welfare caseloads in Germany and Switzerland. *Publius: The Journal of Federalism, 46*(4), 596–622.

Bonoli, G., & Trein, P. (2017). *ESPN country profile: Switzerland*. Brussels: European Commission.

Bonoli, G., & Vuille, S. (2013). *L'accueil de jour des enfants dans le Canton de Vaud*. Lausanne: Fondation pour l'Accueil de Jour de Enfants (FAJE), Research report.

Duell, N., Tergeist, P., Bazant, U., & Cimper, S. (2010). *Activation policies in Switzerland*. Paris: OECD Social Employment and Migration Working Papers.

FSO (Federal Statistical Office). (2016). *Pauvreté et privations matérielles des enfants*. Neuchatel: Federal Statistical Office.

Hemerijck, A. (Ed.). (2017). *Social investment and its critics*. Oxford: Oxford University Press.

Leimgruber, M. (2008). *Solidarity without the state? Business and the shaping of the Swiss welfare state, 1890–2000*. Cambridge: Cambridge University Press.

Morel, N., Palier, B., & Palme, J. (Eds.). (2012). *Towards a social investment welfare state?: Ideas, policies and challenges*. Bristol: The Policy Press.

OECD (Organisation for Economic Co-operation and Development). (2011). *Doing better for families*. Paris: OECD.

Schlanser, R. (2011). *Qui utilise les crèches en Suisse? Logiques sociales du recours aux structures d'accueil collectif pour la petite enfance*. Lausanne: IDHEAP, Cahier No. 264.

SKOS (Schweizerische Konferenz für Sozialhilfe). (2015). *SKOS-Richtlinien* (in German, French and Italian). Berne: SKOS.

Vontobel, W. (2000, December 1). Die Saülen-Scheinheiligen: Pech hat, wer in einem Kleinbetieb arbeitet. *CASH*.

CHAPTER 19

Health Policy

Philipp Trein

19.1 Introduction

Health policy entails the regulation, financing, and provision of a wide range of medical and non-medical services to prevent and cure diseases. This complex task makes it one of the most multifaceted and expensive fields of public policy. Strong professional interests and autonomies, expensive treatments, equity of access, quality concerns, and increasing costs render policymaking challenging. In Switzerland, health policymaking occurs against the background of direct democracy, decentralized federalism, liberalism, consensual policymaking, and subsidiarity. This system grants subnational policymakers, voters, as well as private actors considerable access, voice, and influence on decisions in health policy.

In terms of macro-indicators related to health, Switzerland can only partly be considered a success story. The majority of the Swiss population is satisfied with the country's health care system (FOPH 2016a). From a medical point of view, Switzerland has a high life expectancy rate at birth (83 as of 2015), median childhood mortality (3.9, 2015), low rates of preventable mortality (159 per 100,000 in 2013), and rather low cancer death rates (223.5 per 100,000 in 2013). However, it also has rather high

P. Trein (✉)
IEPHI, University of Lausanne, Lausanne, Switzerland
e-mail: josefphilipp.trein@unil.ch

A. Ladner et al. (eds.), *Swiss Public Administration*, Governance and Public Management,
https://doi.org/10.1007/978-3-319-92381-9_19

suicide rates (12.2 per 100,000 as of 2013, with a historically even higher rate) compared to other Organization for Economic Co-operation and Development (OECD) countries (OECD 2016). The main challenge for Switzerland is rising costs for health and long-term care, as well as issues in the distribution of these costs. In 2015, Switzerland spent 11.5 percent of its gross domestic product (GDP) on health policy (the OECD average is 9 percent), and 3.7 percent of these expenditures were out-of-pocket contributions from patients, as compared to an average of 2.4 percent in the OECD (2016). Health insurance carriers pay for most health expenditures, whereas cantons and municipalities cover the largest share of the health expenditures by the state (FOPH 2017a). The biggest challenge is the rising health care burden for the population, since health insurance premiums continually increase (FOPH 2017b) and a considerable share of the population relies on cantonal subsidies to pay their health insurance fees (FOPH 2014a).

The next section discusses the institutional foundations of Swiss health policy. Then, I present the constellations of the politico-administrative and private actors in Swiss health policy and discuss the resulting political conflicts. This chapter then turns to current challenges for health policymakers in Switzerland.

19.2 Institutional Foundations

National health policy is based on a health insurance law adopted in 1994 and in force since 1996 (LAMal; 'Loi fédérale sur l'assurance maladie'), which replaced the earlier law of 1911. The reform in 1994 signaled a change from a voluntary health insurance system to a universal and mandatory health insurance system. This switch came late in comparison to other European countries (Uhlmann and Braun 2011). The main responsibility for health policy rests with the Federal Office of Public Health (FOPH), founded in 1893, and originally responsible mainly for public health, especially health promotion and illness prevention. Responsibility for health insurance would only be transferred to the FOPH in 2003 (Trein 2018).

A comparative assessment of health care systems suggests that Swiss health care policy follows a collective negotiation logic, in which subnational public actors (such as cantons) as well as private actors (such as health insurance bodies, professional organizations, private hospitals, or the pharmaceutical industry) possess considerable influence and lobbying power. Hierarchy and market logics are less important, although the Swiss system shares important similarities with the US health care system, one which emphasizes market elements in the financing and provision of health care (Böhm et al. 2013).

Historically, three organizational principles have shaped actor constellations and the institutions of the Swiss health system: federalism, liberalism, and subsidiarity (Sager et al. 2010; Vatter and Rüefli 2014, 828).

- **Federalism:** Switzerland is a 'coming together' federation, in which the subnational governmental units (cantons) formed the national government. Originally, the cantons had the power to make policy over health issues, and only gradually and selectively transferred health policymaking to the national level. In principle, Switzerland has 26 different health systems and health policies, and policies adopted at the cantonal level often preceded national regulations. This was true for health insurance itself (Uhlmann and Braun 2011), for the implementation of alcohol policy (Sager 2003, 2004) and tobacco control policy (Trein 2017). Cooperation between cantons always played an important role for national health policy as well, with the Conference of Cantonal Public Health Directors (CPHD) that has existed since 1919 (Trein 2018). Thus, the decentralized federal structure impeded the creation of national health legislation longer than in other countries where subnational governments had less policy competencies.
- **Liberalism:** Health policy in Switzerland has a strong liberal element. This means that policies constraining the liberties of individuals and businesses are notoriously unpopular. Citizens and elites, particularly in the central and eastern part of the country, prefer a small but effective state instead of a large redistributive machinery. Support for a limited state also affected the creation of a national health insurance scheme. Since the early twentieth century, population and elites have repeatedly opposed, and more significantly, voted against policy proposals that aimed at creating a national health insurance law or that called for creating a public health insurance organization operated by the state (Alber and Bernardi-Schenkluhn 1992). In 2014, voters rejected a popular initiative demanding the establishment of a public health insurance organization[1] (Trein

[1] The title of the popular initiative was Eidgenössische Volksinitiative 'Für eine öffentliche Krankenkasse': https://www.admin.ch/ch/d/pore/vi/vis401.html, accessed October 26, 2017.

2018). Liberalism also guided the design of the national health insurance law in 1994, which made health insurance coverage mandatory but nevertheless had private providers offering the health insurance packages. Interestingly, insurers are not allowed to make profits with the basic insurance package, and, despite competition for insurance contracts, are required to accept all applications for basic health care coverage regardless of gender, age, or pre-existing medical conditions (Uhlmann and Braun 2011). The prevalence of liberal values also played a role in the failure of proposals aimed at introducing preventive health policies. In 1993, for example, voters and parliament rejected a popular initiative calling for a complete ban on alcohol and tobacco advertising (Cornuz et al. 1996), and more recently, a national framework law to create a preventive health care policy failed after several rounds in the national parliament (APS 2012; Fontana 2012).

- **Subsidiarity:** Subsidiarity means that social or political issues should be dealt with at the lowest possible level of government. This implies that local non-state actors should be brought in to deal with policy problems, and is a reason non-state actors play an important role in health policymaking and in local delivery of health or long-term care services. In Switzerland, for example, non-governmental organizations such as the Swiss Cancer League or the Swiss Lung League assist patients and create health promotion programs. Historically, health insurance was first provided, following the subsidiarity principle, by local health insurance providers, but their numbers have dwindled and national companies offer contracts in many cantons (Trein 2018). Politically, subsidiarity also implies that the providers of health services, whether these are doctors or pharmaceutical companies, also have an important role to play, and as a result they, too, are often consulted in the policymaking process.

19.3 Competencies of Actors

The main politico-administrative actors (Knoepfel et al. 2011) in the Swiss health care system include the national political executive and its associated administrative units, most notably the FOPH, the federal parliament, with its various political parties, the cantonal governments, and administrative units, particularly the departments of health and the cantonal public health officers (*Kantonsärzte*), the cantonal parliaments and parties, and the municipalities. In addition, private actors regulate important areas in health policy and, thus, functionally occupy roles as politico-administrative actors.

19.3.1 Federal Government, Cantons, and Municipalities

The federal government is responsible for public health matters, in particular those related to infectious diseases and epidemics. It is thus responsible for health protection, prevention, and cure, and in addition, more general health care policy. This includes passing framework legislation, setting out the catalog of benefits covered by health insurances, admitting drugs to the country and setting the prices of health care services, ensuring health care quality, subsidizing health insurances, and providing oversight (Vatter and Rüefli 2014, 835).

The cantons are responsible for implementing federal health policies, including public health protection in cases of infectious diseases. Furthermore, they are in charge of implementing health insurance policies, providing health care infrastructure (e.g., the planning of hospitals, approving labor agreements in the health sector, and implementing health insurance subsidies). In addition, cantons also put their own health policy legislation into place, meaning they are responsible for the provision of health services, for planning and building public hospitals, and for regulating the providers of ambulant care (admitting into practice and controlling services provided). Furthermore, the cantons collaborate at the national and regional levels over health policy. At the national level, the cantons cooperate in the CPHD on a variety of topics, including health occupations or health insurance. There are also regional conferences (East, Central, Northwest, and West Switzerland) of cantonal health directors (Füglister 2012; Vatter and Rüefli 2014, 836).

The federal government and the cantons share a number of competencies in health policy, particularly in promoting health, preventing non-communicable diseases, and in health education. Furthermore, both levels of government share responsibility for the education of health personnel, and in regulating and recognizing the various health professions.

The municipalities also have competencies in health policymaking, mostly in providing complementary health care services in long-term care. Compared to the national and cantonal levels, the scope of these competencies is small. They may well become more important in the future, as expenditures for long-term care are very likely to increase (Trein 2016; Vatter and Rüefli 2014, 835–836).

19.3.2 Coordination Between Different Levels of Government

The mixture of shared and separated competencies in health policies creates coordination problems between levels of government. On the one hand, the national government has an incentive to shift policy competencies and costs to the lower levels of government. On the other hand, cantons may implement national policies and use funds related to health care in ways other than those intended by the national government, for example, when implementing policies in ways that fit the interests of a given cantonal government. Thus, federalism limits the ability of the national government to steer Swiss health policymaking (Vatter and Rüefli 2014, 845–846). Consequently, the federal government needs to incentivize cantons to cooperate and to negotiate, if or when necessary. This happens indirectly through the CPHD, in which the national government participates, but also via regional health ministers' conferences. The national coordination platform *Dialog Nationale Gesundheitspolitik* serves, amongst other things, as a forum for exchanging information and creating common national strategies (Füglister 2012; FOPH 2017c).

19.3.3 Private Actors

Private actors play an important role in Swiss policymaking and implementation, owing to the principles of liberalism and subsidiarity noted previously. In principle, health service providers (e.g., doctors, health insurance bodies, or pharmacies) compete for patients. Compared to countries like the Netherlands or Germany, Switzerland has more competition in its health care market (Hammer et al. 2008; Blenk et al. 2016).

Private actors are collectively organized in several areas of health care policy. Health care providers have the right to organize into peak interest organizations, which in turn are entitled to negotiate collective agreements about prices. Thus, sovereignty in wage bargaining is a key element of the Swiss health care system (Sager et al. 2010; Böhm et al. 2012, 64), though public authorities do control, and approve, the collective wage agreements reached.

Private providers of health care services include doctors, private hospitals, and pharmaceutical companies, which all are well-connected in the national parliament. Together with public hospitals, they form a block of interests often opposed to health insurance bodies when it comes to the pricing of health services (Vatter and Rüefli 2014, 839–840). On the other hand, other coalitions may form, such as when private providers and health insurance bodies make common cause in opposition to patients and their interest representatives, for example, with respect to introducing a national unified health insurance. In addition, private actors play an important role in public health and prevention (Achtermann and Berset 2006). Interestingly, preventive health policies promulgated by the state are quite unpopular among citizens and elites alike.

19.3.4 Relationship Between Public and Private Actors

Private actors play a dual role both as rule-makers and as rule-takers in some parts of health policy, and one of the most important cleavages in Swiss health policy lies in the conflict between providers and financing agents. Private actors are important on both sides, whereas public actors take on the role of an arbitrator in the conflicts between health insurance bodies and health care providers. These disputes, for example, about changes to hospital financing or changes in the rules concerning the admissibility of drugs or adjustments in reimbursement stipulations in the national health insurance laws, turn into strong conflicts between private actors—rather than conflicts between private and public actors (Vatter and Rüefli 2014, 839–840).

The reclusive role of the state, especially of the federal government, in health care policy affects public action regarding preventive health issues. The Federal Office for Public Health pushes for encompassing preventive health policies, but these measures are unpopular among center-right and right-wing parties and lack substantial political support from powerful private health care actors, such as the medical profession or health insurance organizations. These private actors have especially a professional interest in preventative health policies but politically preventative health policy is less important for the medical profession and other private actors of the health care sector. Since they enjoy a strongly institutionalized position in Swiss health policy, they do not need an additional clout and have no incentive to make encompassing non-medical preventive health policies, for example, tobacco control, a high political priority (Trein 2018).

19.4 Current Policy Challenges and Related Political Conflicts

19.4.1 Health Care

In the health care literature, authors distinguish four different policy goals: cost containment, equity, liberty, and the quality of health care services. These four policy goals exist in every health system (Uhlmann and Braun 2011, 23) and policymakers need to balance them, as they may be in conflict with one another. Establishing a national health insurance law created (relatively) equal access to health care services, and these have been supported by public subsidies for health insurance premiums for low-income individuals (Beck et al. 2003). Nevertheless, the Swiss system remains highly regressive; low-income and middle-class households need to dedicate a considerably larger share of their income to health care than rich ones do (De Pietro et al. 2015, 232, 237). Therefore, if health expenditures continue to rise, this may disproportionately affect vulnerable groups such as the poor or low-income retirees.

In Switzerland, health insurance premiums have increased by a yearly average of 4.2 percent from 1996 to 2014. This is 40 percent every ten years, more than the average household income increase in this period (Vatter and Rüefli 2014, 846). General health expenditures increased from 5.3 to 7.5 percent of GDP from 1995 to 2015, according to the Swiss government (Fig. 19.1). These figures differ slightly from the numbers reported by the OECD, which uses a different basis for calculation, but they show the same trend. Thus, like elsewhere, cost control and financial sustainability are central problems for health policy in Switzerland.

To deal with increasing health care costs, left-leaning political actors have proposed a single public health insurance agency (*Einheitskasse*) with regional sub-agencies. Proponents argue that such a system would create a simpler, cost-effective, and more transparent health system (Forster 2013). The national parliament (Sda 2013) objected to the proposal, and in September 2014, voters rejected a popular initiative on the subject. Nevertheless, the topic of public health insurance re-appeared on the political agenda in 2017, since politicians from the French-speaking cantons submitted a popular initiative proposing to give cantons the option to increase public control over health insurance premiums. They argued that the cantonal governments should have the competencies to set health insurance premiums and that this would help to keep cost under control (Kucera 2017).

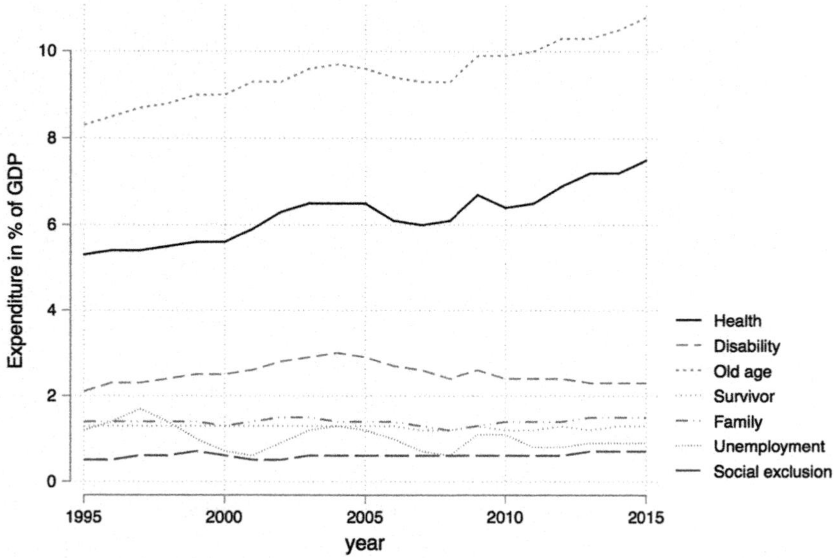

Fig. 19.1 Swiss health expenditure in comparison with other policy sectors. (Source: Social Expenditure Statistics, Swiss Confederation)

Cost containment also played an important role in other proposed reforms to health care, most notably in a proposal to change hospital funding and practices. The idea was to make prices more transparent across Switzerland and to reduce the overall length of treatment. This proposal resulted in tough conflicts between providers and health insurers, at the expense of the interests of patients and overall cost containment (FOPH 2014a, b; Kessler 2014; Weber 2015; Strupler 2018). Other initiatives, such as the proposal to increase the regulation of the managed care market,[2] argued that they too would improve cost containment in the Swiss health system (Vatter and Rüefli 2014, 846). Furthermore, a 2012 legislative proposal regarding managed care failed in a popular referendum (Schoch 2012).

[2] Switzerland has a rather liberal market for managed care models. These have cheaper rates than the standard health insurance model but patients are limited to specific networks of doctors, Health Maintenance Organizations, and telemedicine. The share of patients using the (cheaper) non-standard model of health insurance has increased over the years (Forum Managed Care 2010).

Against this background, (at least) four potentially overlapping reform strategies are possible, if not even probable. First, one could limit the increase of health expenditure by creating a (public) single payer system and by regulating prices. Due to the institutional path dependency in health policy, this is very unlikely to happen. Second, due to the aging population, health expenditures will naturally reduce. This, too, is very unlikely to happen any time soon. Third, health care coverage will progressively be reduced, and out-of-pocket co-payments will increase. This is likely to happen and is already taking place through rising health insurance premiums. Fourth, one could increase tax-financed subsidies for patients, resulting in an incremental transformation—by stealth—into a largely tax-financed health insurance system. This is very likely to happen and is already the case in the existing cantonal subsidies for insurance premiums.

19.4.2 Prevention and Public Health

The second major policy challenge in the field of health policy concerns preventive health policies, in particular, preventing complicated illnesses brought about through non-communicable diseases. The lack of coherent national preventive health policies and the lack of framework legislation at the national level are key problems in the Swiss health system.

A recent effort to create a national framework law for preventive health failed due to resistance from conservative and market-oriented parties. Certain economic groups also brought strong influence to bear on parliament, resulting in the upper chamber failing to approve the funding that would have been needed (APS 2012). This failure was all the more far-reaching, as the proposed law would have permitted a comprehensive preventive health policy to be created, which would have included other areas such as mental health. Such an action would be important since more than 40 percent of the recipients of disability insurance suffer from psychological illnesses (FOPH 2017d).

A better integration of preventive aspects into health policy formulation is now part of the federal government's comprehensive national health strategy (Gesundheit 2020), which defines 12 priorities and 36 specific policy measures to be put into place after 2016 (FOPH 2016b). In addition, the cantons have engaged in their own public health measures, for example concerning tobacco prevention (Trein 2017).

19.4.3 Long-Term Care[3]

A third important challenge for Swiss health policy concerns long-term care. The main problem is that the number of individuals in need of such care is likely to increase sharply. Long-term care is a cantonal responsibility, and they can delegate these competencies to the municipalities or to private organizations—an option they use frequently (OECD 2016).

Health insurances, cantons, and municipalities share the costs for long-term care. The health insurances have to cover a ceiling amount for ambulatory and stationary long-term care, which is fixed by the federal government. Patients have to pay a maximum of 20 percent of the ceiling fixed by the federal government. The cantons (and municipalities) have to cover the rest (FOPH 2016c). Furthermore, measures to compensate individuals caring for their dependent relatives are limited, and so are policies to (re)integrate those who have cared for a dependent relative back into the labor market. Those who take care of dependent relatives—often women—typically reduce their working hours in order to provide this care, but do so without adequate financial compensation or guarantees that they will be reintegrated into the labor market after the period of caregiving is over. Currently, the federal government is developing policies to deal with this problem.

Against this background, long-term care poses a major policy challenge for Swiss health policy. Policymakers will need to deal with the demand for more long-term care in the Swiss context of decentralized federalism, subsidiarity, and liberalism. These principles will make it difficult to formulate a national policy for long-term care, not least because private actors will certainly play an important role, and redistributive elements will need to be kept to a necessary minimum.

19.4.4 Actor Constellations in the Response to These Policy Challenges

In dealing with these policy challenges, the actor constellations and political traditions of Switzerland are likely to result in the following pattern of health policymaking.

The federal government will continue to provide framework legislation and overall strategies. Due to cost pressures and rising health care costs, the national government might need to use decrees to reform health policy, as they did in the 1980s. Changes to paradigms, such as creating a

[3] This section is based on a report written by the author about support for people of working age who have dependent relatives (Trein 2016).

national law for preventive health, are unlikely to occur due to resistance from the conservative/liberal majority in the national parliament. They are often unwilling to support large reforms that grant funds to the statist provision of health services, regardless of what kind they are. How national policymakers will address long-term care—whether through a new national law, cantonal solutions, or co-financing between health care funds and disability insurance—remains to be seen.

The cantons are likely to implement innovative health policies on their own, whether in preventive care or in terms of health insurance. A stronger role for the state in health insurance matters is more popular in the French-speaking than in the German-speaking cantons, leading to divergence between the different cantonal health systems. This also applies to the role that the state takes vis-à-vis private providers of health care financing and to what extent the state regulates potentially unhealthy individual behavior. On the other hand, if the cantons shared common interests, they are likely to work together and learn from one another in the various intercantonal conferences and, if necessary, to coordinate their opposition against the federal government.

Private actors, notably the providers of health and long-term care services as well as health insurance bodies, are likely to retain a strong role in health policy and will try to pursue their interests. These might be regarding cost containment measures or be in efforts to shift the costs for risks to the public sector. The self-organizing principle gives private actors and interest groups considerable influence, and their strong position in the national parliament ensures that these actors will continue to have significant veto power in future proposed reforms of the health care system.

19.5 Conclusion

Historically, federalism, subsidiarity, liberalism, and direct democracy have shaped Swiss health policy, and are important organizational and institutional pillars even now. This context means that policymakers, and voters, are suspicious about having a strong state determine health policy: various levels of government share policy competencies, and private actors, especially health insurance and health service providers but not patients, enjoy considerable influence.

This leads to coordination problems between different levels of government. It also means strong lobbying by interest groups in the health sector, opposition against restricting individual liberties (however this notion is interpreted), and an overall limited steering capacity on the part of the state in health policy. The main policy challenge for Swiss health policy-makers concerns financial stability and rising costs. In the Swiss context, decision-makers need to pay particular attention to trying to contain increases in health care expenditures and to ensure that higher costs do not shift disproportionately and burden vulnerable groups such as the poor and the elderly.

References

Achtermann, W., & Berset, C. (2006). *Gesundheitspolitiken in der Schweiz: Potential für eine nationale Gesundheitspolitik, Analyse und Perspektiven* (Band 1). Bern: Bundesamt für Gesundheit.

Alber, J., & Bernardi-Schenkluhn, B. (1992). *Westeuropäische Gesundheitssysteme im Vergleich: Bundesrepublik Deutschland, Schweiz, Frankreich, Italien, Großbritannien*. Frankfurt a. M.: Campus Verlag.

APS (Année Politique Suisse) (2012). Annee politique suisse 1966–2017. Sozialpolitik; Gesundheit, Sozialhilfe, Sport. Institut für Politikwissenschaft, Universität Bern. https://anneepolitique.swiss. Accessed 30 Nov 2017.

Beck, K., Spycher, S., Holly, A., & Gardiol, L. (2003). Risk adjustment in Switzerland. *Health Policy, 65*(1), 63–74.

Blenk, T., Knötig, N., & Wüstrich, T. (2016). *Die Rolle des Wettbewerbs im Gesundheitswesen: Erfahrungen aus Deutschland, den Niederlanden und der Schweiz, WISO DISKURS* (Vol. 1). Bonn: Friedrich-Ebert-Stiftung.

Böhm, K., Schmid, A., Götze, R., Landwehr, C., & Rothgang, H. (2012). *Classifying OECD healthcare systems: A deductive approach*. TranState working papers, SFB 597. Bremen: University of Bremen.

Böhm, K., Schmid, A., Götze, R., Landwehr, C., & Rothgang, H. (2013). Five types of OECD healthcare systems: Empirical results of a deductive classification. *Health Policy, 113*(3), 258–269.

Cornuz, J., Burnand, B., Kawachi, I., Gutzwiller, F., & Paccaud, F. (1996). Why did Swiss citizens refuse to ban tobacco advertising? *Tobacco Control, 5*(2), 149–153.

De Pietro, C., Camenzind, P., Sturny, I., Crivelli, L., Edwards-Garavoglia, S., Spranger, A., Wittenbecher, F., & Quentin, W. (2015). Switzerland: Health system review. *Health Systems in Transition, 17*(4), 1–288.

Federal Office for Public Health (FOPH). (2014a). Krankenversicherung: Monitoring Prämienverbilligung. https://www.bag.admin.ch/bag/de/home/themen/versicherungen/krankenversicherung/krankenversicherung-versicherte-mit-wohnsitz-in-der-schweiz/praemienverbilligung/monitoring-praemienverbilligung.html. Accessed 22 Feb 2018.

Federal Office for Public Health (FOPH). (2014b). Bundesrat genehmigt neue Tarifstruktur für stationäre Leistungen. https://www.news.admin.ch/message/index.html?lang=de&msg-id=55423. Accessed 1 June 2015.

Fontana, K. (2012, September 27). Die Vorlage ist endgültig vom Tisch. *Neue Zürcher Zeitung*.

FOPH. (2016a). Schweizer Bevölkerung ist zufrieden mit der Gesundheitsversorgung. https://www.admin.ch/gov/de/start/dokumentation/medienmitteilungen.msg-id-64545.html. Accessed 13 Feb 2017.

FOPH. (2016b). Bund, Kantone und Privatsektor vereint gegen nichtübertragbare Krankheiten. https://www.admin.ch/gov/de/start/dokumentation/medienmitteilungen.msg-id-64667.html. Accessed 14 Feb 2017.

FOPH. (2016c). Bisheriger Wohnkanton soll ungedeckte Pflegekosten übernehmen. https://www.bag.admin.ch/bag/de/home/themen/versicherungen/krankenversicherung/krankenversicherung-revisionsprojekte/nachbesserung-pflegefinanzierung-stellungnahme-bundesrat.html Accessed 23 Mar 2018.

FOPH. (2017a). Finanzierung. https://www.bfs.admin.ch/bfs/de/home/statistiken/gesundheit/kosten-finanzierung/finanzierung.html. Accessed 24 Oct 2017.

FOPH. (2017b). Wachstum der Gesundheitskosten: Standardprämie 2018 steigt um 4,0 Prozent. https://www.bag.admin.ch/bag/de/home/aktuell/news/news-28-09-2017.html. Accessed 22 Feb 2018.

FOPH. (2017c). Dialog Nationale Gesundheitspolitik – ständige Plattform von Bund und Kantonen. https://www.bag.admin.ch/bag/de/home/themen/strategien-politik/nationale-gesundheitspolitik/dialog-nationale-gesundheitspolitik-staendige-plattform-bund-kantonen.html. Accessed 31 Oct 2017.

FOPH. (2017d). IV-Statistik. https://www.bsv.admin.ch/bsv/de/home/sozialversicherungen/iv/statistik.html. Accessed 30 Oct 2017.

Forster, C. (2013, September 21). Einheitskassen-Initiative ohne Gegenvorschlag. *Neue Zürcher Zeitung*.

Forum Managed Care. (2010). Ärztenetze in der Schweiz 2010 – auf dem Sprung zu Integrierter Versorgung. Retrieved from https://www.fmh.ch/files/pdf6/SAEZ_D.pdf. Accessed 22 Feb 2018.

Füglister, K. (2012). *Policy laboratories of the federal state? The role of intergovernmental cooperation in health policy diffusion in Switzerland*. Baden-Baden: Nomos.

Hammer, S., Peter, M., & Trageser, J. (2008). *Wettbewerb im Gesundheitswesen: Auslegeordnung*. Neuchâtel: OBSAN Schweizerisches Gesundheitsobservatorium.

Kessler, M. (2014, October 20). Die Rationierung hat bereits begonnen. *Neue Zürcher Zeitung*.

Knoepfel, P., Larrue, C., Hill, M., & Varone, F. (2011). *Public policy analysis*. Bristol: The Policy Press.

Kucera, A. (2017, April 9). Die Auferstehung der Einheitskasse. *Neue Zürcher Zeitung*.

OECD (Organisation for Economic Co-operation and Development). (2016). *OECD Health at a Glance: Europe 2016. State of health in the EU cycle*. Paris: OECD Publishing.

Sager, F. (2003). Kompensationsmöglichkeiten föderaler Vollzugsdefizite. Das Beispiel der kantonalen Alkoholpräventionspolitiken. *Swiss Political Science Review, 9*(1), 309–333.

Sager, F. (2004). Verwaltung, Politik und Wissenschaft in der kantonalen Alkoholprvention. *Sozial- und Präventivmedizin/Social and Preventive Medicine, 49*(3), 208–215.

Sager, F., Rüefli, C., & Wälti, M. (2010). *Schnittstellen zwischen ambulanter und stationärer Versorgung: Möglichkeiten der Steuerung durch die Kantone*. Neuchâtel: Schweizerisches Gesundheitsobservatorium.

Schoch, C. (2012, June 17). Wuchtiges Nein zur Managed Care Vorlage. *Neue Zürcher Zeitung*.

Sda. (2013, June 24). Support für Einheitskasse. *Neue Zürcher Zeitung*.

Strupler, P. (2018, January 30). Im Gesundheitswesen müssen alle Akteure kostenbewusster warden. *Neue Zürcher Zeitung*.

Swiss Confederation. (1995–2015). Social expenditure statistics. https://www.pxweb.bfs.admin.ch/pxweb/de/px-x-1302020000_101/px-x-1302020000_101/px-x-1302020000_101.px. Accessed 22 Feb 2018.

Trein, P. (2016). *ESPN thematic report on work-life balance measures for persons of working age with dependent relatives – Switzerland*. Brussels: European Social Policy Network/European Commission.

Trein, P. (2017). Europeanisation beyond the European Union: Tobacco advertisement restrictions in Swiss cantons. *Journal of Public Policy, 37*(02), 113–142.

Trein, P. (2018). *Healthy or sick? Coevolution of health care and public health in a comparative perspective*. Cambridge: Cambridge University Press.

Uhlmann, B., & Braun, D. (2011). *Die schweizerische Krankenversicherungspolitik zwischen Veränderung und Stillstand*. Chur: Rüegger Verlag.

Vatter, A., & Rüefli, C. (2014). Gesundheitspolitik. In P. Knoepfl, Y. Papadopoulos, P. Sciarini, A. Vatter, & S. Häusermann (Eds.), *Handbuch der Schweizer Politik* (pp. 827–854). Zürich: Neue Zürcher Zeitung libro.

Weber, B. (2015, November 15). Mehr Wirtschaftlichkeit wäre dringlich. *Neue Zürcher Zeitung*.

CHAPTER 20

Policy Networks and the Roles of Public Administrations

Frédéric Varone, Karin Ingold, and Manuel Fischer

20.1 Introduction

This chapter applies the methodological tools of formal social network analysis (SNA) to illustrate the multiple functions currently performed by public administration(s) in steering public policy. Public policy itself is defined as 'a series of intentionally coherent decisions or activities taken or carried out by different public—and sometimes—private actors, whose resources, institutional links and interests vary, with a view to resolving in a targeted manner a problem that is politically defined as collective in nature' (Knoepfel et al. 2011: 24). From this perspective, a public administration is a public actor that must unconditionally coordinate its own actions with

F. Varone (✉)
Department of Political Science and International Relations, University of Geneva, Geneva, Switzerland
e-mail: frederic.varone@unige.ch

K. Ingold
Institute of Political Science, University of Bern, Bern, Switzerland
e-mail: karin.ingold@ipw.unibe.ch

M. Fischer
Department Environmental Social Sciences, Eawag, Dübendorf, Switzerland
e-mail: manuel.fischer@eawag.ch

A. Ladner et al. (eds.), *Swiss Public Administration*, Governance and Public Management,
https://doi.org/10.1007/978-3-319-92381-9_20

those of parliamentary and governmental officials, courts, interest groups, political parties and scientific experts in order to co-produce a policy for a sector or to resolve a collective problem. In fact, in current political systems, no actor alone (including a politico-administrative actor) controls all the resources needed to take unilateral action (Berardo and Scholz 2010).

The empirical examples discussed in this chapter illustrate how classical public administration (e.g., those following the Weberian ideal type of bureaucracy) has changed and takes on new roles nowadays. On the one hand, in the process of making decisions, an administration at times becomes a policy broker between advocacy coalitions. On the other hand, during the implementation phase, it often agrees to share its regulatory powers with other actors such as independent agencies. Empirical evidence tends to confirm the paradox that it is precisely by renouncing its classical role as the dominant actor in the hierarchy, and by sharing its competences and resources with other actors, that the administration is able to maintain its central role in steering public policy. This thesis is underscored in the literature on the meta-governance of networks or network management (e.g., Klijn 2005; Provan and Kenis 2007; Sørensen and Torfing 2009; Klijn et al. 2010). In fact, the social network analyses presented here demonstrate that public administration remains central and influential and at the heart of policy networks—as long as it can adapt itself to the current conditions influencing public policies and can fulfill new functions (see also Fischer 2017).

SNA describes the relations between actors who jointly develop and implement a public policy; it is also a way to study why and how an administration occupies several roles in succession in carrying out public actions. Different labels have been applied in the public policy and public administration literature to describe the networks among actors. The first, 'policy networks', is more in line with political negotiation theories and theories of decision-making processes. Private and public actors exchange information and other resources relevant to taking action, in order to increase their influence on the final outcome of the decision-making process (Leifeld and Schneider 2012; Knoke et al. 1996). This exchange is organized within the policy networks and is often presented as a non-hierarchical approach to public sector decision-making (Kenis and Schneider 1991; Laumann and Knoke 1987). It highlights the horizontal relationships between different actors where no clear hierarchy between them exists, and it focuses on the influence administrative units exert in formulating public policies.

The second, 'collaborative networks', is derived more from the public management literature and focuses on the implementation of public policies.

It tries to explain the quality and efficiency of services provided by a public administration, often at the local or regional level (Shrestha 2013; Schalk et al. 2010; Provan and Kenis 2007). Linked to the theoretical discourse about network governance and collaborative governance (Ansell and Gash 2007), this approach emphasizes the self-organizing, non-hierarchical character of actors involved in policy implementation and the resolution of local collective action problems or natural resource management (Lubell et al. 2014). These two currents are perfectly complementary (Lecy et al. 2014) and make it possible to recognize, if not understand, the different facets of administrative work during the different stages of the public policy cycle. This chapter focuses on the policy formulation and policy implementation stages (for a discussion of 'upstream' agenda-setting and 'downstream' policy evaluation, see Varone et al. 2016).

The 'formulation' stage corresponds to the clarification and stabilization phases (at least temporarily) in the logic of intervention which underpins public policy. This process, which leads to adopting a legislative and regulatory framework, engenders specific choices of objectives, instruments (e.g., prescriptions, incentives or information), institutional arrangements and procedures to be followed to resolve the problem under consideration.

The 'implementation' stage corresponds to the application of the policy which has been legitimized, hence to the production of administrative outputs in specific situations (e.g., a building permit, a subsidy for solar panels or training in ecological farming practices). Most of the time, this phase is quite complex, because a variety of potential snares exist, including the non-execution or very selective application of certain legislative or regulatory provisions by street-level bureaucrats with discretionary powers (Lipsky 1980). The territorial differentiation inherent to federalism also creates implementation issues, whether in a decentralized country or in a multilevel governance system of the kind found at the European level.

At each of these stages of the policy cycle, the administration can assert itself, which it may do either more or less proactively; it is central in the configuration of actors and influences the content of public policy. More generally, an SNA allows one to study the activity, centrality, and influence of an actor. This analysis is precisely aimed at providing theoretical and methodological tools for determining the real scope of an administrative unit with respect to the process and content of public policy, but also for determining the scope of other actors involved in the sectoral network.

The following sections summarize, for the policy formulation and policy implementation stages, the concepts reflecting the particular roles of an administration; it also discusses empirical measurements of that roles. This is illustrated using case studies of policies to combat global warming as well as to liberalize the formerly government-controlled telecommunications sector. These two public policies are chosen because they have a number of interesting characteristics: strong internationalization (there are global debates both about climate and about ways to open the telecommunications sector in Europe to greater competition), a high degree of conflict (there are strong disagreements between state and private sector actors), and they are characterized by innovations with respect to the specific instruments (e.g., tradable certificates, licenses and market regulation) and actors (e.g., the creation of independent regulatory agencies) chosen. In a nutshell, global climate and telecommunications policies reflect, in an ideal-typical manner, the current changes to the framework conditions the state faces.

In these two case studies, we have recourse to some classic SNA indicators (see Table 20.1) for quantifying the structure of a network and the significance of an administrative actor within it.

Table 20.1 Key variables in SNA

Variables	*Definition of the empirical measurement used*
Density	Network density corresponds to the proportion of observed ties as compared to all theoretically possible ties in the network.
Degree centrality	Centrality assesses the relational position of a given node in the overall network. Many different indicators of centrality exist. Degree centrality measures the number of incoming (in-degree) and outgoing ties (out-degree) of a node.
Betweenness centrality	Betweenness centrality is another popular measure of centrality. It takes into account the degree to which a node is located on the shortest path between any two other nodes in the network. Nodes with high betweenness centralities are potentially important bridging actors or brokers in the network.
Eigenvector centrality	Eigenvector centrality is based on degree centrality; it counts the number of other nodes a given node is connected to. It also takes into account the centrality of the nodes a given node is related to by giving more weight to more central nodes.
Clique analysis	A clique is a set of nodes in which every node is connected to every other node. It is a subset of a network with maximum internal density.
Core–periphery	A core–periphery structure is characterized by a set of nodes in the core of the network that are strongly inter-connected and a set of nodes in the periphery of the network that are weakly related to nodes of the core. This represents an ideal-typical structure to which empirically observed networks can be compared to.
Structural equivalence	Two nodes are structurally equivalent (or similar) if they have the same (or a similar) relational profile to the rest of the nodes in the network.

See also Wassermann and Faust (1994)

20.2 Policy Formulation: Brokering and the Choice of Instruments

The most studied aspect of public policy in political science is the design phase. Numerous theories of decision-making processes have tried to explain changes in the choice of objectives and the instruments used in public policy; these explanations cross administrative, governmental and parliamentary domains. In fact, the measures used to intervene, whose implementation is supposed to make it possible to achieve the objectives of the policy as well as contribute to resolving the collective problem, delineate the perimeter of the targeted groups. This is the point in time when public policy becomes concrete and directly tangible for all actors involved. Each private actor can then anticipate whether or not they are targeted by the measure (or instrument) and whether or not they should change their behavior. The calibration of policy instruments is therefore one of the elements which best characterize the design or formulation of a public policy. The instruments selected determine the degree of state 'interventionism', but they also determine the rights directly granted to the various targeted actors or the obligations imposed on them. They also determine the nature and quality of the expected administrative outputs (e.g., authorizations to be granted, prohibitions or penalties to be imposed, subsidies to be allocated, taxes to be levied and information campaigns to be carried out). It is therefore not surprising that the choice of instruments is fiercely contested in the political arena.

The relevant literature proposes various theoretical hypotheses about the links between the configuration of the actors on the one hand and the choice of instruments on the other. Bressers and O'Toole (1998), for example, suggest that the degree of connection between private and public policy stakeholders (e.g., the density of relationships within the political network) as well as their degree of cohesion (e.g., shared political preferences) decisively determines the type of instrument introduced. They suggest an elevated connection and a strong cohesion, resulting from a strong link between the government and the groups targeted by a public policy, which means that a wide variety of instruments can be introduced. This will tend to favor the target groups by granting subsidies and providing information. By contrast, a network with weak cohesion and connections will likely lead to a politics influenced by abstract or normative values—and a lack of room to maneuver in the target groups (Bressers and O'Toole 1998: 230–32).

In a quite different vein, the *Advocacy Coalition Framework* developed by Sabatier and Jenkins-Smith (1993) proposes that the choice of instruments results from a conflict between different coalitions of actors. Each coalition, or each group of advocates for a cause (e.g., those who favor and those who oppose the use of nuclear energy), shares the same belief and value systems and coordinates their efforts. An SNA analysis can be useful for identifying the advocacy coalitions as well as understanding the relations between them (Ingold 2011; Fischer 2014). The work done inside a coalition results in a preference for one combination of instruments over another (e.g., the public licensing and financing of nuclear power plants versus prohibiting such plants and imposing obligation on the private plants' owners to bear the dismantling costs). According to this theoretical model, different administrative units either can be members of different coalitions (competing to assert their value systems and their own instruments) or may act as intermediaries between the coalitions. In this latter case, a public administration body aims above all to reduce the level of conflict between the coalitions and mediate between them so as to identify possible compromise solutions. As they are not part of any coalition advocating a particular cause, these administrative bodies are referred to as 'policy brokers' in the literature (Sabatier and Jenkins-Smith 1993; Ingold and Varone 2012).

A specific example illustrates how such brokering works (Stovel and Shaw 2012), and beyond that, how SNA accounts for it empirically. The case in question was the political struggle over global warming measures to be taken in Switzerland between 1990 and 2010 (Ingold 2011; Ingold and Varone 2012). Following the signing of the Kyoto Protocol (adopted late in 1997 and in force as of early 2005), which set a 2012 target of reducing greenhouse gas emissions by 8% relative to 1990 values, Swiss climate change policy was articulated in passing a first CO_2 emissions law in 2000. This law called on the private market to take voluntary action to reduce greenhouse gas emissions by 10% within two years. Should this prove insufficient, an incentive tax on CO_2 emissions would be introduced.

This choice of instruments reflects the fact that two advocacy coalitions were bitterly opposed: one was pro-market (it included industry, transportation, the energy sector, and the right-wing parties) and only supported voluntary measures, while the other was pro-environment (it included environmental associations, left-wing parties and the Federal Office for the Environment) and called for an immediate introduction of the CO_2 tax. In the event, voluntary measures soon showed their limitations, and the CO_2 law was revised already in 2005. It seems logical to expect an automatic implementation of the CO_2 incentive tax, but its revision led to a very different result. The second law combined a CO_2 tax on fuel, as the pro-environment had called for in the first law, with a 'climate penny' tax levied on fuels, an instrument proposed by the pro-market coalition. This unexpected solution was the result of a compromise negotiated between the two coalitions, thanks to the subtle work and brokerage of a public administration body—in this case the Swiss Federal Office of Energy (SFOE), which intervened to find an amicable solution and prevent an escalation of the conflict between the two coalitions.

In this example, network analysis is a powerful tool for identifying the SFOE as a public policy broker. It shows first that the SFOE does not belong to either of the competing advocacy coalitions. Each coalition brings together actors with a similar profile in terms of conflict structures (vis-à-vis members of the opposing coalition) and cooperation (with members of their own coalition). The SFOE's profile is quite distinct from that of the members of either (cause-driven) coalition. Second, the SFOE possesses a high 'reputational power', meaning the actors in conflict give it credence in its mediation work. No less than 83% of the stakeholder actors declared the SFOE to be a very influential player in the decision-making process. Third—and this empirical observation is critical here—network analysis showed the SFOE to be often found at the interface between the actors who belonged to the pro-environment versus those who belonged to the pro-market coalition. In other words, the actors in conflict only collaborated indirectly and through the intermediary SFOE. This is indicated by the 'betweenness centrality' indicator, which measures the frequency with which the SFOE is found on the geodesic path between two actors who are otherwise not connected. By way of summary, Fig. 20.1 shows the morphology of the collaborative network in Swiss climate policy; the SFOE (the large gray node at the center) maintained collaborative relationships with a multitude of actors from the two camps.

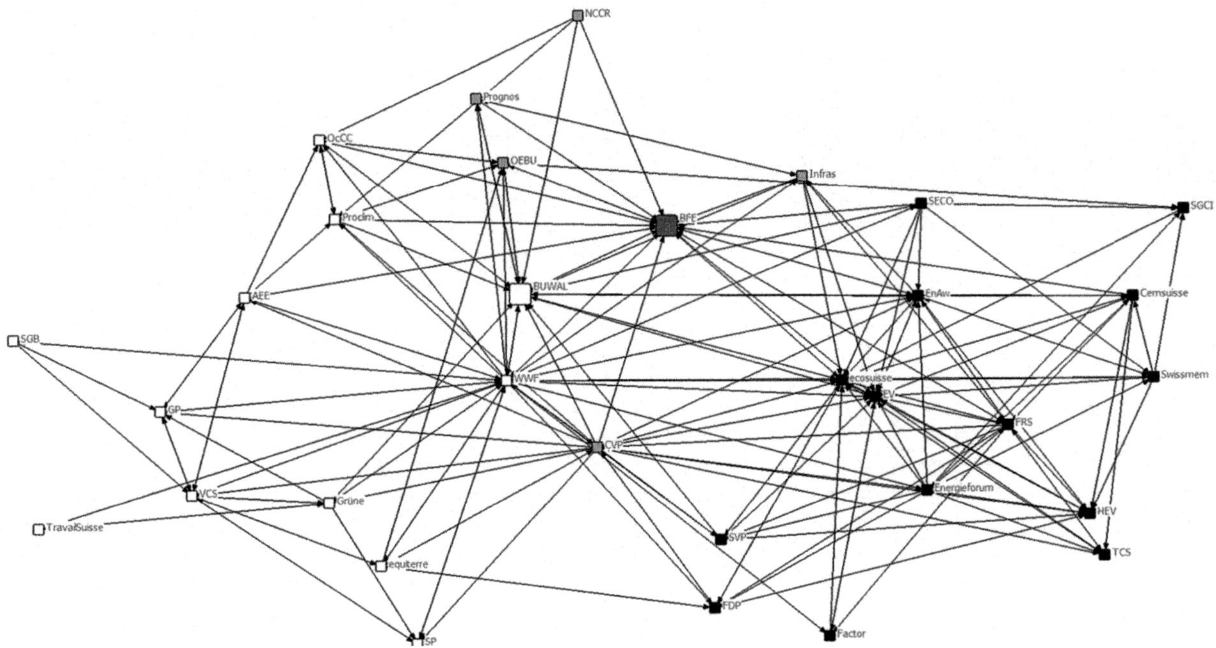

Fig. 20.1 The policy network in Swiss climate policy (2002–2005). (Nodes correspond to actors and ties to collaborative relations between them. White nodes are members of the pro-environment coalition, black nodes members of the pro-market coalition, and gray nodes are mostly administrative entities or scientific bodies which cannot be attributed to either competing coalitions. The larger gray node represents the SFOE, the mediator between the two coalitions. The larger white node is the Swiss Federal Office for the Environment (FOEN), part of the pro-environment coalition, and the leading administrative unit in this policy field. Source: Own illustration)

20.3 Policy Implementation: Encouraging a Network and Co-producing Services

The implementation phase puts public administrations in direct contact with representatives of civil society, including, first and foremost, the groups targeted by the policy instruments. To study the interdependencies and the strategic games played by these actors, one needs to identify the institutional arrangement employed in the implementation. One can also call this the structured set of administrative and parastatal organizations formally charged with implementing the relevant public policy. It is crucial that one understands the many dimensions of this inter-organizational network, as it allows one to comprehend the ability of the public administration to implement the envisaged instruments. Or put differently, to understand its inability to overcome the resistance of the target groups or the problems in application it encounters.

An implementation arrangement involves diverse administrative entities whose numbers vary. Such an arrangement is characterized by a high level of coordination both horizontally (between units) and vertically (between municipal, regional, central, and international levels), but it can, on the contrary, also be characterized by considerable fragmentation. In addition, a low degree of openness to strictly political actors implies a degree of professionalism and neutrality in implementation decisions. Greater permeability, meaning more openness to interests and interference on the part of (e.g., local) politicians, can result in politicization and unpredictability in the implementation. Finally, because public policy is often carried out by administrative units which have also participated in the formulation and execution of other sectoral policies, the question of coordination between sectors (e.g., those in which the state intervenes) is a further important issue. The evidence is that of numerous inter-ministerial conflicts; they become the subjects of administrative, political or even judicial arbitration.

Without going into all the facets of an inter-organizational network, the literature is in agreement on at least one point: a public administration nowadays often shares its regulatory powers and sees itself less a monopoly player than a co-producer of administrative outputs Moreover, an administration may be limited to encouraging (or invigorating) a network composed of parastatal or private actors to whom it delegates regulatory tasks and competencies (Provan and Kenis 2007). This phenomenon is particularly evident in the wake of New Public Management (NPM)-inspired reforms which, for example, lead to creating independent regulatory agencies. Many studies using a network perspective indicate that the efficiency and effectiveness of an administrative arrangement for delivering public services is highly dependent on the context, available resources, and existing administrative control mechanisms (Provan and Milward 1995; Ingold and Fischer 2014).

To illustrate the significance of inter-organizational networks and to show how traditional administrative structures have to share their prerogatives (in implementation contexts), the second example focuses on the emergence of independent regulatory agencies. In the wake of opening certain public services previously regarded as state monopolies (e.g., telecommunications, electricity, postal services or railways) to competition, most industrialized democracies instituted national regulatory agencies, also called sector-specific regulators. At least in theory, these new entities enjoyed broad independence vis-à-vis elected officials, as they were called upon to impartially manage the competition between operators, both public and private, and ensure universal service provision. Such regulatory agencies were added on to existing administrative entities, densifying the implementation mechanisms introduced by policies to liberalize public service provision.

In the telecommunications sector in Switzerland, the Federal Communications Commission is the incarnation of a national regulatory agency, one which has intervened in the network of co-regulators, alongside the Federal Office of Communication (a classical public administration body), the Competition Commission, the Swiss price regulator, and the courts charged with resolving the inevitable conflicts that arise between users, operators and/or co-regulators. Figure 20.2 outlines the relationship between all the actors in the (now liberalized) sector, relations which can be studied in greater detail using network analysis tools.

A formal network analysis of the links between actors in this realm shows that the Federal Communications Commission and the Federal Office of Communication are the two main co-producers of regulations for this sector. They both have the highest 'reputational power' and are the most central in this network. The 'classical' administrative unit, the Federal Office of Communication, also has the highest level of 'betweenness centrality' among all the actors. It can therefore exercise a great deal of control over the flow of information and benefits by having bargaining power relative to the other actors (Fischer et al. 2012; Ingold et al. 2013; Varone and Ingold 2011). In addition, the Communications Commission is strongly interlinked with the Office of Communication and other regulators,

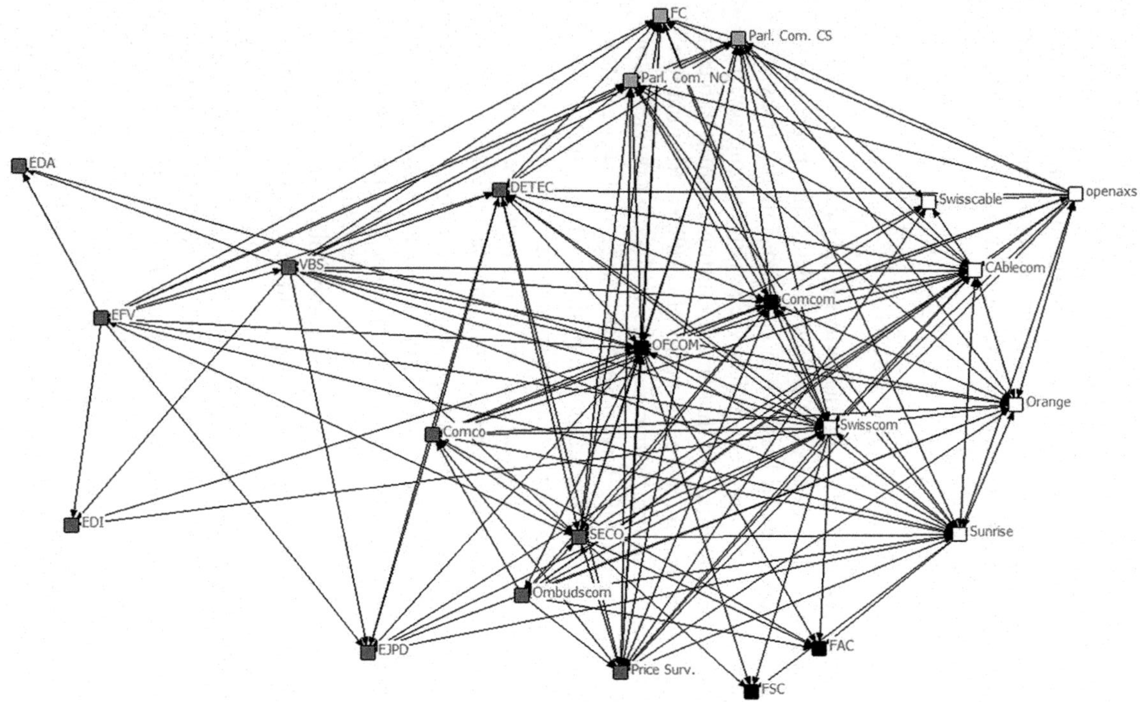

Fig. 20.2 The collaborative network in the telecommunications sector (2010). (Nodes correspond to actors and ties to collaboration relations among them. The two black nodes in the center are the two main regulators in the telecommunications sector: the Federal Office of Communication and the Federal Communications Commission. The two black nodes at the bottom are the key law courts. The dark gray nodes are co-regulators and public agencies; the light gray nodes at the top represent the Federal Council and two parliamentary commissions. The white nodes are the operators. Source: Own illustration)

though it appears much more independent vis-à-vis the elected authorities and other operators in this sector (Maggetti et al. 2013). Thus, the sector-specific national regulatory agency (e.g., the Communications Commission) must deal with a 'classical' administrative unit in order to exercise its regulatory powers. This example reflects the major transformation co-regulation has brought about in numerous sectors, and beyond that, the role co-production plays in the delivery of public services by 'classical' administrative bodies.

20.4 Conclusion

This chapter has shown how public administration(s), in order to maintain a decisive influence over the conduct of public policies, has been transformed and assumes new roles, at least when compared to the tasks and sovereign competencies under an ideal-typical Weberian bureaucracy. The two examples discussed above indicate that an administrative entity can cast itself in turn as a broker and mediator in political conflicts (formulation) and as a co-producer of administrative services and network facilitator (implementation). The results of a formal SNA also suggest that these new roles do not entail a loss of public administration influence. On the contrary: it is by adapting and also abandoning a state-centric vision and hierarchical position, as well as finding a place within a policy network as a broker, facilitator, or co-producer, that public administration is able to maintain its ability to significantly influence the content of public policies.

This observation, perhaps a little paradoxical, is certainly valid beyond the politics of contestation around global warming or the liberalizing of telecommunications. Indeed, policy networks are an undeniable reality in many sectors where the state intervenes to solve collective problems. Political decision-makers, administrative elites, and academic researchers experience this on a daily basis, and it is therefore reasonable to devote more sustained attention to the SNA approach (see Kapucu et al. 2017; Lecy et al. 2014 or Fischer 2017 for an up-to-date overview of the state of empirical research), one which helps in identifying the new roles inhabited by public administration.

Of course the emergence and consolidation of policy networks are certainly not the only transformations public administration has undergone, including in the context of NPM-inspired reforms. However, by highlighting the interdependence of public administrative units and other actors (which include private actors) in public policy, the network approach suggests that there are perhaps some intrinsic limitations inherent to certain other reforms which are underway, especially if they are confined to modifying the internal functioning of public administration and/or reinforcing institutional egoism. One can think here of contemporary performance contracts and performance indicators, essential tools of the NPM approach, which have been negotiated under several governments, and which generally do not take into account that public action is developed and implemented in inter-organizational networks, not in isolated administrative units which are protected by 'their' respective service contracts.

At the same time, we make no claim that policy networks are a panacea, either in theory or in practice. There is no definitive answer for whether the participation of administrative organs in policy networks improves the relevance, effectiveness and efficiency of public policies or not. While some authors highlight how public administration could profit from network-based management (Klijn 2005), others remain cautious or even skeptical (McGuire and Agranoff 2011). A number of significant normative issues, including legitimacy, are also raised by the question of how democratically anchored policy networks are. Responsibility ultimately lies with elected decision-makers, even if delegating decision-making powers can benefit the work of public administration (Sørensen and Torfing 2005).

References

Ansell, C., & Gash, A. (2007). Collaborative governance in theory and practice. *Journal of Public Administration Research and Theory, 18*(4), 543–571.

Berardo, R., & Scholz, J. T. (2010). Self-organizing policy networks: Risk, partner selection, and cooperation in estuaries. *American Journal of Political Science, 54*(3), 632–649.

Bressers, H. T. A., & O'Toole, L. J., Jr. (1998). The selection of policy instruments: A network-based perspective. *Journal of Public Policy, 18*(3), 213–239.

Fischer, M. (2014). Coalition structures and policy change in a consensus democracy. *Policy Studies Journal, 42*(3), 344–366.

Fischer, M. (2017). Institutions and policy networks in Europe. In J. N. Victor, M. Lubell, & A. Montgomery (Eds.), *Oxford handbook of political networks* (pp. 833–854). Oxford: Oxford University Press.

Fischer, M., Ingold, K., Sciarini, P., & Varone, F. (2012). Impacts of market liberalization on regulatory network: A longitudinal analysis of the Swiss telecommunications sector. *Policy Studies Journal, 40*(3), 435–457.

Ingold, K. (2011). Network structures within policy processes: Coalitions, power, and brokerage in Swiss climate policy. *Policy Studies Journal, 39*(3), 435–459.

Ingold, K., & Fischer, M. (2014). Drivers of collaboration to mitigate climate change: An illustration of Swiss climate policy over 15 years. *Global Environmental Change, 24*, 88–98.

Ingold, K., & Varone, F. (2012). Treating policy brokers seriously: Evidence from the climate policy. *Journal of Public Administration Research and Theory, 22*(2), 319–346.

Ingold, K., Varone, F., & Stokman, F. (2013). A social network-based approach to assess de facto independence of regulatory agencies. *Journal of European Public Policy, 20*(10), 1464–1481.

Kapucu, N., Hu, Q., & Khosa, S. (2017). The state of network research in public administration. *Administration & Society, 49*(8), 1087–1120.

Kenis, P., & Schneider, V. (1991). Policy networks and policy analysis: Scrutinizing a new analytical toolbox. In B. Marin & R. Mayntz (Eds.), *Policy networks: Empirical evidence and theoretical considerations* (pp. 25–59). Boulder: Westview Press.

Klijn, E. (2005). Designing and managing networks: Possibilities and limitations for network management. *European Political Science, 4*(3), 328–339.

Klijn, E., Steijn, B., & Edelenbos, J. (2010). The impact of network management on outcomes in governance networks. *Public Administration, 88*(4), 1063–1082.

Knoepfel, P., Larrue, C., Hill, M., & Varone, F. (2011). *Public policy analysis.* Bristol: The Policy Press.

Knoke, D., Pappi, F. U., Broadbent, J., & Tsujinaka, Y. (1996). *Comparing policy networks: Labor politics in the US, Germany, and Japan.* Cambridge: Cambridge University Press.

Laumann, E. O., & Knoke, D. (1987). *The organizational state: Social choice in national policy domains.* Madison: University of Wisconsin Press.

Lecy, J. D., Mergel, I. A., & Schmitz, H. P. (2014). Networks in public administration: Current scholarship in review. *Public Management Review, 16*(5), 643–665.

Leifeld, P., & Schneider, V. (2012). Information exchange in policy networks. *American Journal of Political Science, 56*(3), 731–744.

Lipsky, M. (1980). *Street-level bureaucracy.* New York: Russel Sage.

Lubell, M., Robins, G., & Wang, P. (2014). Network structure and institutional complexity in an ecology of water management games. *Ecology and Society, 19*(4), 23.

Maggetti, M., Ingold, K., & Varone, F. (2013). Having your cake and eating it, too: Can regulatory agencies be both independent and accountable? *Swiss Political Science Review, 19*(1), 1–25.

McGuire, M., & Agranoff, R. (2011). The limitations of public management networks. *Public Administration, 89*(2), 265–284.

Provan, K. G., & Kenis, P. (2007). Modes of network governance: Structure, management, and effectiveness. *Journal of Public Administration Research and Theory, 18*(2), 229–252.

Provan, K. G., & Milward, B. H. (1995). A preliminary theory of interorganizational network effectiveness: A comparative study of four community mental health systems. *Administrative Science Quarterly, 40*(1), 1–33.
Sabatier, P. A., & Jenkins-Smith, H. (1993). *Policy change and learning. An advocacy coalition approach*. Boulder: Westview Press.
Schalk, J., Torenvlied, R., & Allen, J. (2010). Network embeddedness and public agency performance: The strength of strong ties in Dutch higher education. *Journal of Public Administration Research and Theory, 20*(3), 629–653.
Shrestha, M. K. (2013). Self-organizing network capital and the success of collaborative public programs. *Journal of Public Administration Research and Theory, 23*(2), 307–329.
Sørensen, E., & Torfing, J. (2005). The democratic anchorage of governance networks. *Scandinavian Political Studies, 28*(3), 195–218.
Sørensen, E., & Torfing, J. (2009). Making governance networks effective and democratic through metagovernance. *Public Administration, 87*(2), 234–258.
Stovel, K., & Shaw, L. (2012). Brokerage. *Annual Review of Sociology, 38*(1), 139–158.
Varone, F., & Ingold, K. (2011). L'indépendance des agences nationales de régulation. In F. Bellanger & T. Tanquerel (Eds.), *Les autorités administratives indépendantes* (pp. 37–61). Zurich: Schulthess Verlag.
Varone, F., Ingold, K., & Fischer, M. (2016). Administration et réseaux d'action publique. In D. Giauque & Y. Emery (Eds.), *L'acteur et la bureaucratie* (pp. 115–140). Québec: Presses de l'Université de la Laval.
Wasserman, S., & Faust, K. (1994). *Social network analysis: Methods and applications*. Cambridge: Cambridge University Press.

CHAPTER 21

Factors Contributing to the Strong Institutionalization of Policy Evaluation in Switzerland

Katia Horber-Papazian and Marion Baud-Lavigne

21.1 Introduction

At the end of the 1980s, the evaluation of public policy in Switzerland was largely conducted by academics (Horber-Papazian and Thévoz 1990); nowadays, it has gained international recognition. The most recent comparison (Jacob et al. 2015) places Switzerland among the top three countries, along with Canada and Finland, on the basis of the following criteria: the existence of evaluations in different policy domains, professional competency in evaluation, the presence of a national discourse about evaluation, the existence of a national evaluation society, the institutionalization of evaluation in government and parliament, the existence of evaluation in the highest auditing institution, that a plurality of institutions or evaluators conduct evaluations in different areas, and finally

K. Horber-Papazian (✉) • M. Baud-Lavigne
IDHEAP, University of Lausanne, Lausanne, Switzerland
e-mail: katia.horber-papazian@unil.ch; marion.baud-lavigne@unil.ch

A. Ladner et al. (eds.), *Swiss Public Administration*, Governance and Public Management,
https://doi.org/10.1007/978-3-319-92381-9_21

that a certain proportion of evaluations focus on impact and outcome rather than output and process.

A finding of this kind justifies that one takes interest in examining factors which have favored this institutionalization. Our thesis is that the strong institutionalization of public policy evaluation since the 1990s can be explained by a convergence of conducive factors. They include a context favorable to conducting evaluations, a variety of actors at the interface between differing universes, the incorporation and inclusion of an obligation to evaluate into the national Constitution, the emergence of political strategies which use evaluation to achieve political goals (including using clauses in laws that call for evaluation), and the use of the results of evaluations both in politics and in public administration. As data on cantonal and communal evaluation practices are both poor and quite disparate, the following discussion focuses on the federal level.

21.2 A Context Favorable to Evaluation

Many factors were responsible for putting questions about the effectiveness of state action, the implementation of governmental decisions, and the auditing methods being used onto the political agenda in the late 1980s and early 1990s. One of these was a crisis in public finance. Another was a larger debate about the role, or place, of the state in the context of the rise in 'neoliberal' ideology. Many public projects, particularly in the area of infrastructure, were called into question at the time, and there was also a loss of confidence in relations between the federal parliament and the executive. Deficits in public policy implementation had been identified by various national research programs. Finally, voters were calling for more efficiency and more transparency in actions undertaken by the state.

The combination of these factors led numerous actors, especially those at the interface between social universes and in contact with one another, to engage in reflections which began to converge. Their discourse first sensitized the communities to which these actors belonged about the important space which evaluation could occupy in the public policy cycle and then led to them becoming active in the process of institutionalizing such evaluations.

21.3 The Actors at the Interface Between Academic, Administrative, and Political Worlds

21.3.1 The Federal Department of Justice and Police

At the instigation of the author of the first thesis about legislative evaluation in Switzerland (Mader 1985), the Federal Department of Justice and Police created a working group in 1987 (the *Arbeitsgruppe Gesetzesevaluation*—AGEVAL) whose goal was to analyze the utility and value of policy evaluation in the Swiss federal government. The group brought federal and cantonal officials together with academic researchers. Following a proposal contained in the final report of this working group (Arbeitsgruppe Gesetzesevaluation 1991), an 'evaluation network in the federal administration' was brought to life in 1995. This group is still active and allows participants, who may be officials, clients, or users, to share their knowledge about, and experiences with, the results of evaluations.

In 1987, the Federal Department of Justice and Police also suggested that a national research program be launched to study the 'Efficiency of Governmental Actions' (NRP 27). Its principal goal was to identify assessment tools or methods most suited to the Swiss context. It was also an effort to increase knowledge about the effects different types of evaluations had on state activity, one coordinated by an administrator in the Federal Office of Justice who would later become the first president of the Swiss Evaluation Society (SEVAL). Thus, this Federal Department played a central role in promoting the use of evaluation within the federal administration and gave impetus to conducting further research on evaluation.

21.3.2 The Federal Parliament and Parliamentary Control of the Administration

Since the 1980s, the Control Committees in both houses of parliament, oversight committees which review the work conducted by the Federal Council and the federal administration, have 'worked to reinforce this supervision' and have 'demanded that, in addition to the criteria of legality, regularity and appropriateness in taking action on the part of government and administration, that the effectiveness of the measures taken by the state be controlled in a more systematic manner' (Bättig and Schwab 2015, 2).

In 1990, the parliament decided to set up a specialized evaluation body, the Parliamentary Control of the Administration (PCA). This body is responsible, in particular, for carrying out analyses of the effectiveness of public policies and public services on behalf of the Control Committees of the two houses. Today it has eight employees (six FTEs) specialized in evaluation, and it works completely independently; it can also call on external experts.

The work of the PCA serves as the basis for reports prepared by the Control Committees and recommendations they make to the executive, which is required to answer. If they are not satisfied with the response, the Committees can demand fuller answers. At the same time, if they believe that the results of the evaluation show important steps that need to be taken, the Committees can require the government to submit propositions for legislative revisions through a motion or propose those revisions themselves through a parliamentary initiative.

It is also the parliament, and more particularly the Committees, which requested including Article 170 into the new 1999 Constitution. It stipulates that 'the Federal Assembly shall ensure that federal measures are evaluated with regard to their effectiveness'. By including such a broad clause in the Constitution, the parliament was a pioneer (Bussmann 2007). One result is that evaluation has shifted from being a tool for parliamentary oversight to being an instrument which covers all parliamentary activities, including legislative. The relevant literature thus widely accepts that Art. 170 sends or is a strong signal from parliament about the importance of the term 'evaluation' and about the importance of evaluation in legislative activity (Bussmann 2008; Horber-Papazian 2006, 135). Of all the parliaments considered in the aforementioned international comparison, the Swiss parliament has most institutionalized evaluation.

21.3.3 The Swiss Federal Audit Office

The revision of the Financial Control Act in 1994 extended the powers of the Swiss Federal Audit Office (SFAO) in line with the guidelines of the International Organization of Supreme Audit Institutions; it also encouraged the use of evaluations. This means the SFAO needs to examine whether resources are being used in an economical fashion and if the cost–benefit relationship is advantageous; it must also ensure that the budgeted expenditures are having the desired effect. In 2002, a new competency center focusing on performance audit and evaluation was created within the SFAO. It has the power to examine the effects and implementation of high-expenditure federal policies, and it can propose ways action taken by the Confederation can be made more efficient. In exercising this oversight, it assists the joint finance delegation of both parliamentary chambers, a body which, like the Federal Council, can entrust it with mandates to conduct summative and retrospective evaluations.

Like the PCA, the SFAO can approach topics in an intersectoral perspective. By contrast, it is the SFAO which formulates the recommendations which are given to the evaluated bodies—or more rarely, to political bodies like the Federal Council or parliaments (Crémieux and Sangra 2015). To avoid duplication, the SFAO and the PCA coordinate their activities in making their annual plans for conducting evaluations. Drafting such plans is required by the Financial Control Act. Helpfully, the evaluation criteria these actors focus on are not the same. The PCA focuses on the implementation of federal policies from a legal point of view, as well as with respect to appropriateness and effectiveness,[1] while the SFAO concentrates on fiscal oversight with respect to (financial) regularity, legality, and profitability.[2]

Finally, following the federal model, it is worth noting that the cantons of Geneva and Vaud have each introduced their own Court of Auditors to serve their cantonal parliaments and cantonal executives.

21.3.4 The Administrative Units

Evaluation activity in various administrative units helped institutionalize it. However, there are notable differences between these units, the most active of which have been the State Secretariat for Economic Affairs, the Federal Office of Public Health, the Federal Office for Professional Education and Technology, the Federal Office for Education and Science, the Federal Social Insurance Office, and the Swiss Agency for Development and Cooperation (Balthasar 2015). Balthasar and Strotz (2017) have noted an increase in the institutionalization of evaluation functions within the federal administration between 1999 and 2015, particularly in creating positions specifically devoted to evaluation. However, the total number of evaluations carried out within, or on behalf of, the federal administration has remained stable during this period, at about 80 per year (Balthasar 2015).

[1] Art. 10 Order on the Parliament's administration, in combination with Art. 52 Parliamentary Act.

[2] Art. 5 Financial Control Act.

Data on evaluation practices at the cantonal level are too sparse to allow a similar inventory. However, as at the federal level, there appears to be a culture of evaluation in certain domains (e.g., training and health), where evaluations are more common than in others (Wirths and Horber-Papazian 2016). The phenomenon of 'implementing federalism', where the Confederation calls on the cantons to carry out directives on fighting unemployment or controlling migration but then also requires them to report on their actions, appears to have an influence on cantonal evaluation practices (Horber-Papazian and Rosser, forthcoming). At the municipal level, one can observe more and more towns evaluating measures taken in social policy, the planning of public space, policy toward youths, or sustainable development, all of which are in their sphere of competence. At both cantonal and municipal levels, evaluations are usually outsourced.

21.3.5 The Swiss Evaluation Society

SEVAL was created in 1996 with the aim of encouraging dialogue, exchanging information, and sharing evaluation experiences among politicians, administrators, university researchers, and consulting firms. It also intended to promote the dissemination of evaluation practices and to encourage quality. It currently has more than 500 members and helps create a favorable climate for evaluation in the country. SEVAL organizes an annual congress, holds brief courses, and supports the creation of working groups which focus on specific issues. It has also supported the development of quality standards for Switzerland and contributed to disseminating them; these standards were most recently revised in 2016 by a SEVAL working group. The Swiss standards were based on the Program Evaluation Standards originally drafted in the USA by the Joint Committee on Standards for Educational Evaluation (Widmer and Neuenschwander 2004). A debate has been underway in SEVAL for some time now about the professionalization of evaluators (Horber-Papazian 2015).

21.3.6 Universities and Higher Education Institutions

The earliest developments in the academic study of evaluation were made in French-speaking Switzerland. Centre d'étude, de technique et d'évaluation législatives (CETEL), the Center for Legislative Study, Technique, and Evaluation at the University of Geneva, was a forerunner in research on the effect of laws (Delley et al. 1982). The first seminar which brought together political leaders, administrative heads, and key researchers, however, was organized by the Urban and Regional Planning Community at Lausanne's Ecole polytechnique fédérale de Lausanne (EPFL) in 1988; it gave rise to the first volume devoted to the evaluation of public policies in Switzerland (Horber-Papazian 1990).

In 1992, Institut de hautes études en administration publique (IDHEAP), the Swiss Graduate School of Public Administration, was the first to offer a 15-day postgraduate course devoted to public policy evaluation (Bergman et al. 1998). Since then, evaluation courses have been offered in various social science degree programs at Swiss universities and universities of applied sciences. A postgraduate degree and a master's degree in evaluation are offered by the University of Bern, for example, and various other shorter courses are available, largely meant for political and administrative actors.

As far as research is concerned, it is regrettable that once the national research program 'Efficiency of Governmental Actions' (NRP 27) ended in 1997, after ten years' work, it took another 16 years for a successor project to emerge. In 2013, researchers from the Universities of Bern, Geneva, Lausanne (IDHEAP), Lucerne, and Zurich launched a new national project entitled 'Policy Evaluation in the Swiss Political System—Roots and Fruits'. The conclusions from this research, some of which are included here, were published in a collective work edited by Fritz Sager, Thomas Widmer, and Andreas Balthasar (2017). Apart from their implication in teaching and research, academics employed at Swiss universities are quite active in publishing in the major international evaluation journals (Jacob 2015).

21.3.7 Evaluators

It is the evaluators themselves who are among the most important players in the development of evaluation in the country; the SEVAL website at present lists 202 evaluators and 28 institutions which give out mandates to conduct evaluations.[3] The vast majority of these are in German-speaking Switzerland (only 33 are active in the French-speaking part of the country), and so it is also in the German-speaking area that one finds the most important evaluation offices. This can certainly be explained by their proximity to federal institutions, the largest providers of evaluation mandates. The SEVAL list indicates that the largest numbers of active evaluators in French-speaking Switzerland are associated with university institutes.

[3] As of the beginning of February, 2018.

Evaluators in Switzerland are generally very well trained and have extensive professional experiences both in terms of how many evaluations they have completed and how many years' practice they have (Pleger et al. 2017).

21.4 The Available Resources for Constitutionally Mandated Evaluations

The resources available for evaluation in Switzerland are another aspect which helps explain its institutionalization. If one refers to resources, one means not just the demonstrated competence shown by evaluators and the structures and organizations, but also the consensus that there is a need for evaluation. As many of these were addressed already, the rest of this section looks at available financial and legal resources.

21.4.1 Financial Resources

No official data exist on the financial resources allocated to evaluations. However, all evaluations conducted at the federal level are included in a national database (ARAMIS), and so Balthasar (2015) has used this database to calculate that in the 2009–2012 period: 31.6 million Swiss francs was spent at the federal level on evaluations, or around 8 million Swiss francs per year. This is equivalent to the annual amount spent between 1999 and 2002, he notes, and hence the absolute amount spent in the federal administration for evaluations has remained essentially unchanged from 1999 to 2012.

21.4.2 Legal Resources

21.4.2.1 Article 170 of the Federal Constitution

The incorporation of an obligation to evaluate the impact of measures taken by the state is one of the criteria for determining the degree to which evaluation is institutionalized (Jacob et al. 2015). As noted above, Art. 170 of the Federal Constitution reflects the importance accorded to evaluation in Switzerland. The report of the interdepartmental working group in the Swiss federal administration on the 'evaluation of effectiveness' (IDEKOWI 2004) underscores that this article refers to all forms of state action, regardless of juridical basis (e.g., whether in the constitution, or a law, federal decree, ordinance, or directive). It also applies to all organs—parliament, executive, administration, courts, external bodies, and cantons inasmuch as they implement measures of the Confederation—which originate such state action. The phrase ***dass die Massnahmen des Bundes auf ihre Wirksamkeit überprüft werden*** ('that federal measures are evaluated with regard to their effectiveness') meant, in the eyes of this working group, that the most open approach possible has been chosen, one that includes both prospective and retrospective evaluation, monitoring, controlling, and quality control (IDEKOWI 2004, 11).

21.4.2.2 Evaluation Clauses Incorporated into Legislation

Article 170 of the Federal Constitution played a catalyzing role, particularly in defining 'sectoral' evaluation clauses (meaning in laws related to specific public policies) at the federal level, and in both general and sectoral clauses at the cantonal level. Among 262 evaluation clauses found at federal and cantonal levels in 2015 (Wirths and Horber-Papazian 2016), 80% came into force after Art. 170 became part of the Federal Constitution. Today, 14 cantons have followed the Confederation and introduced general evaluation clauses into their own constitutions. With the exception of Nidwalden, all other cantons have integrated a general clause into their political practice; it is applicable to the entirety of their legislation. For both cantons and federal government, evaluation clauses appear in nine out of ten cases already at the point when laws are being drafted, and this is even more so at the federal than at the cantonal level (Wirths and Horber-Papazian 2016, 496). A comparison between the cantons and the Confederation also reveals an important detail: it is at the cantonal level that political actors introduce the most clauses, mainly in the committees.

This is particularly true in Geneva. On the one hand, this can be explained by the strong links between academic actors, active in working to increase awareness of the importance of legislative evaluation, and the political world. On the other hand, it is also the result of the creation, in Geneva, of an 'External Commission for Public Policy Evaluation' in 1995. This permanent body, external to the administration and composed of actors from civil society, can be called upon by the government and parliament, and has the power to launch its own inquiries. Its activities were transferred to the Court of Auditors (*Cour des Comptes*) in 2013. The strong presence of a culture of evaluation in Geneva is also reflected in the results of a recent survey of Swiss parliaments (Eberli et al. 2014). Elsewhere, 20% of the parliamentarians surveyed said that they had proposed including an evaluation clause—but in Geneva it was 57%.

21.4.2.3 Evaluation Clauses as a Strategic Resource in the Political Decision-Making Process

The possibility of using a tool such as evaluation clauses, or calling for an evaluation, evidently has an influence on parliamentary debates. An analysis conducted in the Geneva parliament showed that, aside from reducing uncertainty in politically new domains or creating the possibility of controlling the actions of the executive, parliamentarians who proposed adding evaluation clauses could obtain a consensus. The prospect of a (subsequent) evaluation gave opponents a means to have their objections be taken into account and could lead, when necessary, to modifications, or even the cancelation of the legislation under consideration (Horber-Papazian and Rosser, forthcoming).

The survey conducted by Eberli et al. (2014) also reveals that parliamentarians make more calls for evaluations than they use their results. This can certainly be explained by the fact that, in the great majority of cases, it is up to the administration to launch the evaluations called for in evaluation clauses. When the evaluation clauses have a 'low normative density', that is, when they only define few elements like the object of or the criteria for evaluation (Wirths 2016), the administration's resulting room for maneuver means it can define the evaluation questions of interest for it. The focus is therefore on managerial issues, and the results of such evaluations are generally not discussed among parliamentarians: they tend to be more interested in questions of relevance and impact.

21.4.2.4 The Freedom of Information Act

Since their introduction, the SEVAL standards have encouraged transparency in evaluations. The 2004 introduction of the Freedom of Information Act in the Administration (FoIA) at the national level (implemented at the cantonal level) has made it possible to significantly strengthen such transparency, particularly because one can generalize access to the results of public policy evaluations. This act 'seeks to promote transparency with regard to the mandate, organization and activities of the administration' and contains an article specifically about evaluation: Access to reports on the evaluation of the performance of the Federal Administration and the effectiveness of its measures is guaranteed' (Art. 8(5), FoIA). This transparency can thus be active. Those who mandate an evaluation publicize the evaluations through various channels, including their websites, publications, or even press conferences. Yet it can also be passive, in which case the report must be communicated to the person (or agency) which requested it.

21.5 Utilization of Evaluation Results

Among the factors contributing to strong institutionalization is that the results of evaluations are actually used. An analysis conducted by the SFAO focused on the specific effects of 115 evaluation clauses introduced from 2006 to 2009 (Swiss Federal Audit Office 2011); it showed that these resulted in 62 actual evaluations. In 45% of the cases, their purpose was to improve the implementation of the measures. In 35% of the cases, their main purpose was to provide information, in the accountability reports, on their implementation status, while 9% of the evaluations led to a modification of the law. The remaining cases served to justify the continuation and financing of programs and measures taken by the Confederation.

Other analyses examining the utilization of administration-initiated evaluations have also found that they have had effects. At the federal level, Balthasar (2015) notes that more than 65% of those responsible feel that among the evaluations that they have seen to completion, the use of the results has been high. This accords with the analysis of Bättig and Schwab (2015, 10), who find that 'following nearly all PCA evaluations, corrective measures related to the recommendations of the Control Committees can be identified. In any case, the scope of these measures may differ'. The same is true for evaluations conducted within the audit and evaluation unit of the SFAO. One analysis of implementation found that among 15 evaluations containing 100 recommendations, 55% were applied, 24% were partly implemented, and 21% were not implemented at all (Crémieux and Sangra 2015).

If it is important that an evaluation allows for adjustments in implementing a public policy, then it is essential that the results can also be used. Policymakers should be able to move from 'single-loop' learning, which involves the administration, to 'double-loop' learning, integrating political decision-makers and giving them an opportunity to reconsider the objectives and formulation of a public policy (Leeuw et al. 1994). An extract from a PCA annual report provides reassurance on this point:

> The results of the PCA's work are taken into consideration in diverse ways in the parliamentary and executive decision-making process. The Control Committees made numerous recommendations to the Federal Council or initiated legislative revisions based on PCA evaluations. (...) Moreover, evaluation results are regularly mentioned in parliamentary interventions and debates, or mentioned by the Federal Council in its messages calling for revisions of the law (2014, 5).

A similar analysis was conducted at the cantonal level by Geneva's Court of Auditors. Its annual report indicated that of its seven published evaluations from 2014 to 2017, three led to modifications of the law that has either entered into force or are still under review by the cantonal legislature (Court of Auditors 2017).

These various analyses indicate the importance of institutional legitimacy in order that evaluation results be taken into account. To reinforce the use of evaluation results, the external bodies which mandate evaluations increasingly turn to advisory groups. These are often composed of those who are in some sense the 'constituents' of an evaluation, such as communal or cantonal politicians, or the representatives of groups the evaluations concern. Such advisory groups are kept informed about the different stages of the evaluation, the results of the analyses, and are consulted about the clarity, feasibility, and acceptability of the recommendations. This facilitates the process of learning about the content of the evaluation, reduces apprehensions it may engender, and serves as a means to explain a not small part of the recommendations which are to be implemented both at the political and administrative levels.

21.6 What Can One Learn from the Swiss Example with Respect to the Institutionalization of Public Policy Evaluation?

Diverse factors have contributed to the institutionalization of public policy evaluation in Switzerland, as this chapter has highlighted. What stands out most, in international comparison, is *the place evaluation occupies in the functioning of the federal parliament*. The Swiss parliament is composed of militia politicians concerned about their prerogatives in the area of executive oversight. They saw evaluation as an additional tool that could strengthen the means at their disposal to exert control, and thereby their power to intervene. By creating a structure, the *PCA*, composed of professionals who carry out evaluations on topics chosen by its Control Committees, parliament has a powerful tool at its disposal which allows it to respond to questions of interest, and these are related to the appropriateness, legality, and effectiveness of the measures taken and implemented. By reserving the right to make recommendations to the government, which must take a position on the subject, the parliament gives evaluations a strong political dimension. This is reinforced by the competence it has to *control the implementation of its recommendations.* Indeed, it even has the power to replace executive decisions—on the basis of parliamentary initiatives—by its own proposals, which can include repealing or enacting laws should the government not propose amendments. This is certainly one explanation for why, at the federal level, evaluation not only has effects in terms of implementing public policies but also in terms of political decisions.

The (at times) close relations between the different actors involved in an evaluation, and especially between academics and administrative officials, which result from mutual learning and the links between theory and practice it permits, are another strong explanatory factor for the institutionalization of evaluation. It is, in fact, common in Switzerland that senior officials teach classes on evaluation practice at institutions of higher education. Academics whose research focuses on evaluation may well also be contracted to conduct evaluations, enriching their teaching and strengthening their ties to other actors in this world. For their part, politicians increasingly have training in evaluation and are prepared to discuss the effects of their decisions not just in terms of political values or sensibilities, but relative to data collected and analyzed in a rigorous and independent manner.

The procedural institutionalization of evaluation brought about by introducing *a general evaluation clause in the Federal Constitution*, from which specific clauses have been derived and are now found in most legislation, has had a significant effect on the dissemination of evaluation through various political policy domains. Anchoring evaluation in the juridical texts has also meant that the influence of evaluation has been extended to the cantonal level. With one exception, all the cantons have followed Art. 170 in the Federal Constitution and integrated a general evaluation clause into their own constitutions.

Moreover, *the strategic utilization of evaluation clauses* in political debates is an element which has strengthened parliamentarians' control over actions taken by the state, particularly in terms of the relevance and effectiveness of the measures taken. This aspect might be even further increased should they understand the full interest they (potentially) have in proposing clauses with 'high normative density' of a kind which maintains control over the evaluation criteria.

The guarantee of access to evaluation reports which is given by the *Freedom of Information Act* is an important step, as it allows citizens who wish to inform themselves about the effectiveness of actions taken by public administrations—notably bodies whose tasks citizens finance. A public administration thus then moves from seeming to be a mysterious, all-powerful 'black box' to become an institution that is accountable to the citizens.

Finally, the issue SEVAL recently raised about the *accreditation* of evaluators makes it possible to question the training which is currently available. It certainly reinforces the idea of providing short-term training to enable evaluators to keep abreast of developments, especially from the point of view of new evaluation methods.

These generally positive points should not obscure that financial resources allocated for evaluation at the federal level have stagnated for many years. It is also true that while one can say that evaluation is strongly institutionalized at the federal level, data on evaluation practices at levels below it are lacking; one thus cannot make a reliable diagnosis of where evaluation stands, say, at the cantonal level. Finally, even if the Freedom of Information Act requires that evaluations be made accessible, this does not mean they are known beyond the immediate circle of those they concern. At present, the results of evaluations are not sufficiently disseminated to the general public; it is also rare to find them mentioned in the press (Stucki and Schlaufer 2017). If the press does report on them, then often in truncated or even biased ways (Horber-Papazian and Bützer 2008).

So in addition to maintaining its rank as the country in which evaluation is most highly institutionalized, Switzerland faces another challenge: finding a way to enable evaluation to promote an enlightened democratic debate.

References

Arbeitsgruppe Gesetzesevaluation. (1991). *Die Wirkungen staatlichen Handelns besser ermitteln: Probleme, Möglichkeiten, Vorschläge. Schlussbericht an das Eidgenössische Justiz- und Polizeidepartement.* Bern: EDMZ.

Balthasar, A. (2015). L'utilisation de l'évaluation par l'administration fédérale. In K. Horber-Papazian (Ed.), *Regards croisés sur l'évaluation en Suisse* (pp. 115–132). Lausanne: PPUR.

Balthasar, A., & Strotz, C. (2017). Verbreitung und Verankerung von Evaluation in Bundesverwaltung. In F. Sager, T. Widmer, & A. Balthasar (Eds.), *Evaluation im politischen System der Schweiz* (pp. 89–117). Zurich: Neue Zürcher Zeitung libro.

Bättig, C., & Schwab, P. (2015). La place de l'évaluation dans le cadre du contrôle parlementaire. In K. Horber-Papazian (Ed.), *Regards croisés sur l'évaluation en Suisse* (pp. 1–23). Lausanne: PPUR.

Bergman, M. M., Cattacin, S., & Läubli-Loud, M. (1998). *Evaluators evaluating evaluators: Peer-assessment and training opportunities in Switzerland*. Geneva: RESOP-Université de Genève.

Bussmann, W. (2007). Institutionalisierung der Evaluation in der Schweiz. Verfassungsauftrag, Konkretisierungsspielräume und Umsetzungsstrate-gie. In H. Schäffer (Ed.), *Evaluierung der Gesetze / Gesetzesfolgenabschätzung (II)* (pp. 1–20). Vienna: Manzsche Verlags und Universitätsbuchhandlung.

Bussmann, W. (2008). The emergence of evaluation in Switzerland. *Evaluation, 14*(4), 499–506.

Court of Auditors. (2017). *Rapport annuel d'activité 2017. Tome 2: Annexes*. Geneva: République et Canton de Genève.

Crémieux, L., & Sangra, E. (2015). La place de l'évaluation dans le cadre du Contrôle fédéral des finances. In K. Horber-Papazian (Ed.), *Regards croisés sur l'évaluation en Suisse* (pp. 37–57). Lausanne: PPUR.

Delley, J.-D., Morand, C.-A., Derivaz, R., & Mader, L. (1982). *Le droit en action – Etude de mise en œuvre de la loi Furgler*. St-Saphorin: Georgi.

Eberli, D., Bundi, P., Frey, K., & Widmer, T. (2014). *Befragung: Parlamente und Evaluationen. Ergebnisbericht*. Zurich: Universität Zürich.

Horber-Papazian, K. (Ed.). (1990). *Evaluation des politiques publiques en Suisse. Pourquoi? Pour qui? Comment?* Lausanne: PPUR.

Horber-Papazian, K. (2006). La place de l'évaluation des politiques publiques en Suisse. In J.-L. Chappelet (Ed.), *Contributions à l'action publique/Beiträge zum öffentlichen Handeln* (pp. 131–144). Lausanne: PPUR.

Horber-Papazian, K. (2015). *Regards croisés sur l'évaluation en Suisse*. Lausanne: PPUR.

Horber-Papazian, K., & Bützer, M. (2008). Dissemination of evaluation reports in newspapers: The case of CEPP evaluations in Geneva, Switzerland. In R. Boyle, J. D. Breul, & P. Dahler-Larsen (Eds.), *Open to the public: Evaluation in the public* (pp. 43–66). New Brunswick: Transaction Publishers.

Horber-Papazian, K., & Rosser, R. (forthcoming). From law to reality – A critical view on the institutionalization of evaluation in the Swiss Canton of Geneva's parliament. In J.-E. Furubo & N. Stame (Eds.), *The evaluation enterprise*. London: Routledge.

Horber-Papazian, K., & Thévoz, L. (1990). Switzerland: Moving towards evaluation. In R. C. Rist (Ed.), *Program evaluation and the management of government* (pp. 133–143). New Brunswick: Transaction Publishers.

IDEKOWI. (2004). *Efficacité des mesures prises par la Confédération. Proposi-tions de mise en œuvre de l'art. 170 de la Constitution fédérale dans le contexte des activités du Conseil fédéral et de l'administration fédérale*. Bern: Office fédéral de la justice.

Jacob, S. (2015). La recherche sur l'évaluation en Suisse. In K. Horber-Papazian (Ed.), *Regards croisés sur l'évaluation en Suisse* (pp. 267–284). Lausanne: PPUR.

Jacob, S., Speer, S., & Furubo, J.-E. (2015). The institutionalization of evaluation matters: Updating the international atlas of evaluation 10 years later. *Evaluation, 21*(1), 6–31.

Leeuw, F. L., Rist, R. C., & Sonnichsen, R. C. (Eds.). (1994). *Can governments learn? Comparative perspectives on evaluation and organizational learning*. New Brunswick: Transaction Publishers.

Mader, L. (1985). *L'évaluation législative – Pour une analyse empirique des effets de la législation*. Geneva: Université de Genève.

PCA. (2014). *Rapport annuel 2013 du Contrôle parlementaire de l'administration*. Berne: Services du Parlement.

Pleger, L., Wittwer, S., & Sager, F. (2017). Wer sind die Evaluierenden in der Schweiz? In F. Sager, T. Widmer, & A. Balthasar (Eds.), *Evaluation im politischen System der Schweiz* (pp. 189–208). Zurich: Neue Zürcher Zeitung libro.

Sager, F., Widmer, T., & Balthasar, A. (Eds.). (2017). *Evaluation im politischen System der Schweiz*. Zurich: Neue Zürcher Zeitung libro.

Stucki, I., & Schlaufer, C. (2017). Die Bedeutung von Evaluationen im direktdemokratischen Diskurs. In F. Sager, T. Widmer, & A. Balthasar (Eds.), *Evaluation im politischen System der Schweiz* (pp. 279–310). Zurich: Neue Zürcher Zeitung libro.

Swiss Federal Audit Office. (2011). *Umsetzung der Evaluationsklauseln in der Bundesverwaltung*. Bern: Contrôle fédéral des finances.

Widmer, T., & Neuenschwander, P. (2004). Embedding evaluation in the Swiss Federal Administration: Purpose, institutional design and utilization. *Evaluation, 10*(4), 388–409.

Wirths, D. (2016). Procedural institutionalization of the evaluation through legal basis: A new typology of evaluation clauses in Switzerland. *Statute Law Review, 38*(1), 23–39.

Wirths, D., & Horber-Papazian, K. (2016). Les clauses d'évaluation dans le droit des cantons suisses: leur diffusion, leur contenu et la justification à l'origine de leur adoption. *LeGes, 2016*(3), 485–502.

Index[1]

[1] Note: Page numbers followed by 'n' refer to notes.

A. Ladner et al. (eds.), *Swiss Public Administration*, Governance and Public Management,
https://doi.org/10.1007/978-3-319-92381-9

Q

R

U

V

W

Printed by Printforce, the Netherlands